Understanding Nonsuicidal Self-Injury

Understanding Nonsuicidal Self-Injury

Origins, Assessment, and Treatment

Edited by Matthew K. Nock

American Psychological Association
Washington, DC

Published by
American Psychological Association
750 First Street, NE
Washington, DC 20002
www.apa.org

To order
APA Order Department
P.O. Box 92984
Washington, DC 20090-2984
Tel: (800) 374-2721; Direct: (202) 336-5510
Fax: (202) 336-5502; TDD/TTY: (202) 336-6123
Online: www.apa.org/books/
E-mail: order@apa.org

In the U.K., Europe, Africa, and the Middle East, copies may be ordered from
American Psychological Association
3 Henrietta Street
Covent Garden, London
WC2E 8LU England

Typeset in Goudy by Circle Graphics, Columbia, MD

Printer: Edwards Brothers, Inc., Ann Arbor, MI
Cover Designer: Watermark Design Office, Alexandria, VA
Technical/Production Editor: Devon Bourexis

The opinions and statements published are the responsibility of the authors, and such opinions and statements do not necessarily represent the policies of the American Psychological Association.

Library of Congress Cataloging-in-Publication Data

Understanding nonsuicidal self-injury : origins, assessment, and treatment / edited by Matthew K. Nock. — 1st ed.
     p. ; cm.
  Includes bibliographical references and index.
  ISBN-13: 978-1-4338-0436-6
  ISBN-10: 1-4338-0436-0
  1. Self-injurious behavior. I. Nock, Matthew. II. American Psychological Association.
  [DNLM: 1. Self-Injurious Behavior—psychology. 2. Self-Injurious Behavior—therapy.
  WM 165 U547 2009]
  RC569.5.S48U53 2009
  616.85′82—dc22
                                                                                    2008039895

British Library Cataloguing-in-Publication Data

A CIP record is available from the British Library.

Printed in the United States of America
First Edition

For Keesha

CONTENTS

CONTRIBUTORS

Caroline B. Browne, BA, University of North Carolina, Chapel Hill
Christine B. Cha, BA, Harvard University, Cambridge, MA
Caroline Cozza, BA, Duke University, Durham, NC
Leonard A. Doerfler, PhD, Assumption College, Worcester, MA
Armando R. Favazza, MD, University of Missouri—Columbia School of Medicine, Columbia
Marina Gershkovich, BA, Cornell University, New York, NY
John D. Guerry, MA, University of North Carolina, Chapel Hill
Keith Hawton, DSc, DM, FRCPsych, Centre for Suicide Research, University of Oxford, Oxford, England
Colleen M. Jacobson, PhD, Columbia Presbyterian Medical Center, Columbia University, New York, NY
E. David Klonsky, PhD, Stony Brook University, Stony Brook, NY
James K. Luiselli, EdD, ABPP, BCBA, The May Institute, Randolph, MA
Thomas R. Lynch, PhD, University of Exeter, Exeter, Devon, England
Alec L. Miller, PsyD, Montefiore Medical Center, Albert Einstein College of Medicine, Bronx, NY
Jennifer J. Muehlenkamp, PhD, University of North Dakota, Grand Forks

Cory F. Newman, PhD, ABPP, Center for Cognitive Therapy, University of Pennsylvania, Philadelphia

Matthew K. Nock, PhD, Harvard University, Cambridge, MA

Mitchell J. Prinstein, PhD, University of North Carolina, Chapel Hill

Amanda Purington, BS, Cornell University, New York, NY

Diana Rancourt, MA, University of North Carolina, Chapel Hill

Karen Rodham, PhD, University of Bath, Bath, England

Curt A. Sandman, PhD, University of California, Irvine

Leo Sher, MD, Columbia University College of Physicians and Surgeons; New York State Psychiatric Institute, New York

Barbara Stanley, PhD, Columbia University College of Physicians and Surgeons; New York State Psychiatric Institute; City University of New York—John Jay College, New York

Barent W. Walsh, PhD, The Bridge of Central Massachusetts, Worcester

Anna Weinberg, BA, Stony Brook University, Stony Brook, NY

Janis Whitlock, PhD, MPH, Cornell University, New York, NY

Tuppett M. Yates, PhD, University of California, Riverside

ACKNOWLEDGMENTS

I would like to express my deep admiration and appreciation to the contributors to this volume for producing such outstanding chapters. I also thank my research assistants, Christine Cha, Tara Deliberto, Halina Dour, Robin Hertzbach, and Alayna Harned, for their invaluable help with reading, researching, organizing, and reading some more. This book would not have made it to press without them. Finally, I am deeply grateful to Susan Reynolds, Genevieve Gill, Devon Bourexis, and the amazing team in the American Psychological Association's Books department who expertly shepherded this project from initial idea to published volume.

Understanding Nonsuicidal Self-Injury

INTRODUCTION

MATTHEW K. NOCK

Self-injurious behaviors are one of the most concerning—and perplexing—of all human behaviors. Particularly puzzling are instances in which people hurt themselves with no intention of dying. If not to die, why would people do such a thing? Instances of nonsuicidal self-injury (NSSI) have been reported for centuries but appear to have increased dramatically since the late 1980s. With this increase comes an amplified need to understand why NSSI occurs and what effective assessments and treatments can be used to address it. Until now, however, the field has lacked an authoritative, comprehensive volume on the topic, and most researchers, scholars, and clinicians are unaware of recent scientific findings about NSSI. How prevalent is NSSI? What factors influence its occurrence? Why do people purposely hurt themselves if they do not want to die, and what can one do to help them?

The purpose of this book is to provide comprehensive, state-of-the-art information on the origins, assessment, and treatment of NSSI. The contributors are among the world's leading researchers, scholars, and clinicians on the topic. The chapters form an integrative and interdisciplinary volume written for a broad audience.

This book was written primarily for researchers, scholars, clinicians, and graduate students in clinical psychology and related fields, including psychiatry, counseling psychology, school psychology, social work, nursing, education, and anthropology. It will also be of interest to other readers with a personal interest in NSSI who want to familiarize themselves with the most current research and clinical approaches. Each chapter is written in an accessible way (i.e., jargon-free and to the point) but without sacrificing complex information on each topic. This book provides readers with detailed information about the most up-to-date scientific findings and clinical approaches available on NSSI. There has been a virtual explosion of research and clinical advances on this behavior since the late 1990s. With each chapter written by a leader in a respective area of the field, this book synthesizes and summarizes this new information. It is important to also mention what the reader will not find in this book: It does not contain self-help advice, personal narratives, or unsupported opinions about NSSI. Information of this sort can be found in other books on this topic for those who are interested.

This book is organized into three general parts that address the following overarching questions: (a) What is NSSI? (b) Why do people engage in NSSI? and (c) What are the most effective ways to assess and treat NSSI? Part I begins with a chapter (chap. 1), coauthored by myself and Armando R. Favazza, the author of the seminal text on NSSI (*Bodies Under Siege: Self-Mutilation and Body Modification in Culture and Psychiatry*, 1996), on the definition and classification of NSSI. One of the biggest obstacles to scientific and clinical work on this topic has been confusion about how to define and classify episodes of self-injurious behavior. In chapter 1, we address this and related issues, providing the definitions and terminology used throughout the rest of the book. In chapter 2, Favazza puts NSSI into historical and cultural perspective, providing examples of self-injury across various times and places in a way that challenges some popular notions about NSSI. Chapter 2 is less research focused than the other chapters in the book; Favazza instead presents an intriguing and provocative introduction to NSSI from a cultural anthropological perspective. In chapter 3, Karen Rodham and Keith Hawton review what is currently known about the epidemiology of NSSI, addressing the following questions: (a) How frequently does NSSI occur? and (b) Is it more common among younger people, women, and people of a particular race? The information in the chapter will be of great interest to researchers, clinicians, and the public alike, given the importance of these questions.

Part II of this book includes six chapters addressing, from several perspectives, why people engage in NSSI. Part II is likely to be of interest to all potential readers of this book (i.e., researchers, clinicians, students, and laypersons) because of the general importance of this issue. In chapter 4, Christine B. Cha and I present a model of the psychological factors proposed to cause NSSI. We describe how NSSI can actually be rewarding for some people by helping them to regulate negative thoughts and feelings and by helping them to communicate with the people around them. We also discuss how factors such as childhood maltreatment, mental disorders such as depression and anxiety, and negative social interactions can increase the likelihood that a person will engage in NSSI. Expanding on this last point in much greater detail, Mitchell J. Prinstein, John D. Guerry, Caroline B. Browne, and Diana Rancourt, in chapter 5, present an interpersonal model of NSSI that describes how social factors can have a powerful influence over people's decision to engage in NSSI. Interpersonal factors have been largely understudied in the NSSI literature, and Prinstein and colleagues provide a thorough and thought-provoking review of how social factors can act as triggers for NSSI, can provide a model of NSSI for others to follow, and can reinforce NSSI once it is performed. Moving from social to biological issues, in chapter 6, Leo Sher and Barbara Stanley provide a revealing and accessible explanation of the biological factors that appear to influence NSSI. They synthesize prior work to help explain how NSSI may be biologically rewarding and why people who engage in NSSI often feel little or no pain during the act.

The final three chapters of Part II review special topics and populations that have received increased attention among NSSI researchers. In chapter 7, Tuppett M. Yates provides a detailed analysis of the developmental pathways that can lead from child maltreatment to engagement in NSSI. Yates describes how negative experiences early in life can lead to problems in how one views oneself, how one responds to stress, and how a person regulates or manages his or her thoughts and feelings. Janis Whitlock, Amanda Purington, and Marina Gershkovich, in chapter 8, present new data on the influence of media and the Internet on NSSI. They provide compelling data on the increased attention NSSI has received in the media and make the case that this increase may be partly responsible for the apparent rise in NSSI in recent decades. NSSI often occurs among those with developmental disabilities, and in fact, NSSI is well studied and effectively treated in this group. However, there has historically been little cross talk between researchers and clinicians working on NSSI among those with developmental disabilities and those who are developing typically. In an effort to bridge this gap, it is fortunate that James K. Luiselli, who has done leading work on NSSI among those with developmental disabilities, has contributed chapter 9, in which he covers both the differences and the similarities observed between NSSI in these two populations. I believe there is much one can learn from this, and future, communication across these areas of scientific and clinical work.

Part III provides new information about the assessment and treatment of NSSI. It will be of interest to both researchers and clinicians interested in this problem and presents diverse theoretical and practical approaches to the topic. In the first chapter of Part III (chap. 10), E. David Klonsky and Anna Weinberg provide a thorough overview of the methods and measures that should be considered in the assessment of NSSI. Chapter 10 is a must-read for anyone doing scientific or clinical work with people engaging in NSSI. In chapter 11, Cory F. Newman describes how cognitive therapy can be used to treat NSSI. Cognitive therapy is one of the only psychological treatments shown to decrease the likelihood of suicide attempts and is one of the most promising treatments for NSSI. Another promising treatment for NSSI is dialectical behavior therapy (DBT), which is described in detail in chapters 12 and 13. Thomas R. Lynch and Caroline Cozza, in chapter 12, provide a detailed and accessible explanation of the behavioral model of NSSI, which leads into a discussion of the essentials of DBT, many of which derive directly from the behavioral model. Chapter 12 is an excellent introduction to DBT for those new to this approach but will be a valuable read for even the most seasoned DBT clinicians as well because of the presentation of the behavioral model underlying DBT and the linkages made to behavior therapy more broadly. In chapter 13, Alec L. Miller, Jennifer J. Muehlenkamp, and Colleen M. Jacobson review special issues that arise in treating NSSI among adolescents. Their focus on DBT provides a nice complement to chapter 12, and their discussion of how to engage adolescents in treatment, how to involve the family, and how to manage difficult situations that can arise provides useful information for anyone working with self-injurious adolescents.

Many adolescents and young adults who engage in NSSI are treated in residential treatment centers; however, few studies have examined what is actually done in such settings or how effective such treatment is. In chapter 14, Barent W. Walsh and Leonard A. Doerfler fill this major gap in the literature by describing an award-winning residential treatment program that focuses on decreasing NSSI. They present new data on the therapeutic effects of their residential approach, providing an important advance in this new research area. Curt A. Sandman, in chapter 15, summarizes what is currently known about the effectiveness and mechanism of action of pharmacological treatments for NSSI. It is an area of great interest and promise, but a relatively small amount of research has been done on the topic to date. In fact, Sandman did much of the existing work in this area, and it is fortunate that he has provided this expert review on an important area of research.

In addition to summarizing the most important research findings in each area, the contributors make specific recommendations for future scientific work and describe the implications for clinical practice in each area. Experts in their field, they have done a superb job in each regard, and as a result, this volume not only provides current information about scientific and clinical advances in the understanding and treatment of NSSI but also presents a road map for the most important work needed to understand, assess, and treat NSSI more effectively.

REFERENCE

Favazza, A. R. (1996). *Bodies under siege: Self-mutilation and body modification in culture and psychiatry* (2nd ed.). Baltimore: Johns Hopkins University Press.

I

WHAT IS NONSUICIDAL SELF-INJURY?

1

NONSUICIDAL SELF-INJURY: DEFINITION AND CLASSIFICATION

MATTHEW K. NOCK AND ARMANDO R. FAVAZZA

Nonsuicidal self-injury (NSSI) is the direct, deliberate destruction of one's own body tissue in the absence of suicidal intent. NSSI is direct in that the ultimate outcome of the self-injury occurs without intervening steps. For instance, cutting one's own skin with a razor is direct self-injury, whereas smoking tobacco or taking an overdose of medication, behaviors that indirectly lead to negative health outcomes through chemical processes in the body, are not considered to be NSSI. NSSI is deliberate in that self-injury is intended by the individual, rather than accidental. Destruction of one's own body tissue is required in this definition, although it is acknowledged that the actual physical harm caused by NSSI can vary significantly. There are some socially or culturally sanctioned behaviors that cause destruction or modification of body tissue, such as tattooing or ear piercing in Western cultures. Such behaviors are not classified or studied as harmful or deviant behaviors requiring intervention and are not the focus of this book (see Favazza, 1996, and chap. 2 of this volume for a detailed discussion of various forms of culturally sanctioned self-injury). Before going into more detail about NSSI, it is important to consider this behavior in the context of, and to distinguish it from, other forms of self-injurious thoughts and behaviors.

SELF-INJURIOUS THOUGHTS AND BEHAVIORS

The term *self-injurious thoughts and behaviors* (SITB) refers to a broad class of experiences in which people think about or engage in behavior that directly and deliberately injures themselves. SITB are among the most dangerous and concerning behaviors encountered by researchers and clinicians. For this reason, an increasing amount of scientific and clinical work is dedicated to understanding SITB and improving the ability to detect, predict, and prevent them. Unfortunately, a major obstacle to these scientific and research efforts is that vague and inconsistent terms and definitions are used to refer to different forms of SITB. This is problematic for scientific efforts because it limits the reliability and validity of SITB constructs examined in research studies. It is problematic for clinical efforts because it creates confusion among clinicians regarding what the client actually did and for what they are most at risk. For example, it is not uncommon for researchers or clinicians to use terms such as *deliberate self-harm* to refer to both nonsuicidal (e.g., cutting, burning) and suicidal (e.g., suicide attempts) self-injury. Similarly, terms such as *suicidality* are often used without specifying whether one is describing self-injurious thoughts or behaviors. Overall, it is important that authors and clinicians use clear and consistent terms and definitions when referring to SITB in order to advance research in this area most efficiently and to increase the effectiveness of clinical assessment and interventions.

The development of clear terms, definitions, and guidelines for what are considered SITB and how one should distinguish their various forms has been hindered at least to some degree by the lack of inclusion of such behaviors in the *Diagnostic and Statistical Manual of Mental Disorders* (*DSM–IV*; 4th ed.; American Psychiatric Association, 1994). The reason for this is that SITB are conceptualized by many as simply behaviors rather than mental disorders (although one also could make similar arguments about many diagnoses currently included in the *DSM–IV*, such as trichotillomania, encopresis, drug and alcohol abuse, etc.). Instead, engagement in SITB appears in the *DSM–IV* as only a symptom of Borderline Personality Disorder, a symptom of Major Depression (in the case of suicidal ideation and attempts), and under Stereotypic Movement Disorder. Given that many of those who engage in SITB in their various forms do not meet diagnostic criteria for these diagnoses (Favazza, 1989; Favazza & Conterio, 1989; Nock, Joiner, Gordon, Lloyd-Richardson, & Prinstein, 2006), these diagnoses are often inappropriate. We suggest that Impulse-Control Disorder Not Otherwise Specified may be most appropriate in many cases, especially in instances of NSSI. Some have proposed that repetitive NSSI in particular be included in the DSM as a new diagnosis (e.g., deliberate self-harm syndrome; Favazza, 1996; Favazza & Rosenthal, 1993; Muehlenkamp, 2005; Pattison & Kahan, 1983); however, this inclusion has not yet been made.

Over the years, different classification systems and definitions have been proposed for the various manifestations of SITB (Beck et al., 1973; Nock, Holmberg, Photos, & Michel, 2007; Nock, Wedig, Janis, & Deliberto, 2008; O'Carroll et al., 1996; Posner, Oquendo, Gould, Stanley, & Davies, 2007; Silverman, Berman, Sanddal, O'Carroll, & Joiner, 2007a, 2007b; Simeon & Favazza, 2001). It is important to note that research has supported several of the distinctions proposed among these various constructs. For instance, different types of SITB (e.g., suicidal ideation vs. suicide attempts vs. NSSI) have been shown to have different base rates, correlates, courses, and responsiveness to treatment (e.g., see Brown et al., 2005; Kessler, Berglund, Borges, Nock, & Wang, 2005; Linehan, Armstrong, Suarez, Allmon, & Heard, 1991; Nock & Kazdin, 2002; Nock & Kessler, 2006). The empirical demonstration of such differences highlights the need to classify and define SITB in a way that incorporates these distinctions.

A classification system for SITB based on current research and clinical observations is presented in Figure 1.1. In classifying SITB, the first major distinction that must be made is between suicidal thoughts and behaviors, in which there is intent to die, and nonsuicidal SITB, in which there is no intent to die. Suicidal self-injury is a higher risk behavior, and death is more likely in such incidents. In addition, those who self-injure with intent to die are more likely to subsequently die by suicide (Harriss, Hawton, & Zahl, 2005; Hjelmeland, 1996).

Suicidal Self-Injurious Thoughts and Behaviors

Suicidal self-injury can be further classified into one of several subcategories. *Suicidal ideation* refers to thoughts of engaging in behavior intended to end one's own life. This is distinguished from passive thoughts of death or dying. A *suicide plan* refers to the formulation of a specific method through which one intends to die. Although a suicide plan is also a cognitive construct

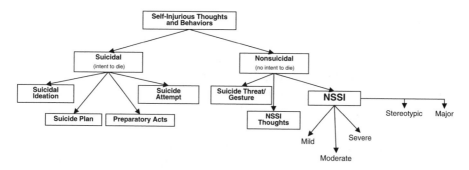

Figure 1.1. Classification of self-injurious thoughts and behaviors. NSSI = nonsuicidal self-injury.

related to thinking of killing oneself, most people who report suicidal ideation and plans report being able to clearly distinguish between the two. A *suicide attempt* refers to engagement in potentially self-injurious behavior in which there is at least some intent to die. It is recommended that clinicians and researchers assess intent to die among those who report making a "suicide attempt," because recent research has demonstrated that many people who make such reports indicate that they actually had no intent to die from their behavior (Nock & Kessler, 2006). Such behavior should instead be classified as NSSI, which is reviewed in more detail later in the chapter.

Researchers and clinicians who work with self-injurious individuals will note that in many cases, suicidal behaviors do not fit neatly into one of the aforementioned categories. For instance, a person may take action beyond formulating a plan (e.g., purchases a firearm with the intent of using it in the future) but not go so far as to make a suicide attempt. In an effort to capture and classify such behaviors, several more nuanced categories of suicidal behaviors have been articulated that fall between suicide plans and suicide attempts. The general category of *preparatory acts* refers to behaviors in which an individual takes actual steps toward making a suicide attempt but stops short of actually engaging in injurious behavior, such as in the earlier example of buying a firearm (Posner et al., 2007). Instances in which the individual prepares to engage in a suicide attempt but at the last minute stops him- or herself before doing so are referred to as *aborted suicide attempts* (Barber, Marzuk, Leon, & Portera, 1998; Marzuk, Tardiff, Leon, Portera, & Weiner, 1997). Instances in which the individual prepares to engage in a suicide attempt but at the last minute is stopped by someone else before doing so (e.g., person removes the gun or pills from the potential suicide attempter) are referred to as *interrupted suicide attempts* (Posner et al., 2007).

Nonsuicidal Self-Injurious Thoughts and Behaviors

Nonsuicidal SITB can also be further classified into several subcategories. A *suicide threat* or *suicide gesture* refers to a statement or behavior in which people lead others to believe they intend to kill themselves when they really have no intention of doing so (Nock & Kessler, 2006; O'Carroll et al., 1996). The term *suicide gesture* was initially used to describe the behavior of soldiers who intentionally injured themselves without wanting to die but instead to escape active military duty (Fisch, 1954; Tucker & Gorman, 1967), and thus some believe the term has taken on a pejorative meaning and so should not be used (Silverman et al., 2007b). Others have argued that it is not appropriate to suggest that someone is using self-injurious behavior simply as a means to influence others. However, we note that this term accurately captures the behavior described, that we certainly do not propose that all self-injury is performed only for the purposes of communication (or *secondary gain*), and that many individuals do, however, report making such threats and gestures purely for the purposes of communicating with others (Martinson, 2007; Nock et al., 2007, 2008).

NSSI thoughts refer to instances in which people think about or have urges to engage in NSSI. *NSSI*, as mentioned in the opening paragraph of this chapter, refers to direct, deliberate destruction of body tissue in the absence of any intent to die. NSSI differs from suicide threats or gestures in that the person does not engage in the behavior for the purpose of leading others to believe he or she wants to die. Although actual harm (i.e., destruction of body tissue) must occur for a behavior to be considered NSSI, that is not necessarily true of a suicide gesture. The lack of suicidal intent associated with NSSI deserves special comment. Behavior is only classified as NSSI if there is evidence that intent to die is completely absent. The assessment of intent to die is difficult and currently relies on an individual's explicit self-report. Nevertheless, this report should be used to classify behavior as NSSI if there is zero-level intent to die and should be used to classify behavior as suicidal self-injury (i.e., either a suicide attempt or a suicide death) if there is some intent to die. This categorical distinction based on presence versus absence of intent to die does not capture the variability that undoubtedly exists in individuals' intent to die, but it is consistent with expert consensus in this area (O'Carroll et al., 1996; Silverman et al., 2007a, 2007b) and is considered the most appropriate method of classification until more sophisticated methods of measuring intent to die are available.

Although most researchers and clinicians would agree with our definition of *NSSI*, some have used slightly different definitions or alternative terms for this behavior. The significant variability in the terms and definitions used in past research and practice has introduced confusion and has stunted scientific advancement in this area. Alternative terms used for this behavior in the literature include *self-mutilation, deliberate self-harm, self-cutting,* and *parasuicide*. We propose use of the term *NSSI* instead of these for several reasons. First, although we have used the terms *self-mutilation* and *self-mutilative behavior* in our own work (Favazza, 1996; Nock & Prinstein, 2004, 2005), we believe the term *NSSI* is more accurate and more appropriate. Two definitions of *mutilate* are (a) "to cut up or alter radically so as to make imperfect" and (b) "to cut off or permanently destroy a limb or essential part of; cripple" (Merriam-Webster's Collegiate Dictionary, 2005, p. 820), suggesting a high degree of harm and permanence that is not necessarily characteristic of this behavior. In addition, the term *self-mutilation* is often viewed as having a negative connotation, and people who engage in this behavior have lobbied for use of the term *self-injury* instead (Martinson, 2007).

Second, other terms, such as *deliberate self-harm* and *parasuicide*, are quite general; although they clearly indicate the deliberate nature of the self-injury, these terms do not convey the nonsuicidal nature of the behavior. This introduces a lack of clarity when making comparisons across studies, because some authors have used these terms to refer to self-injury in which there is no intent to die (i.e., NSSI), others have used them for behavior in which there is clear intent to die (i.e., suicide attempts), and still others have used these terms to describe all self-injurious behavior without distinguishing between those with and without intent to die (i.e., both NSSI and suicide attempts). This is problematic given that prior work has demonstrated clear differences between those with and without intent to die, with the former engaging in self-injurious behavior of greater lethality and being more likely ultimately to die by suicide (Brown, Henriques, Sosdjan, & Beck, 2004; Harriss & Hawton, 2005; Nock & Kessler, 2006). Moreover, this confusion makes it difficult to compare results across studies and hinders communication among researchers and clinicians. We believe the term *NSSI* more clearly and accurately defines this behavior and minimizes the possibility of confusion, and therefore this term is used throughout this volume.

The primary focus of this volume, and of most current research on this behavior, is on NSSI among normally developing, nonpsychotic individuals. It is notable, however, that two additional subtypes of NSSI exist and are the focus of some study as well. *Stereotypic NSSI* refers to self-injury that is performed at high frequency (sometimes thousands of episodes per hour), typically without any implements, and with each individual behavior causing only minor physical injury. Stereotypic NSSI occurs almost exclusively among individuals with developmental disabilities or neuropsychiatric disorders such as Tourette's disorder and Lesch–Nyhan syndrome. A prototypic example is a child with mental retardation who engages in repetitive head banging or tongue and finger biting. Stereotypic NSSI is covered in greater detail in chapter 9 of this volume. In contrast, *major NSSI* refers to self-injury that is performed at low frequency (sometimes only once in a person's lifetime), typically although not necessarily with an implement, and with each individual episode causing severe physical injury. Major NSSI occurs most often among those with psychotic disorders or within the context of substance or alcohol intoxication. A prototypic example is an adult with a psychotic disorder who enucleates an eye or castrates himself in response to command auditory hallucinations.

NSSI that occurs among normally developing, nonpsychotic individuals is much more prevalent than stereotypic or major NSSI. To be sure, the actual prevalence of NSSI is not known because nationally representative studies have not included assessments of these behaviors. However, data are available on the rates of NSSI from several smaller studies ($Ns = 400$–$2,000$) and from community- and clinic-based studies. These data reveal consistent estimates of the rate of NSSI: Approximately 7.7% of preadolescents (Hilt, Nock, Lloyd-Richardson, & Prinstein, 2008), 13.9% to 21.4% of adolescents and young adults (Muehlenkamp & Gutierrez, 2004; Ross & Heath, 2002; Zoroglu et al., 2003), and 4% of adults (Briere & Gil, 1998; Klonsky, Oltmanns, & Turkheimer, 2003) report a lifetime history of NSSI. It is important to note, however, that although NSSI is distinct from suicide attempts, recent studies indicate that 50% to 75% of those with a history of NSSI make a suicide attempt at some point (often through overdose; Favazza & Conterio, 1988; Nock et al., 2006), highlighting the importance of studying NSSI in greater detail.

Favazza (1996) proposed further distinguishing instances of NSSI among normally developing, nonpsychotic individuals as being either *compulsive* (i.e., mild, ritualistic behaviors such as hair pulling in trichotillomania); *episodic* (i.e., NSSI performed every so often, with no strong identification with being a self-injurer, such as the adolescent who engages in NSSI only a few times and then stops); or *repetitive* (i.e., NSSI performed on a more regular basis, often accompanied by identification with the behavior, such as the adolescent who engages in NSSI approximately once per week). Although there is no clear boundary between episodic and repetitive NSSI, these proposed categories highlight important distinctions among different manifestations of NSSI. Researchers and clinicians may also wish to use modifiers such as *mild* (e.g., low frequency, low severity of injury), *moderate* (e.g., moderate severity, such as that requiring medical treatment), and *severe* (e.g., high frequency and severe injury, such as that causing scarring or permanent disfigurement) when classifying NSSI, as is done with psychiatric disorders such as major depressive episodes. Several recent studies provide empirical support for such a distinction (e.g., see Klonsky & Olino, 2008; Whitlock, Muehlenkamp, & Eckenrode, 2007). However, here too, there are as yet no clear boundaries for distinguishing among modifiers.

CONCLUSION

Although the terms and definitions outlined in this chapter for SITB in general, and NSSI in particular, are imperfect and evolving in nature, they provide a clear and consistent structure for classifying and studying SITB. The field has advanced beyond using only the terms *suicidal ideation* and *suicide attempts* to describe all SITB and now allows for careful study of these complex behaviors. In addition, recent research demonstrating important differences between suicidal self-injury and NSSI has moved the field beyond the use of vague and general terms such as *parasuicide* and *deliberate self-harm*. Moving forward, more research is necessary to advance understanding of NSSI. Each of the subsequent chapters of this volume is aimed at addressing this goal.

REFERENCES

American Psychiatric Association. (1994). *Diagnostic and statistical manual of mental disorders* (4th ed.). Washington, DC: Author.

Barber, M. E., Marzuk, P. M., Leon, A. C., & Portera, L. (1998). Aborted suicide attempts: A new classification of suicidal behavior. *American Journal of Psychiatry, 155*, 385–389.

Beck, A. T., Davis, J. H., Frederick, C. J., Perlin, S., Pokorny, A. D., Schulman, R. E., et al. (1973). Classification and nomenclature. In H. L. P. Resnick & B. C. Hathorne (Eds.), *Suicide prevention in the seventies* (pp. 7–12). Washington, DC: U.S. Government Printing Office.

Briere, J., & Gil, E. (1998). Self-mutilation in clinical and general population samples: Prevalence, correlates, and functions. *American Journal of Orthopsychiatry, 68*, 609–620.

Brown, G. K., Henriques, G. R., Sosdjan, D., & Beck, A. T. (2004). Suicide intent and accurate expectations of lethality: Predictors of medical lethality of suicide attempts. *Journal of Consulting and Clinical Psychology, 72*, 1170–1174.

Brown, G. K., Ten Have, T., Henriques, G. R., Xie, S. X., Hollander, J. E., & Beck, A. T. (2005). Cognitive therapy for the prevention of suicide attempts: A randomized controlled trial. *Journal of the American Medical Association, 294*, 563–570.

Favazza, A. R. (1989). Why patients mutilate themselves. *Hospital and Community Psychiatry, 40*, 137–145.

Favazza, A. R. (1996). *Bodies under siege: Self-mutilation and body modification in culture and psychiatry* (2nd ed.). Baltimore: Johns Hopkins University Press.

Favazza, A. R., & Conterio, K. (1988). The plight of chronic self-mutilators. *Community Mental Health Journal, 24*, 22–30.

Favazza, A. R., & Conterio, K. (1989). Female habitual self-mutilators. *Acta Psychiatrica Scandanavica, 79*, 283–289.

Favazza, A. R., & Rosenthal, R. J. (1993). Diagnostic issues in self-mutilation. *Hospital and Community Psychiatry, 44*, 134–140.

Fisch, M. (1954). The suicidal gesture: A study of 114 military patients hospitalized because of abortive suicide attempts. *American Journal of Psychiatry, 111*, 33–36.

Harriss, L., & Hawton, K. (2005). Suicidal intent in deliberate self-harm and the risk of suicide: The predictive power of the Suicide Intent Scale. *Journal of Affective Disorders, 86*, 225–233.

Harriss, L., Hawton, K., & Zahl, D. (2005). Value of measuring suicidal intent in the assessment of people attending hospital following self-poisoning or self-injury. *The British Journal of Psychiatry, 186*, 60–66.

Hilt, L. M., Nock, M. K., Lloyd-Richardson, E., & Prinstein, M. J. (2008). Longitudinal study of nonsuicidal self-injury among young adolescents: Rates, correlates, and preliminary test of an interpersonal model. *Journal of Early Adolescence, 28*, 455–469.

Hjelmeland, H. (1996). Verbally expressed intentions of parasuicide: II. Prediction of fatal and nonfatal repetition. *Crisis, 17*, 10–14.

Kessler, R. C., Berglund, P., Borges, G., Nock, M., & Wang, P. S. (2005). Trends in suicide ideation, plans, gestures, and attempts in the United States, 1990–1992 to 2001–2003. *The Journal of the American Medical Association, 293,* 2487–2495.

Klonsky, E. D., & Olino, T. M. (2008). Identifying clinically distinct subgroups of self-injurers among young adults: A latent class analysis. *Journal of Consulting and Clinical Psychology, 76,* 22–27.

Klonsky, E. D., Oltmanns, T. F., & Turkheimer, E. (2003). Deliberate self-harm in a nonclinical population: Prevalence and psychological correlates. *The American Journal of Psychiatry, 160,* 1501–1508.

Linehan, M. M., Armstrong, H. E., Suarez, A., Allmon, D., & Heard, H. L. (1991). Cognitive–behavioral treatment of chronically parasuicidal borderline patients. *Archives of General Psychiatry, 48,* 1060–1064.

Martinson, D. (2007). *Bill of rights for people who self-harm.* Retrieved November 9, 2007, from http://www.enotalone.com/article/2997.html.

Marzuk, P. M., Tardiff, K., Leon, A. C., Portera, L., & Weiner, C. (1997). The prevalence of aborted suicide attempts among psychiatric in-patients. *Acta Psychiatrica Scandanavica, 96,* 492–496.

Merriam-Webster's Collegiate Dictionary (11th ed.). (2005). Springfield, MA: Merriam-Webster.

Muehlenkamp, J. J. (2005). Self-injurious behavior as a separate clinical syndrome. *American Journal of Orthopsychiatry, 75,* 324–333.

Muehlenkamp, J. J., & Gutierrez, P. M. (2004). An investigation of differences between self-injurious behavior and suicide attempts in a sample of adolescents. *Suicide and Life-Threatening Behavior, 34,* 12–23.

Nock, M. K., Holmberg, E. B., Photos, V. I., & Michel, B. D. (2007). Self-Injurious Thoughts and Behaviors Interview: Development, reliability, and validity in an adolescent sample. *Psychological Assessment, 19,* 309–317.

Nock, M. K., Joiner, T. E., Jr., Gordon, K. H., Lloyd-Richardson, E., & Prinstein, M. J. (2006). Non-suicidal self-injury among adolescents: diagnostic correlates and relation to suicide attempts. *Psychiatry Research, 144,* 65–72.

Nock, M. K., & Kazdin, A. E. (2002). Examination of affective, cognitive, and behavioral factors and suicide-related outcomes in children and young adolescents. *Journal of Clinical Child and Adolescent Psychology, 31,* 48–58.

Nock, M. K., & Kessler, R. C. (2006). Prevalence of and risk factors for suicide attempts versus suicide gestures: Analysis of the National Comorbidity Survey. *Journal of Abnormal Psychology, 115,* 616–623.

Nock, M. K., & Prinstein, M. J. (2004). A functional approach to the assessment of self-mutilative behavior. *Journal of Consulting and Clinical Psychology, 72,* 885–890.

Nock, M. K., & Prinstein, M. J. (2005). Clinical features and behavioral functions of adolescent self-mutilation. *Journal of Abnormal Psychology, 114,* 140–146.

Nock, M. K., Wedig, M. M., Janis, I. B., & Deliberto, T. L. (2008). Self-injurious thoughts and behaviors. In J. Hunsely & E. Mash (Eds.), *A guide to assessments that work* (pp. 158–177). New York: Oxford University Press.

O'Carroll, P. W., Berman, A. L., Maris, R. W., Moscicki, E. K., Tanney, B. L., & Silverman, M. M. (1996). Beyond the Tower of Babel: A nomenclature for suicidology. *Suicide and Life-Threatening Behavior, 26*, 237–252.

Pattison, E. M., & Kahan, J. (1983). The deliberate self-harm syndrome. *American Journal of Psychiatry, 140*, 867–872.

Posner, K., Oquendo, M. A., Gould, M., Stanley, B., & Davies, M. (2007). Columbia Classification Algorithm of Suicide Assessment (C-CASA): Classification of suicidal events in the FDA's pediatric suicidal risk analysis of antidepressants. *The American Journal of Psychiatry, 164*, 1035–1043.

Ross, S., & Heath, N. (2002). A study of the frequency of self-mutilation in a community sample of adolescents. *Journal of Youth and Adolescence, 31*, 67–77.

Silverman, M. M., Berman, A. L., Sanddal, N. D., O'Carroll P. W., & Joiner, T. E., Jr. (2007a). Rebuilding the Tower of Babel: A17d nomenclature for the study of suicide and suicidal behaviors. Part 1: Background, rationale, and methodology. *Suicide and Life-Threatening Behavior, 37*, 248–263.

Silverman, M. M., Berman, A. L., Sanddal, N. D., O'Carroll P, W., & Joiner, T. E., Jr. (2007b). Rebuilding the Tower of Babel: A revised nomenclature for the study of suicide and suicidal behaviors. Part 2: Suicide-related ideations, communications, and behaviors. *Suicide and Life-Threatening Behavior, 37*, 264–277.

Simeon, D., & Favazza, A. R. (2001). Self-injurious behaviors: Phenomenology and assessment. In D. Simeon & E. Hollander (Eds.), *Self-injurious behaviors: Assessment and treatment* (pp. 1–28). Washington, DC: American Psychiatric Association.

Tucker, G. J., & Gorman, E. R. (1967). The significance of the suicide gesture in the military. *The American Journal of Psychiatry, 123*, 854–861.

Whitlock, J., Muehlenkamp, J. J., & Eckenrode, J. (2007). *Variation in non-suicidal self-injury: Identification of latent classes in a community population of* young adults. Manuscript submitted for publication.

Zoroglu, S. S., Tuzun, U., Sar, V., Tutkun, H., Savaçs, H. A., Ozturk, M., et al. (2003). Suicide attempt and self-mutilation among Turkish high school students in relation with abuse, neglect and dissociation. *Psychiatry and Clinical Neurosciences, 57*, 119–126.

2

A CULTURAL UNDERSTANDING OF NONSUICIDAL SELF-INJURY

ARMANDO R. FAVAZZA

In this chapter, I present an understanding of nonsuicidal self-injury (NSSI) and body modification from the perspective of cultural psychiatry. Unlike the other chapters in this book, the content of this chapter is primarily based on anthropological, historical, and clinical observational data. Knowledge about the importance of body modification rituals as culturally sanctioned methods of achieving physical healing, spirituality, and social stability may assist clinicians in their attitudes toward and encounters with patients who engage in NSSI. Although NSSI has existed since the earliest days of humankind, speculations about its apparent increased prevalence are presented.

From a cultural psychiatry perspective, *behavior* is considered to be determined by the interplay among a person's environment, life experiences, and biological endowment. *Culture* is the matrix within which these psychological, social, and biological forces operate and become meaningful to human beings. Culture provides an overall consistency to a society's patterns and components over generations. It helps organize diversity and mediate between the forces of stability and conformity and those of new ideas and actions. Culture is not a thing that a person has but an ongoing process created by shared interpersonal experiences that reverberate throughout a society and affect its institutions and the daily life of its members. Matter is neutral; molecules and energies are meaningless until they are personally interpreted, explained, and accepted as reality through the cultural process. Concepts such as social class, mind, biology, and psychology do not materially exist, yet they are accepted as useful in Western societies through the cultural process.

EARLY CONSIDERATIONS OF NONSUICIDAL SELF-INJURY FROM A CULTURAL PSYCHIATRY PERSPECTIVE

In 1980, I was asked by a resident to present some wise cultural psychiatric comments at a grand rounds at my university. The patient, a typical mid-Missouri "cutter," had made many visits to the emergency room and had been hospitalized several times because of her multiple cuts. The resident informed me that his presentation would focus on her behavior as a form of attenuated suicide. I looked through notes from my residency, as well as numerous textbooks, but I could find nothing useful. What was I to say? The patient was evidently intelligent and certainly knew how to kill herself, yet she never did. As luck would have it, I was reading a book about a group of Sufi healers known as the Hamadsha (Crapanzano, 1973). In their healing ceremonies, patients sat in a large circle while the healers, moved by rhythmic music, went into a swirling trance dance. Then, each healer took a knife and slashed his own head. As the blood gushed, the patients were given pieces of bread soaked in the blood to eat. The blood of the Hamadsha was thought to possess healing properties. In Western culture, cutters are deviant, yet among the Hamadsha, healers cut themselves to treat the ill. It got me to thinking.

My attention turned to the Gospel of Mark, in which Jesus met a demon-possessed man in Gadara. The townspeople kept him shackled and chained in the cemetery, but he could not be tamed, and constantly broke free from his bonds. "And always, night and day, he was in the mountains and in the tombs, crying out and cutting himself with stones" (Mark 5:5). This was the earliest case of a repetitive cutter that I have found. Jesus discovered that the man was possessed by a demon called "Legion: for we are many." Jesus exorcised Legion and gave the spirits permission to enter 2,000 swine, which then violently ran into the sea and committed suicide by drowning. It is one hell of a story. The man must have had unconscious suicidal urges, but he did not kill himself. Why? One cannot be sure, but maybe the reason was that he cut himself.

Suddenly I had plenty to say at the grand rounds discussion. The audience was befuddled when I suggested that self-cutting might represent a morbid form of self-help and that NSSI was not quite the senseless, horrific act we had all thought it to be. Perhaps it was a phenomenon worthy of study in its own right. For me, the obvious place to start the process of understanding was by studying the role of culturally sanctioned body modification.

CULTURAL ORIGINS OF HUMAN BODY MODIFICATION

The influences of culture on the human body are myriad. The ability to speak a particular language, for example, depends on a culture-specific neural organization that influences cognitive processing and creation of cognitive schema so as to structure a person's perception and experience of the world (Castillo, 1995; Sperry, 1987).

Culturally sanctioned behaviors that alter or destroy body tissue are found throughout the world and across the millennia. The oldest graphic evidence is found in more than 20,000-year-old imprints in the cave of Gargas in southern France. Although many caves in the region contain such imprints, only in the Gargas cave are the hands missing the tips of four fingers, with only the thumb being spared.

Body modification rituals are not alien to the human condition; rather, they are culturally and psychologically embedded in profound, elemental experiences especially connected to healing, spirituality, and social orderliness. Unlike practices, these rituals are traditional and reflect the history, spiritualism, and beliefs of a society. They affect the individual, but because they are woven into the fabric of social life, they also frequently affect the entire community.

Body modification rituals and NSSI are similar in their shared purposefulness (except in the case of severe mental retardation in which cognitive capacity is minimal and in some cases of illness such as the Lesch–Nyhan syndrome with an overwhelming biological imperative). The identical purpose that these behaviors serve is an attempt to correct or prevent pathological, destabilizing conditions that threaten the community, the individual, or both. Examples of such conditions include (a) individual or epidemic disease; (b) crop failure; (c) widespread sinfulness; (d) angry gods, spirits, or ancestors; (e) failure of boys and girls to accept adult responsibilities when they mature; (f) loosening of clear social role distinctions; (g) loss of group identity and destructiveness; (h) immoral behaviors; (i) ecological disasters; (j) male–female, intergenerational, interclass, intertribal, and interpersonal conflicts; and (k) overwhelming anxiety, depersonalization, fluctuating emotions, and other mental conditions. I do not mean to imply that NSSI is unidimensional or that the social and personal explanations for it are invalid, nor do I wish to minimize the suffering and morbidity that it causes. However, I do contend that at the deepest, irreducible level, the behaviors are prophylactic and salubrious for groups and individuals threatened by death, disorganization, disease, and discomfort. Especially significant for an understanding of NSSI are rituals involving healing, religion, and social orderliness.

Physical Healing

It may seem counterintuitive to destroy or alter body tissue to foster better health and healing, but there are precedents in scientific medicine such as the amputation of an extremity to prevent the spread of gangrene or the destruction of areas in the brain to treat Parkinson's disease and some forms of epilepsy (in rare cases, almost half of a brain may be removed). An ancient practice throughout much of the world involved trephination, a surgical procedure in which the skull was opened with a circular cut, the plug lifted, and the brain exposed. Thousands of trephined skulls have been found, some with multiple holes. Trephination was used to treat severe headaches, epilepsy, vertigo, coma, delirium, and mental illness. One common rationale for the practice was to allow evil spirits to escape through the hole.

I previously referred to the Moroccan Sufi healers, the Hamadsha, who cure persons possessed by jinn spirits. When insulted or injured, the jinn may strike a person blind, deaf, mute or paralyzed, or they may possess offenders and cause them to lose consciousness, to talk in tongues, to have convulsions and tremors, and to manifest abrupt, meaningless changes in activity or speech. Aisha Qandisha, a libidinous, quick-tempered jinn, is important to the Hamadsha; her fondness for blood compels her followers to cut themselves. While in a trance induced by loud and fast music and by twirling and jumping up and down, the Hamadsha slash their own heads with axes and knives, often while seeing a vision of Aisha Qandisha slashing her head. The flow of blood quiets her and allows the healers to smear their blood on the ailing body parts of patients' bodies and also give them bread or sugar cubes soaked in the healer's blood, which is thought to possess a miraculous, saintly healing force.

A particularly informative demonstration of the connection of body modification and healing is found in shamanism. The lineage of priests and physicians traces back to shamans, wise men and women who have devoted their lives to healing the illnesses and reversing the misfortunes of the people of their community. They accomplish this through personal contact with the spirit world, a dangerous world populated by horrific demons.

The greatest student of shamanism, Mircea Eliade (1973), described the most important moments of this process, which demands shamanic initiates to endure and resolve a crisis and a sickness, and then to be "resurrected" as new persons with the power to heal. In a sequence of mystical events, the initiates are eviscerated, tortured, dismembered, and reduced to a skeleton as demons scrape the flesh from their bones, tear out their eyeballs, and remove their bodily fluids. They are then transported to Hell, where their bodies are finely chopped and the pieces distributed to diseased spirits. In Hell, amid great suffering, the initiates learn the secrets of healing. When their bones are covered with new flesh and their bodies are given new blood, they ascend to

Heaven to be consecrated by God before returning to the natural world with a new persona, that of a true shaman. These experiences are mystical, yet they are perceived to be absolutely real.

Although there are variations of this process, a basic theme that exists throughout the world is that body modification is a stepping stone to wisdom, special capacities for healing oneself and others, and a higher level of existence. Shamans allow their bodies to be dismembered and stripped down to the bare bones, and then reconstructed so that they emerge as wiser and healthier persons. Seen from this ancient perspective, the behaviors of persons who engage in NSSI begin to assume a significance that goes beyond the phenomenon of self-injury as merely a method of temporarily alleviating anxiety, depression, depersonalization, and other unpleasant experiences.

Spirituality

In many totally disparate religious traditions mortification of the body is a primary pathway to salvation and to a better relationship with God. During the festival of Husain, for example, large masses of Shiite Moslems flagellate themselves while recalling his words: "Trial, afflictions, and pains, the thicker they fall on man, the better they prepare him for his journey heavenward" (Bowker, 1970, p. 131). In Hinduism, the god Siva is the force of both creation and destruction that demands sacrifice and suffering. Ascetic men, known as sadhus, are revered in India because of their willingness to endure bodily privation to achieve holiness. Some of these gaunt figures may stand on one leg for decades. Some even stretch their penises by using weights until they are able to tie their member into a bow, rendering it totally useless as a sexual organ. At festivals, such as the one devoted to Lord Murugan, devotees go into a trance, pierce their tongues and cheeks with thick pins, and carry heavy religious objects fastened to their bodies by hooks, the better to please their lord.

The *Tibetan Book of the Dead* (Lingpa, 1975) describes a series of meditations on death and birth. The bardo retreat, which takes place in total darkness for 7 weeks, is the most dangerous yet rewarding meditation. The meditator feels detached from the world; at first the peaceful divinities are envisioned along with the eternal peace of the cosmos. However, the wrathful deities of mutilation then appear as a sign of cosmic passion and aggression.

> With teeth biting the lower lip, glassy-eyed, their hair tied on top of their heads, chanting "Strike!" and "Kill!", licking up brains, tearing heads from bodies, pulling out internal organs: in this way they will come.
>
> When projections like this appear do not be afraid. You have a mental body of unconscious tendencies, so even if you are killed and cut into pieces, you cannot die. (Lingpa, 1975, p. 69)

Perfect, instantaneous enlightenment occurs when the meditator understands that he is projecting these horrible images from within himself. After death comes rebirth into another womb. This profound bardo experience is believed to lead sinners to the secret path of wisdom.

The Sun Dance is the index ritual of Native American Plains Indians culture. It lasts for 8 days and is characteristic of buffalo hunting tribes. Participants, the bravest of the braves, volunteer, but the entire tribe cooperates because everyone benefits from the suffering and mutilation of the dancers. At the climax of the ritual, the warrior dancers have pieces of wood with attached leather thongs inserted under the muscles of their chest. The thongs are attached by ropes to the top of the Sacred Pole, and the dancers are hoisted into the air while gazing at the sun. They then struggle until the skewers tear open their muscles and rip through their flesh. The pure of heart able to withstand this religious ordeal are expected to receive a vision that would clarify the meaning and course of their lives.

Alexander (1953) commented on this ritual:

> Possibly, in a more mystical sense, here is shown the drama of all embodied human life—for more than one religion and philosophy, from the ancients onward have depicted man as snared in the flesh, there to suffer and endure, and if by the prowess of his spirit enduring to the end, escaped and triumphant in a new and more spiritual vision. Assuredly there is here an elemental coincidence between the essential elements of Indian and Neo-Platonic or even Christian thinking. (p. 148)

The theme of healing through wounding is a foundation stone of the Judeo-Christian tradition. In Jewish Scripture, Jeremiah (12:1) asked God, "Why is it that the wicked live so prosperously? Why do scoundrels enjoy peace?" Bowker (1970) described the answer that emerged as "perhaps the supreme contribution of Israel to a human response to suffering, that suffering can be made redemptive, that it can become the foundation of better things, collectively, if not individually" (p. 51). Thus, Isaiah described the Suffering Servant, which is a metaphor for the people of Israel:

> Ours were the sufferings he bore, ours the sorrows he carried. But we thought of him as someone punished, struck by God, and afflicted. Yet he was wounded for our transgressions, crusted for our sins. On him lies a punishment that brings us peace, and through his wounds we are healed. (53:4–6)

In Christian Scripture, Jesus was both the Messiah and the Suffering Servant.

> Christ also suffered for you, leaving you an example, that you should follow in his steps. . . . He himself bore our sins in his body on the tree, that we might die to sin and live to righteousness. By his wounds you have been healed. (1 Peter 2:24)

Christ's willingness to be mutilated and killed was an act of redeeming love that was followed by his victorious resurrection. It afforded humankind the opportunity to establish a right relationship with God that involved holding certain beliefs, participating in certain rituals, and following certain rules of conduct. In considering self-injury, two passages are especially portentous:

> It is inevitable that scandal should occur! Nonetheless, woe to the man through whom scandal comes! If your hand or foot is your undoing, cut it off and throw it from you! Better to enter life maimed or crippled than be thrown with two hands or feet into endless fire. If your eye is your downfall, gouge it out and cast it from you! Better to enter life with one eye than be thrown into Gehenna. (Matthew 18:7–9)

> And I [Jesus] say to you, whoever divorces his wife, except for sexual immorality, and marries another, commits adultery. . . . His disciples said to Him, "If such is the case of a man with his wife, it is better not to marry." But He said to them, "All cannot accept this saying, but only those to whom it has been given. For there are eunuchs who were born thus from their mother's womb, and there are eunuchs who were made eunuchs by man, and there are eunuchs who have made themselves eunuchs for the kingdom of heaven's sake. He who is able to accept it, let him accept it." (Matthew 19:9–12)

It should be clear from the examples provided that body modification, in addition to its role in physical healing, also is a pathway through which humankind can achieve spiritual healing, appease the gods, and win their favor.

Social Orderliness

Social orderliness permits a society to function comfortably. Through natural disasters, wars, and rapid innovations, especially technological ones, cultural forces may not be able to preserve order. When this occurs, social life may crumble and even disintegrate with resulting morbidity in all aspects of social life as persons lose their moral compass and become more susceptible to physical and mental disturbances. Culture, however, especially through its rituals, serves to preserve social orderliness while allowing for slowly progressive innovations.

Rituals with the goal of preserving social orderliness involve the highest degree of tissue destruction and modification. This is especially evident in coming-of-age or rites-of-passage ceremonies. Many of these rituals are ancient, going back to the Stone Age, which is the earliest known period of human culture. For communal life to function smoothly, children must progress to adulthood, and a bloody rite-of-passage ritual is the defining moment of this change, signifying that adolescents are ready to accept their new social roles and the status of an adult.

Gould (1969) described this process in which the urethra is cut open with a stone from the tip of the urethral meatus to a point above the scrotum (among the Bardi tribe, the skin is also removed from the entire penis). The resulting artificial hypospadias sometimes heals near the base of the scrotum, so some groups such as the Pidjandjana, add transverse cuts in the area. It should be noted the ritual hypospadias that is created has a religious connotation because it emulates the bifid penis of the totemic kangaroo (Cawte, 1974).

Among the Tiv in Nigeria, genealogy is central to social organization. It determines territorial rights, suitability of marriage partners, land usage, and many rules of personal behavior. In times of intratribal conflicts, certain rituals involving sacred objects are performed by a secret group of elders. These sacred objects are carved statues of women and are seen by only a few select Tiv. The decorations on these statues duplicate the scarification patterns inscribed on the bodies of girls at puberty. The scars represent Tiv family, heritage, land, traditions, genealogy, and myths. According to Lincoln (1981), the scarification

> may represent the structure of time, placing the pubescent girl at the intersection of past and future. Beyond that, it may be taken as a picture of genealogical descent, whereby she is shown to be heir of the ancestors, bearer or descendents, and guarantor of the lineage's continuity. (p. 48)

The scarification transforms the girl into a woman and into a sacred object on whom the group's fertility depends. The scars serve to anchor time and space and to ensure the continuity of communal life.

The male–female relationship is central to the stability of a society. Although the rise of Western feminism in the 20th century has helped to elevate the status and prerogatives of women, in most of the world, men have controlled female behavior. In China, for example, foot binding of women allowed men to keep them prisoners by limiting their mobility (Levy, 1967). The process began in early childhood when a bandage was tightly wrapped around a girl's feet, sparing only the large toe. The object was to break many of the foot bones, to bend the toes into the sole of the foot, and to bring the sole and heel as close together as possible. Toes sometime sloughed off secondary to infection. The pain continued for a year and then diminished as the feet became numb. With such crippled feet, women could not walk alone or "run around."

Another method used to control female behavior is infibulation. Its other name, pharaonic circumcision, attests to its early origins. This body modification ritual, practiced in numerous African countries such as Kenya, Sudan, Somalia, Ethiopia, Egypt, and Nigeria, involves girls between ages 8 to 11 years. The entire clitoris is removed, as are the labia minora and majora and the mons veneris. The vagina is then sewn shut except for a small opening to permit the flow of menstrual blood (Hosken, 1978). An infibulated woman is a guaranteed virgin because the ordeal creates a chastity belt forged out of the woman's own flesh. The procedure is rationalized by the belief that an uncircumcised woman is unclean, is unfit to be a mother or wife, and has an offensive smell that comes from her clitoris. Deprived of the ability to have an orgasm, an infibulated woman is less likely to be unfaithful to her husband. In cultures in which infibulation is practiced, men often have a fear of female sexuality, which is thought to be so powerful that it must be cut away so that communal life may continue in an orderly and unthreatened manner.

RECENT WESTERN PERSPECTIVES ON BODY MODIFICATION

NSSI involves the direct, deliberate destruction or alteration of body tissue. Up until the 1980s, NSSI was mainly regarded as a senseless, sometimes horrific act. An exception was instances in which it was understood as a manipulation designed to achieve a secondary gain, such as a prisoner who cuts his arms in a bid to be relocated, persons who cut themselves in an attempt to keep a spouse or lover from ending their relationship, or patients who injured themselves in an attempt to instill guilt in a therapist who was planning to leave on a vacation.

In terms of prevalence per 100,000 persons per year, the fairly constant suicide rate in the United States is about 13, whereas the rate of NSSI is estimated to be about 1,200 persons (Favazza & Conterio, 1989; see also chap. 3, this volume), yet the literature on the former is extensive compared with the meager literature on the latter. Most publications on NSSI were and continue to be case reports and small group studies with a major emphasis on wrist cutting to the exclusion of the other types of NSSI as well as consideration of a classification or overall perspective on self-injurious behavior. Two of the best early articles were by Graff and Mallin (1967) and Simpson (1975). The former reviewed the literature and described the typical wrist cutter as

> an attractive, intelligent, unmarried young woman who is either promiscuous or overtly afraid of sex, easily addicted and unable to relate to others. . . . She slashes her wrists indiscriminately and repeatedly at the slightest provocation, but she does not commit suicide. She feels relief with the commission of her act. (Graff & Mallin, 1967, p. 38)

The latter compared 24 wrist cutters with a control group of persons who had overdosed. The cutters differed significantly from the control participants in having (a) major mood instability; (b) complaints of emptiness; (c) a strong interest or job in a paramedical field; (d) excessive use of alcohol and drugs; (e) a history of an eating disorder; (f) negative reactions to menarche and menstruation; (g) a history of surgery or hospitalization in early childhood; (h) a home broken by divorce, death, and parental deprivation;

(i) difficulties in verbalizing emotions and needs; (j) a tendency to elope from the hospital; and (k) a pattern of painless cutting and bleeding after a period of depersonalization, followed by relaxation and repersonalization.

Unfortunately, these and other articles made little impact on mental health professionals. Neither did the first book devoted to NSSI: an excellent but little-read study by two psychologists of a repressive Canadian correctional institution for adolescent girls in which 86% of the inmates carved their skin (Ross & McKay, 1979). The investigators concluded that "carving was the girls' way of expressing independence, autonomy, and personal freedom. . . . It was a very adequate way of controlling their social environment" (Ross & McKay, 1979, p. 224). Carving thus provided the girls with a sense of power, satisfaction, and control of their lives.

Until the mid-1990s NSSI was known as self-mutilation (SM), and the topic was deemed unworthy of study by most researchers. Both laypersons and mental health professionals were uneasy with the concept of SM for several reasons. Like anorexia and bulimia nervosa decades earlier, it was thought to be quite rare. Those who would self-mutilate, especially skin cutters, had the reputation of being difficult, unthankful patients. Despite the pleadings of family members and the best efforts of therapists, cutters just would not stop harming themselves. Indeed, a large portion of the literature dealt with the troublesome countertransference they created in everyone who tried to help them. Also, SM was a general term that covered a variety of behaviors. It had a mysterious aura that was best left alone. It was too edgy to even contemplate.

The first person who attempted to consider the totality of SM was Karl Menninger. In his 1938 best seller, *Man Against Himself*, he devoted a chapter to the topic and proposed the first classification: organic, psychotic, neurotic, and religious. His typology never caught on. Readers were taken more with his notions that local self-destruction was a form of partial suicide to avert total suicide and that, because castration is the prototype of all SM, any substituted organ is invariably an unconscious representation of the genital.

H. G. Morgan's *Death Wishes?* (1979) deals with some forms of SM, but the first modern examination of SM was conducted by Mansell Pattison (Pattison & Kahan, 1983). He developed an understanding of self-damaging behaviors on the basis of three variables. The *direct–indirect* variable concerns time and awareness, the *lethality* variable considers the possibility of the behavior resulting in death, and the *repetition* variable refers to the number of times that the behavior occurs. He proposed a deliberate self-harm syndrome, such as chronic skin-cutting, that was direct, repetitive, and had a low lethality. Finally, someone was beginning to address SM in a systematic manner.

The short answer as to why persons engage in NSSI could be that rapid, albeit temporary, relief from troublesome emotions and thoughts is often achieved. The longer answer is that in many cases of major and impulsive NSSI participants both consciously and unconsciously might be seen as tapping into traditions that attempt to foster healing spirituality, and the establishment of orderliness in one's life. How this process might occur is speculative. NSSI has been recorded in all cultures since the earliest days of humankind. Perhaps it is passed on like universally recognized but relatively expressed personality traits such as neuroticism, extroversion, and even psychoticism. Perhaps, like altruism, it can be understood in terms of social evolution. More fancifully, it might be embedded in the Jungian collective unconscious.

Bodies Under Siege: Self-Mutilation and Body Modification in Culture and Psychiatry (Favazza, 1996) is the major sourcebook for both body modification rituals and cases of NSSI. It contains hundreds of cases that demonstrate the examples of the longer answer (e.g., eye enucleation to better one's relationship with God, self-castration to "cure" the perceived illness of homosexuality). Even persistent skin scratching has been interpreted psychodynamically as a mechanism for ridding the body of badness and contamination, such as sexual conflicts. It should be noted that after psychotic acts of NSSI, such as eye enucleation or self-castration, many patients are quite calm, at peace with themselves, and feel relieved and no longer conflicted because they have removed a burdensome organ.

An interesting perspective on Western adolescent skin cutting can be seen vis-à-vis the body modification ordeals in rites-of-passage rituals. Children are transformed into adults when they overcome their fears and allow themselves to be subjected to pain and mutilation. The process induces a peak emotional process that "has the potential to mature consciousness by wasting the innocence of childhood and giving birth to the heightened self-awareness and greater consciousness of adulthood" (Morinis, 1985, p. 167). To gain acceptance into the orderly adult world, the adolescent initiates must agree to surrender part of their autonomy as symbolized by the mutilation. By voluntarily accepting the ordeal, adolescents give visible notice of relinquishing their childhood ways. It is the price that must be paid to partake of adult communal life.

Western adolescents with mental illness who have difficulty with maturing into adults may cut themselves to escape feelings of loneliness and abandonment and to attain the heightened self-awareness that often leads to change and maturity. The cuts may be desperate, primitive attempts to achieve social acceptance and integration into the adult world. They are pacts, unconscious and sealed with blood, indicating the adolescents' desire to be reconciled with society. In fact, when the cuts are discovered, they do force those people in an adolescent's social network to reconsider their relationship with both the cutter and themselves. In some cases, the reconsideration is constructive, even integrative. In other cases, unfortunately, the psychopathology that exists among the network members results in intensified alienation; almost half of cutters have been abused by relatives (Favazza & Conterio, 1989).

Suicidal behavior in which the goal is death is often understandable (e.g., when a person suffers from severe chronic pain, or is diagnosed with a fatal illness, or is profoundly depressed). People mourn the death of those who commit suicide, but in almost all cases, the image of the dead person, no matter how much loved, slowly dims over time. Self-injury in which the goal is not death but rather the betterment of a troubled life is galling. Those who have strived to treat individuals who repetitively self-injure have produced, until very recently, a remarkable literature of negative countertransference as epitomized in the following:

> Of all disturbing patient behaviors, self-mutilation is the most difficult to understand and treat. . . . The typical clinician (including myself) treating a patient who self-mutilates is often left feeling a combination of helpless, horrified, guilty, furious, betrayed, disgusted, and sad. (Frances, 1987, p. 316)

How is one to understand such strong words from an experienced, highly respected psychiatrist? It is frustrating to work intensively with patients who have impulse disorders or AIDS or massive burn wounds or a terminal illness, but those who self-injure seem to be in a class of their own. It is difficult to love someone who self-mutilates. Their very presence seems to threaten the mental and physical integrity of those around them. The power of self-injury to mystify, horrify, and unman even seasoned therapists seem to derive from more than what are generally considered to be the sources of countertransference.

Podvoll (1969) was onto something when he wrote,

> The self-mutilator can incorporate into his actions patterns which, to a greater or lesser degree, remain unarticulated in most of us. That is, such patients already exist in muted intensities with a patient's social field. As such, he may even perform a service to his culture in his dramatic expression of those patterns which are felt to be intolerable within the self. Still other patterns invoked are those that illicit silent levels of admiration and envy. The history of these images reaches at least as far back as the Passion of the Cross and has prevailed among some of the most respected members of our culture. (p. 219)

In addition to the standard psychological reasons, I propose an additional one, not found in other chapters of this book, to explain the profoundly unsettling effect of self-injury on those who witness or have to deal with it. I believe that self-injury rattles one's equanimity because its bloody tendrils reach out to touch the Sacred, which is a holy and scary space that has existed in the human mind since the beginnings of recorded time. The construct of the Sacred involves veneration of a mysterious spiritual power, distinct from the reality of the profane world, that governs the universe, bestows blessings and curses upon humankind, and endures in myths. In the seminal book *Violence and the Sacred*, bloody sacrifice is shown to be the central core of all myth as well as the genesis of tragedy and the source and function of ritual which serves to deflect the primal brutality of violence from human consciousness (Girard, 1972/1977). The ancient origins of sacred violence can be traced back to the most early, deeply layered, and prestigious myths in all cultures—namely, myths of creation.

Lincoln (1975) reconstructed the basic Proto-Indo European mythologem of the creation of the world as recounted in the classic texts of the *Rigveda* (India), the *Greater Bundahism* (Iran), and the *Prose Edda* (Scandinavia). In this primal mythologem, creation is born of violence in the form of sacrifice and mutilation. The sacrifice of this Primordial Being was the origin of the world, and from his mutilation, society and social order were established. Over the millennia, this myth in its various elaborations has been, and continues to be, reenacted in countless religious rituals. The self-injurious acts of some persons with mental illness become demystified in light of this mythic process. Their bodies become a microcosm of the vaster cosmos, and the urge to self-injure becomes an unconscious reenactment of the cosmogonic myth in which chaos is averted and a new order established. However, self-injury offers only a temporary respite from illness rather than a permanent cure because the sacrificial death of the Primordial Being is not fulfilled. The person with mental illness sacrifices a body part or a portion of blood to achieve a modicum of well-being. A partial sacrifice achieves only a partial peace.

In his famous description of the Holy or the Sacred, the theologian Rudolph Otto (1917/1958) had to revert to the Latin *mysterium tremendum et fascinosum*, eerie, numinous, astounding, feelings of wonderment and dread. These feelings are supposedly primary, unique, underived from anything else, and compose the basic factor and impulse underlying the process of religious evolution. At any rate, the terrain of the Sacred is replete with sacrifice and suffering, with the blood of the martyrs, the hearts of victims ripped from their bodies, the beheaded offerings to Kali the Black Goddess, the body parts of Osiris, and the two most widespread and revered religious symbols, the Cross of Christ's Passion and phallic stones that represent the self-severed penis of Siva. This dreadful panorama of the Sacred is so fearsome that religions often sanitize it to protect its devotees. Catholics, for example, believe that the bloodless communion wafer they ingest is truly the blood and flesh of Jesus. Similar transubstantiation of rice cakes into flesh was practiced among the ancient Aryans of India, and in the Aztec sacrificial ritual called "killing the God Huitzlopochtli so that it might be eaten," images of the god made of dough and the blood of children were eaten. Indeed, many religious practices may serve to deflect the attention of devotees away from the blood core of the Sacred.

As behavioral scientists, we are content (and often therapeutically effective) to focus on measurable behaviors. Few are able to look beyond the objective behavior of a self-injurious act and to confront its inner, violent, sacred core directly. Such a confrontation is too unsettling, so we distance ourselves from individuals who self-injure by developing a protective counter-transference. However, some shamans have the ability to see the wounds of those who self-injure as an opening to the Sacred, and a few priests can, as can those persons who have endured the Tibetan bardo retreat, and perhaps some wise therapists. What they see cannot be measured, but it can be felt deeply and empathically.

The act of NSSI is understood as a morbid form of self-help that provides generally temporary respite from troublesome feelings and thoughts. Examination of the behavior from a cultural perspective provides a deeper insight that may facilitate the way behavioral psychologists understand and interact with clients who self-injure. The individual human body mirrors the collective social body, and each creates and sustains the other. Psychosis, neurosis, disordered personality, and all the symptoms associated with personal mental illness defy a comprehensive understanding unless one also considers the psychological, social, cultural, and physical integrity of the communal "body." The eternal struggles between men and women, parents and children, friends and foes, humankind and the environment, the flesh and the spirit are played out through the myths and personal dramas of cutting, dismemberment, and reassembly—of wounding and healing.

NSSI is more than a simple deviant act. It is also the expression of a struggle to lead a normal life. Cutting the skin may release "bad blood" as well as provide an opening into the interior. Everyday life is mostly lived on the surface, but the examined life that gets to the heart of things often necessitates the painful process of dissection. For most, dissection is a metaphor for introspection and intellectual self-examination, but for others, it is a literal, physical act. Certainly one can entertain the notion that extirpation of pathological thoughts, emotions, and behaviors might be achieved as well by cutting their roots as by poisoning and chasing them away with drugs, by chanting psychomantras, by providing interpretive insights, or by redirecting them into more socially acceptable forms. As I concluded in *Bodies Under Siege* (1996),

> It is easy to forget that dripping blood may accompany birth as well as death. The scars of the process are more than the artless artifacts of a twisted mind. They signify an ongoing battle and that all is not lost. As befits one of nature's triumphs, scar tissue is a magical substance, a physiological and psychological mortar that holds flesh and spirit together when a difficult world threatens to tear us apart. Self-injurers seek what we all seek: an ordered life, spiritual peace—maybe even salvation—and a healthy mind in a healthy body. Their desperate methods are upsetting

to those of us who try to achieve those goals in a more tranquil manner, but the methods rest firmly on the dimly perceived bedrock of the human experience. (pp. 322–323)

CURRENT CULTURAL INFLUENCES ON BODY MODIFICATION

Most body modification practices, unlike rituals, are performed to promote beauty and to enhance sexuality; to signify membership in a particular group; to mimic the behavior of highly publicized athletes, rock stars, and actors who have tattoos and piercings; or to express rebelliousness and individuality. Examples of these behaviors are earlobe piercing to affix jewelry, insertion of nipple rings, tattoos to indicate membership in a gang or fraternity, and a simple tattoo on the ankle. The widespread fad of body piercing and tattooing in Western nations may often be the result of dissatisfaction with an increasingly bureaucratic and computer-driven society in which people are identified by numbers and passwords and in which artificial products are replacing "the real thing" and the living of life is passively experienced by watching television, listening to music through headphones for hours on end, and interacting mainly with virtual figures while playing videogames. Other factors that may play a role include the increase in fragmented family life through divorce and both parents working that often results in bored children with time on their hands. The quality of communication with peers has deteriorated as high-tech options, such as text messaging or instant messaging, have become prominent (Kraut et al., 1998; Van den Eijnden, Meerkerk, Vermulst, Spijkerman, & Engels, 2008). The social acceptability of NSSI is evidenced by the expanding number of Internet sites and chat rooms devoted to both body modification and deviant behaviors such as cutting and even amputation. In my experience, contagion often plays a role in high school NSSI in that small groups of students may cluster together to compare and sometimes escalate their acts of NSSI. A large portion of a recent book on treating NSSI is devoted to its detection and treatment in high school (Walsh, 2006). Body piercing has probably contributed to the increased prevalence of deviant skin cutting simply because allowing someone to pierce one's body lowers the fear threshold and makes it easier to cut oneself or, at least, to contemplate doing it. Also, unpublished data that I have collected on 173 students who have attended an accredited school for body piercing from 2004 to the present reveal that 58% have a history of self-cutting. Their choice of profession appears to be an instance of sublimation.

There seems to be a relative increase in NSSI, although the behavior was closeted until the 1990s (Ross & Heath, 2000). In my opinion, the primary factor in this increase has been media attention given to prominent persons ranging from Princess Diana to actor Johnny Depp, who were or are cutters.

Also, almost every popular television news and talk show (e.g., *20/20, The Oprah Winfrey Show, Phil Donahue, Dr. Phil, Dateline*) has devoted many hours to this topic. *Time, Newsweek, The New York Times,* and numerous other newspapers and magazines (especially those popular with women and teenagers) have published articles on cutters. In a 1989 study of 234 females who self-injure, 95% said that they just "stumbled on" the behavior (Favazza & Conterio, 1989, p. 286). In contrast, in my clinical encounters since the late 1990s with more than 500 individuals who self-injure, almost all have said that they learned about the behavior from the media or from friends who got the idea from television shows, magazines, and movies.

CONCLUSION

Thorough understanding of the psychological, biological, and social forces that result in NSSI can be achieved only by also considering the overarching influence of culture, which reveals the multilayered complexity of the behavior. NSSI may be understood as a morbid form of self-help in that it does provide temporary respite from a host of psychopathological symptoms. In many cases, however, it additionally may represent a desperate attempt by those who self-injure to experience healing, social stability, and some measure of spirituality. An awareness of these understandings may positively impact the approach of therapists who treat such individuals whose behaviors typically illicit feelings of countertransference.

REFERENCES

Alexander, H. B. (1953). *The world's rim: Great mysteries of the North American Indians.* Lincoln: University of Nebraska Press.

Bowker, J. (1970). *Problems of suffering in the religions of the world.* Cambridge, England: Cambridge University Press.

Castillo, R. (1995). Culture, trance, and the mind–brain. *Anthropology of Consciousness, 6,* 17–34.

Cawte, J. (1974). *Medicine is the law.* Honolulu: University Press of Hawaii.

Cohn, N. (1958). *The pursuit of the millennium.* New York: Basic Books.

Crapanzano, V. (1973). *The Hamadsha.* Berkeley: University of California Press.

Eliade, M. (1973). *Rites and symbols of initiation.* New York: Harper & Row.

Favazza, A. R. (1996). *Bodies under siege: Self-mutilation and body modification in culture and psychiatry (2nd ed.).* Baltimore: Johns Hopkins University Press.

Favazza A. R., & Conterio K. (1989). Female, habitual self-mutilators. *Acta Psychiatrica Scandinavcia, 79,* 283–289.

Frances, A. (1987). Introduction to the section on self-mutilation. *Journal of Personality Disorder, 1,* 316.

Girard, R. (1977). *Violence and the sacred* (P. Gregory, Trans.). Baltimore: Johns Hopkins University Press. (Original work published 1972)

Gould, R. (1969). *Yiwara: Foragers of the Australian Desert*. New York: Scribner.

Graff, H., & Mallin, R. (1967). The syndrome of the wrist cutter. *American Journal of Psychiatry, 124,* 36–42.

Hosken, F. (1978). The epidemiology of female genital mutilation. *Tropical Doctor, 8,* 150–156.

Keller, M. (1970). The great Jewish drink mystery. *British Journal of Addiction, 64,* 287–296.

Kraut, R., Patterson, M., Lundmark, V., Kiesler, S., Mukopadhyay, T., & Scherlis, W. (1998). Internet paradox: A social technology that reduces social involvement and psychological well-being. *American Psychologist, 53,* 1017–1031.

Levy, H. (1967). *Chinese footbinding: The history of a curious erotic custom*. New York: Bell.

Lincoln, B. (1975). The Indo-European myth of creation. *History of Religion, 15,* 121–145.

Lincoln, B. (1981). *Emerging from the chrysalis*. Cambridge, MA: Harvard University Press.

Lingpa, K. (1975). *The Tibetan book of the dead: The great liberation through hearing in the bardo* (F. Fremantle & C. Trungpa, Trans.). London: Shambhala.

Menninger, K. (1938). *Man against himself*. New York: Harcourt, Brace, World.

Morgan, H. G. (1979). *Death wishes?* New York: Wiley.

Morinis, A. (1985). The ritual experience. *Ethos, 13,* 150–174.

Otto, R. (1958). *The idea of the holy* (J. W. Harvey, Trans.). New York: Oxford University Press. (Original work published 1917)

Pattison, M., & Kahan J. (1983). The deliberate self-harm syndrome. *American Journal of Psychiatry, 140,* 867–872.

Podvoll, E. (1969). Self-mutilation within a hospital setting. *British Journal of Medical Psychology, 42,* 213–221.

Ross, R., & McKay, H. (1979). *Self-mutilation*. Lexington, MA: Lexington Books.

Ross, S., & Heath N. (2000). A study of the frequency of self-mutilation in a community sample of adolescents. *Journal of Youth and Adolescence, 1,* 67–77.

Simpson, C. A. (1975). The phenomenology of self-mutilation in a general hospital setting. *Canadian Psychiatric Association Journal, 20,* 429–434.

Sperry, R. (1987). Structure and significance of the consciousness revolution. *The Journal of Mind and Behavior, 8,* 37–65.

Van den Eijnden, R. J., Meerkerk, G. J., Vermulst, A. A., Spijkerman, R., & Engels, R. C. (2008). Online communication, compulsive Internet use, and psychosocial well-being among adolescents: A longitudinal study. *Developmental Psychology, 44,* 655–665.

Walsh, B. (2006). *Treating self-injury*. New York: Guilford Press.

3

EPIDEMIOLOGY AND PHENOMENOLOGY OF NONSUICIDAL SELF-INJURY

KAREN RODHAM AND KEITH HAWTON

An understanding of the epidemiology and phenomenology of non-suicidal self-injury (NSSI) is vital for researchers, clinicians, and policymakers interested in this problem. The outcomes of recent studies have provided data that answer basic questions concerning these aspects of NSSI. For example, rates are much higher among adolescents and young adults than among children and older adults. Also, studies demonstrate higher rates among females, although the behavior is more common than previously thought among males. In this chapter, we provide an overview of the information currently available concerning the epidemiology and the phenomenology of NSSI. We conclude with an agenda for future work in this area directed at addressing gaps in our current knowledge.

CHALLENGES IN DETERMINING PREVALENCE OF NONSUICIDAL SELF-INJURY

The process of establishing the prevalence of self-injury is complicated for several reasons. First is the lack of consensus on terms and definitions of the behavior in existing studies. Second, and related, is that terms used to describe self-injury are sometimes left undefined. Third, data collection methods have previously tended to be based on hospital presentations; however, it is now recognized that much NSSI occurs in the community and does not come to clinical attention.

Earlier in this book, Nock and Favazza highlighted that finding an acceptable definition for self-injury has proved complicated (see chap. 1). In addition to the range of inconsistent terms used by researchers to describe self-injurious behaviors, there is also debate about which specific behaviors should be classified as constituting self-injury (e.g., see Mental Health Foundation, 2006; Platt et al., 1992). For example, both Jacobsen and Gould (2007) and Claes and Vandereycken (2007) noted that whereas in the United States the term *deliberate self-harm* is used to refer to NSSI, in the United Kingdom the same term is used in its broader sense and refers to any purposeful, nonlethal self-injurious act performed with or without suicidal intent; this would therefore include the act of taking an overdose (something not included in the definition of *NSSI*), as well as acts of attempted suicide. This lack of consensus about terms and definitions among researchers and clinicians is proving problematic because this makes it difficult to compare and interpret prevalence rates. In this chapter, in addition to discussing NSSI, *deliberate self-harm* (with or without suicidal intent) is defined as

> an act with a non-fatal outcome in which an individual deliberately did one or more of the following: initiated behavior which they intended to cause self-harm; ingested a substance in excess of the prescribed or generally recognized therapeutic dose; ingested a recreational or illicit drug that was an act the person regarded as self-harm; ingested a non-ingestible substance or object. (Hawton, Rodham, & Evans, 2006, p. 29)

Until researchers and clinicians reach agreement as to the definition and labeling of NSSI, it is difficult to present a clear epidemiological picture of the behavior.

An additional problem is that in many published articles, researchers have provided no definition for the behavior. This makes comparison of findings impossible because of the uncertainty as to whether like is being compared with like. A further complication is that researchers who do define the term they have used do not always explain its meaning to participants. This means that reliance is then placed entirely on the participants' interpretation of the question(s) asked. This issue is further magnified if participants are simply required to tick a box as a means of indicating that they have self-injured. We argue that researchers should include an explanation of the term being used and that they ask participants to describe in their own words the self-injurious behavior(s) in which they have engaged. This allows the investigators to determine whether participants' behaviors correspond with predetermined criteria (Hawton,

Rodham, & Evans, 2006). In doing this, researchers are able to exclude from analysis cases in which participants have clearly misunderstood what is meant by self-injury. This procedure also enables them to gain insight into how participants' experiences, definitions, and perceptions of self-injury may differ from those held by the research community (Laye-Gindhu & Schonert-Reichl, 2005).

Another important issue concerns how data are collected. Until now much research has relied on data collected by means of monitoring presentations to hospital and other clinical settings. Such monitoring is useful to demonstrate the requirements for hospital service provision, follow trends over time, and evaluate prevention strategies (Hawton, Bale, et al., 2006). However, concerns have been raised about generalizing results from research based on clinical samples to the general population (e.g., see Laye-Gindhu & Schonert-Reichl, 2005). A large-scale community study of adolescents revealed that only 6.3% of those engaging in self-cutting (with or without suicidal intent) reported presenting to a general hospital (Hawton, Harriss, Simkin, Bale, & Bond, 2004). Furthermore, in the United States, the Centers for Disease Control and Prevention (2004) reported that only 2.9% of adolescents who reported making a suicide attempt in the preceding year said that this behavior had resulted in presentation to a doctor or nurse, whereas in Canada, Rhodes, Bethell, and Bondy (2006) reported that less than 1 in 3 of those who took part in the research had had contact with the health service. In short, the findings of these studies suggest that hospital-based studies may exclude a significant proportion of those who engage in NSSI but have not reached the attention of the clinical services.

METHODS OF NONSUICIDAL SELF-INJURY

NSSI was defined by Nock, Joiner, Gordon, Lloyd-Richardson, and Prinstein (2006) as the "direct, deliberate destruction of one's own body tissue in the absence of intent to die" (see chap. 1, this volume). Typical methods used by those engaging in NSSI include skin cutting, burning, hitting, severe skin scratching, and interfering with wound healing (Briere & Gil, 1998; Favazza, 1998; Favazza & Conterio 1989; Klonsky, 2007; Muehlenkamp, 2005). Klonsky (2007) highlighted research suggesting that skin cutting is the most common method, occurring in between 70% to 90% of individuals who engage in NSSI, followed by banging or hitting (21%–44%) and burning (15%–35%; Briere & Gil, 1998; Nijman et al., 1999). It is also apparent that many individuals tend to use more than one method (Favazza & Conterio, 1989; Gratz, 2001; Herpetz, 1995).

Estimates of rates of NSSI have ranged widely from 400 to 1,400 cases per 100,000 annually (Favazza, 1998; Pattison & Kahan, 1983). Most studies have focused on clinical cases, and estimates range between 4% and 20% (Briere & Gil, 1998) for adult psychiatric inpatients and up to 40% for adolescent inpatients (Darche, 1990; Hurry, 2000). Muehlenkamp (2005) noted that although few studies have been conducted on the prevalence of NSSI in community samples, the evidence to date suggests that the occurrence of self-injurious behaviors is increasing, especially among adolescents and college and university students. To support her assertion, she referred to work completed by the Centre for Suicide Research in the United Kingdom, where hospital presentation rates have been monitored over many years (Hawton, Fagg, & Simkin, 1996; Hawton, Fagg, Simkin, Bale, & Bond, 1997), as well as work completed in the United States that focused on students (Gratz, 2001). Additional evidence was cited by Hawton, Rodham, and Evans (2006), who highlighted an increase in rates of deliberate self-harm (including NSSI and drug overdose) in recent years (O'Loughlin & Sherwood, 2005).

One recent prospective study was conducted by Zanarini, Frankenburg, Hennen, Reich, and Silk (2005) to assess the course of NSSI in adults (ages 18–35) who met the criteria for borderline personality disorder (BPD). At baseline, 81% of the participants indicated that they had engaged in NSSI within the previous 2 years, whereas only 26% reported doing so at a 6-year follow-up, thereby suggesting that NSSI decreases over time, at least among people with BPD. Clearly more studies of this type conducted on community samples would enable researchers to explore the course of NSSI over time, assess risk factors for continuing to engage in NSSI, and to assess whether different explanations that individuals offer for engaging in NSSI are associated with different outcomes.

Age

Researchers have explored the prevalence of NSSI at different stages of the lifespan; typically children and adolescents, young adults, and older people have been focused on. The following section outlines in more detail some of the key findings that have been reported for these three groups.

Children and Adolescents

Recent studies have reported an average age of onset of between 12 and 14 years (see Table 3.1; see also Kumar, Pepe, & Steer, 2004; Muehlenkamp & Guttierrez, 2004; Nock & Prinstein, 2004; Ross & Heath, 2002); earlier studies suggested that NSSI is rare in children under age 14 and usually

TABLE 3.1
The Prevalence of Nonsuicidal Self-Injury (NSSI) in Children and Adolescents

Author/location	Methodology	Outcome assessed	Time frame	N	Age (yrs)	Notes
Brent et al. (1993)/ United States	Case control study, psychological autopsy vs. semistructured psychiatric interviews	Completed suicide vs. matched community control	N/A	67 participants who had completed suicide (85% male); 67 matched control participants, (85% male)	Mean (suicide group): 17.1 Mean (control group): 17.3	A significantly greater percentage of those who had completed suicide had engaged in past suicidal behavior compared with the control participants (25.8% vs. 1.5%).
Fergusson Horwood, Ridder, and Beautrais (2005)/ New Zealand	25-year longitudinal study	Suicidal ideation and suicide attempt	Lifetime	1,025 (50% male)	Range: 18–25	Of participants in the study, 21.2% reported experiencing suicidal thoughts or making a suicide attempt by age 18.
Hawton, Houston, and Shepperd (1999)/ United Kingdom	Study of coroners' inquest notes, general practitioners' records, and psychiatric case notes	Completed suicide	N/A	174 (85% male)	Range: 13–24	A prior history of deliberate self-harm (including NSSI) was found in 44.8% of participants.

(continues)

TABLE 3.1
The Prevalence of Nonsuicidal Self-Injury (NSSI) in Children and Adolescents   (Continued)

Author/location	Methodology	Outcome assessed	Time frame	N	Age (yrs)	Notes
Hawton and Harriss (in press)/ United Kingdom	Study of all patients presenting to the hospital following deliberate self-harm 1995 through 2004.	Deliberate self-harm	N/A	3,628 (40% male)	Range: 10–80+	The article highlights that studies providing overall gender ratios for deliberate self-harm may conceal changes in the ratio across the life span.
Hawton, Zahl, and Weatherall (2003)/ United Kingdom	Mortality follow-up study of patients who had presented to the hospital following deliberate self-harm 1978 through 1997.	Deliberate self-harm, particularly suicide	N/A	11,583 (40% male)	Range: 10–55+	Three hundred (2.6%) had died by suicide at follow-up. In both sexes, the authors noted a marked escalation in risk of suicide with increasing age at the time of the initial deliberate self-harm episode.
Herpertz (1995)/ Germany	Study of patients admitted to psychiatric care over 2-year period	Self-injurious behavior (presence of suicidal intent unknown)	N/A	54 (13% male)	Range: 16–57 Mean, female: 27 Mean, male: 25	Peak age of onset of the behavior was 18 to 24.

Study/Country						Results
Houston, Hawton, and Shepperd (2001)/ United Kingdom	Psychological autopsy	Completed suicide vs. undetermined death	N/A	27 (93% male; death recorded as suicide, $n = 24$; death recorded as undetermined, $n = 3$); subsample of 22 were matched (age and sex) with a group that had survived deliberate self-harm	Range: 15–24	Results showed strong links to psychiatric disorders in those who had committed suicide. Comparison of the suicide group with age- and sex-matched participants who had survived deliberate self-harm showed that participants in the suicide group used more dangerous methods and that a markedly greater proportion of them lived alone.
Jacobson and Gould (2007)/ United States	Review article	NSSI	Lifetime	25 articles	Articles were included if they focused on children and adolescents (age not specifically reported).	The review reports a lifetime prevalence of NSSI ranging from 13.0% to 23.2%.
Klonsky (2007)/ United States	Review article	NSSI	Lifetime	18 studies included	Range: 15–37	Reports a range of lifetime NSSI instances from 3.4 (Soloff, Lis, Kelly, Cornelius, & Ulrich, 1994) to 50.0 (Favazza & Conterio, 1989).

(continues)

Author/location	Methodology	Outcome assessed	Time frame	N	Age (yrs)	Notes
Kumar, Pepe, and Steer (2004)/ United States	Cross-sectional study of adolescent psychiatric inpatients	Self-cutting (absence of conscious suicidal intent)	Lifetime	50 (38% male)	Range: 13–17	Results show no gender differences among adolescent inpatients when reporting reasons for self-cutting, and self-reported depression scores were positively associated with the number of motivations for self-injury.
Marttunen, Aro, and Lönnqvist (1993)/Finland	Review of psychological autopsy studies	Completed suicide, prior episodes of deliberate self-harm	N/A	298 (from 7 studies)	Range: 9–20	The article notes that before suicide, one third of cases had carried out a previous nonfatal act of self-harm (NSSI not reported separately).
Muehlemkamp and Gutierrez (2002)/ United States	Survey of high school students	NSSI	Lifetime	390 (45% male)	Mean: 16.27	Of the students enrolled, 15.9% had engaged in NSSI.

Study/Country	Sample	Measure	Timeframe	N	Age	Findings
Muehlenkamp and Gutierrez (2004)/United States	Suicide screening at a U.S. high school	NSSI	Past year	540 (38% male)	Mean: 15.3	Fifteen percent of participants reported that the NSSI began at age 13; 28.4% reported onset at age 14.
Nock and Prinstein (2004)/United States	Clinical interviews with adolescent inpatients	NSSI	Past year	108 (30% male)	Mean: 14.8	Most individuals began engaging in NSSI in early adolescence (mean age: 12.8).
Nock, Joiner, Gordon, Lloyd-Richardson, and Prinstein (2006)/United States	Clinical interviews with adolescent inpatients who had engaged in NSSI in previous 12 months	NSSI	Past year	89 (26% male)	Range: 12–17 Mean: 14.7	Noted a surprisingly high rate of suicide attempts in those adolescents engaging in recent NSSI. More than 70% reported a lifetime history of at least one suicide attempt.
Ross and Heath (2002)/United States	Community sample of high school students	NSSI	Lifetime	440	Range: 12–16 Mean: 14	Of participants who engaged in NSSI, 59% said they began to do so at age 12; 24% were age 11 or younger.

appears between ages 14 and 24 (Favazza & Conterio, 1989; Herpetz, 1995). Indeed, Skegg (2005) reported that in the United States, the most common age for first onset of deliberate self-harm is 16. More recently, in a survey of school pupils in Australia, the onset of deliberate self-harm was associated with pubertal stage (normally late or completed puberty). Additional risk factors for deliberate self-harm were depression, alcohol abuse, and sexual activity (Patton et al., 2007).

Regardless of age of onset, following an episode of self-injury, repetition of the behavior is common. For example, Klonsky (2007) noted that estimates for the average number of lifetime instances of NSSI range from 3.4 to 50.0. In their recent review, Jacobson and Gould (2007) also highlighted the range in levels of reported frequency with which adolescents engage in NSSI and suggested that further research is necessary to clarify the risk factors for repetition of NSSI.

Long-term follow-up of older adolescents who have engaged in deliberate self-harm indicates a high rate of suicide attempts in young adulthood and other adverse mental health outcomes, especially depression (Fergusson, Horwood, Ridder, & Beautrais, 2005), as well as risk of actual suicide (Hawton & Harriss, 2007; Hawton, Zahl, & Weatherall, 2003). Indeed, Nock et al. (2006) noted that although NSSI and suicide attempts are distinct behavioral phenomena, they often co-occur within individuals (Brown, Comtois, & Linehan, 2002; Dulit, Fyer, Leon, Brodsky, & Frances, 1994). Studies of young people who have died by suicide also highlight the association between self-injury and suicide. For example, in an investigation of suicide in 174 young people ages 13 to 24, 44.8% were known to have a prior history of deliberate self-harm, often through NSSI (Hawton, Houston, & Shepperd, 1999). Similarly, in psychological autopsy studies of young people who had died by suicide (which included interviews with relatives), between a quarter and two thirds had carried out previous nonfatal acts of deliberate self-harm (Brent et al., 1993; Houston, Hawton, & Shepperd, 2001; Marttunen, Aro, & Lönnqvist, 1993).

Young Adults

Young adults between ages 18 and 25 are thought to be in the highest risk group for engaging in NSSI (see Table 3.2). For example, Favazza, DeRosear, and Conterio (1989) found that 12% of college students had engaged in NSSI. Other researchers have reported rates of deliberate self-harm ranging from 5% to 13% (e.g., see Nada-Raja, Skegg, Langley, Morrison, & Showerby, 2004; Skegg, Nada-Raja, Dickson, Paul, & Williams, 2003). However, in a random survey of 3,000 college students, Whitlock, Eckenrode, and Silverman (2006) found a lifetime NSSI prevalence of 17%. Other smaller studies of college students have reported NSSI rates ranging from

TABLE 3.2

The Prevalence of Nonsuicidal Self-Injury (NSSI) in Young Adults

Author/location	Methodology	Outcome assessed	Time frame	N	Age (yrs)	Notes
Favazza, DeRosear, and Conterio(1989)/ United States	Survey of those reporting engaging in NSSI	NSSI	Lifetime	254 (5% male)	Mean: 28	Of the 254 college students surveyed, 12% reported engaging in NSSI.
Gratz, Conrad, and Roemer (2002)/ United States	Survey of under- graduate psychology students	NSSI	Lifetime	133 (33% male)	Range: 18–49 Mean: 22.73	A history of NSSI was reported by 38% of participants.
Nada-Raja, Skegg, Langley, Morrison, and Sowerby (2004)/ New Zealand	Birth cohort study	Deliberate self-harm	Lifetime, past year	966 (51% male)	26	Lifetime prevalence of deliberate self-harm was 13%, and lifetime prevalence of suicide attempts was 9% of sample; 3% of sam- ple reported self-injury (mostly without suicidal intent) in the past year.
Skegg, Nada-Raja, Dickson, Paul, and Williams(2003)/ New Zealand	Birth cohort study inter- viewing those age 26	Deliberate self-harm	Lifetime	946	26	Opposite-sex attraction (men = 7%, women = 13%), minor same-sex attraction (men = 29%, women 19%), persist- ent major same-sex attraction (men = 38%, women = 44%).

(continues)

TABLE 3.2
The Prevalence of Nonsuicidal Self-Injury (NSSI) in Young Adults   (Continued)

Author/location	Methodology	Outcome assessed	Time frame	N	Age (yrs)	Notes
White, Trepal-Wollenzier, and Nolan (2002)/ United States	Review article on self-injury among college students	NSSI	N/A	N/A	Range: 18–22	Stated that "traditional college-age" (i.e., 18–22) students fall in the range of the highest risk of NSSI.
Whitlock, Eckenrode, and Silverman (2006)/ United States	Internet-based survey	NSSI	Lifetime	2,875 (44% male)	Range (73% of sample): 18–24 Range (27% of sample): 24+	Lifetime prevalence was 17%; past year prevalence was 7.3%.

12% to as high as 38% (e.g., see Gratz, Conrad, & Roemer, 2002; Muehlenkamp & Guttierez, 2004).

Older Adults

Studies of deliberate self-harm among older individuals (i.e., those over age 60) have tended to include relatively small (Hepple & Quinton, 1997; Lamprecht, Pakrasi, Gash, & Swann, 2005) and sometimes unrepresentative clinical samples (see Table 3.3). Furthermore, Hawton and Harriss (2006) noted that they have often been based on case-note review rather than prospectively identified. Also, much of the work with this population has tended to focus on behaviors that include, but do not focus exclusively on, NSSI. Nevertheless, it has been suggested that self-injurious behavior in older people is often associated with high suicidal intent (Conwell, 1997; Draper, 1996; Sakinofsky, 2000). In a 20-year prospective study of 730 patients ages 60 and older who presented to a general hospital in the United Kingdom following deliberate self-harm (the prevalence of self-poisoning and self-injury was reported separately), Hawton and Harriss (2006) found that 8.5% of the sample who presented over the 10-year period had engaged in self-injury alone, 88.6% had self-poisoned, and 2.9% had both self-injured and self-poisoned. They concluded deliberate self-harm in older people was closely related to suicide and that, as a consequence, all self-injurious behaviors in older people must be taken seriously, with admission to a general hospital bed and mandatory careful assessment paying special attention to those with a history of such behavior. Given the serious implications of the existing research, it is clear that further attention focusing explicitly on older individuals who engage in NSSI is warranted.

Gender

Although suicide death is more common among males than females, findings from studies of hospital admissions suggest that average rates of suicide ideation, suicide attempts, and NSSI are consistently higher among females than males (see Table 3.4; see also Hawton, Harriss, et al., 2003; Kerfoot, Dyer, Harrington, & Woodham, 1996; Schmidtke et al., 1996). Furthermore, Hawton, Rodham, Evans, and Weatherall (2002) found that reports of deliberate self-harm (with or without suicidal intent) were nearly 4 times as frequent in girls compared with boys who participated in their large-scale community study of 15- and 16-year-olds. The results from other community-based studies suggest that this pattern is internationally consistent (E. Evans, Hawton, Rodham, & Deeks, 2005). Similarly for the adult population, Ogundipe (1999) and Suyemoto (1998) suggested that self-injurious behavior is more common among women.

TABLE 3.3
The Prevalence of Nonsuicidal Self-Injury in Older Adults

Author/location	Methodology	Outcome assessed	Time frame	N	Age (yrs)	Notes
Conwell (1997)/United States	Review	Suicide attempts	Not mentioned	N/A	Range: 65+	Notes that self-injurious behaviors in older people is often associated with high suicidal intent.
Draper (1996)/Australia	Review	Deliberate self-harm	Not mentioned	2,180 (40% male)	Range: 55+	A range of 75% to 100% of older people in the studies who self-harmed had high suicidal intent.
Hawton and Harriss (2006)/United Kingdom	20-year prospective investigation and follow-up of patients presenting to hospital after deliberate self-harm	Deliberate self-harm	N/A	730 (37% male)	Range: 60+	Of the total sample, 8.4% had engaged in deliberate self-harm.
Hepple and Quinton (1997)/United Kingdom	Prospective investigation and follow-up of patients presenting to general hospital following suicide attempt	Suicide attempt	Average length of follow-up = 3.5 years	100 (36% male)	Range: 65+	Of the total sample, 2% had engaged in self-injury (presence of suicidal intent unknown).
Lamprecht, Pakrasi, Gash, and Swann (2005)/United Kingdom	Older people presenting to hospital following a deliberate self-harm episode	Deliberate self-harm	N/A	84 (40% male)	Mean (male): 72.5 Mean (female): 75.3	Overdose was the method of choice in 93% of deliberate self-harm episodes. Only 6% ($n = 5$) engaged in self-cutting.
Sakinofsky (2000)/Canada	Reviewed prospective follow-up studies of attempted suicide	Suicide attempt	Review	29 studies (participants' sex not reported for all studies)	Range: 13–88	Concluded that an older age sample generally reports higher suicidal intent.

TABLE 3.4

Gender Differences in the Prevalence of Nonsuicidal Self-Injury (NSSI)

Author/location	Methodology	Outcome assessed	Time frame	N	Age (yrs)	Notes
Briere and Gil (1998)/ United States	Study 1: General population survey Study 2: Clinical sample	Self-mutilation (presence of suicidal intent unknown)	Study 1: Past 6 months Study 2: Past 6 months	Study 1: 927 (50% male) Study 2: 390 (22% male)	Mean (Study 1): 46 Mean (Study 2): 36	Study 1: 4.0% had at least occasionally self-mutilated, 0.3% reported doing so often. Study 2: 21% had at least occasionally self-mutilated, 8% reported doing so often.
Cooper et al. (2006)/United Kingdom	Study of presentations to hospital	Deliberate self-harm	4 years	7,185 (45% male)	Range: 15–65	Of the total sample, 16.6% of males and 9.5% of females presented following deliberate self-injury.
Evans, Hawton, Rodham, and Deeks (2005)/ United Kingdom	Review article	Deliberate self-harm	Lifetime	513,188	Mean: 15.7 (not reported in all studies included)	The average prevalence rate was 9.7% and was significantly higher among female participants.
Hawton, Rodham, Evans, and Weatherall (2002)/United Kingdom	Community survey	Deliberate self-harm	Past year	6,020	Range: 15–16	Of the total sample, 3.2% of male vs. 11.2% of female participants reported deliberate self-harm.
Hawton, Harriss, et al. (2003)/United Kingdom	Study of hospital presentations	Deliberate self-harm	N/A	8,590	Range: 15–55+	Rates were significantly higher among female participants in all age brackets. Gender ratio (M:F) was 1.6:1.26.

(continues)

TABLE 3.4

Gender Differences in the Prevalence of Nonsuicidal Self-Injury (NSSI) (Continued)

Author/location	Methodology	Outcome assessed	Time frame	N	Age (yrs)	Notes
Hawton, Harriss, Simkin, Bale, and Bond (2004)/ United Kingdom	Study of hospital presentations	Deliberate self-harm (self-cutting and self-poisoning: only methods included)	N/A	14,892	Range: 15+	A greater proportion of males presented following self-cutting or self-poisoning (12.9% vs. 7.9%).
Horrocks, Price, House, and Owens (2003)/ United Kingdom	Accident and Emergency (A&E) records for people over age 12 who attended 2 A&E departments over an 18-month period after deliberate self-harm	Deliberate self-harm	Previous 18 months	3,239	Range: 12–75	Males were significantly more likely to have hit things (deliberate self-harm) compared to females (10.7% versus 3.7%).
Kerfoot, Dyer, Harrington, and Woodham (1996)/ United Kingdom	Comparison of overdose cases with community and psychiatric control participants	Self-poisoning method only	Most recent episode	40 (15% males)	Mean: 14.9	Self-poisoning was more frequent among girls. Of those who had self-harmed, 85% were girls.

Study/Country	Type of study/source	Definition	Time frame	Sample	Age	Findings
Klonsky, Oltmanns, and Turkheimer (2003)/United States	Survey	NSSI	Lifetime	1,986 (62% male)	Mean: 20	Of the total sample, 2.5% of men vs 1.7% of women reported engaging in NSSI.
Ogundipe (1999)/United Kingdom	Letter to The British Journal of Psychiatry	Nonfatal deliberate self-harm	N/A	N/A	N/A	Reported that nonfatal deliberate self-harm is more common in females.
Schmidtke et al. (1996)/Germany	Study of hospital presentations in 13 European countries	Suicide attempt	Lifetime	16,394	Range: 15+	Reported that in 15 out of 16 centers, the rates were higher among females. The average ratio of male-to-female rates for individuals age 15 or older was 1:1.5.
Stanley, Winchel, Molcho, Simeon, and Stanley (1992)/United States	Review of the phenomenological and biochemical evidence	Deliberate self-harm	N/A	N/A	N/A	Highlighted that research with adults in clinical settings have reported inconsistent findings.
Suyemoto (1998)/United States	Review article	NSSI	Not given	Not given	Not given	Suggested that majority of those engaging in NSSI are female.
Zlotnick, Mattia, and Zimmerman (1999)/United States	Patient survey	NSSI	Past 3 months	256 (42% male)	Mean: 40.58	Women were slightly more likely to engage in NSSI (67% vs. 53%).

However, Muehlenkamp (2005) noted that although it is widely believed women are more likely than men to engage in NSSI, the picture is unclear because studies of adults in clinical settings have reported inconsistent results (e.g., see Briere & Gil, 1998; Stanley, Winchel, Molcho, Simeon, & Stanley, 1992; Zlotnick, Mattia, & Zimmerman, 1999). Furthermore, in a study of presentations to a general hospital following deliberate self-harm over a 23-year period, Hawton et al. (2004) reported that similar proportions of male (83.3%) and female (89.1%) patients presented following self-poisoning (with or without suicidal intent), and a greater proportion of male participants presented following self-cutting (with or without suicidal intent; 12.9% vs. 7.9%). In the United Kingdom, similar findings were also reported by Horrocks, Price, House, and Owens (2003) in Leeds and Cooper et al. (2006) in Manchester. Although further research is necessary before strong conclusions can be drawn, it appears that deliberate self-harm by males is more common than was previously thought.

Ethnicity

In their review of the international literature, J. Evans, Evans, Morgan, Hayward, and Gunnell (2005) reported that the association between ethnicity and self-injurious thoughts and behaviors (with and without suicidal intent) found in American adolescents suggested that the prevalence of suicidal phenomena is higher in both Native American and Hispanic adolescents than in either Black or White adolescents. This trend was found in the majority of studies in which this association was investigated. Similarly, studies in the United Kingdom have suggested that rates of deliberate self-harm (including NSSI) among young South Asian women are higher than in the White population (Bhugra, Desai, & Baldwin, 1999; Cooper et al., 2006; Merrill & Owens, 1986). However, significant differences tend to be reported in only the studies with relatively large sample sizes, suggesting that nonsignificant findings may be the result of inadequate power (i.e., insufficient numbers to detect a difference) but also that differences are not large. There also appears to be a general trend for suicide to be more frequent in indigenous native populations (e.g., see W. Evans, Smith, Hill, Albers, & Neufeld, 1996).

One important factor to consider when exploring NSSI and ethnicity concerns how ethnic groups are categorized. The ethnicity of the minority will vary greatly from one geographic area to another. Thus, what constitutes a "minority" needs to be specified. For example, Neeleman and Wessely (1999) found that in London, suicidal behavior was more frequent in ethnic groups living in areas where they were in the minority than those who lived in areas in which they constituted a much larger part of the local population. Thus, the social experience of being part of a minority group may be an important factor, and it is important to be mindful of this when considering the generalizability of findings.

International Differences

There have been few attempts to conduct multicenter studies of NSSI. However, in the early 1990s, a collaborative multicenter study was conducted on self-injurious behaviors (with and without suicidal intent) in 16 areas in Europe (Platt et al., 1992). In all the areas, the same methodology, definition, and case-finding criteria were used to identify deliberate self-harm (i.e., parasuicide) presentations to general hospitals in those ages 15 and older. The term *parasuicide* was defined as

> an act with a non-fatal outcome, in which an individual deliberately initiates a non-habitual behavior that without intervention from others, will cause self-harm, or deliberately ingests a substance in excess of the prescribed or generally recognized therapeutic dosage, and which is aimed at realising changes which the subject desired via the actual or expected physical consequences. (Platt et al., 1992, p. 99)

Although this definition is close to that for deliberate self-harm and includes suicide attempts, the findings warrant inclusion in this chapter.

The study showed substantial variation in annual rates of parasuicide between different areas in Europe, with up to sevenfold differences. For example, for male participants, the rates varied between 327 (per 100,000) in Helsinki (Finland) and 46 in Guipuzcoa (Spain), and in female participants, they varied between 542 (per 100,000) in Cergy-Pontoise (France) and 72 in Guipuzcoa. Overall, it was found that in general, high rates were found in northern European regions and low rates in Mediterranean regions (Platt et al., 1992).

More recently, the Child and Adolescent Self-Harm in Europe Study has been completed. This collaboration of centers in the United Kingdom, Ireland, the Netherlands, Belgium, Norway, Hungary, and Australia used the same questionnaire in community surveys to collect data from adolescents predominantly ages 15 and 16 (Hawton, Rodham, & Evans, 2006). Specific findings have been reported for Norway (Ystgaard, Reinholdt, Husby, & Mehlum, 2003), Hungary (Fekete, Voros, & Osvath, 2004), Ireland (Sullivan, Arensman, Keeley, Corcoran, & Perry, 2004), and Australia (DeLeo & Heller, 2004). Comparing the findings from the seven countries, Hawton, Rodham, and Evans (2006) noted that there are strikingly similar rates of deliberate self-harm among male and female residents of the United Kingdom, Ireland, Belgium, Norway, and Australia. They also reported that in the year before the survey, rates of deliberate self-harm of any kind ranged from 9.1% to 11.8% for female participants and from 2.5% to 4.4% for male participants.

Far lower rates of deliberate self-harm were found in the Netherlands (males = 1.7%; females = 3.7%) and Hungary (males = 1.7%; females = 5.9%). It is interesting to note that adolescents from the Netherlands had the lowest reported rates of thoughts of deliberate self-harm of all seven countries involved in the multicenter study. It is therefore possible to conclude that in the Netherlands, levels of deliberate self-harm phenomena are generally low. In contrast, the levels of thoughts of deliberate self-harm among adolescents from Hungary were the highest. This may suggest that in Hungary, there are greater barriers to translation of thoughts of deliberate self-harm into actual acts than in certain other European countries, which may reflect cultural differences in terms of both social attitudes toward deliberate self-harm and availability of methods.

Thus, multicenter studies of adolescents and adults as well as reviews of community studies have cited both similarities and differences in reported prevalence rates of deliberate self-harm. It is, however, important not simply to take these figures at face value. In other words, it may be that the different subgroups within each country's populations differ in terms of the proportions most likely to engage in NSSI. Such an argument is similar to that put forward by Neeleman and Wessely (1999) and highlights the necessity of looking beyond the global prevalence rates reported for each country.

FUTURE DIRECTIONS

Much work in this field to date has been cross-sectional in nature, providing a snapshot in time from which to establish the prevalence of NSSI and to identify correlates of NSSI. Longitudinal studies are required to identify the causal direction of these relationships. In particular, prospective studies using rigorous qualitative and quantitative methodologies would allow one to explore the meaning that self-injury has for those who engage in NSSI. Tapping into this information would enable one to develop a greater understanding of a range of issues, including why it is that some individuals engage in NSSI repeatedly, whereas for others the behavior is used as a more short-term form of coping. Also, more needs to be known about how and why individuals first decide to engage in NSSI and what influences their specific choice of method of NSSI. Further, it would be valuable to learn more about how NSSI functions as a coping strategy.

Much of what is currently known about NSSI has come from research conducted with clinical populations. This phenomenon needs to be explored in more community-based studies, taking into account gender, ethnicity, and life stage. In particular, attention should be focused on adolescent communities, for it is in adolescence when NSSI begins. Thus, it would be sensible to follow cohorts of young people over time (ideally before they begin to engage in NSSI). This would enable researchers perhaps to identify differences among those who develop NSSI compared with those who do not. Given the conclusion drawn by Jacobson and Gould (2007) in their review of the research addressing the epidemiology and phenomenology of NSSI among adolescents—namely, that NSSI is increasing in prevalence among teenagers—continued research exploring causal factors and assessing preventive and intervention strategies is clearly required.

In addition, older adults have been relatively neglected in terms of NSSI research and should be investigated with regard to the extent and nature of this behavior. Much of the work conducted in older adults has involved clinical samples and has not focused solely on NSSI but explored broader self-harming behaviors (with or without suicidal intent). The findings of this research clearly link self-injurious behaviors with suicide. It is therefore important to explore whether there are parallel implications for older people in the community who engage in NSSI.

In this chapter, we provided an overview of the information currently available concerning the epidemiology and phenomenology of NSSI and deliberate self-harm. We demonstrated that although links have been identified between NSSI and age, gender, and ethnicity, there is much room for further exploration and study. If the field is to move forward and to begin considering more complex questions, there is a need for the research and clinical communities to take stock and reach consensus concerning the meaning, definition, and measurement of NSSI, together with the terminology used to describe it, to be able to compare and interpret findings confidently across studies.

There are several important directions for future research in this area. First, to place research on NSSI and other forms of deliberate self-harm on a sound footing, consensus must be reached on terminology and definitions of the behavior. Second, cross-sectional studies have identified correlates of NSSI. More longitudinal studies are required to identify the causal direction of these correlates and to identify other risk factors. Such prospective studies could also help elucidate the developmental processes and events that may be involved in the occurrence of NSSI and factors that may contribute to its cessation. Third, little research has been conducted on NSSI among older adults. Studies of prevalence and risk factors could be incorporated into broader community surveys and follow-up studies and into investigation of adult populations. Fourth, it appears that NSSI may be becoming more common, especially in adolescents. Regular cross-sectional surveys, conducted as part of a broader investigation of mental health and well-being issues, would help track the extent to which this is occurring. Fifth, further work, both qualitative and quantitative, is necessary to explore the meanings that self-injury has for those who engage in NSSI. This type of investigation may also elucidate factors that trigger NSSI and those that reduce the desire to hurt oneself without suicidal intent.

REFERENCES

Bhugra, D., Desai, M., & Baldwin, D. (1999). Attempted suicide in West London: I. Rates across ethnic communities. *Psychological Medicine, 29*, 1125–1130.

Brent, D. A., Perper, J., Moritz, G., Allman, C., Friend, A., Roth, C., et al. (1993). Psychiatric risk factors for adolescent suicide: A case control study. *Journal of the American Academy of Child & Adolescent Psychiatry, 32*, 521–529.

Briere, J., & Gil, E. (1998). Self-mutilation in clinical and general population samples: Prevalence, correlates, and functions. *American Journal of Orthopsychiatry, 68*, 609–620.

Brown, M. Z., Comtois, K. A., & Linehan, M. M. (2002). Reasons for suicide attempts and nonsuicidal self-injury in women with borderline personality disorder. *Journal of Abnormal Psychology, 111*, 198–202.

Centers for Disease Control and Prevention. (2004). Youth Risk Behavior Surveillance—United States, 2003. *MMWR: Morbidity and Mortality Weekly Report, 53*(No. SS2).

Claes, L., & Vandereycken, W. (2007). Self-injurious behavior: Differential diagnosis and functional differentiation. *Comprehensive Psychiatry, 48*, 137–144.

Conwell, Y. (1997). Management of suicidal behavior in the elderly. *Psychiatric Clinics of North America, 20*, 667–683.

Cooper, J., Husain, N., Webb, R., Waheed, W., Kapur, N., Guthrie, E., & Appleby, L. (2006). Self-harm in the UK: Differences between South Asians and Whites in rates, characteristics, provision of service and repetition. *Social Psychiatry & Psychiatric Epidemiology, 41*, 782–788.

Darche, M. A. (1990). Psychological factors differentiating self-mutilating and non-self mutilating adolescent inpatients females. *Psychiatric Hospital, 21*, 31–35.

De Leo, D., & Heller, T. S. (2004). Who are the kids who self-harm? An Australian self-report school survey. *The Medical Journal of Australia, 181*, 140–144.

Draper, B. (1996). Attempted suicide in old age. *International Journal of Geriatric Psychiatry, 11*, 577–587.

Dulit, R. A., Fyer, M. R., Leon, A. C., Brodsky, B. S., & Frances, A. J. (1994). Clinical correlates of self-mutilation in borderline personality disorder. *The American Journal of Psychiatry, 151*, 1305–1311.

Evans, E., Hawton, K., Rodham, K., & Deeks, J. (2005). The prevalence of suicidal phenomena in adolescents: A systematic review of population-based studies. *Suicide and Life-Threatening Behavior, 35*, 239–250.

Evans, J., Evans, M., Morgan, H., Hayward, A., & Gunnell, D. (2005). Crisis card following self-harm: 12 month follow-up of a randomised controlled trial. *The British Journal of Psychiatry, 187*, 186–187

Evans, W., Smith, M., Hill, G., Albers, E., & Neufeld, J. (1996). Rural adolescent views of risk and protective factors associated with suicide. *Crisis Intervention, 3*, 1–12.

Favazza, A. R. (1998). The coming of age of self-mutilation. *The Journal of Nervous and Mental Disease, 186*, 259–268.

Favazza, A. R., & Conterio, K. (1989). Female habitual self-mutilators. *Acta Psychiatrica Scandinavica, 79*, 238–239.

Favazza, A. R., DeRosear, L., & Conterio, K. (1989). Self-mutilation and eating disorders. *Suicide and Life-Threatening Behavior, 19*, 352–361.

Fekete, S., Voros, V., & Osvath, P. (2004). Suicidal behavior and psychopathology in adolescents—results of a self-report survey among 15 and 16-year old adolescent people in Hungary. *European Neuropsychopharmacology, 14*(Suppl. 3), 365–365.

Fergusson, D. M., Horwood, L. J., Ridder, E. M., & Beautrais, A. L. (2005). Suicidal behavior in adolescence and subsequent mental health outcomes in young adulthood. *Psychological Medicine, 35*, 983–993.

Gratz, K. L. (2001). Measurement of deliberate self-harm: Preliminary data on the Deliberate Self-Harm Inventory. *Journal of Psychopathology and Behavioral Assessment, 23*, 253–263.

Gratz, K. L., Conrad, S. D., & Roemer, L. (2002). Risk factors for deliberate self-harm among college students. *American Journal of Orthopsychiatry, 72*, 128–140.

Hawton, K., Bale, L., Casey, D., Shepherd, A., Simkin, S., & Harriss, L. (2006). Monitoring deliberate self-harm presentations to general hospitals. *Crisis, 27*, 157–163.

Hawton, K., Fagg, J., & Simkin, S. (1996). Deliberate self-poisoning and self-injury in children and adolescents under 16 years of age in Oxford, 1976–1993. *The British Journal of Psychiatry, 169*, 202–208.

Hawton, K., Fagg, J., Simkin, S., Bale, E., & Bond, A. (1997). Trends in deliberate self-harm in Oxford, 1985–1995. *The British Journal of Psychiatry, 171*, 556–560.

Hawton, K., & Harriss, L. (2006). Deliberate self-harm in people aged 60 years and over: Characteristics and outcome of a 20-year cohort. *International Journal of Geriatric Psychiatry, 21*, 572–581.

Hawton, K., & Harriss, L. (2007). Deliberate self-harm in young people: Characteristics and subsequent mortality in a 20-year cohort of patients presenting to hospital. *Journal of Clinical Psychiatry, 68*, 1574–1583.

Hawton, K., Harriss, L., Hall, S., Simkin, S., Bale, E., & Bond, A. (2003). Deliberate self-harm in Oxford, 1990–2000: A time of change in patient characteristics. *Psychological Medicine, 33*, 987–996.

Hawton, K., Harriss, L., Simkin, S., Bale, E., & Bond, A. (2004). Self-cutting: Patient characteristics compared with self-poisoners. *Suicide and Life-Threatening Behavior, 34*, 199–208.

Hawton, K., Houston, K., & Shepperd, R. (1999). Study of 174 cases, aged under 25 years, based on coroners' and medical records. *The British Journal of Psychiatry, 175*, 271–276.

Hawton, K., Rodham, K., & Evans, E. (2006). *By their own young hand: Deliberate self-harm and suicidal ideas in adolescents*. London: Jessica Kingsley.

Hawton, K., Rodham, K., Evans, E., & Weatherall, R. (2002, November 23). Deliberate self-harm in adolescents: Self-report survey in schools in England. *BMJ, 325*, 1207–1211.

Hawton, K., Zahl, D., & Weatherall, R. (2003). Suicide following self-harm: Long term follow-up of patients who presented to a general hospital. *The British Journal of Psychiatry, 182*, 537–542.

Hepple, J., & Quinton, C. (1997). One hundred cases of attempted suicide in the elderly. *The British Journal of Psychiatry, 171*, 42–46.

Herpertz, S. (1995). Self-injurious behavior: Psychopathological and nosological characteristics in subtypes of self-injurers. *Acta Psychiatrica Scandinavica, 91*, 57–68.

Horrocks, J., Price, S., House, A., & Owens, D. (2003). Self-injury attendances in the accident and emergency department: Clinical database study. *The British Journal of Psychiatry, 183*, 34–39.

Houston, K., Hawton, K., & Shepperd, R. (2001). Suicide in young people aged 15–24: A psychological autopsy study. *Journal of Affective Disorders, 63*, 159–170.

Hurry, J. (2000). Deliberate self-harm in children and adolescents. *International Review of Psychiatry, 1*, 31–36.

Jacobsen, C. M., & Gould, M. (2007). The epidemiology and phenomenology of non-suicidal self-injurious behavior among adolescents: A critical review. *Archives of Suicide Research, 11*, 129–147.

Kerfoot, M., Dyer, E., Harrington, V., & Woodham, A. (1996). Correlates and short term course of self-poisoning in adolescents. *The British Journal of Psychiatry, 168*, 38–42.

Klonsky, E. D. (2007). The functions of deliberate self-injury: A review of the evidence. *Clinical Psychology Review, 27*, 226–239.

Klonsky, E. D., Oltmanns, T. F., & Turkheimer, E. (2003). Deliberate self-harm in a nonclinical population: Prevalence and psychological correlates. *The American Journal of Psychiatry, 160*, 1501–1508.

Kumar, G., Pepe, O., & Steer, R. A. (2004). Adolescent psychiatric inpatients' self-reported reasons for cutting themselves. *The Journal of Nervous and Mental Diseases, 192*, 830–836.

Lamprecht, H. C., Pakrasi, S., Gash, A., & Swann, A. G. (2005). Deliberate self-harm in older people revisited. *International Journal of Geriatric Psychiatry, 20*, 1090–1096.

Laye-Gindhu, A., & Schonert-Reichl, A. (2005). Nonsuicidal self-harm among community adolescents: Understanding the "Whats" and "Whys" of self-harm. *Journal of Youth and Adolescence, 34*, 447–457.

Marttunen, M. J., Aro, H. M., & Lönnqvist, J. K. (1993). Adolescence and suicide: A review of psychological autopsy studies. *European Child & Adolescent Psychiatry, 2*, 10–18.

Mental Health Foundation. (2006). *Truth Hurts: Report of the National Inquiry into self-harm among young people*. London: Mental Health Foundation.

Merrill, J., & Owens, J. (1986). Ethnic differences in self-poisoning: A comparison of Asian and White groups. *The British Journal of Psychiatry, 148*, 708–712.

Muehlenkamp, J. J. (2005). Self-injurious behavior as a separate clinical syndrome. *American Journal of Orthopsychiatry, 75*, 324–333.

Muehlenkamp, J. J., & Gutierrez, P. (2004). An investigation of the differences between self-injurious behavior and suicide attempts in a sample of adolescents. *Suicide and Life-Threatening Behavior, 34,* 12023.

Nada-Raja, S., Skegg, K., Langley, J., Morrison, D., & Sowerby, P. (2004). Self-harmful behaviors in a population-based sample of young adults. *Suicide and Life-Threatening Behavior, 34,* 177–186.

Neeleman, J., & Wessely, S. (1999). Ethnic minority suicide: A small area geographical study in South London. *Psychological Medicine, 29,* 429–436.

Nijman, H. L. I., Dautzenberg, M., Merckelbach, H. L. G., Juang, P., Wessel, I., & Campo, J. (1999). Self-mutilating behavior in psychiatric inpatients. *European Psychiatry, 14,* 4–10.

Nock, M. K., Joiner, T. E., Gordon, K. H., Lloyd-Richardson, E., & Prinstein, M. J. (2006). Nonsuicidal injury among adolescents: Diagnostic correlates and relation to suicide attempts. *Psychiatry Research, 144,* 65–72.

Nock, M. K., & Prinstein, M. J. (2004). A functional approach to the assessment of self-mutilative behavior. *Journal of Consulting and Clinical Psychology, 72,* 885–890.

Ogundipe, L. O. (1999). Suicide attempts vs. deliberate self-harm. *The British Journal of Psychiatry, 175,* 90.

O'Loughlin, S., & Sherwood, J. (2005). A 20-year review of trends in deliberate self-harm in a British town, 1981–2000. *Social Psychiatry & Psychiatric Epidemiology, 40,* 446–453.

Pattison, E. M., & Kahan, J. (1983). The deliberate self-harm syndrome. *American Journal of Psychiatry, 140,* 867–872.

Patton, G. C., Hemphill, S. A., Beyers, J., Bond, L., Toumbourou, J. W., McMorris, B. J., & Catalano, R. F. (2007). Pubertal stage and deliberate self-harm in adolescents. *Journal of the American Academy of Child & Adolescent Psychiatry, 46,* 508–514.

Platt, S., Bille-Brahe, U., Kerkhof, A., Schmidtke, A., Bjerke, T., Crepet, P., et al. (1992). Parasuicide in Europe: The WHO/EURO multicentre study on parasuicide. Introduction and preliminary analysis for 1989. *Acta Psychiatrica Scandinavica, 85,* 97–104.

Rhodes, A. E., Bethell, J., & Bondy, S. J. (2006). Suicidality, depression and mental health service use in Canada. *The Canadian Journal of Psychiatry, 51,* 35–41.

Ross, S., & Heath, N. (2002). A study of the frequency of self-mutilation in a community sample of adolescents. *Journal of Youth and Adolescence, 31,* 67–77.

Sakinofsky, I. (2000). Repetition of suicidal behavior. In K. Hawton & K. van Heeringen (Eds.), *The International Handbook of Suicide and Attempted Suicide* (pp. 385–404). Chichester, England: Wiley.

Schmidtke, A., Bille-Brahe, U., De Leo, D., Kerkhof, A., Bjerke, T., Crepet, P., et al. (1996). Attempted suicide in Europe: Rates, trends and sociodemographic characteristics of suicide attempters during the period 1989–1992: Results of the WHO/EURO Multicentre Study on Parasuicide. *Acta Psychiatrica Scandinavica, 93,* 327–338.

Skegg, K. (2005, October 22–28). Self-harm. *The Lancet, 366,* 1471–1483.

Skegg, K., Nada-Raja, S., Dickson, N., Paul, C., & Williams, S. (2003). Sexual orientation and self-harm in men and women. *American Journal of Psychiatry, 160,* 541–546.

Soloff, P. H., Lis, J. A., Kelly, T., Cornelius, J., & Ulrich, R. (1994). Self-mutilation and suicidal behaviour in borderline personality disorder. *Journal of Personality Disorders, 8,* 257–267.

Stanley, B., Winchel, R., Molcho, R., Simeon, D., & Stanley, M. (1992). Suicide and the self-harm continuum: Phenomenological and biochemical evidence. *International Review of Psychiatry, 4,* 149–155.

Sullivan, C., Arensman, E., Keeley, H. S., Corcoran, P., & Perry, I. J. (2004). *Young people's mental health: A report of the findings from the Lifestyle and Coping Survey.* Cork, Ireland: The National Suicide Research Foundation.

Suyemoto, K. L. (1998). The functions of self-mutilation. *Clinical Psychology Review, 18,* 531–554.

White, V. E., Trepal-Wollenzier, H., & Nolan, J. M. (2002). College students and self-injury: Intervention strategies for counselors. *Journal of College Counseling, 5,* 105–113.

Whitlock, J., Eckenrode, J., & Silverman, D. (2006). Self-injurious behaviors in a college population. *Pediatrics, 117,* 1939–1948.

Ystgaard, M., Reinholdt, N. P., Husby, J., & Mehlum, L. (2003). Villet egenskade blant ungdom [Deliberate self-harm in adolescents]. *Tidsskrift for den Norske laegeforening, 123,* 2241–2245.

Zanarini, M. C., Frankenburg, F. R., Hennen, J., Reich, B., & Silk, K. R. (2005). The McLean study of adult development (MSAD): Overview and implications of the first six years of prospective follow-up. *Journal of Personality Disorders, 19,* 505–523.

Zlotnick, C., Mattia, J. I., & Zimmerman, M. (1999). Clinical correlates of self-mutilation in a sample of general psychiatric patients. *The Journal of Nervous and Mental Disease, 187,* 296–301.

II

WHY DO PEOPLE ENGAGE IN NONSUICIDAL SELF-INJURY?

4

PSYCHOLOGICAL MODELS OF NONSUICIDAL SELF-INJURY

MATTHEW K. NOCK AND CHRISTINE B. CHA

Why do some people purposely and repetitively inflict severe harm on their own body? The psychological literature is replete with speculative accounts of why people engage in nonsuicidal self-injury (NSSI), and there appear to be as many explanations as there are authors on the topic. Notably, however, recent research has begun to evaluate the evidence systematically for various psychological models of NSSI. Converging evidence suggests that NSSI serves several purposes, such as to decrease aversive thoughts and feelings, to increase stimulation, and to communicate with others. In this chapter, we review evidence for the behavioral functions of NSSI as well as evidence for other psychological deficits and dysfunctions present among those who self-injure.

EARLY THEORIES OF NONSUICIDAL SELF-INJURY

Numerous reasons may explain why some people engage in NSSI. Some earlier theoretical models have suggested that NSSI is performed for a wide range of purposes, such as boundary definition, antisuicide, or mastery of penetration and other sexual impulses. For example, the psychoanalytic antisuicide model proposes that individuals engage in NSSI—considered partial or microsuicides—to soothe themselves actively and to avert total suicide (Firestone & Seiden, 1990; Menninger, 1938). In addition to addressing life and death drives, other psychoanalytic models suggest that through displacement, NSSI damaging any part of the body addresses "the unconscious fantasy . . . of destroying the genitals seen as the source of the urges" (Friedman, Glasser, Laufer, Laufer, & Wohl, 1972, p. 182). Unfortunately, there is no research support for such claims.

More recent research has focused largely on describing the psychosocial correlates of NSSI. The result of this research has been the generation of a list of diagnostic and psychosocial characteristics associated with NSSI, including higher levels of suicidal thoughts and behaviors, depression, anxiety, posttraumatic stress, anger, aggressiveness, impulsiveness, loneliness, social isolation, and hopelessness (Darche, 1990; Favazza & Conterio, 1989; Guertin, Lloyd-Richardson, Spirito, Donaldson, & Boergers, 2001). Although this work can be useful for identifying those at increased risk of NSSI, it has added little to the understanding of why it is that some people engage in NSSI. For instance, why exactly are suicide attempts and NSSI related? Why is posttraumatic stress disorder (PTSD) correlated with NSSI? What theoretical models can help explain the observed pattern of relations? By addressing these questions, future work may identify specific targets for intervention for those at heightened risk of NSSI.

A FUNCTIONAL MODEL OF NONSUICIDAL SELF-INJURY

An alternative theoretical approach is to consider what functions NSSI may serve. In contrast to a syndromal approach, which classifies behaviors according to associated signs and symptoms, a functional approach classifies and treats behaviors according to the processes that produce and maintain them (i.e., antecedent and consequent events). For instance, demonstrating that people who engage in NSSI have elevated levels of anxiety represents a finding consistent with a syndromal approach and tells little about why that person engages in NSSI. However, showing that there is an immediate decrease in anxious arousal following NSSI describes a process likely to maintain NSSI in many cases and represents a functional approach. The use of a functional approach has led to impressive advances in the conceptualization, assessment, and treatment of a range of clinically relevant behavior problems (Hayes, Wilson, Gifford, Follette, & Strosahl, 1996).

Drawing on this earlier conceptual work, as well as on earlier empirical research focused on NSSI among those with developmental disabilities (Durand & Crimmins, 1988; Iwata et al., 1994), Nock and Prinstein (2004, 2005) proposed a four-function model (FFM) of NSSI, with functions differing along two dichotomous dimensions: reinforcement that can be either positive (i.e., followed by the presentation of a favorable stimulus) or negative (i.e., followed by the removal of an aversive stimulus), and contingencies that can be either automatic (i.e., intrapersonal) or social (i.e., interpersonal).

The first function proposed in this model, presented schematically in Figure 4.1, is *automatic negative reinforcement* (ANR), in which NSSI is performed to remove or escape from an aversive affective or cognitive state. This is the function most often endorsed by research participants in virtually all studies in this area to date. The second function is *automatic positive reinforcement* (APR), in which NSSI is performed for the purpose of generating feeling. People endorsing this function often report feeling numbness or anhedonia and engaging in NSSI to feel something, which is a rewarding sensation in this context. The third function of NSSI proposed in this model is *social positive reinforcement* (SPR), in which NSSI is performed to get attention or access to resources in the environment. The fourth function is *social negative reinforcement* (SNR), in which NSSI is performed to remove some interpersonal demand.

Several recent theoretical articles have proposed that there are many more functions of NSSI than those proposed in the FFM, such as antisuicide, antidissociation, and boundary definition (e.g., see Klonsky, 2007; Suyemoto, 1998). The proposal of such additional functions is, we believe, the result of a much broader, more colloquial, use of the word *function*. The term *function* has been used for decades in learning theory and behavior therapy, and from this perspective, the study of the function of a behavior refers to an analysis of the antecedent and consequent events hypothesized to cause or maintain a behavior (as in

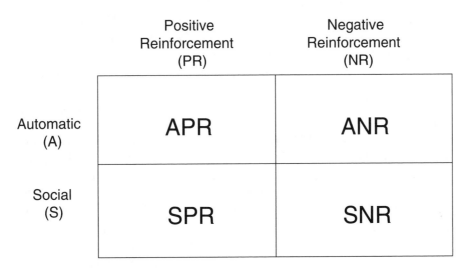

	Positive Reinforcement (PR)	Negative Reinforcement (NR)
Automatic (A)	APR	ANR
Social (S)	SPR	SNR

Figure 4.1. Four-function model.

the FFM). Examinations of such events are referred to as *functional analyses* or *behavioral analyses*. In contrast, some research on the functions of NSSI uses this term more loosely to refer simply to the proposed purpose of a behavior (e.g., boundary definition), without careful operationalization and with no consideration of the antecedents or consequences of the behavior. This differing use of the term *function* is important to bear in mind when reading the research literature in this area and when interacting with clinicians and families.

Evidence Supporting the Four-Function Model of Nonsuicidal Self-Injury

There is substantial empirical support for the four-function model. Evidence has been found through multiple methods, such as self-report studies and physiological and behavioral studies. These studies are reviewed in the sections that follow.

Self-Report Studies

The structure of the FFM has been replicated by independent research groups in both adolescent clinical (Nock & Prinstein, 2004) and community (Lloyd-Richardson, Perrine, Dierker, & Kelley, 2007) samples, as well as in adult clinical samples (Brown, Comtois, & Linehan, 2002) and among those with developmental disabilities (Iwata et al., 1994). Internal consistency reliability has been supported in many of these studies, as has the construct validity of this model. In support of construct validity, one recent study (Nock & Prinstein, 2005) demonstrated that the use of these four functions can help explain the heterogeneous list of correlates of NSSI by showing specific function–correlate relations. For instance, endorsement of the ANR function of NSSI is correlated with the experience of self-reported heightened emotion reactivity and hopelessness, as well as with the experience of greater attempts at thought suppression and suicide—the former being states from which a person may be trying to escape and the latter being methods of escape from intolerable cognitive and affective states (Najmi, Wegner, & Nock, 2007; Nock & Prinstein, 2005). Similarly, the presence of clinical constructs involving anhedonia, inactivity, and psychic numbness (PTSD and major depressive disorder symptoms) is most strongly related to the use of an APR function for NSSI (Nock & Prinstein, 2005; Weierich & Nock, 2008). In addition, the presence of social concerns is most strongly correlated with endorsement of the social functions of NSSI (Nock & Prinstein, 2005). These findings support the FFM but also help gain an understanding of the wide array of correlates of this behavior, and more recent studies are elucidating the mechanisms and moderating factors through which these functions may operate (Hilt, Cha, & Nolen-Hoeksema, 2008; Weierich & Nock, 2008). For instance, some identified mechanisms relating frequency of NSSI and childhood sexual abuse are reexperiencing PTSD symptoms and avoidance and numbing PTSD symptoms, suggesting APR (Weierich & Nock, 2008). Some identified moderators between social functions (i.e., SNR and SPR) and interpersonal distress, and between APR and internal distress, are quality of peer communication and degree of rumination, respectively (Hilt et al., 2008). A major limitation to most prior work in this area, however, is the methodology of self-report itself. This is problematic given the well-known effects of social desirability on reporting (Nederhof, 1985) as well as the limits in people's ability to report accurately on the factors influencing their behavior (Nisbett & Wilson, 1977).

Physiological and Behavioral Studies

If NSSI is maintained by the four functions outlined earlier, then one would expect to see corroborating evidence using methods other than self-report, such as in physiological and behavioral studies. For instance, if people most often engage in NSSI to escape the experience of elevated, aversive arousal, then those who self-injure should show higher physiological arousal in response to stress and a poorer ability to tolerate such distress. A recent laboratory-based study showed just that: People with a recent history of NSSI compared with those with no such history showed higher physiological arousal (i.e., skin conductance level) in response to a stressor as well as a poorer ability to tolerate the stressor, and this effect was strongest for those endorsing an ANR function of NSSI (Nock & Mendes, 2008). These findings complement those from an earlier study on the psychophysiology of NSSI indicating that those who self-injure show decreased arousal when imagining engaging in NSSI (Haines, Williams, Brain, & Wilson, 1995), providing indirect evidence that NSSI may indeed be negatively reinforced by relieving aversive arousal. Physiological or behavioral support for the APR function of NSSI has not yet been reported, perhaps because this function receives less attention in the literature and because of the lower rate of endorsement of this function by those who self-injure (e.g., see Nock & Prinstein, 2004).

Recent research also has begun to use behavioral studies to examine the social functions of NSSI. For instance, Nock and Mendes (2008) also tested several aspects of the social problem-solving skills of those who self-injure that are likely to play an important role in social communication problems that could lead to self-injury. Nock and Mendes reported that adolescents who self-injure demonstrated deficits in some social problem-solving skills but not in others. It is interesting to note that the deficits observed did not pertain to the quantity or quality of solutions generated in response to socially challenging situations. However, when it came time to select specific solutions, individuals who self-injure tended to choose more maladaptive solutions and reported lower self-efficacy for performing constructive solutions. These findings suggest that although those who self-injure have the ability to generate adaptive solutions to socially challenging situations, they ultimately choose a maladaptive response, such as engaging in NSSI for social functions (i.e., SNR and SPR).

WHY USE NONSUICIDAL SELF-INJURY TO SERVE THESE FUNCTIONS?

There are many ways to regulate emotions or communicate with others. For example, one could decrease or distract oneself from aversive thoughts or feelings by exercising, talking to friends, taking a hot shower, or even by using some other potentially maladaptive behavior such as drinking alcohol or using drugs. Similarly, one could use a range of adaptive (e.g., talking) or potentially maladaptive (e.g., screaming, crying) social behaviors to communicate with others. This raises the question of why some individuals select NSSI as a means to accomplish these aims.

Nonsuicidal Self-Injury as Self-Punishment

Given that NSSI is a behavior in which a person by definition abuses or attacks one's own body, it stands to reason that this behavior may be performed as an extreme form of self-deprecation or self-punishment. Thoughts about the self are a surprisingly understudied aspect of self-injury. However, several recent studies support the idea that NSSI may indeed represent attempts at self-punishment. First, those engaging in NSSI often report self-punishment as a reason for this behavior (e.g., see Klonsky, 2007; Nock & Prinstein, 2004; Rodham, Hawton, & Evans, 2004). Second, individuals who self-injure report significantly higher levels of self-criticism than do non-injurers, even after statistically controlling for the presence of depression (Glassman, Weierich, Hooley, Deliberto, & Nock, 2007). Moreover, self-criticism mediates the relation between child maltreatment and NSSI (Glassman, Weirich, Hooley, Deliberto, & Nock, 2007), which suggests a model in which people may engage in NSSI following child maltreatment because they learn to be critical of, or harmful toward, themselves after experiencing earlier physical or emotional abuse. Third, consistent with this model, another recent study revealed that parents of adolescents who self-injure are significantly more hostile and critical in their comments about their children than are parents of noninjurers, and the combination of parent criticism and adolescent criticism was associated with an especially high risk of engaging in NSSI (Wedig & Nock, 2007). Taken together, these findings provide initial support for the role of self-criticism and self-punishment in NSSI; however, much more research is necessary to better understand this potential pathway to NSSI.

Nonsuicidal Self-Injury Is Natural, Effective, and Readily Available

A more parsimonious explanation for why people engage in NSSI is that it is a natural, effective, and readily available strategy for regulating one's cognitive and emotional experiences. Humans are not the only animals to engage in NSSI. Nonhuman primates and some other animals do so as well, and the behavior among such animals is also believed to be done largely for the purposes of self-soothing or self-stimulation (e.g., see Kraemer, Schmidt, & Ebert, 1997). Thus, NSSI represents a coping strategy, albeit a harmful one, that occurs elsewhere in nature for the purpose of emotion regulation, and so making inferences about the reasons that people engage in NSSI that go beyond these parsimonious accounts requires strong evidence. Moreover, NSSI appears to work quickly (i.e., injury brings about immediate changes in attention and physiological arousal) and effectively, and because all that is needed is the body, it can be performed at any time.

Nonsuicidal Self-Injury Provides an Honest Signal of Distress

Another reason for selecting NSSI over some other behavior is that if the goal of NSSI is to communicate with or to influence the behavior of others, then engaging in NSSI is more likely than less severe behaviors to achieve these goals. The reason for this is well-articulated by work on animal signaling, which shows that behaviors that come at a cost to the signaler (i.e., the organism performing the behavior) are much more likely to be believed (i.e., they are considered more honest), otherwise they would not be performed because they would not be to the benefit of the signaler. As an example, if a gazelle is being pursued by a cheetah or some other predator, the gazelle will sometimes engage in stotting behavior, which refers to jumping highly and stiffening the legs. This behavior is believed to function as an honest signal to the predator that the gazelle is of superior fitness and that the cheetah is unlikely to catch that particular gazelle. Stotting decreases the likelihood that the predator will continue to pursue the gazelle (Caro, 1986). Of course, the gazelle could be faking its level of fitness, but to do so would be so costly (i.e., given that stotting decreases the lead distance and expends excess energy, thus increasing the chance of being caught) that it is unlikely most gazelles would take such a risk. Similarly, NSSI is by definition a harmful behavior that comes at a physical (and often social) cost to those who self-injure, and so it provides a loud signal that is more likely to be heard and taken seriously by others because of these costs (Hagen, Watson, & Hammerstein, 2008; Nock, 2008). It is possible that NSSI is selected as a means of communicating with others when less extreme behaviors have been unsuccessful in communicating, and so the person "graduates" to the use of NSSI. This can be the case when NSSI is used for the purpose of either SPR or SNR (see Nock, 2008).

Nonsuicidal Self-Injury as Modeled Behavior

Behaviors are learned in many instances by observing the behaviors performed by those around us. It is likely that modeling the behavior of others plays a significant role in the occurrence of NSSI. Two prime candidates provide models for engaging in NSSI: peers and the media. One recent study simply asked adolescents with a recent history of NSSI where they had learned about the behavior, and the most frequent response was that they learned about NSSI from a peer (38%); however, many adolescents also reported learning about NSSI from media sources (13%), such as television, movies, and magazines (Deliberto & Nock, 2008). The influence of peers and the media is discussed in much greater detail in subsequent chapters (i.e., chaps. 5 and 8, respectively, of this volume).

Obviously, not everyone exposed to the idea of NSSI through peers or the media goes on to engage in the behavior, so an important task for researchers is to identify factors that distinguish those who do from those who do not. One important psychological factor is whether a person identifies with NSSI or believes it to be a favorable behavior in which to engage. For instance, some adolescents may observe several of their friends cutting themselves, but if they think it is a negative behavior that is not at all like them, they may be much less likely to engage in that particular behavior than if they have come to see NSSI as a favorable behavior with which they identify. Consistent with this, one recent study using a performance-based response time test revealed that individuals who self-injure hold more favorable beliefs about NSSI and identify with the behavior significantly more than do noninjurers (Nock & Banaji, 2007). Further addressing the question of why it is that some people decide to engage in NSSI is just one of many important directions for future work in this developing research area.

SPECIFIC RECOMMENDATIONS FOR FUTURE WORK

Clinical Recommendations

There has been a significant increase in research on psychological models of NSSI in recent years, and the findings from many of these studies may be useful to clinicians working with clients who self-injure. Several clinical recommendations follow directly from the work reviewed here.

- *Assess the functions of NSSI.* It is clear that individuals who self-injure do not all consistently use this behavior for the same reason, and it is important that clinicians assess the function of the behavior in each client and attempt to identify the factors or events that maintain the behavior.

- *Use data about functions to guide treatment.* Although treatment research has yet to test the effectiveness of tailoring treatments on the basis of results of functional assessments, it makes good sense for clinicians to do so and to evaluate the effects of such a strategy in each case. For instance, if a clinician determines that a client is engaging in NSSI to decrease or escape from aversive thoughts, it is likely better to focus treatment on teaching cognitive and emotion regulation skills rather than on interpersonal communication skills.
- *Assess and address specific influences on NSSI.* The functional model presented is a contextual one, and as such it is important that clinicians constantly examine and consider the influence of contextual factors that may specifically influence engagement in NSSI. What is the client's self-concept (i.e., Is he or she especially self-critical?)? What is the client's family environment like, and might it contribute to engagement in NSSI? Where did the client learn about NSSI, and is there an ongoing influence of peers or the media?

Research Recommendations

Despite recent progress, however, many questions remain about the factors that influence engagement in NSSI. Although there are many directions for future research in this area, we believe a narrower set of research directions deserve the greatest attention.

- *Conduct objective tests of psychological models.* The majority of research on NSSI to date has relied almost exclusively on self-report measures. Such studies are useful for providing preliminary tests of psychological models, but there is a great need to progress beyond the use of self-report methods to test the psychological processes proposed to influence NSSI. Several recent studies have done so, but much more work is needed in this regard.
- *Examine factors influencing the onset and offset of NSSI.* Functional models of NSSI have focused mostly on factors that maintain this behavior, and little is known about how NSSI develops to begin with or about how and why people stop this behavior. Why do people choose to engage in NSSI over other potential behaviors? How might the factors influencing engagement in the behavior change over time? Why do most people stop engaging in NSSI? What treatments are most effective? What factors outside of treatment have the greatest impact on decreasing the behavior?

- *Test novel models of NSSI.* Prior studies on NSSI have been fairly narrow in focus, often examining the relation between one factor, or a handful of factors, in relation to this behavior problem. Significant advances will come only from examining the contributions and interactions of multiple factors. In this chapter, we presented evidence for the processes believed to maintain NSSI, as well as factors believed to influence the development of this behavior, with a focus on what factors may be specific to the development of NSSI rather than other behavior problems. These factors can be integrated by considering them in the context of a diathesis–stress model (see Figure 4.2). Early environmental and cognitive–emotional–biological factors may operate by predisposing certain individuals to experience emotional over- or underarousal in response to stressful events or to lack the social problem-solving or communication skills required to respond adaptively to a stressful event (see the three circles in Figure 4.2). These factors are all common to many forms of psychopathology and behavior problems, so what may lead one to engage in NSSI? The predisposing factors may have an effect not only by contributing to other predisposing factors or increasing the likelihood of stressful events but also by increasing the odds of using NSSI in particular to regulate these problems. For instance, early emotional abuse and familial criticism may lead to emotion dys-

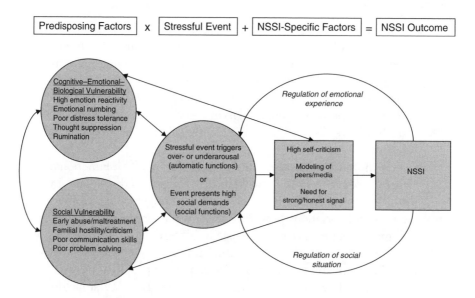

Figure 4.2. Psychological model of the development and maintenance of nonsuicidal self-injury (NSSI).

regulation and poor social problem-solving skills but also in some cases (e.g., if the environment is particularly critical or non-responsive to feedback from the child) to the development of a self-critical cognitive style and perceived need for a strong and honest signal of distress, each increasing the likelihood of NSSI in particular. Although pieces of this model have been supported by prior studies, it is important that future research includes prospective tests of the pathways and interactions proposed.

CONCLUSION

It is important to note that the greatest advances in understanding NSSI may come from the examination of factors or models not mentioned in this chapter. Factors such as impulsiveness and general problem-solving ability have not been shown to distinguish those who engage in NSSI from those who do not and seem to provide little explanatory power for this behavior (Herpertz, Sass, & Favazza, 1997; Janis & Nock, in press; Nock & Mendes, 2008). Moreover, more comprehensive models of NSSI will account for the factors mentioned here and also synthesize recent findings from broader areas of research including interpersonal (see chap. 5, this volume), neurobiological (see chap. 6, this volume), developmental (see chap. 7, this volume), and media (see chap. 8, this volume) influences on this behavior. Theoretical models that synthesize data from these myriad areas are likely to enhance understanding of this dangerous and pervasive behavior problem.

REFERENCES

Brown, M. Z., Comtois, K. A., & Linehan, M. M. (2002). Reasons for suicide attempts and nonsuicidal self-injury in women with borderline personality disorder. *Journal of Abnormal Psychology, 111,* 198–202.

Caro, T. M. (1986). The functions of stotting in Thomson's gazelles: Some tests of the predictions. *Animal Behaviour, 34,* 663–684.

Darche, M. A. (1990). Psychological factors differentiating self-mutilating and non-self-mutilating adolescent inpatient females. *The Psychiatric Hospital, 21,* 31–35.

Deliberto, T. L., & Nock, M. K. (2008). An exploratory study of correlates, onset, and offset of non-suicidal self-injury. *Archives of Suicide Research, 12,* 219–231.

Durand, V. M., & Crimmins, D. B. (1988). Identifying the variables maintaining self-injurious behavior. *Journal of Autism and Developmental Disorders, 18,* 99–117.

Favazza, A. R., & Conterio, K. (1989). Female habitual self-mutilators. *Acta Psychiatrica Scandanavica, 79,* 283–289.

Firestone, R. W., & Seiden, R. H. (1990). Suicide and the continuum of self-destructive behavior. *Journal of American College Health, 38,* 207–213.

Friedman, M., Glasser, M., Laufer, E., Laufer, M., & Wohl, M. (1972). Attempted suicide and self-mutilation in adolescence: Some observations from a psycho-analytic research project. *International Journal of Psychoanalysis, 53,* 179–183.

Glassman, L. H., Weierich, M. R., Hooley, J. M., Deliberto, T. L., & Nock, M. K. (2007). Child maltreatment, non-suicidal self-injury, and the mediating role of self-criticism. *Behaviour Research and Therapy, 45,* 2483–2490.

Guertin, T., Lloyd-Richardson, E., Spirito, A., Donaldson, D., & Boergers, J. (2001). Self-mutilative behavior in adolescents who attempt suicide by overdose. *Journal of the American Academy of Child & Adolescent Psychiatry, 40,* 1062–1069.

Hagen, E. H., Watson, P. J., Hammerstein, P. (2008). Gestures of despair and hope: A view on deliberate self-harm from economics and evolutionary biology. *Biological Theory, 3,* 123–138.

Haines, J., Williams, C. L., Brain, K. L., & Wilson, G. V. (1995). The psychophysiology of self-mutilation. *Journal of Abnormal Psychology, 104,* 471–489.

Hayes, S. C., Wilson, K. G., Gifford, E. V., Follette, V. M., & Strosahl, K. (1996). Experimental avoidance and behavioral disorders: A functional dimensional approach to diagnosis and treatment. *Journal of Consulting and Clinical Psychology, 64,* 1152–1168.

Herpertz, S., Sass, H., & Favazza, A. (1997). Impulsivity in self-mutilative behavior: Psychometric and biological findings. *Journal of Psychiatry Research, 31,* 451–465.

Hilt, L. M., Cha, C. B., & Nolen-Hoeksema, S. (2008). Nonsuicidal self-injury in young adolescent girls: Moderators of the distress-function relationship. *Journal of Consulting and Clinical Psychology, 76,* 63–71.

Iwata, B. A., Pace, G. M., Dorsey, M. F., Zarcone, J. R., Vollmer, T. R., Smith, R. G., et al. (1994). The functions of self-injurious behavior: An experimental-epidemiological analysis. *Journal of Applied Behavior Analysis, 27,* 215–240.

Janis, I. B., & Nock, M. K. (in press). Are self-injurers impulsive? Results from two behavioral laboratory studies. *Psychiatry Research.*

Klonsky, E. D. (2007). The functions of deliberate self-injury: A review of the evidence. *Clinical Psychology Review, 27,* 226–239.

Kraemer, G. W., Schmidt, D. E., & Ebert, M. H. (1997). The behavioral neurobiology of self-injurious behavior in rhesus monkeys: Current concepts and relations to impulsive behavior in humans. *Annals of the New York Academy of Sciences, 836,* 12–38.

Lloyd-Richardson, E. E., Perrine, N., Dierker, L., & Kelley, M. L. (2007). Characteristics and functions of non-suicidal self-injury in a community sample of adolescents. *Psychological Medicine, 37,* 1183–1192.

Menninger, K. (1938). *Man against himself.* New York: Harcourt Brace & World.

Najmi, S., Wegner, D. M., & Nock, M. K. (2007). Thought suppression and self-injurious thoughts and behaviors. *Behaviour Research and Therapy, 45,* 1957–1965.

Nederhof, A. J. (1985). Methods of coping with social desirability bias: A review. *European Journal of Social Psychology, 15,* 263–280.

Nisbett, R. E., & Wilson, T. D. (1977). Telling more than we can know: Verbal reports on mental processes. *Psychological Review, 84,* 231–259.

Nock, M. K. (2008). Actions speak louder than words: An elaborated theoretical model of the social functions of self-injury and other harmful behaviors. *Applied and Preventive Psychology, 12,* 159–168.

Nock, M. K., & Banaji, M. R. (2007). Assessment of self-injurious thoughts using a behavioral test. *The American Journal of Psychiatry, 164,* 820–823.

Nock, M. K., & Mendes, W. B. (2008). Physiological arousal, distress tolerance, and social problem-solving deficits among adolescent self-injurers. *Journal of Consulting and Clinical Psychology, 76,* 28–38.

Nock, M. K., & Prinstein, M. J. (2004). A functional approach to the assessment of self-mutilative behavior. *Journal of Consulting and Clinical Psychology, 72,* 885–890.

Nock, M. K., & Prinstein, M. J. (2005). Clinical features and behavioral functions of adolescent self-mutilation. *Journal of Abnormal Psychology, 114,* 140–146.

Rodham, K., Hawton, K., & Evans, E. (2004). Reasons for deliberate self-harm: Comparison of self-poisoners and self-cutters in a community sample of adolescents. *Journal of the American Academy of Child & Adolescent Psychiatry, 43,* 80–87.

Suyemoto, K. L. (1998). The functions of self-mutilation. *Clinical Psychology Review, 18,* 531–554.

Wedig, M. M., & Nock, M. K. (2007). Parental expressed emotion and adolescent self-injury. *Journal of the American Academy of Child & Adolescent Psychiatry, 46,* 1171–1178.

Weierich, M. R., & Nock, M. K. (2008). Posttraumatic stress symptoms mediate the relation between childhood sexual abuse and nonsuicidal self-injury. *Journal of Consulting and Clinical Psychology, 76,* 39–44.

5

INTERPERSONAL MODELS OF NONSUICIDAL SELF-INJURY

MITCHELL J. PRINSTEIN, JOHN D. GUERRY,
CAROLINE B. BROWNE, AND DIANA RANCOURT

Once considered a behavior restricted to individuals with developmental disabilities or with borderline personality disorder (BPD), nonsuicidal self-injury (NSSI) is a remarkably common phenomenon exhibited by youth and adults with a range of diagnostic profiles. Recent estimates suggest that NSSI occurs at significant rates among preadolescents (7%; Hilt, Nock, Lloyd-Richardson, & Prinstein, 2008), adolescents (12%–15%; Favazza, DeRosear, & Conterio, 1989; Ross & Heath, 2002), and adults (1%–4%; Briere & Gil, 1998; Klonsky, Oltmanns, & Turkheimer, 2003) within community-based samples. Prevalence estimates within clinical samples are notably higher (21%–61% in youth, approximately 21% in adults; Briere & Gil, 1998; Darche, 1990; DiClemente, Ponton, & Hartley, 1991).

These strikingly high rates of NSSI have naturally led to a recent increase in research efforts to identify the possible antecedents or risk factors that precede engagement in these behaviors. In some cases, this work has offered important descriptive data regarding factors that differentiate individuals who do or do not engage in NSSI. Other efforts have offered theoretical frameworks for understanding underlying disturbances or proximal reinforcements that generate and maintain NSSI behavior. This rapidly growing area of research has captured the attention of investigators from various psychological subdisciplines and promises to offer innovative directions for understanding not only the range of behaviors referred to as NSSI but perhaps also the nature by which these behaviors may heterogeneously manifest as part of various forms of psychopathology.

Despite the exciting potential for this area of research, progress toward identifying possible antecedents or risk factors for NSSI has been somewhat mixed, perhaps underscoring the difficulties in conducting this type of work. Evidence to date has come largely from uncontrolled case studies, correlational research, self-reported measures, and cross-sectional designs. Similar limitations are evident in research on other forms of self-injury (e.g., suicidal behaviors). Substantial ethical and legal issues often prohibit a thorough assessment of self-injury, and the importance of ensuring safety among individuals at risk of self-injury can potentially contaminate data from naturalistic longitudinal studies. In many cases, data regarding self-injury are extracted from broader data sets examining psychopathology more generally; research progress regarding NSSI often is dependent on data that may have been collected for a different purpose. Consequently, most extant research on NSSI has offered descriptive information that may be used to generate hypotheses. There is an unfortunate paucity of studies that have rigorously examined theoretically based hypotheses using advanced research or analytic methods.

Nevertheless, several potential models for understanding NSSI have been offered (e.g., see Chapman, Gratz, & Brown, 2006; Nock & Prinstein, 2004, 2005; Suyemoto, 1998). By far, most evidence to date has suggested that individuals may engage in NSSI as a strategy to regulate emotional distress (e.g., see M. Z. Brown, Comtois, & Linehan, 2002; Chapman et al., 2006; Klonsky, 2007; Nock & Prinstein, 2004). Chapman et al. (2006) focused specifically on the reduction of tension or more general negative affect as a primary motivation for engaging in NSSI. Similar theories have been suggested by Nock and Prinstein (2004, 2005), Suyemoto (1998), and Yip (2005). There also is substantial empirical evidence accumulating to support this theory. For example, one study revealed that compared with control participants who did not self-injure, individuals who had engaged in NSSI showed a decrease in psychophysiological arousal and subjective distress during an NSSI imagery task (Haines, Williams, Brain, & Wilson, 1995). These results indicate that NSSI is maintained, at least in part, by its reinforcing tension-reducing qualities.

In addition to a growing consensus that affect regulation is a primary motivation for NSSI, most theorists agree that NSSI is an "overdetermined" behavior (Klonsky, 2007; Lloyd-Richardson, Nock, & Prinstein, 2008; Nock & Prinstein, 2004, 2005; Suyemoto, 1998), serving several functions and reflecting various psychological deficits or limitations. Indeed, substantial research has supported the equifinality of NSSI as an outcome associated with multiple disparate precursors (e.g., see Yates, 2004). Thus, in addition to its emotional regulation functions, it is important to examine other potential models that may be associated with individuals' NSSI. In this chapter, we focus specifically on interpersonal correlates, antecedents, and functions of NSSI. The past research that we present highlights the important role of individuals' interpersonal experiences in understanding NSSI behavior and suggests that for some individuals, or for some incidents, NSSI may be motivated primarily by interpersonal goals.

INTERPERSONAL MODELS OF NONSUICIDAL SELF-INJURY

Interpersonal factors have been implicated as NSSI risk factors in at least four specific models. First, a collection of studies has examined distal interpersonal correlates that are associated with later NSSI behaviors. It is important to note that the majority of prior studies examining distal interpersonal correlates have examined NSSI and interpersonal constructs concurrently, often using retrospective reports of prior interpersonal difficulties to infer possible antecedents or risk factors. This work offers an important initial step but requires replication using alternative methods to better ascertain the temporal nature of associations and to rule out well-known mood-related biases that likely influence recall and interpretation of past experiences.

A second group of studies has examined more proximal interpersonal experiences that may serve as immediate precipitants to NSSI. Third, emerging research has examined specific interpersonal mechanisms that may be impaired among individuals who engage in NSSI. This particular approach is especially exciting for its potential to identify psychological processes that might be intervention targets. Fourth, recent work has posited potential interpersonal functions that may be served by NSSI. These functional models articulate immediate antecedent conditions and consequences that likely reinforce NSSI. Functional models have great potential for explaining etiological factors, as well as processes that serve to maintain or exacerbate NSSI over time. A brief review of each type of interpersonal model is offered in the sections that follow, followed by a detailed discussion of one particular example of an interpersonal function potentially addressed by NSSI that has recently garnered substantial scientific and public attention.

Distal Interpersonal Risk Factors for Nonsuicidal Self-Injury

Perhaps not surprisingly, past research has revealed that individuals who engage in NSSI report substantial prior interpersonal difficulties. The vast majority of these findings pertain specifically to difficulties within the family context, and several studies state that adults who engage in NSSI report histories of physical, sexual, or emotional maltreatment (Crowe & Bunclark, 2000;

Dubo, Zanarini, Lewis, & Williams, 1997; Gratz, 2003, 2006; Silove, George, & Bhavani-Sankaram, 1987; M. A. Simpson, 1975). This association between maltreatment and NSSI is consistent among both male (e.g., see Evren & Evren, 2005; Gratz & Chapman, 2007) and female (e.g., see Favazza & Conterio, 1989) individuals who engage in NSSI. This association has also been revealed among adolescents who engage in NSSI (C. A. Simpson & Porter, 1981).

Some question remains, however, as to whether childhood maltreatment is a unique risk factor for NSSI in particular or a more general predictor of psychopathology. At least some evidence suggests that there are differences in the severity of maltreatment experiences between those who do and those who do not engage in NSSI even within a group of diagnosed individuals such as individuals with BPD (Welch & Linehan, 2002) or those who use substances (Evren & Evren, 2005). In addition, some work suggests that severity of reported maltreatment is associated with the frequency of NSSI episodes within groups of adults diagnosed with BPD (Dubo et al., 1997). However, few studies have examined whether reports of maltreatment may serve as a marker for psychological symptom severity, rather than act as a unique predictor of later NSSI. Studies examining the longitudinal association between distal interpersonal factors and later NSSI are sorely needed.

Theorists have suggested that early relationship disturbances may be associated with later NSSI through various mechanisms (see Yates, 2004, for a review). For example, attachment theorists suggest that maladaptive interpersonal experiences early in childhood leave individuals with a diminished capacity for supportive interpersonal experiences or matured emotional regulation skills later in development. It is interesting to note that this theory offers a hypothesis that is most consistent with an emotional regulation function of NSSI. According to this theory, early interpersonal experiences have an indirect effect on NSSI through an individual's difficulties in coping with negative emotional states; resolution of this emotional distress may be a proximal motivator (or, if successful, a subsequent reinforcement) for NSSI.

Similar to attachment theorists, schema theorists have suggested that core beliefs regarding social isolation and alienation may be a unique risk factor for NSSI. Specifically, higher levels of social isolation and alienation schemas are associated concurrently with higher frequencies of NSSI within a clinical sample (Castille et al., 2007). A psychosomatic approach suggests that early maltreatment contributes to an altered trajectory of self-development; NSSI may be an expression of disrupted boundaries between the self and others (Cohen & Mills, 1999; Yates, 2004). Biological theories suggest that early maltreatment experiences may distort an individual's pain or pleasure sensitivity. Research has suggested that individuals who engage in NSSI or related suicidal behaviors may have higher thresholds for pain than other people (see Orbach, Mikulincer, King, Cohen, & Stein, 1997) and may engage in NSSI as a strategy for feeling generation (M. Z. Brown et al., 2002).

Yates (2004) offered an integrative model accounting for developmental variation in the course of NSSI behavior.

Interpersonal Precipitants of Nonsuicidal Self-Injury

As has been demonstrated for other forms of self-injury (e.g., suicidality; Davila & Daley, 2000), it appears that interpersonal stressors often immediately precede engagement in NSSI. These interpersonal precipitants include intense loneliness, interpersonal rejection or loss, or a recent conflict with a family member, romantic partner, adult authority figure, or peer (e.g., see Hawton & Harriss, 2006). In one interesting study conducted with adolescents in a group treatment home, significantly more incidents of NSSI were noted before the anticipated loss of staff members than during other comparison periods (Rosen, Walsh, & Rode, 1990).

The salience of interpersonal stressors as precipitants for NSSI may help, in part, to understand developmental variation, as well as gender differences, in the prevalence of NSSI. Compared with childhood, adolescence is associated with significant increases in stressful events, particularly within the interpersonal context (Rudolph & Hammen, 1999). Moreover, adolescence is associated with the emergence of gender differences in the frequency and meaning of interpersonal stressors. Compared with younger children of either sex and with adolescent boys, adolescent girls experience significantly higher frequencies of interpersonal stressors (including peer stressors in particular; Rudolph & Hammen, 1999). Adolescent girls also report greater emotional reactivity to interpersonal stressors than do adolescent boys or children of both sexes (Rudolph, 2002). These findings parallel commonly cited developmental and gender differences in the prevalence of NSSI (Jarvis, Ferrence, Johnson, & Whitehead, 1976; Ross & Heath, 2002; Yates, 2004).

Although consistent findings have revealed that interpersonally themed stressors are potent proximal antecedents to NSSI, it is important to note that it is not possible to infer individuals' motivation to engage in NSSI, or the functions served by this behavior, from these data alone. It is highly likely that stressful precipitants, including interpersonal stressors, may produce negative affect, and this elevation in distress leads to engagement in NSSI as a strategy for regulating emotions (Chapman et al., 2006). Interpersonal stressors, and individuals' resulting distress, may also give rise to certain social goals that may motivate or reinforce NSSI. Some of these possibilities are discussed in more detail in the next section.

Interpersonal Mechanisms and Nonsuicidal Self-Injury

In addition to the study of interpersonal constructs as potential risk factors or antecedents for engaging in NSSI, some recent work has suggested interpersonal processes or social deficiencies that may explain why individuals engage in NSSI. To date, this work has focused almost exclusively on social–cognitive models of NSSI. One such model that is especially relevant for understanding NSSI may be derived from a social information processing framework. Typical social information processing theories propose a variety of discrete steps that link individuals' experience of socially themed stimuli to specific behavioral responses (e.g., see Crick & Dodge, 1994; Ingram, 1986; McFall, 1982). Specifically, social–cognitive theories posit that individuals exhibit substantial variation in their encoding of social cues, as well as in the manner in which they interpret these social cues. Prior experiences and contextual factors may produce encoding biases, heightening or attenuating an individual's sensitivity to specific stimuli that are related to a core belief or schema.

Interpretative biases may also distort individuals' perceptions of the causes or salience of encoded social cues. These cognitive interpretations may be specific to each encoded stimulus or may generalize into a broader pattern (i.e., an attributional or explanatory style) that is somewhat consistent across time and contexts (e.g., a depressogenic attributional style; Abramson, Metalsky, & Alloy, 1989). Following the encoding and interpretation of a specific social stimulus, individuals implicitly use their goals for the social interaction to guide the generation, selection, and enactment of a specific behavioral response. Each of these steps again may be informed by prior experiences, contextual cues, or schema. A behavioral response enacted by an individual produces a new social stimulus, thus beginning a new cycle of social information processing.

Much research has suggested that incidents of NSSI often occur in response to specific stressful precipitants, and thus the examination of social information processing mechanisms may be especially useful to understand why individuals exhibit this particular behavioral response. Unfortunately, few studies have addressed this question to date. In our own work, we have hypothesized a cognitive vulnerability–stress model that specifically examines clinically referred adolescents' interpretations of stressful interpersonal experiences as longitudinal predictors of NSSI. Results indicate a significant interaction effect between adolescents' general tendency to interpret stressful experiences as the result of internal, global, and stable causes (i.e., a depressogenic attributional style) and adolescents' interpersonal stressors on increases in NSSI over an 18-month interval. The significance of this interaction effect remained unchanged after accounting for adolescents' depressive symptoms, suggesting that the role of their cognitive interpretations of stressful interpersonal experiences was not mediated by depression (Guerry & Prinstein, 2007).

The majority of research examining social–cognitive mechanisms of NSSI has focused specifically on individuals' ability to generate, select, or enact adaptive behavioral responses to interpersonal stimuli (i.e., social problem-solving skills). Theories suggest that NSSI, and perhaps other forms of self-injury such as suicidal behavior, are the result of an individual's diminished capacity to generate adaptive behavioral strategies in response to a stressful situation. In particular, it is posited that some individuals may become hyperaroused in response to stressful stimuli; this hyperaroused state compromises social problem-solving skills, perhaps even among individuals who would be capable of demonstrating adaptive skills in a less aroused state.

Results have offered some preliminary evidence to support tenets of this theory. However, most research examining the association between social problem-solving skills and NSSI has used questionnaire-based methods. In general, results indicate that individuals who engage in NSSI report poorer social problem-solving skills than those who do not (e.g., see Howat & Davidson, 2002; Kehrer & Linehan, 1996). For example, Howat and Davidson (2002) revealed that geriatric adults who engaged in NSSI (or suicidal behavior) reported significantly poorer social problem-solving skills in response to interpersonal stressors than did adults diagnosed with depression or community control participants. Among female patients with BPD, Kehrer and Linehan (1996) demonstrated that poor self-reported social problem-solving skills are longitudinally associated with NSSI (or suicidal behavior) 4 months later. McAuliffe et al. (2006) revealed that adults who engaged in repeated episodes of NSSI (or suicidal behavior) reported poorer social problem-solving skills than did adults who engaged in a single episode of NSSI or suicidal behavior (see also Andover, Pepper, & Gibb, 2007).

Data from questionnaire-based methods offer important and promising preliminary results. For at least two reasons, however, this procedure makes it difficult to examine the role of social problem-solving skill deficits as a potential risk factor for NSSI in the manner that is most consistent with theoretical hypotheses. First, most questionnaire-based studies assess social problem-solving skills to participants while in an emotionally neutral state. Although this procedure allows for an examination of global social problem-solving skill deficits that are evident even in the absence of distress, it does not allow for an assessment of social problem-solving skills in the manner that most closely simulates the moments that precede NSSI. Data confirm that social problem-solving skills are indeed compromised under conditions of distress (Dodge & Somberg, 1987). Second, self-reported ratings of social problem-solving skills rely on individuals' ability to accurately recall, interpret, and report their own social–cognitive skills. Yet these questionnaires often are administered to research participants for whom a deficit in social–cognitive skills is hypothesized. Thus, these individuals may be particularly poor reporters of their own social problem-solving skills, especially given that these processes are thought to be implicit and sometimes even illogical in nature.

Recent research addressing each of these limitations has offered intriguing evidence that is consistent with the theoretical propositions stated earlier. In a laboratory-based study, Nock and Mendes (2008) compared adolescents with and without prior histories of NSSI on a series of performance-based tasks. Participants completed a performance-based measure of social problem-solving skills both before and after participation in a stress-inducing task. Physiological measures of arousal were also collected throughout adolescents' participation. As predicted, participants with a history of NSSI evidenced greater physiological arousal (measured by skin conductance) than did control participants throughout the stress-inducing task, particularly as the task became increasingly challenging and frustrating. These differences remained significant even after controlling for symptoms of psychopathology.

Several differences were also observed for social problem-solving skills. Although adolescents who did or did not engage in NSSI did not differ in the overall number of solutions they generated to hypothetical scenarios, adolescents who engaged in NSSI reported more maladaptive solutions and lower ratings of self-efficacy for successfully using adaptive solutions than did control participants. Moreover, among both groups, results suggested that following the stress-inducing task, adolescents were less likely to generate solutions to hypothetical dilemmas overall.

Thus, studies examining social information processing mechanisms that may be relevant for NSSI have offered promising results. An important direction for future work will be to determine whether social–cognitive interventions may reduce self-injurious behavior among those at greatest risk of NSSI (Donaldson, Spirito, & Esposito-Smythers, 2005). Although such strategies are incorporated in well-established treatments for BPD (e.g., see Linehan et al., 2006), more work is necessary to examine the efficacy of similar interventions among non-BPD adults and youth at risk of NSSI.

Interpersonal Functions of Nonsuicidal Self-Injury

Functional models of NSSI examine the psychological benefits and reinforcements that are offered by engaging in this unique and dangerous behavior. Functional models, therefore, present the potential for a conceptualization of NSSI from a developmental psychopathology perspective, understanding the course of NSSI over time, as well as the factors that contribute to its onset, maintenance, (de)escalation, and desistance. In our own work, we have articulated a multifaceted functional model to explain NSSI (Nock & Prinstein, 2004, 2005; see also Favazza, 1998; Iwata et al., 1994; Suyemoto, 1998). This model is based on several premises. First, it is posited that there are multiple psychological states or beliefs that may motivate or reinforce NSSI. Second, there is likely intraindividual variability in the functions of

NSSI; disparate functions may motivate engagement in different NSSI behaviors (e.g., skin cutting, burning), across episodes or at different points in development. Third, NSSI shares *functional equivalence* with other manifestations of psychopathology. In other words, NSSI likely serves the same function as do other psychological symptoms and does not often constitute a unique disorder that is unrelated to preexisting psychopathology.

Our functional model suggests that individuals engage in NSSI for either automatic (i.e., internally derived) or social contingencies that are maintained through (perceived or actual) positive or negative reinforcement. The automatic negative reinforcement (ANR) function therefore suggests that individuals engage in NSSI as a strategy for reducing a negative stimulus (e.g., negative affect). Research suggests that this indeed is the most common function endorsed by individuals who engage in NSSI (M. Z. Brown et al., 2002; Chapman et al., 2006; Klonsky, 2007; Nock & Prinstein, 2004, 2005). The automatic positive reinforcement (APR) function suggests that individuals engage in NSSI to generate an internal emotional state (e.g., feeling generation; M. Z. Brown et al., 2002; Klonsky, 2007; Nock & Prinstein, 2005). Consistent with theoretical suppositions, ANR functions of NSSI are associated with psychological symptoms that individuals typically attempt to escape (i.e., suicidal ideation and hopelessness), whereas APR functions of NSSI are associated with symptoms that typically produce numbness and a need for feeling generation (e.g., PTSD and depression; Nock & Prinstein, 2005).

In addition to these two functions that pertain specifically to the affect regulation contingencies of NSSI, Nock and Prinstein (2004, 2005) proposed that some NSSI may be a strategy for managing the social environment (see Briere & Gil, 1998; M. Z. Brown et al., 2002; Claes, Vandereycken, & Vertommen, 2007; Figueroa, 1988; Herpertz, 1995; Himber, 1994; Klonsky, 2007; Laye-Gindhu & Schonert-Reichl, 2005; Nixon, Cloutier, & Aggarwal, 2002; Osuch, Noll, & Putnam, 1999; Rodham, Hawton, & Evans, 2004; Shearer, 1994; Walker, Joiner, & Rudd, 2001). The social positive reinforcement (SPR) function suggests that NSSI is a strategy to elicit a response from others (e.g., to share feelings, to elicit attention), whereas the social negative reinforcement function suggests that NSSI is used to escape from interpersonal task demands (e.g., to avoid punishment or unpleasant activities). Compared with automatic NSSI functions, both social functions of NSSI are associated uniquely with social concerns (e.g., loneliness, socially prescribed perfectionism; Nock & Prinstein, 2005).

Recently, research regarding potential functions of NSSI has begun to proliferate. The vast majority of this work, however, has used narrative accounts of clients or therapists or checklist measures to indicate the reasons that individuals ascribe to NSSI. It is interesting to note that little research has empirically examined whether NSSI is, in fact, followed by specific contingencies or reinforcements. Although individuals' repeated engagement in

NSSI suggests that some reinforcing contingencies must be perceived, in the case of social functions, it is not known whether these perceptions are biased interpretations of NSSI consequences or reflect true changes in the social environment following NSSI.

Narrative accounts of SPR functions generally suggest that, at least initially, NSSI may serve as a form of communication (e.g., see Himber, 1994). For example, Osuch et al. (1999) revealed that individuals who engage in NSSI reported that their behavior was used as a strategy for expressing anger, hurt, to seek revenge, or to elicit support (see also Andover et al., 2007; M. Z. Brown et al., 2002). Klonsky and Olino's (2008) latent class analysis of NSSI characteristics revealed a subgroup of young adults especially likely to endorse social functions of NSSI. These participants were also more likely than others to endorse symptoms of anxiety. Thus, evidence clearly indicates that some individuals who engage in NSSI identify the perceived social effects of their behavior as one potential motivator. There also may be distinct, reinforcing social consequences that motivate repeated acts of NSSI (Carr & McDowell, 1980).

At least one study has provided empirical evidence to support the notion that individuals' NSSI may be followed by changes in the social environment. Using a large community-based sample of preadolescents, Hilt et al. (2008) examined adolescents' reports of their relationship quality with mothers and fathers over two time points, 1 year apart. Results revealed a distinct trajectory of youths' relationship quality with fathers for youths who engaged in NSSI compared with those who did not. Among those who did not self-injure, results suggested no significant change in father–child relationship quality over time. In contrast, those who engaged in NSSI reported a significant increase in father–child relationship quality in the year following their engagement in NSSI. This association remained significant even after controlling for symptoms of depression, suggesting that youths' reports of their relationship quality did not appear to be biased as a function of negative affect or depression-distortion biases. Moreover, results suggested that this association was somewhat unique to NSSI; similar analyses conducted with youth who did or did not engage in other health risk behaviors did not reveal a similar pattern of differences in relationship quality trajectories. Results generally are consistent with contemporary theories regarding other forms of self-injury (e.g., suicidal behaviors). Walker, Joiner, and Rudd (2001) suggested that suicidal behavior can often be followed by periods of increased support from others, thus reifying individuals' beliefs regarding the potential functions of their behavior.

Nonsuicidal Self-Injury Contagion

Studies examining individuals' reports of the social functions that motivate or reinforce NSSI rarely cite a desire to conform to others' expectations and behaviors. However, there is substantial accumulating evidence to suggest that NSSI is a behavior subject to peer influence, perhaps particularly among adolescents. Most of this work has characterized patterns of NSSI among individuals in a closed psychiatric treatment facility. Among vulnerable individuals (e.g., those with diagnoses of depression or BPD), the presence of a single patient who engages in NSSI appears to be associated with increased episodes of NSSI among others (Ghaziuddin, Tsai, Naylor, & Ghaziuddin, 1992; Rada & James, 1982; Raine, 1982; Rosen & Walsh, 1989; Taiminen, Kallio-Soukainen, Nokso-Koivisto, Kaljonen, & Kelenius, 1998; Walsh & Rosen, 1985). Recent work has also confirmed that adolescents actively engage in Internet discussions about NSSI, both normalizing this behavior and sharing specific strategies for forms of NSSI (Whitlock, Powers, & Eckenrode, 2006). Clearly, the contagion of NSSI among vulnerable groups presents a large public health concern, yet little empirical research examining processes of peer influence have been conducted.

Peer influence among adolescents has been examined extensively with regard to other health risk behaviors. Research has clearly demonstrated that one of the most consistent and potent correlates of adolescents' engagement in health risk behavior is their perception that close friends or high-status peers engage in similar behaviors. Such effects have been revealed for peer influence on substance use, including use of alcohol (see Bosari & Carey, 2001; Hawkins, Catalano, & Miller, 1992, for reviews), nicotine (Alexander, Piazza, Mekos, & Valente, 2001; Urberg, Degirmencioglu, & Pilgrim, 1997), and marijuana (e.g., see Andrews, Tildesley, Hops, & Li, 2002; Wills & Cleary, 1999); weight-related behaviors (e.g., dieting, binge eating; Paxton, Schutz, Wertheim, & Muir, 1999); as well as other injurious behaviors, such as aggression (e.g., see Vitaro, Tremblay, Kerr, Pagani, & Bukowski, 1997), illegal behavior (e.g., see Paetsch & Bertrand, 1997), sexual risk behavior (Billy & Udry, 1985; Prinstein, Meade, & Cohen, 2003), and suicidal thoughts and behaviors (Brent et al., 1993; Prinstein, Boergers, & Spirito 2001).

Theorists suggest that the association between adolescents' and their peers' health risk behaviors is due to two processes of homophily (Kandel, 1978). First, adolescents are likely to affiliate with others who endorse similar attitudes and engage in similar behaviors (i.e., referred to as *selection effects*). Second, exposure to peers' behaviors is associated with increases in adolescents' own behavior over time (i.e., *socialization effects*). Research examining potential peer influence effects requires a longitudinal assessment of health risk behavior to differentiate selection from socialization effects. Unfortunately, this type of research has rarely been conducted. Findings from studies that have documented clinical observations of NSSI on inpatient units, however, appear to be preliminarily suggestive of socialization effects. Individuals within an inpatient setting typically are unfamiliar with one another and do not appear to have formed friendships on the basis of similar self-injurious characteristics. Several clinical reports also suggest clustering of NSSI over time. NSSI behavior initially is evident for a single individual or within a small group of patients, and then later it is exhibited by a larger number of patients who had not previously engaged in this behavior (Rosen & Walsh, 1989; Taiminen et al., 1998).

Our own recent work has examined whether peer influence may also occur outside of an inpatient setting. Specifically, our work has examined whether the NSSI behavior of adolescents' best friends may be a prospective predictor of adolescents' own NSSI behavioral trajectories over time. Findings have yielded promising results. Within a community-based sample of youth at the adolescent transition, best friends' own reports of their engagement in NSSI was prospectively associated with increasing levels of target adolescents' own NSSI over a 2-year period. It is important to note that this effect was not based merely on adolescents perceptions of their friends behavior (i.e., a common procedure in past research that is often confounded by adolescents' perceptual biases; see Prinstein & Wang, 2005) but adolescents' friends' actual reported behavior (Prinstein, Guerry, & Rancourt, 2007). Within a clinically referred sample, a reciprocal, transactional model was supported over three time points, suggesting that adolescents' NSSI is longitudinally associated with increases in self-injurious behavior (with or without suicidal intent) among their closest friends; subsequently, friends' self-injurious behavior longitudinally predicts increases in adolescents' NSSI (Prinstein et al., 2007).

Several theoretical models have been offered to understand why peer socialization may occur (Prinstein & Dodge, 2008). Two of these are briefly reviewed here. Social psychological theories suggest that individuals may emulate the behavior of admired others in an attempt to maintain a favorable self-image (Cohen & Prinstein, 2006; Gibbons & Gerrard, 1997; Turner, 1991). This theory is particularly relevant for understanding peer influence effects in adolescence. Developmental research suggests that, compared with younger children, adolescents participate in peer interactions more frequently (B. B. Brown, 1990). Adolescents rely on feedback from peers as a primary basis for the development of their self-concept and thus are motivated to engage in behaviors that they believe will earn them favorable status among peers (Harter, Stocker, & Robinson, 1996; Steinberg & Silverberg, 1986). Thus, if adolescents believe that their close friends or high-status peers endorse NSSI as an adaptive and appropriate behavior, they may be especially likely to emulate that behavior, perhaps especially in a manner that will be observable among those who will confer rewards.

Behavioral theories suggest that adolescents may emulate behavior through social modeling or positive reinforcements among peers. In a particularly interesting line of peer influence research, Granic and Dishion (2003) revealed that the manner in which adolescents discuss deviant acts among close friends may serve to reinforce and increase aggressive and illegal behavior over time (i.e., referred to as *deviancy training*). In initial work, it was revealed that deviant adolescent–friend dyads were especially likely to offer verbal or nonverbal positive reinforcements (e.g., nodding, laughing) following utterances that pertained to illegal or aggressive behavior but less reinforcement following prosocial or neutral utterances. An opposite pattern of findings was revealed for nondeviant dyads. Moreover, the extent to which adolescents and their best friends engaged in this pattern of discussion was longitudinally associated with arrest rates 2 years later (Granic & Dishion, 2003). Such behavioral theories suggest that engagement in a health risk behavior (e.g., NSSI) therefore can be motivated or maintained to earn social rewards, including immediate social rewards communicated in the verbal planning or retelling of health risk acts. Unfortunately, no research to date has examined these potential mechanisms to explain how peer influence of NSSI occurs.

CONCLUSION

Overall, emerging evidence suggests that numerous potential models incorporate adults' and adolescents' interpersonal experiences as relevant for understanding and perhaps treating NSSI. This is an area that requires substantial additional attention in future research and clinical efforts. Perhaps most crucial for investigators in this area will be the examination of NSSI using prospective, longitudinal methods incorporating assessments of NSSI from multiple informants. Second, recent research has offered promising support for the use of laboratory-based methods for examining mechanisms and consequences of NSSI, or similar behaviors, in vivo. To best understand proximal contingencies that individuals associate with these unique, atypical, and dangerous behaviors, it is essential to study the processes surrounding them in real time and with careful momentary measurements. A final high-priority direction for research on NSSI pertains to the importance of a developmental psychopathology perspective. It is widely agreed that NSSI may be particularly common among adolescents. Yet studies of NSSI most often involve adults or convenience samples of college-age students. This work has offered an essential contribution to the literature but precludes the testing of developmentally based hypotheses regarding specific competencies or contingencies that may be most relevant to the period in which individuals first learn to engage in NSSI.

Research efforts on NSSI have yielded important insights that may guide clinical practice. Perhaps most important, research has revealed that NSSI is remarkably common and widespread. Identification of this covert and harmful behavior will require more consistent and reliable assessment of NSSI behaviors and possible risk factors. This will be especially true as NSSI becomes more commonly discussed by the media (see chap. 8, this volume) and individuals become more accustomed to discussion of this phenomenon. Given the equifinality of NSSI, it will be particularly important to assess risk among individuals with a wide range of presenting symptoms and risk factors. Second, as noted earlier, findings have begun to suggest that social–cognitive approaches for conceptualizing NSSI may be useful, particularly when considering social information processes in the context of stress. These ideas should be more thoroughly integrated into treatment approaches. Remarkably few randomized controlled trials of self-injury have been conducted; this is a high priority for clinical research and practice. Third, models that have elucidated the functions served by NSSI suggest that assessments and treatments will need to consider carefully the immediate antecedents and contingencies of this behavior and how the heterogeneity of these functions may reflect different symptoms of psychopathology. NSSI is not a disorder in its own right but appears to be a manifestation of many possible disturbances and a behavior that is perpetuated by other known diagnoses.

REFERENCES

Abramson, L. Y., Metalsky, G. I., & Alloy, L. B. (1989). Hopelessness depression: A theory-based subtype of depression. *Psychological Review, 96,* 358–372.

Alexander, C., Piazza, M., Mekos, D., & Valente, T. (2001). Peers, schools, and adolescent cigarette smoking. *Journal of Adolescents Health, 29,* 22–30.

Andover, M. S., Pepper, C. M., & Gibb, B. E. (2007). Self-mutilation and coping strategies in a college sample. *Suicide and Life-Threatening Behavior, 37,* 238–243.

Andrews, J. A., Tildesley, E., Hops, H., & Li, F. (2002). The influence of peers on young adult substance use. *Health Psychology, 21,* 349–357.

Billy, J. O. G., & Udry, J. R. (1985). The influence of male and female best friends on adolescent sexual behavior. *Adolescence, 20,* 21–32.

Bosari, B., & Carey, K. B. (2001). Peer influences on college drinking: A review of the research. *Journal of Substance Abuse, 20,* 21–32.

Brent, D. A., Perper, J. A., Moritz, G., Allman, C., Schweers, J., Roth, C., et al. (1993). Psychiatric sequelae to the loss of an adolescent peer to suicide. *Journal of the American Academy of Child & Adolescent Psychiatry, 32,* 509–517.

Briere, J., & Gil, E. (1998). Self-mutilation in clinical and general population samples: Prevalence, correlates, and functions. *American Journal of Orthopsychiatry, 68,* 609–620.

Brown, B. B. (1990). Peer groups and peer cultures. In S. S. Feldman & G. R. Elliott (Eds.), *At the threshold: The developing adolescent* (pp. 171–196). Cambridge, MA: Harvard University Press.

Brown, M. Z., Comtois, K. A., & Linehan, M. M. (2002). Reasons for suicide attempts and nonsuicidal self-injury in women with borderline personality disorder. *Journal of Abnormal Psychology, 111,* 198–202.

Carr, E. G., & McDowell, J. J. (1980). Social control of self-injurious behavior of organic etiology. *Behavior Therapy, 11,* 402–409.

Castille, K., Prout, M., Marcyk, G., Schmidheiser, M., Yoder, S., & Howlett, B. (2007). The early maladaptive schemas of self-mutilators: Implications for therapy. *Journal of Cognitive Psychotherapy, 21,* 58–71.

Chapman, A. L., Gratz, K. L., & Brown, M. Z. (2006). Solving the puzzle of deliberate self-harm: The experiential avoidance model. *Behaviour Research and Therapy, 44,* 371–394.

Claes, L., Vandereycken, W., & Vertommen, H. (2007). Self-injury in female versus male psychiatric patients: A comparison of characteristics, psychopathology and aggression regulation. *Personality and Individual Differences, 42,* 611–621.

Cohen, G. L., & Prinstein, M. J. (2006). Peer contagion of aggression and health-risk behavior among adolescent males: An experimental investigation of effects on public conduct and private attitudes. *Child Development, 77,* 967–983.

Crick, N. R., & Dodge, K. A. (1994). A review and reformulation of social information-processing mechanisms in children's social adjustment. *Psychological Bulletin, 115,* 74–101.

Crowe, M., & Bunclark, J. (2000). Repeated self-injury and its management. *International Review of Psychiatry, 12,* 48–53.

Darche, M. A. (1990). Psychological factors differentiating self-mutilating and non-self-mutilating adolescent inpatient females. *Psychiatric Hospital, 21,* 31–35.

Davila, J., & Daley, S. E. (2000). Studying interpersonal factors in suicide: Perspectives from depression research. In T. E. Joiner, Jr. & M. D. Rudd (Eds.), *Suicide science: Expanding the boundaries* (pp. 175–200). New York: Kluwer Academic/Plenum.

DiClemente, R. J., Ponton, L. E., & Hartley, D. (1991). Prevalence and correlates of cutting behavior: Risk for HIV transmission. *Journal of the American Academy of Child & Adolescent Psychiatry, 30,* 735–739.

Dodge, K. A., & Somberg, D. R. (1987). Hostile attributional biases among aggressive boys are exacerbated under conditions of threats to the self. *Child Development, 58,* 213–224.

Donaldson, D., Spirito, A., & Esposito-Smythers, C. (2005). Treatment for adolescents following a suicide attempt: Results of a pilot trial. *Journal of the American Academy of Child & Adolescent Psychiatry, 44,* 113–120.

Dubo, D. E., Zanarini, M. C., Lewis, R. E., & Williams, A. A. (1997). Childhood antecedents of self-destructiveness in borderline personality disorder. *The Canadian Journal of Psychiatry, 42,* 63–69.

Evren, C., & Evren, B. (2005). Self-mutilation in substance-dependent patients and relationship with childhood abuse and neglect, alexithymia and temperament and character dimensions of personality. *Drug and Alcohol Dependence, 80,* 15–22.

Favazza, A. R. (1998). The coming of age of self-mutilation. *The Journal of Nervous and Mental Disease, 186,* 259–268.

Favazza, A. R., & Conterio, K. (1989). Female habitual self-mutilators. *Acta Psychiatrica Scandinavica, 79*, 283–289.

Favazza, A. R., DeRosear, L., & Conterio, K. (1989). Self-mutilation and eating disorders. *Suicide and Life-Threatening Behavior, 19*, 352–261.

Figueroa, M. D. (1988). A dynamic taxonomy of self-destructive behavior. *Psychotherapy: Theory, Research, Practice, Training, 25*, 280–287.

Ghaziuddin, M., Tasi, L. Y., Naylor, M. W., & Ghaziuddin, N. (1992). Mood disorder in a group of self-cutting adolescents. *Acta Paedopsychiatrica, 55*, 103–105.

Gibbons, F. X., & Gerrard, M. (1997). Predicting young adults' health risk behavior. *Journal of Personality and Social Psychology, 69*, 505–517.

Granic, I., & Dishion, T. J. (2003). Deviant talk in adolescent friendships: A step toward measuring a pathogenic attractor process. *Social Development, 12*, 314–334.

Gratz, K. L. (2003). Risk factors for and functions of deliberate self-harm: An empirical and conceptual review. *Clinical Psychology: Science and Practice, 10*, 192–205.

Gratz, K. L. (2006). Risk factors for deliberate self-harm among female college students: The role and interaction of childhood maltreatment, emotional inexpressivity, and affect intensity/reactivity. *American Journal of Orthopsychiatry, 76*, 238–250.

Gratz, K. L., & Chapman, A. L. (2007). The role of emotional responding and childhood maltreatment in the development and maintenance of deliberate self-harm among male undergraduates. *Psychology of Men & Masculinity, 8*, 1–14.

Guerry, J. D., & Prinstein, M. J. (2007, November). *Longitudinal prediction of nonsuicidal self-injury: Examination of a cognitive vulnerability-stress model*. Philadelphia: Association for Behavioral and Cognitive Therapies.

Haines, J., Williams, C. L., Brain, K. L., & Wilson, G. V. (1995). The psychophysiology of self-mutilation. *Journal of Abnormal Psychology, 104*, 471–489.

Harter, S., Stocker, C., & Robinson, N. S. (1996). The perceived directionality of the link between approval and self-worth: The liabilities of a looking glass self-orientation among young adolescents. *Journal of Research on Adolescence, 6*, 285–308.

Hawkins, J. D., Catalano, R. F., & Miller, J. Y. (1992). Risk and protective factors for alcohol and other drug problems in adolescence and early adulthood: Implications for substance abuse prevention. *Psychological Bulletin, 112*, 64–105.

Hawton, K., & Harriss, L. (2006). Deliberate self-harm in people aged 60 years and over: Characteristics and outcome of a 20-year cohort. *International Journal of Geriatric Psychiatry, 21*, 572–581.

Herpertz, S. (1995). Self-injurious behavior: Psychopathological and nosological characteristics in subtypes of self-injurers. *Acta Psychiatrica Scandinavica, 91*, 57–68.

Hilt, L. M., Nock, M. K., Lloyd-Richardson, E., & Prinstein, M. J. (2008). Longitudinal study of nonsuicidal self-injury among young adolescents: Rates, correlates, and preliminary test of an interpersonal model. *Journal of Early Adolescence, 28*, 455–469.

Himber, J. (1994). Blood rituals: Self-cutting in female psychiatric inpatients. *Psychotherapy, 31*, 620–631.

Howat, S., & Davidson, K. (2002). Parasuicidal behavior and interpersonal problem solving performance in order adults. *British Journal of Clinical Psychology, 41*, 375–386.

Ingram, R. E. (Ed.). (1986). *Information processing approaches to clinical psychology*. San Diego, CA: Academic Press.

Iwata, B. A., Pace, G. M., Dorsey, M. F., Zarcone, J. R., Vollmer, T. R., Smith, R. G., et al. (1994). The functions of self-injurious behavior: An experimental-epidemiological analysis. *Journal of Applied Behavior Analysis, 27*, 215–240.

Jarvis, G. K., Ferrence, R. G., Johnson, F. G., & Whitehead, P. C. (1976). Sex and age patterns in self-injury. *Journal of Health and Social Behavior, 17*, 145–154.

Kandel, D. B. (1978). Homophily, selection, and socialization in adolescent friendships. *American Journal of Sociology, 84*, 427–436.

Kehrer, C. A., & Linenhan M. M. (1996). Interpersonal and emotional problem solving skills and parasuicide among women with borderline personality disorder. *Journal of Personality Disorders, 10*, 153–163.

Klonsky, E. D. (2007). The functions of deliberate self-injury: A review of the evidence. *Clinical Psychology Review, 27*, 226–239.

Klonsky, E. D., & Olino, T. M. (2008). Identifying clinically distinct subgroups of young adult self-injurers: A latent class analysis. *Journal of Consulting and Clinical Psychology, 76*, 22–27.

Klonsky, E. D., Oltmanns, T. F., & Turkheimer, E. (2003). Deliberate self-harm in a nonclinical population: Prevalence and psychological correlates. *The American Journal of Psychiatry, 160*, 1501–1508.

Laye-Gindhu, A., & Schonert-Reichl, K. A. (2005). Nonsuicidal self-harm among community adolescents: Understanding the "whats" and "whys" of self-harm. *Journal of Youth and Adolescence, 34*, 447–457.

Linehan, M. M., Comtois, K. A., Murray, A. M., Brown, M. Z., Gallop, R. J., Heard, H. L., et al. (2006). Two-year randomized controlled trial and follow-up of dialectical behavior therapy vs therapy by experts for suicidal behaviors and borderline personality disorders. *Archives of General Psychiatry, 63*, 757–766.

Lloyd-Richardson, E. E., Nock, M. K., & Prinstein, M. K. (2008). Functions of adolescent non-suicidal self-injury. In M. K. Nixon & N. Heath (Eds.), *Self-injury in youth: Essential guide to assessment and intervention* (pp. 29–41). New York: Routledge.

McAuliffe, C., Corcoran, P., Keeley, H. S., Arensman, E., Bille-Brahe, U., DeLeo, D., et al. (2006). Problem-solving ability and repetition of deliberate self-harm: A multicentre study. *Psychological medicine, 36*, 45–55.

McFall, R. M. (1982). A review and reformulation of the concept of social skills. *Behavioral Assessment, 4*, 1–33.

Nixon, M. K., Cloutier, P. F., & Aggarwal, S. (2002). Affect regulation and addictive aspects of repetitive self-injury in hospitalized adolescents. *Journal of the American Academy of Child & Adolescent Psychiatry, 41*, 1333–1339.

Nock, M. K., & Mendes , W. B. (2008). Physiological arousal, distress tolerance, and social problem-solving deficits among adolescent self-injurers. *Journal of Consulting and Clinical Psychology, 76,* 28–38.

Nock, M. K., & Prinstein, M. J. (2004). A functional approach to the assessment of self-mutilative behavior. *Journal of Consulting and Clinical Psychology, 72,* 885–890.

Nock, M. K., & Prinstein, M. J. (2005). Contextual features and behavioral functions of self-mutilation among adolescents. *Journal of Abnormal Psychology, 114,* 140–146.

Orbach, I., Mikulincer, M., King, R., Cohen, D., & Stein, D. (1997). Thresholds and tolerance of physical pain in suicidal and nonsuicidal adolescents. *Journal of Consulting and Clinical Psychology, 65,* 646–652.

Osuch, E. A., Noll, J. G., & Putnam, F. W. (1999). The motivations for self-injury in psychiatric inpatients. *Psychiatry, 62,* 334–346.

Paetsch, J. J., & Bertrand, L. D. (1997). The relationship between peer, social, and school factors, and delinquency among youth. *Journal of School Health, 67,* 27–32.

Paxton, S. J., Schutz, H. K., Wertheim, E. H., & Muir, S. L. (1999). Friendship clique and peer influences on body image concerns, dietary restraint, extreme weight-loss behaviors, and binge eating in adolescent girls. *Journal of Abnormal Psychology, 108,* 255–266.

Prinstein, M. J., Boergers, J., & Spirito, A. (2001). Adolescents' and their friends' health-risk behavior: Factors that alter or add to peer influence. *Journal of Pediatric Psychology, 26,* 287–298.

Prinstein, M. J., & Dodge, K. A. (2008). *Understanding peer influence in children and adolescents.* New York: Guilford Press.

Prinstein, M. J., Guerry, J. D., & Rancourt, D. (2007, November). Peer contagion of adolescent nonsuicidal self-injury: Support from two longitudinal studies. In M. J. Prinstein & M. K. Nock (Cochairs), *A closer look at functional models of nonsuicidal self-injury: Results from multi-method investigations.* Symposium conducted at the meeting of the Association for Behavioral and Cognitive Therapies, Phildelphia, PA.

Prinstein, M. J., Meade, C. S., & Cohen, G. L. (2003). Adolescent sexual behavior, peer popularity, and perceptions of best friends' sexual behavior. *Journal of Pediatric Psychology, 28,* 243–249.

Prinstein, M. J., & Wang, S. S. (2005). False consensus and adolescent peer contagion: Examining discrepancies between perceptions and actual reported levels of friends' deviant and health risk behaviors. *Journal of Abnormal Child Psychology, 33,* 293–306.

Rada, R. T., & James, W. (1982). Urethral insertion of foreign bodies: A report of contagious self-mutilation in a maximum-security hospital. *Archives of General Psychiatry, 39,* 423–429.

Raine, W. J. B. (1982). Self-mutilation. *Journal of Adolescence, 5,* 1–13.

Rodham, K., Hawton, K., & Evans, E. (2004). Reasons for deliberate self-harm: Comparison of self-poisoners and self-cutters in a community sample of adolescents. *Journal of the American Academy of Child & Adolescent Psychiatry, 43,* 80–87.

Rosen, P. M., & Walsh, B. W. (1989). Patterns of contagion in self-mutilation epidemics. *The American Journal of Psychiatry, 146,* 656–658.

Rosen, P. M., Walsh, B. W., & Rode, S. A. (1990). Interpersonal loss and self-mutilation. *Suicide and Life-Threatening Behavior, 20,* 177–184.

Ross, S., & Heath, N. (2002). A study of the frequency of self-mutilation in a community sample of adolescents. *Journal of Youth and Adolescence, 311,* 67–77.

Rudolph, K. D. (2002). Gender differences in emotional responses to interpersonal stress during adolescence. *Journal of Adolescent Health, 30,* 3–13.

Rudolph, K. D., & Hammen, C. (1999). Age and gender as determinants of stress exposure, generation, and reactions in youngsters: A transactional perspective. *Child Development, 70,* 660–677.

Shearer, S. L. (1994). Phenomenology of self-injury among inpatient women with borderline personality disorder. *The Journal of Nervous and Mental Disease, 182,* 524–526.

Silove, D., George, G., & Bhavani-Sankaram, V. (1987). Parasuicide: Interaction between inadequate parenting and recent interpersonal stress. *Australian and New Zealand Journal of Psychiatry, 21,* 221–228.

Simpson, C. A., & Porter, G. L. (1981). Self-mutilation in children and adolescents. *Bulletin of the Menninger Clinic, 45,* 428–438.

Simpson, M. A. (1975). The phenomenology of self-mutilation in a general hospital setting. *Canadian Psychiatric Association Journal, 20,* 429–434.

Steinberg. L. D., & Silverberg, S. B. (1986). The vicissitudes of autonomy in early adolescence. *Child Development, 57,* 841–851.

Suyemoto, K. L. (1998). The functions of self-mutilation. *Clinical Psychology Review, 18,* 531–554.

Taiminen, T. J., Kallio-Soukainen, K., Nokso-Koivisto, H., Kaljonen, A., & Kelenius, H. (1998). Contagion of deliberate self-harm among adolescent inpatients. *Journal of the American Academy of Child & Adolescent Psychiatry, 37,* 211–217.

Turner, J. (1991). *Social Influence.* Bristol, England: Open University Press.

Urberg, K. A., Degirmencioglu, S. M., & Pilgrim, C. (1997). Close friend and group influence on adolescent cigarette smoking and alcohol use. *Developmental Psychology, 33,* 834–844.

Vitaro, F., Tremblay, R. E., Kerr, M., Pagani, L., & Bukowski, W. M. (1997). Disruptiveness, friends' characteristics, and delinquency in early adolescence: A test of two competing models of development. *Child Development, 68,* 676–689.

Walker, R. L., Joiner, T. E., Jr., & Rudd, M. D. (2001). The course of post-crisis suicidal symptoms: How and for whom is suicide "cathartic"? *Suicide and Life-Threatening Behavior, 31,* 144–152.

Walsh, B. W., & Rosen, P. (1985). Self-mutilation and contagion: An empirical test. *The American Journal of Psychiatry, 142*, 119–120.

Welch, S. S., & Linehan, M. M. (2002). High-risk situations associated with para-suicide and drug use in borderline personality disorder. *Journal of Personality Disorders, 16*, 561–569.

Whitlock, J. L., Powers, J. L., & Eckenrode, J. (2006). The virtual cutting edge: The Internet and adolescent self-injury. *Developmental Psychology, 42*, 407–417.

Wills, T. A., & Cleary, S. D. (1999). Peer and adolescent substance use among 6th–9th graders: Latent growth analyses of influence versus selection mechanisms. *Health Psychology, 18*, 453–563.

Yates, T. M. (2004). The developmental psychopathology of self-injurious behavior: Compensatory regulation in posttraumatic adaptation. *Clinical Psychology Review, 24*, 35–74.

Yip, K. (2005). A multi-dimensional perspective of adolescents' self-cutting. *Child and Adolescent Mental Health, 10*, 80–86.

6

BIOLOGICAL MODELS OF NONSUICIDAL SELF-INJURY

LEO SHER AND BARBARA STANLEY

Nonsuicidal self-injury (NSSI) is a serious behavioral condition that afflicts millions of individuals around the world. It occurs frequently in individuals diagnosed with borderline personality disorder (BPD), a disorder characterized by self-injurious behavior, impulsivity, and emotional lability. Up to 75% of individuals with BPD engage in NSSI, which is often regarded as manipulative, attention seeking, and not life-threatening (Bongar, Peterson, Golann, & Hardiman, 1990; Feldman, 1988). Although suicidal behavior and NSSI are distinct behaviors, NSSI is a significant risk factor for suicide attempts and suicide. Approximately 55% to 85% of those who self-injure have made at least one suicide attempt (Fyer, Frances, Sullivan, Hurt, & Clarkin, 1988; Stone, 1990). Whereas the lifetime suicide rate for those who self-injure is unknown, the suicide rate for those with BPD is 8% to 10% (Frances, Fyer, & Clarkin, 1986; Stone, Hurt, & Stone, 1987). The high co-occurrence of suicidal behavior and NSSI suggests that they may share a common biology. Other diagnoses associated with NSSI are antisocial personality disorder, dissociative identity disorder, posttraumatic stress disorder, anorexia nervosa, bulimia nervosa, depression, autism, mental retardation, alcohol abuse, and Lesch–Nyhan syndrome (Favazza, 1989; Feldman, 1988; Nock, Joiner, Gordon, Lloyd-Richardson, & Prinstein, 2006; Roy, 1978; Winchel & Stanley, 1991).

Most individuals who repetitively self-injure have problems with other forms of impulsivity (Lacey & Evans, 1986). In a study of alcoholic women, 25% cut themselves deliberately, 16% had an eating disorder, half described impulsive physical violence, and half acknowledged a period of promiscuity (Evans & Lacey, 1992). Fichter, Quadflieg, and Rief (1994) reported on 32 "multi-impulsive bulimics"; among their impulsive behaviors were NSSI (75%), shoplifting (78%), alcohol dependence (34%), drug abuse (22%), and sexual promiscuity (53%). These findings are consistent with those of Favazza and Conterio (1989), in which about half of those who repetitively self-injure develop or have a history of eating disorders, and at least 20% develop or have a history of episodic alcohol or substance abuse and kleptomania.

The expression of NSSI is not limited to human populations (Bayne, Haines, Dexter, Woodman, & Evans, 1995; Tiefenbacher, Novak, Lutz, & Meyer, 2005). Spontaneously occurring NSSI has also been described in many nonhuman primates, including the great apes, Old World monkeys, New World monkeys, and prosimians, again suggesting a biological component.

Several hypotheses have been formulated as to why humans in particular engage in self-injurious behavior. These hypotheses arise from various theoretical orientations, ranging from behavioral (e.g., negative and positive reinforcement hypothesis, self-stimulation hypothesis) and psychodynamic (e.g., anxiety or hostility reduction) to neurobiological (e.g., serotonergic, dopaminergic, and opioidergic hypotheses; Stanley & Brodsky, 2005; Winchel & Stanley, 1991). Given the heterogeneity of conditions and disorders associated with NSSI in humans, it is likely that self-injury has more than one etiology and does not simply represent a single entity or syndrome. In this chapter, we focus on the neurobiological mechanisms of NSSI.

ROLE OF OPIOIDS IN NONSUICIDAL SELF-INJURY

Endogenous opioids have been implicated in the expression of NSSI in several psychiatric and developmental disorders, including BPD, mental retardation, and autism (Schmahl, McGlashan, & Bremner, 2002; Tiefenbacher et al., 2005). Evidence for such a role is based on (a) the partial success of opioid antagonist treatment to ameliorate NSSI (Casner, Weinheimer, & Gualtieri, 1996; Kars, Broekema, Glaudemans-van Gelderen, Verhoven, & Van Ree, 1990), (b) reports of altered pain sensitivity during episodes of NSSI (Kemperman, Russ, & Shearin, 1997; Russ, Campbell, Kakuma, Harrison, & Zanine, 1999), and (c) findings of altered endogenous opioid levels in individuals with NSSI (Coid, Allolio, & Rees, 1983; Sandman, Hetrick, Taylor, & Chicz-DeMet, 1997).

Opioid deficiency could result from chronic and severe childhood stress and trauma, such as abuse, neglect, and loss. There is a high incidence of childhood trauma in those who inflict NSSI. Traumatic events may alter or reset physiological levels of opioids or may create a deficiency state. Another possibility is that there is habituation to high levels of endogenous opioids in childhood caused by recurrent exposure to physical or sexual abuse.

Russ, Roth, Kakuma, Harrison, and Hull (1994) did not directly examine the opioid system but suggested that it may play an important role in NSSI. Russ, Shearin, Clarkin, Harrison, and Hull (1993) classified patients with BPD into two groups on the basis of whether they did or did not experience pain during self-injurious episodes. This study found that ratings of depression, anxiety, impulsiveness, dissociation, and trauma symptoms were higher in the women who did not experience pain while injuring themselves, as were the number of suicide attempts and the prevalence of childhood sexual abuse. Russ et al. (1992) also found that women with BPD who reported that they did not feel pain during episodes of NSSI experienced significantly less pain in response to a standard laboratory pain stimulus than did those who reported that they did feel pain during self-injurious episodes. These results are suggestive of biological subtypes of patients with BPD who self-injure. The notion that there are different biological subtypes of BPD is consistent with the data suggesting that different opioid receptors may play different roles in NSSI.

There is a well-established relationship between pain perception and endogenous opioids. Beta-endorphin and met-enkephalin are agonists at mu-opioid receptors and are related to stress-induced analgesia and thermal pain perception (Akil et al., 1984; Schmauss, 1987; Watkins & Mayer, 1982). Met-enkephalin is also involved in saliency, reward, and motivational behavior (Chen, Mestek, Liu, Hurley, & Yu, 1993). Several studies have demonstrated that reward is influenced by activation of ventral pallidum mu-opioid receptors (Steiner & Gerfen, 1998). Mu-opioid receptors are widely distributed throughout the human central nervous system, with a particularly dense location in the basal ganglia, cortical structures, thalamic nuclei, spinal cord, and specific nuclei in the brainstem (Cross, Hille, & Slater, 1987). This explains their multiple roles in pain perception and behavior.

Dynorphin is associated with kappa receptor activity and attendant chemical and pressure pain perception (Mogil et al., 2003). Steiner and Gerfen (1998) suggested that the specific function of dynorphin and enkephalin is to dampen excessive activation of projection neurons by dopamine and other neurotransmitters and that dynorphin is involved in the mechanisms of behavioral sensitization. Consequently, the roles of beta-endorphin, met-enkephalin, and dynorphin may differ in NSSI because they play different roles in pain perception in behavior.

Evidence consistent with a role for endogenous opioids in the expression of NSSI in monkeys has been found (Tiefenbacher et al., 2005). Rhesus monkeys engaging in NSSI preferentially direct their self-biting activity toward body areas that can be associated with acupuncture and acupressure analgesia

(Marinus, Chase, & Novak, 2000). A similar relationship has also been demonstrated for people engaging in NSSI (Symons & Thompson, 1997). Acupuncture- and acupressure-induced analgesia in humans is thought to be at least partly mediated by the release of endogenous opioids, particularly met-enkephalin (Ulett, Han, & Han, 1998). Monkeys also show acupuncture-induced analgesia that can be reversed with opioid antagonist treatment (Ha, Tan, Fukunaga, & Aochi, 1981; Liu, Han, & Su, 1990). Together, these findings raise the possibility that in some monkeys, self-directed biting might serve to release and self-administer endogenous opioids. Indeed, monkeys with a veterinary record of self-inflicted wounding showed significantly reduced levels of beta-endorphin-like immunoreactivity in blood plasma, and met-enkephalin-like immunoreactivity in cerebrospinal fluid compared with monkeys without such record (Tiefenbacher et al., 2003). Monkeys may therefore engage in self-directed biting specifically to release met-enkephalin or beta-endorphin.

If the endogenous opioid system is central to repetitive self-injury, then treatment with a long-acting opioid antagonist could block the reward of enhanced endogenous opioids caused by such behaviors and subsequently lead to their extinction. Several reports found that naloxone or naltrexone could be useful in diminishing NSSI (Sandman, Touchette, Lenjavi, Marion, & Chicz-DeMet, 2003; Symons, Thompson, & Rodriguez, 2004; see also chap. 13, this volume). Naltrexone has few effects in the absence of opioids (Reisine & Pasternak, 1996), suggesting that effective treatment (i.e., resulting in reduced NSSI) engages the endogenous opioid system. Not surprisingly, not all individuals expressing NSSI are positive responders to naltrexone (Sandman et al., 1993, 1998; Sandman, Hetrick, Taylor, Marion, & Chicz-DeMet, 2000; Thompson, Hackenberg, Cerutti, Baker, & Axtell, 1994), and in fact, a small minority may increase their engagement in NSSI (Sandman et al., 1998).

Attempts to explain the variation in individual response patterns to naltrexone led to the search for biological markers that predicted treatment efficacy. In a series of studies, researchers reported that (a) baseline levels of beta-endorphin were positively related to changes in behavior (Clinical Global Impressions) after treatment with naltrexone in five young children with autism (Ernst et al., 1993), (b) C-terminal beta-endorphin levels (a fragment of the larger beta-endorphin molecule) decreased after naltrexone only in good responders (Bouvard et al., 1995), (c) increased NSSI and positive response to naltrexone in some participants were related to high levels of endogenous opiates (Scifo et al., 1996), and (d) participants responding with decreased beta-endorphin levels after treatment with naltrexone had better and more pervasive behavioral improvement than did participants who did not have physiological changes after naltrexone (Cazzullo et al., 1999). In a placebo-controlled crossover study, Sandman et al. (1997) found that participants with the highest change in plasma levels of beta-endorphin after NSSI had the most positive (and significant) response to the high dose (2 mg/kg) of naltrexone.

Duman et al. (2004) suggested that paroxetine, a selective serotonin reuptake inhibitor (SSRI) antidepressant drug, induced an antinociceptive effect following administration. This antinociception was significantly inhibited by naloxone, an opioid receptor antagonist, suggesting the involvement of opioidergic mechanisms. This demonstrates the interaction between the serotonergic and opioid systems in the brain. This interaction may play a role in the pathophysiology of NSSI.

NSSI in the context of BPD is often followed by mood enhancement. Specifically, a decrease in negative affect, an increase in positive affect, and an increase in dissociative symptoms were reported (Kemperman et al., 1997). Simeon et al. (1992) suggested that self-mutilation could act as self-healing through restoration of positive affect, however brief. Studies have demonstrated that the activation of mu-opioid receptor–mediated neurotransmission suppresses fear and stress responses to noxious threatening stimuli and mother–infant separation (Kalin, Shelton, & Barksdale, 1988, 1989). The mu-opioid receptors also contribute to regulation of emotional memory (Quirarte, Galvez, Roozendaal, & McGaugh, 1998). In humans, the regional activation of mu-opioid neurotransmission is centrally implicated in the suppression of the affective qualities of a pain stressor and in the negative internal affective states induced by that challenge (Zubieta et al., 2002, Zubieta, Heitzeg, et al., 2003). Zubieta, Ketter, et al. (2003) demonstrated dynamic changes in mu-opioid neurotransmission in response to an experimentally induced negative affective state. The direction and localization of these responses confirm the role of mu-opioid receptors in the regulation of affective experiences in humans. It is worth noting that endogenous opioids may mediate the mood-enhancing effect of exercise (Zubieta et al., 2002; Zubieta, Heitzeg, et al., 2003), and aerobic exercise has been associated with decreased engagement in NSSI (Wallenstein & Nock, 2007). Our study demonstrated that those with BPD who self-injure have lower CSF levels of endogenous opioids compared those with BPD who do not engage in NSSI (Stanley, Sher, Wilson, Ekman, & Mann, 2008).

In summary, multiple lines of evidence suggest that endogenous opioids are involved in the pathogenesis of NSSI. Future studies of the role of opioids in the biological mechanisms of NSSI may lead to the development of new treatment modalities.

SEROTONIN AND NONSUICIDAL SELF-INJURY

Dysregulation in serotonergic neurotransmission has been proposed to play a role in the expression of NSSI (Herpertz, Sass, & Favazza, 1997; New et al., 1997; Simeon et al., 1992). Biological studies implicate reduced serotonergic neurotransmission in both inwardly and outwardly directed aggressive behaviors, especially impulsive ones (Stein, Hollander, & Liebowitz, 1993). This finding pertains to patients with a history of attempted suicide (Asberg, 1986; Coccaro et al., 1989; Traskman, Asberg, Bertilsson, & Sjostrand, 1981), to impulsive violent offenders (Linnoila et al., 1983; O'Keane et al., 1992), to individuals with antisocial personality disorder and substance abuse (Moss, Yao, & Panzak, 1990), and to individuals with personality disorders who cut or burn themselves (Simeon et al., 1992). Relevant psychopathological features claimed to be associated with reduced central serotonergic activity are assaultiveness and dysphoria (Moss et al., 1990), irritability (Coccaro & Kavoussi, 1991; Coccaro & Siever, 1995), trait impulsivity (Barratt, 1994), and state depression (Asberg et al., 1984; Meltzer & Lowry, 1987).

An increased serotonergic action within the striatum has been suggested as being crucial in the appearance of self-injurious behavior in Lesch–Nyhan syndrome (Davanzo, Belin, Widawski, & King, 1998; Pellicer, Buendia-Roldan, & Pallares-Trujillo, 1998). Abnormalities of serotonin metabolism have also been described in Gilles de la Tourette syndrome, which frequently has NSSI as a feature (Sandyk & Bamford, 1988). SSRIs have been shown to be effective in controlling NSSI in both Prader–Willi syndrome and Lesch–Nyhan syndrome (Antochi, Stravrakaki, & Emery, 2003). SSRIs reduced NSSI in some individuals with BPD (Antochi et al., 2003; Markovitz & Wagner, 1995; New et al., 1997). As noted earlier, Duman et al. (2004) suggested that paroxetine induced an antinociceptive effect following administration. This finding supports the notion that the serotonergic system is involved in the neurobiology of pain perception.

Altered serotonin system function has also recently been implicated in the expression of NSSI in rhesus monkeys (Tiefenbacher et al., 2005). Treatment with the serotonin precursor L-tryptophan resulted in significant reductions in rates of self-directed biting in rhesus monkeys with a history of self-inflicted wounding (Weld et al., 1998). These findings raise the possibility that high levels of self-biting in monkeys could be due to a deficiency in serotonergic transmission.

THE DOPAMINERGIC SYSTEM AND NONSUICIDAL SELF-INJURY

There is relatively limited evidence that altered dopaminergic system function may be associated with NSSI. In particular, reductions in basal ganglia dopamine have been proposed to play a role in the expression of NSSI and stereotypy in individuals with developmental disorders and Lesch–Nyhan disease (C. A. Turner & Lewis, 2002). Lloyd et al. (1981) demonstrated that central nervous system dopamine and its metabolites are markedly lower in patients with Lesch–Nyhan syndrome. Such reductions could, in turn, lead to supersensitivity of postsynaptic dopaminergic receptors. There are several rodent and primate models that implicate sensitization of postsynaptic D1, and possibly also D2, receptors in the development of NSSI (Breese, Criswell, & Mueller, 1990; Okamura, Murakami, Yokoyama, Nakamura, & Ibata, 1997; Yokoyama & Okamura, 1997). Sokol, Campbell, Goldstein, and Kriechman (1987) reported on a group of patients with attention-deficit/hyperactivity disorder in whom self-biting behavior was elicited by administration of stimulants (i.e., dextroamphetamine and methylphenidate). The authors proposed that the dopamine agonist activity of these stimulants in a supersensitive dopaminergic system resulted in NSSI. However, the efficacy of neuroleptics (i.e., dopamine antagonists) to reduce NSSI in individuals with developmental disorders has been marginal.

HYPOTHALAMIC–PITUITARY–ADRENAL AXIS AND NONSUICIDAL SELF-INJURY

The hypothalamic–pituitary–adrenal (HPA) stress system has been implicated in NSSI (Sandman et al., 2000). Adverse early experience and lifetime trauma have been linked to long-lasting changes in peripheral (i.e., HPA) and central (i.e., brain corticotropin-releasing hormone) stress response systems (Kanter et al., 2001; Yehuda, Halligan, Golier, Grossman, & Bierer, 2004). Such experiences are also important risk factors in the development and expression of NSSI (Briere & Gil, 1998; Zlotnick et al., 1997). However, existing studies assessing alterations in peripheral and central stress response systems in people with NSSI have been limited (Symons, Sutton, Walker, & Bodfish, 2003; Verhoeven et al., 1999). One exception is a case report of a patient with BPD by Sachsse, Von der Heyde, and Huether (2002). The authors examined the relationship between episodes of NSSI and fluctuations in levels of nocturnal urinary cortisol excretion and found significant increases in urinary cortisol directly preceding an episode of NSSI, followed by an immediate return to baseline.

Proopiomelanocortin (POMC) is probably involved in the pathophysiology of NSSI (Sandman et al., 1997, 2000). In humans, most POMC is produced in the pars distalis of the anterior pituitary but also by hypothalamic neurons and neurons in the amygdala and pituitary stalk. The POMC molecule is a well-characterized bioinactive protein-like molecule that is converted by enzymes into biologically active fragments, including beta-endorphin and adrenocorticotrophin (ACTH; Bertagna, 1994; Bicknell, Savva, & Lowry, 1996; Boutillier et al., 1995; Sandman, Spence, & Smith, 1999; Seidah & Chretien, 1992; Seidah et al., 1991).

Sandman et al. (1997) reported that plasma levels of beta-endorphin were elevated and dissociated from plasma levels of ACTH immediately after a self-injuring act. The uncoupled pattern following NSSI was unexpected because the degree of association between these two stress peptides usually increases with stress, exertion, or pain (Forman, Cavalieri, Estilow, & Tatarian, 1990; Guiffre, Udelsman, Listwak, & Chrousos, 1988; Holson, Scallet, Ali, Sullivan, & Gough, 1988; Knigge, Matzen, Bach, Bang, & Warberg, 1989; Oltras, Mora, & Vives, 1987; Recher, Willis, Smit, & Copolov, 1988; Shutt, Smith, Wallace, Connell, & Fell, 1988; Strand, 1999). This observation demonstrates the relationship between the HPA system and endogenous opioids.

GENETIC FINDINGS RELATED TO NONSUICIDAL SELF-INJURY

Several findings indicate a potential role of genetic factors in the etiology and pathogenesis of self-injurious behavior. NSSI is a recognized clinical feature of Lesch–Nyhan syndrome, a rare X-linked recessive metabolic disorder with hyperuricemia (Pellicer et al., 1998). The biochemical alterations that accompany this syndrome arise from a lack of the enzyme hypoxanthine-guanine phosphoribosyltransferase, which is related to purine metabolism. NSSI also has been described in laboratory animals, with suggestions that this reflects a genetic predisposition (Iglauer et al., 1995). For example, Iglauer et al. (1995) suggested a genetic predisposition for the observed compulsive NSSI in laboratory rabbits. A duplication of part of the long arm of chromosome 22 (22q11.2–q13.1) together with a pericentric inversion of the same chromosome is associated with particular phenotypic features that include persistent self-injury (Prasher et al., 1995). A genetic polymorphism of the enzyme catechol-O-methyl transferase, also located in chromosome 22q11, is associated with alterations in mu-opioid receptor binding and in the release of endogenous opioids and with enhanced affective response to a pain stressor (Zubieta, Heitzeg, et al., 2003; Zubieta, Ketter, 2003). Zammarchi, Savelli, Donati, and Pasquini (1994) reported a case of NSSI in a patient with Mucolipidosis III, a lysosomal disease in which self-mutilation had not been previously described.

It has recently been shown that the T allele of GN3 is a risk factor for NSSI and that it remains so even when the impact of childhood sexual abuse and BPD is taken into account (Joyce et al., 2006). The T allele (C825T) of GN3 located in exon 10 affects splicing and is associated with a deletion of 41 amino acids, altered structure, and enhanced signal transduction to a variety of stimuli, including adrenergic stimuli (Farfel, Bourne, & Iiri, 1999). This T allele is also associated with hypertension, obesity, and increased antihypertensive response to thiazide diuretics (Siffert, 2000; S. T. Turner, Schwartz, Chapman, & Boerwinkle, 2001) and thus is not specific to NSSI.

BIOLOGICAL MODEL OF NONSUICIDAL SELF-INJURY

We propose a homeostasis model of self-injury that incorporates several aspects of current theoretical perspectives (Figure 6.1; Stanley et al., 2008). In our model, individuals who self-injure may have chronically lower levels of endogenous opioids. The self-injury may be viewed as attempting to restore their levels of endogenous opioids to more normal levels. As we suggested earlier, opioid deficiency could result from chronic and severe childhood stress and trauma, such as abuse, neglect, and loss. Severe traumas may create a permanent deficiency state or habituation to higher levels of endogenous opioids. Therefore, patients with histories of abuse may require increased levels of endorphins to cope with stress as adults.

Our model is consistent with the observations that painful stimuli and other highly stressful conditions can increase levels of endogenous opioids in the central nervous system and result in the development of a phenomenon known as stress-induced analgesia (Basbaum & Fields, 1984; Helmstetter & Fanselow, 1987). These neurochemical alterations may be associated with NSSI. Coid et al. (1983) studied patients reporting absence of pain during NSSI. Their mean plasma met-enkephalin level was elevated shortly after their hospitalization for NSSI but returned to normal range after at least 2 months of abstinence from NSSI. This suggests that elevated met-enkephalin levels could be a pain response to NSSI. Stress-induced analgesia may play a role in the pathogenesis of NSSI. The trauma of battle, attack by a predator, and even everyday stress often reduce the perception of pain. This phenomenon, called stress-induced analgesia, was first recognized by researchers after World War II.

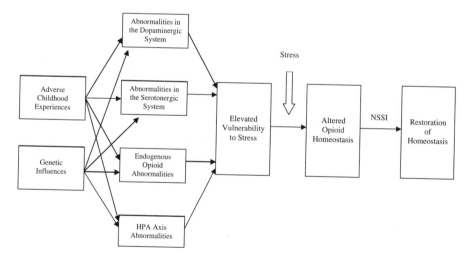

Figure 6.1. Biological model of nonsuicidal self-injury (NSSI). HPA = hypothalamic–pituitary–adrenal.

Stress-induced analgesia may play a role in the apparent pain insensitivity of individuals who engage in NSSI.

CONCLUSION

In this chapter, we reviewed data suggesting that NSSI has a biological basis. Adverse early experience followed by later repeated stressful events can result in lasting alterations in neuropeptide and neuroendocrine systems associated with the regulation of stress. Genetic factors may also contribute to this pathology. Although the important and traumatic effects of childhood abuse should not be underestimated, a cause-and-effect relationship between abuse and NSSI should not be automatically assumed. Abuse may serve to elicit symptoms in a person already at risk, but frequent histories of such trauma may also reflect a familial predisposition to impulsive and aggressive behavior. An interplay of both factors suggests a possibility that those who are biologically endowed with a vulnerability to NSSI may also have a greater probability of being raised in a familial environment in which the stressors that might elicit such behavior—such as childhood physical, sexual, or emotional abuse—are more likely to occur.

Endogenous opioids may play a key role in the pathophysiology of NSSI. Further studies of the neurobiology of NSSI are necessary. In particular, research is needed to understand more fully the role of endogenous opioids in the neurobiology in self-injury. Other areas of investigation should include a better understanding of the experience of pain and relief from pain, both emotional and physiological, in individuals with BPD.

REFERENCES

Akil, H., Watson, S. J., Young, E., Lewis, M. E., Khachaturian, H., & Walker, J. M. (1984). Endogenous opioids: Biology and function. *Annual Review of Neuroscience, 7*, 223–255.

Antochi, R., Stravrakaki, C., & Emery, P. C. (2003). Psychopharmacological treatments in persons with dual diagnosis of psychiatric disorders and developmental disabilities. *Postgraduate Medical Journal, 79*, 139–146.

Asberg, M. (1986). Biochemical aspects of suicide. *Clinical Neuropharmacology, 9*, 374–376.

Asberg, M., Bertilosson, L., Martensson, B., Scalia-Tombia, G. P., Thoren, P., & Traskman, L. (1984). CSF monoamine metabolites in melancholia. *Acta Psychiatrica Scandinavica, 69*, 201–219.

Barratt, E. S. (1994). Impulsiveness and aggression. In J. Monahan & H. Stedman (Eds.), *Violence and mental disorder: Developments in risk assessment* (pp. 61–80). Chicago: University of Chicago Press.

Basbaum, A. I., & Fields, H. L. (1984). Endogenous pain control systems: Brainstem spinal pathways and endorphin circuitry. *Annual Review of Neuroscience, 7,* 309–338.

Bayne, K., Haines, D., Dexter, S., Woodman, D., & Evans, C. (1995). Nonhuman primate wounding prevalence: A retrospective analysis. *Lab Animal, 24,* 40–44.

Bertagna, X. (1994). Proopiomelanocortin-derived peptides. *Endocrinology and Metabolism Clinics of North America, 23,* 467–485.

Bicknell, A. B., Savva, D., & Lowry, P. J. (1996). Pro-opiomelanocortin and adrenal function. *Endocrine Research, 22,* 385–393.

Bongar, B., Peterson, L. G., Golann, S., & Hardiman, J. J. (1990). Self-mutilation and the chronically suicidal patient: An examination of the frequent visitor to the psychiatric emergency room. *Annals of Clinical Psychiatry, 2,* 217–222.

Boutillier, A. L., Monnier, D., Lorang, D., Lundblad, J. R., Roberts, J. L., & Loeffler, J. P. (1995). Corticotropin-releasing hormone stimulates propiomelanocortin transcription by cFos-dependent and -independent pathways: Characterization of an AP1 site in exon 1. *Molecular Endocrinology, 9,* 745–755.

Bouvard, M. P., Leboyer, J. M., Launay, J., Recasens, C., Plumet M. H., Waller-Perotte D., et al. (1995). Low-dose naltrexone effects on plasma chemistries and clinical symptoms in autism: A double-blind, placebo-controlled study. *Psychiatry Research, 58,* 191–201.

Breese, G. R., Criswell, H. E., & Mueller, R. A. (1990). Evidence that lack of brain dopamine during development can increase the susceptibility for aggression and self-injurious behavior by influencing D1-dopamine receptor function. *Progress in Neuro-Psychopharmacology & Biological Psychiatry, 14*(Suppl.), 65–80.

Briere, J., & Gil, E. (1998). Self-mutilation in clinical and general population samples: Prevalence, correlates, and functions. *American Journal of Orthopsychiatry, 68,* 609–620.

Casner, J. A., Weinheimer, B., & Gualtieri, C. T. (1996). Naltrexone and self-injurious behavior: A retrospective population study. *Journal of Clinical Psychopharmacology, 16,* 389–394.

Cazzullo, A. G., Musetti, M. C., Musetti, L., Bajo, S., Sacerdote, P., & Panerai, A. (1999). Beta-endorphin levels in peripheral blood mononuclear cells and long-term naltrexone treatment in autistic children. *European Neuropsychopharmacology: Journal of the European College of Neuropsychopharmacology, 9,* 361–363.

Chen, Y., Mestek, A., Liu, J., Hurley, J. A., & Yu, L. (1993). Molecular cloning and functional expression of a μ-opioid receptor from rat brain. *Molecular Pharmacology, 44,* 8–12.

Coccaro, E. F., & Kavoussi, R. (1991) Biologic and pharmacologic aspects of borderline personality disorder. *Hospital and Community Psychiatry, 42,* 1029–1033.

Coccaro, E. F., & Siever, L. J. (1995). The neuropsychopharmacology of personality disorders. In F. E. Bloom & D. J. Kupfer (Eds.), *Psychopharmacology: The fourth generation of progress* (pp. 1567–1579). New York: Raven Press.

Coccaro, E. F., Siever, L. J., Klar, H. M., Maurer, G., Cochrane, K., Cooper, T. B., et al. (1989). Serotonergic studies in patients with affective and personality disorders. *Archives of General Psychiatry, 46*, 587–599.

Coid, J., Allolio, B., & Rees, L. H. (1983, September 3). Raised plasma metenkephalin in patients who habitually mutilate themselves. *The Lancet, 2*, 545–546.

Cross, A. J., Hille, C., & Slater, P. (1987). Subtraction autoradiography of opiate receptor subtypes in human brain. *Brain Research, 418*, 343–348.

Davanzo, P. A., Belin, T. R., Widawski, M. H., & King, B. H. (1998). Paroxetine treatment of aggression and self-injury in persons with mental retardation. *American Journal on Mental Retardation, 102*, 427–437.

Duman, E. N., Kesim, M., Kadioglu, M., Yaris, E., Kalyoncu, N. I., & Erciyes, N. (2004). Possible involvement of opioidergic and serotonergic mechanisms in antinociceptive effect of paroxetine in acute pain. *Journal of Pharmacology Sciences, 94*, 161–165.

Ernst, M., Devi, L., Silva, R. R., Gonzalez, M. N., Small, A. M., Malone, R. P., & Campbell, M. (1993). Plasma beta-endorphin levels, naltrexone, and haloperidol in autistic children. *Psychopharmacology Bulletin, 29*, 221–227.

Evans, C., & Lacey, J. H. (1992). Multiple self-damaging behaviour among alcoholic women: A prevalence study. *The British Journal of Psychiatry, 161*, 643–647.

Farfel, Z., Bourne, H. R., & Iiri, T. (1999). The expanding spectrum of G protein diseases. *The New England Journal of Medicine, 340*, 1012–1020.

Favazza, A. R. (1989). Why patients mutilate themselves. *Hospital and Community Psychiatry, 40*, 137–145.

Favazza, A. R., & Conterio, K. (1989). Female habitual self-mutilators. *Acta Psychiatrica Scandinavica, 79*, 283–289.

Feldman, M. D. (1988). The challenge of self-mutilation: A review. *Comprehensive Psychiatry, 29*, 252–269.

Fichter, M. M., Quadflieg, N., & Rief, W. (1994). Course of multi-impulsive bulimia. *Psychological Medicine, 24*, 591–604.

Forman, L. J., Cavalieri, R., Estilow, S., & Tatarian, G. T. (1990). The elevation of immunoreactive B-endorphin in old male rats is related to alterations in dopamine and serotonin. *Neurobiology of Aging, 11*, 223–227.

Frances, A., Fyer, M., & Clarkin, J. (1986). Personality and suicide. *Annals of the New York Academy of Sciences, 487*, 281–293.

Fyer, M. R., Frances, A. J., Sullivan, T., Hurt, S. W., & Clarkin, J. (1988). Suicide attempts in patients with borderline personality disorder. *The American Journal of Psychiatry, 145*, 737–739.

Guiffre, K. A., Udelsman, R., Listwak, S., & Chrousos, G. P. (1988). Effects of immune neutralization of corticotropin-releasing hormone, adrenocorticotropin, and B-endorphin in the surgically stressed rat. *Endocrinology, 122*, 306–310.

Ha, H., Tan, E. C., Fukunaga, H., & Aochi, O. (1981). Naloxone reversal of acupuncture analgesia in the monkey. *Experimental Neurology, 73*, 298–303.

Helmstetter, F. J., & Fanselow, M. S. (1987). Effects of naltrexone on learning and performance of conditional fear-induced freezing and opioid analgesia. *Physiology & Behavior, 39*, 501–505.

Herpertz, S., Sass, H., & Favazza, A. (1997). Impulsivity in self-mutilative behavior: Psychometric and biological findings. *Journal of Psychiatric Research, 31*, 451–465.

Holson, R. R., Scallet, A. C., Ali, S. F., Sullivan, P., & Gough, B. (1988). Adrenocortical, B-endorphin and behavioral responses to graded stressors in differentially reared rats. *Physiology & Behavior, 42*, 125–130.

Iglauer, F., Beig, C., Dimigen, J., Gerold, S., Gocht, A., Seeburg, A., et al. (1995). Hereditary compulsive self-mutilating behaviour in laboratory rabbits. *Lab Animal, 29*, 385–393.

Joyce, P. R., McKenzie, J. M., Mulder, R. T., Luty, S. E., Sullivan, P. F., Miller, A. L., & Kennedy, M. A. (2006). Genetic, developmental and personality correlates of self-mutilation in depressed patients. *Australian and New Zealand Journal of Psychiatry, 40*, 225–229.

Kalin, N. H., Shelton, S. E., & Barksdale, C. M. (1988). Opiate modulation of separation-induced distress in non-human primates. *Brain Research, 440*, 285–292.

Kalin, N. H., Shelton, S. E., & Barksdale, C. M. (1989). Behavioral and physiologic effects of CRH administered to infant primates undergoing maternal separation. *Neuropsychopharmacology, 2*, 97–104.

Kanter, E. D., Wilkinson, C. W., Radant, A. D., Petrie, E. C., Dobie, D. J., McFall, M. E., et al. (2001). Glucocorticoid feedback sensitivity and adrenocortical responsiveness in posttraumatic stress disorder. *Biological Psychiatry, 50*, 238–245.

Kars, H., Broekema, W., Glaudemans-van Gelderen, I., Verhoeven, W. M., & Van Ree, J. M. (1990). Naltrexone attenuates self-injurious behavior in mentally retarded subjects. *Biological Psychiatry, 27*, 741–746.

Kemperman, I., Russ, M. J., & Shearin, E. (1997). Self-injurious behavior and mood regulation in borderline patients. *Journal of Personality Disorders, 11*, 146–157.

Knigge, U., Matzen, S., Bach, F., Bang, P., & Warberg, J. (1989). Involvement of histaminergic neurons in the stress-induced release of pro-opiomelanocortin-derived peptides in rats. *Acta Endocrinologica, 120*, 533–539.

Lacey, J. H., & Evans, C. D. (1986). The impulsivist: A multi-impulsive personality disorder. *British Journal of Addiction, 81*, 641–649.

Linnoila, M., Virkkunen, M., Scheinin, M., Nuutila, A., Rimon, R., & Goodwin, F. K. (1983). Low cerebrospinal fluid 5-hydroxyindoleacetic acid concentration differentiates impulsive from non-impulsive violent behavior. *Life Sciences, 33*, 2609–2614.

Liu J. L., Han, X. W., & Su, S. N. (1990). The role of frontal neurons in pain and acupuncture analgesia. *Science in China: Series B. Chemistry, 33*, 938–945.

Lloyd, K. G., Hornykiewicz, O., Davidson, L., Shannak, K., Farley, I., Goldstein, M., et al. (1981). Biochemical evidence of dysfunction of brain neurotransmitters in the Lesch–Nyhan syndrome. *The New England Journal of Medicine, 305*, 1106–1111.

Marinus, L. M., Chase, W. K., & Novak, M. A. (2000). Self-biting behavior in rhesus macaques (*Macaca mulatta*) is preferentially directed to body areas associated with acupuncture analgesia. *American Journal of Primatology, 51,* 71–72.

Markovitz, P. J., & Wagner, S. C. (1995). Venlafaxine in the treatment of borderline personality disorder. *Psychopharmacology Bulletin, 31,* 773–777.

Meltzer, H. Y., & Lowry, M. T. (1987). The serotonin hypothesis of depression. In H. Y. Meltzer (Ed.), *Psychopharmacology: Third generation of progress* (pp. 513–526). New York: Raven Press.

Mogil, J. S., Wilson, S. G., Chesler, E. J., Rankin, A. L., Nemmani, K. V., Lariviere, W. R., et al. (2003). The melanocortin-1 receptor gene mediates female-specific mechanisms of analgesia in mice and humans. *Proceedings of the National Academy of Sciences of the United States of America, 100,* 4867–4872.

Moss, H. B., Yao, J. K., & Panzak, G. (1990). Serotonergic responsivity and behavioral dimensions in antisocial personality disorder with substance abuse. *Biological Psychiatry, 28,* 325–338.

New, A. S., Trestman, R. L., Mitropoulou, V., Benishay, D. S., Coccaro, E., Silverman J., & Siever, L. J. (1997). Serotonergic function and self-injurious behavior in personality disorder patients. *Psychiatry Research, 69,* 17–26.

Nock, M. K., Joiner, T. E., Gordon, K., Lloyd-Richardson, E., & Prinstein, M. J. (2006). Non-suicidal self-injury among adolescents: Diagnostic correlates and relation to suicide attempts. *Psychiatry Research, 144,* 65–72.

Okamura, H., Murakami, T., Yokoyama, C., Nakamura, T., & Ibata, Y. (1997). Self-injurious behavior and dopaminergic neuron system in neonatal 6-hydroxy-dopamine-lesioned rat: 2. Intracerebral microinjection of dopamine agonists and antagonists. *The Journal of Pharmacology and Experimental Therapeutics, 280,* 1031–1037.

O'Keane, V., Moloney, E., O'Neill, H., O'Connor, A., Smith, C., & Dinan, T. G. (1992). Blunted prolactin responses to d-fenfluramine in sociopathy: Evidence for subsensitivity of central serotonergic function. *The British of Journal Psychiatry, 160,* 643–646.

Oltras, C. M., Mora, F., & Vives, F. (1987). B-endorphin and ACTH in plasma: Effects of physical and psychological stress. *Life Sciences, 40,* 1683–1686.

Pellicer, F., Buendia-Roldan, I., & Pallares-Trujillo, V. C. (1998). Self-mutilation in the Lesch–Nyhan syndrome: A corporal consciousness problem?—A new hypothesis. *Medical Hypotheses, 50,* 43–47.

Prasher, V. P., Roberts, E., Norman, A., Butler, A. C., Krishnan, V. H., & McMullan, D. J. (1995). Partial trisomy 22 (q11.2–q13.1) as a result of duplication and pericentric inversion. *Journal of Medical Genetics, 32,* 306–308.

Quirarte, G. L., Galvez, R., Roozendaal, B., & McGaugh, J. L. (1998). Norepinephrine release in the amygdala in response to footshock and opioid peptidergic drugs. *Brain Research, 808,* 134–40.

Recher, H., Willis, G. L., Smit, G. C., & Copolov, D. L. (1988). B-endorphin, corticosterone, cholesterol and triglyceride concentrations in rat plasma after stress, cingulotomy or both. *Pharmacology Biochemistry and Behavior, 31,* 75–79.

Reisine, T., & Pasternak, G. (1996). Opioid analgesics and antagonists. In J. G. Hardman, L. E. Limbird, P. B. Molinoff, R. W. Ruddon, & A. G. Gilman (Eds.), *The pharmacological basis of therapeutics* (pp. 521–556). New York: McGraw-Hill.

Roy, A. (1978). Self-mutilation. *British Journal of Medical Psychology, 51,* 201–203.

Russ, M. J., Campbell, S. S., Kakuma, T., Harrison, K., & Zanine, E. (1999). EEG theta activity and pain insensitivity in self-injurious borderline patients. *Psychiatry Research, 89,* 201–214.

Russ, M. J., Roth, S. D., Kakuma, T., Harrison, K., & Hull, J. W. (1994). Pain perception in self-injurious borderline patients: Naloxone effects. *Biological Psychiatry, 35,* 207–209.

Russ, M. J., Roth, S. D., Lerman, A., Kakuma, T., Harrison, K., Shindledecker, R. D., et al. (1992). Pain perception in self-injurious patients with borderline personality disorder. *Biological Psychiatry, 32,* 501–511.

Russ, M. J., Shearin, E. N., Clarkin, J. F., Harrison, K., & Hull, J. W. (1993). Subtypes of self-injurious patients with borderline personality disorder. *The American Journal of Psychiatry, 150,* 1869–1871.

Sachsse, U., Von der Heyde, S., & Huether, G. (2002). Stress regulation and self-mutilation. *The American Journal of Psychiatry, 159,* 672.

Sandman, C. A., Hetrick, W. P., Taylor, D. V., Barron, J. L., Touchette, P., Lott, I., et al. (1993). Naltrexone reduces self-injury and improves learning. *Experimental and Clinical Psychopharmacology, 1,* 242–258.

Sandman, C. A., Hetrick, W. P., Taylor, D. V., & Chicz-DeMet, A. (1997). Dissociation of POMC peptides after self-injury predicts responses to centrally acting opiate blockers. *American Journal on Mental Retardation, 102,* 182–199.

Sandman, C. A., Hetrick, W., Taylor, D. V., Marion S., & Chicz-DeMet, A. (2000). Uncoupling of proopiomelanocortin (POMC) fragments is related to self-injury. *Peptides, 21,* 785–791.

Sandman, C. A., Spence, M. A., & Smith, M. (1999). Proopiomelanocortin (POMC) disregulation and response to opiate blockers. *Mental Retardation and Developmental Disabilities Research Review, 5,* 314–321.

Sandman, C. A., Thompson, T., Barrett, R. P., Verhoeven, W. M. A., McCubbin, J. A., Schroeder, S. R., & Hetrick, W. P. (1998). Opiate blockers. In M. Aman & S. Reiss (Eds.), *Consensus handbook on psychopharmacology* (pp. 291–302). Unpublished handbook, Nisonger Center, Ohio State University, Columbus.

Sandman, C. A., Touchette, P., Lenjavi, M., Marion, S., & Chicz-DeMet, A. (2003). Beta-endorphin and ACTH are dissociated after self-injury in adults with developmental disabilities. *American Journal on Mental Retardation, 108,* 414–424.

Sandyk, R., & Bamford, C. R. (1988). Opioid-serotoninergic dysregulation in the pathophysiology of Tourette's syndrome. *Functional Neurology, 3,* 225–235.

Schmahl, C. G., McGlashan, T. H., & Bremner, J. D. (2002). Neurobiological correlates of borderline personality disorder. *Psychopharmacology Bulletin, 36,* 69–87.

Schmauss, C. (1987). Spinal kappa-opioid receptor-mediated antinociception is stimulus specific. *European Journal of Pharmacology, 137,* 197–205.

Scifo, R., Cioni, M., Nicolosi, A., Batticane, N., Tirolo, C., Testa, N., et al. (1996). Opioid-immune interactions in autism: Behavioural and immunological assessment during a double-blind treatment with naltrexone. *Annali dell'Istituto Superiore di Sanita, 32*, 351–359.

Seidah, N. G., & Chretien, M. (1992). Proprotein and prohormone convertases of the subtilisin family. *Trends in Endocrinology and Metabolism, 3*, 133–140.

Seidah, N. G., Marcinkiewicz, M., Benjannet, S., Gaspar, L., Beaubien, G., Mattei, M. G., et al. (1991). Cloning and primary sequence of a mouse candidate prohormone convertase PC1 homologous to PC2, Furin, and KEX 2: Distinct chromosomal localization and messenger RNA distribution in brain and pituitary compared to PC2. *Molecular Endocrinology, 15*, 111–122.

Shutt, D. A., Smith, A. I., Wallace, C. A., Connell, R., & Fell, L. R. (1988). Effect of myiasis and acute restraint stress on plasma levels of immunoreactive B-endorphin, adrenocorticotrophin (ACTH) and cortisol in sheep. *Australian Journal of Biological Sciences, 41*, 297–301.

Siffert, W. (2000). G protein beta3 subunit 825T allele, hypertension, obesity, and diabetic nephropathy. *Nephrology, Dialysis, Transplantation, 15*, 1298–1306.

Simeon, D., Stanley, B., Frances, A., Mann, J. J., Winchel, R., & Stanley, M. (1992). Self-mutilation in personality disorders: Psychological and biological correlates. *The American Journal of Psychiatry, 149*, 221–226.

Sokol, M. S., Campbell, M., Goldstein, M., & Kriechman, A. M. (1987). Attention deficit disorder with hyperactivity and the dopamine hypothesis: Case presentations with theoretical background. *Journal of the American Academy of Child & Adolescent Psychiatry, 26*, 428–433.

Stanley, B., & Brodsky, B. (2005). Suicidal and self-injurious behavior in borderline personality disorder: A self-regulation model. In J. G. Gunderson & P. D. Hoffman (Eds.), *Understanding and treating borderline personality disorder: A guide for professionals and families* (pp. 43–63). Washington, DC: American Psychiatric Press.

Stanley, B., Sher, L., Wilson, S., Ekman, R., & Mann, J. J. (2008). *Nonsuicidal self-injurious behavior, endogenous opioids and monoamine neurotransmitters.* Manuscript submitted for publication.

Stein, D. J., Hollander, E., & Liebowitz, M. R. (1993). Neurobiology of impulsivity and the impulse control disorders. *The Journal of Neuropsychiatry and Clinical Neurosciences, 5*, 9–17.

Steiner, H., & Gerfen, C. R. (1998). Role of dynorphin and enkephalin in the regulation of striatal output pathways and behavior. *Experimental Brain Research, 123*, 60–76.

Stone, M. H. (1990). *The fate of borderline patients: Success, outcome, and psychiatric practice.* New York: Guilford Press.

Stone, M. H., Hurt, S., & Stone, D. (1987). The PI 500: Long-term follow-up of borderline inpatients meeting *DSM–III* criteria: I. Global outcomes. *Journal of Personality Disorders, 1*, 291–298.

Strand, F. L. (1999). *Neuropeptides: Regulators of physiological processes*. Cambridge: MIT Press.

Symons, F. J., Sutton, K. A., Walker, C., & Bodfish, J. W. (2003). Altered diurnal pattern of salivary substance P in adults with developmental disabilities and chronic self-injury. *American Journal on Mental Retardation, 108*, 13–18.

Symons, F. J., Thompson, A., & Rodriguez, M. C. (2004). Self-injurious behavior and the efficacy of naltrexone treatment: A quantitative synthesis. *Mental Retardation and Developmental Disabilities Research Reviews, 10*, 193–200.

Symons, F. J., & Thompson, T. (1997). Self-injurious behaviour and body site preference. *Journal of Intellectual Disability Research, 41*, 456–468.

Thompson, T., Hackenberg, T., Cerutti, D., Baker, D., & Axtell, S. (1994). Opioid antagonist effects on self-injury in adults with mental retardation: Response form and location as determinants of medication effects. *American Journal on Mental Retardation, 99*, 85–102.

Tiefenbacher, S., Marinus, L. M., Davenport, M. D., Pouliot, A. L., Kaufman, B. M., Fahey, M. A., et al. (2003). Evidence for a endogenous opioid involvement in the expression of self-injurious behavior in rhesus monkeys. *American Journal of Primatology, 60*(Suppl. 1), 103.

Tiefenbacher, S., Novak, M. A., Lutz, C. K., & Meyer, J. S. (2005). The physiology and neurochemistry of self-injurious behavior: A nonhuman primate model. *Frontiers in Bioscience, 10*, 1–11.

Traskman, L., Asberg, M., Bertilsson, L., & Sjostrand, L. (1981). Monoamine metabolites in CSF and suicidal behavior. *Archive of General Psychiatry, 38*, 631–636.

Turner, C. A., & Lewis, M. H. (2002). Dopaminergic mechanisms in self-injurious behavior and related disorders. In S. R. Schroeder, M. L. Oster-Granite, & T. Thompson (Eds.), *Self-injurious behavior: Genes–brain–behavior relationships* (pp. 165–179). Washington, DC: American Psychological Association.

Turner, S. T., Schwartz, G. L., Chapman, A. B., & Boerwinkle, E. (2001). C825T Polymorphism of the G protein beta3-subunit and antihypertensive response to a thiazide diuretic. *Hypertension, 37*, 739–743.

Ulett, G. A., Han, S., & Han, J. S. (1998). Electroacupuncture: Mechanisms and clinical application. *Biological Psychiatry, 44*, 129–138.

Verhoeven, W. M., Tuinier, S., van den Berg, Y. W., Coppus, A. M., Fekkes, D., Pepplinkhuizen, L., & Thijssen, J. H. (1999). Stress and self-injurious behavior: Hormonal and serotonergic parameters in mentally retarded subjects. *Pharmacopsychiatry, 32*, 13–20.

Wallenstein, M. B., & Nock, M. K. (2007). Physical exercise for the treatment of non-suicidal self-injury: Evidence from a single-case study. *The American Journal of Psychiatry, 164*, 350–351.

Watkins, L. R., & Mayer, D. J. (1982). Involvement of spinal opioid systems in foot-shock-induced analgesia: Antagonism by naloxone is possible only before induction of analgesia. *Brain Research, 242*, 309–326.

Weld, K. P., Mench, J. A., Woodward, R. A., Bolesta, M. S., Suomi, S. J., & Higley, J. D. (1998). Effect of tryptophan treatment on self-biting and central nervous system serotonin metabolism in rhesus monkeys (*Macaca mulatta*). *Neuropsychopharmacology, 19*, 314–321.

Winchel, R. M., & Stanley, M. (1991). Self-injurious behavior: A review of the behavior and biology of self-mutilation. *The American Journal of Psychiatry, 148*, 306–317.

Yehuda, R., Halligan, S. L., Golier, J. A., Grossman, R., & Bierer, L. M. (2004). Effects of trauma exposure on the cortisol response to dexamethasone administration in PTSD and major depressive disorder. *Psychoneuroendocrinology, 29*, 389–404.

Yokoyama, C., & Okamura, H. (1997). Self-injurious behavior and dopaminergic neuron system in neonatal 6-hydroxydopamine-lesioned rat: 1. Dopaminergic neurons and receptors. *The Journal of Pharmacology and Experimental Therapeutics, 280*, 1016–1030.

Zammarchi, E., Savelli, A., Donati, M. A., & Pasquini, E. (1994). Self-mutilation in a patient with Mucolipidosis III. *Pediatric Neurology, 11*, 68–70.

Zlotnick, C., Shea, M. T., Recupero, P., Bidadi, K., Pearlstein, T., & Brown, P. (1997). Trauma, dissociation, impulsivity, and self-mutilation among substance abuse patients. *American Journal of Orthopsychiatry, 67*, 650–654.

Zubieta, J.-K., Heitzeg, M. M., Smith, Y. R., Bueller, J. A., Xu, K., & Xu, Y. (2003, February 21). COMT val158met genotype affects μ-opioid neurotransmitter responses to a pain stressor. *Science, 299*, 1240–1243.

Zubieta, J.-K., Ketter, T. A., Bueller, J. A., Xu, Y., Kilbourn, M. R., Young, E. A., & Koepper, R. A. (2003). Regulation of human affective responses by anterior cingulate and limbic μ-opioid neurotransmission. *Archives of General Psychiatry, 60*, 1145–1153.

Zubieta, J.-K., Smith, Y. R., Bueller, J. A., Xu, Y., Kilbourn, M. R., Jewett, D. M., et al. (2002). μ-opioid receptor-mediated antinociceptive responses differ in men and women. *Journal of Neuroscience, 22*, 5100–5107.

7

DEVELOPMENTAL PATHWAYS FROM CHILD MALTREATMENT TO NONSUICIDAL SELF-INJURY

TUPPETT M. YATES

In the face of dramatic and apparently rising rates of nonsuicidal self-injury (NSSI), empirical and clinical scholars—including myself and many of the contributors to this book—have come together in search of clear methods for identifying, understanding, and treating NSSI. However, in our haste to focus empirical and clinical lenses of inquiry on self-injury, our knowledge about the descriptive psychopathology of NSSI has outpaced our understanding of the processes that underlie its emergence, maintenance, or desistance over time (i.e., the developmental psychopathology of self-injurious behavior; see Yates, 2004, for a discussion). Across descriptive studies of NSSI and main effect models of its etiology, NSSI has emerged as a shared end point of numerous and structurally varied developmental paths, many of which originate in adverse childhood experiences. Emphasizing developmental pathways and processes, this chapter draws on the integrative paradigm of developmental psychopathology to understand apparent relations between child maltreatment and NSSI.

The extant literature supports the assertion that NSSI is associated with traumatic experiences in childhood, including chronic illness or major surgery, parental loss or deprivation, and maltreatment (Briere & Gil, 1998; van der Kolk, Perry, & Herman, 1991). Childhood experiences of malevolent

117

caregiving consistently emerge as an especially powerful initiating condition for pathways toward self-injurious outcomes with up to 79% of those who self-injure reporting a childhood history of abuse or neglect (van der Kolk et al., 1991; see also Favazza & Conteiro, 1989; Low, Jones, MacLeod, Power, & Duggan, 2000; Wiederman, Sansone, & Sansone, 1999). These findings join the vast literature documenting a host of deleterious effects of maltreatment and providing support for research programs that identify specific processes carrying individuals toward and away from particular pathological outcomes in the aftermath of maltreatment (Cicchetti & Valentino, 2006).

This chapter speaks to recent calls for theoretically informed, developmental process models of maltreatment and its effects broadly, and to the pressing need to clarify pathways between maltreatment and NSSI in particular. The first section of the chapter reviews evidence of relations between child maltreatment (i.e., child sexual abuse, child physical abuse, child neglect, and child emotional abuse) and NSSI. The second section introduces a developmental psychopathology framework and an organizational perspective on development to illustrate the salience of the caregiving milieu for understanding current and prospective adaptation. Building on this foundation, this section summarizes the theoretical justification and empirical support for three putative process pathways between child maltreatment and NSSI. First, a *representational path* may carry individuals toward NSSI through internalized representations of the self as defective, of others as malevolent, and of relationships as dangerous following recurrent patterns of negative transactions in the early caregiving milieu. Second, either in isolation or in concert with representational vulnerabilities, maltreatment may thwart children's emerging integrative, symbolic, and reflective affect processing capacities. This, in turn, increases the probability of a *regulatory path* toward self-injurious behaviors. Third, maltreatment may initiate neurobiological alterations and physiological cascades that contribute to a *reactive path* toward NSSI. The chapter concludes with a discussion of the empirical and clinical implications of a developmental process perspective for future research and practice.

MAIN EFFECT MODELS OF CHILD MALTREATMENT AND NONSUICIDAL SELF-INJURY

Over the past 20 years, scientific understanding of the effects of child maltreatment in various developmental domains (e.g., biology, cognition, self-development, attachment) has grown considerably, with particularly notable gains in the areas of neuroendocrinology and physiology. Maltreatment negatively influences developmental processes across multiple levels, including the self-system (e.g., self–other distinctions, body image, self-representation), affect regulation and impulse control (e.g., behavior toward self and others, dissociation, memory), relational patterns (e.g., distrust, rejection sensitivity, withdrawal), and neurophysiology (e.g., sympathetic and parasympathetic arousal modulation, brain structure; see Cicchetti & Valentino, 2006, for a review). Thus, it is not surprising that child maltreatment is associated with a range of disorders across both internalizing (e.g., anxiety, depression) and externalizing (e.g., aggression, substance abuse) dimensions of behavior (Briere & Elliott, 2003; Mullen, Martin, Anderson, Romans, & Herbison, 1996), as well as with NSSI (Santa Mina & Gallop, 1998; Yates, Carlson, & Egeland, 2008).

Retrospective relations between child sexual abuse and NSSI have been widely observed and almost entirely replicated in published research (e.g., see Boudewyn & Huser Liem, 1995; Noll, Horowitz, Bonanno, Trickett, & Putnam, 2003; van der Kolk et al., 1991; Zlotnick, Shea, & Pearlstein, 1996). This relation is especially pronounced in cases of intrafamilial abuse, especially parent–child incest. Percentages of incest survivors who engage in NSSI range from 17% (Briere & Zaidi, 1989) to 25% (Albach & Everaerd, 1992) to 58% (de Young, 1982).

Relative to sexual abuse, fewer studies have examined the role of child physical abuse in the etiology of NSSI, and still fewer have studied the potential contribution of child neglect or emotional maltreatment to self-injurious outcomes. Published reports support a relation between a history of child physical abuse and NSSI (e.g., see Carroll, Schaffer, Spensley, & Abramowitz, 1980; Green, 1978; van der Kolk et al., 1991; Wiederman et al., 1999; cf. Boudewyn & Huser Liem, 1995). Studies evaluating the role of child neglect in NSSI have yielded equivocal findings, with some reporting significant relations (e.g., see Dubo, Zanarini, Lewis, & Williams, 1997; Lipschitz et al., 1999; van der Kolk et al., 1991), but others not (e.g., see Wiederman et al., 1999). With respect to emotional maltreatment, recent studies demonstrating predictive relations between child-directed parental criticism and NSSI among high school students suggest that negative emotional exchanges in the family may contribute to adolescent NSSI (Wedig & Nock, 2007; Yates, Tracy, & Luthar, 2008). However, the potential contribution of child emotional abuse to NSSI awaits further clarification.

Beyond main effect models, few studies have examined whether and how different forms of maltreatment shape developmental pathways toward NSSI. Preliminary evidence suggests that specific forms of maltreatment are differentially related to NSSI (Lipschitz et al., 1999; Wiederman et al., 1999). In a study of individuals with personality disorders, for example, Dubo et al. (1997) found that both child sexual abuse and child neglect individually explained variation in NSSI. However, when considered together, sexual abuse predicted suicidal behavior, whereas neglect emerged as the strongest predictor of NSSI. With respect to the specific features of maltreatment, the association between child maltreatment and NSSI is strongest in cases in which there has been an extended period of abuse, perpetrated by a person known to the victim, and, in the case of sexual abuse, involving the use of force or penetration (e.g., see Trickett, Noll, Reiffman, & Putnam, 2001).

In addition to the heterogeneity of maltreatment experiences, recent studies point to meaningful differences in NSSI as a function of its form, frequency, function, etiology, or a combination of these. For example, a recent study of child maltreatment and NSSI in a community sample suggested specific pathways between child physical abuse and NSSI that occurs intermittently and subserves primarily interpersonal functions (e.g., seeking attention, communicating with others), whereas child sexual abuse appeared more salient in recurrent NSSI that subserves primarily intrapsychic functions related to self-soothing, self-regulation, or self-punishment (Yates, Carlson, & Egeland, 2008). The possibility that different kinds of maltreatment may differentially predict specific kinds of NSSI (as categorized on the basis of form, frequency, or function) introduces yet another level of complexity to this area of research. Moreover, the preponderance of retrospective methods in this work brings the need for longitudinal studies of pathways toward and away from NSSI into full relief. Even in the context of prospective data, however, demonstrating the etiological contribution of maltreatment to NSSI does little to facilitate understanding of the processes involved in its initiation, maintenance, or desistance over time.

DEVELOPMENTAL PROCESS MODELS OF CHILD MALTREATMENT AND NONSUICIDAL SELF-INJURY

Classical approaches to NSSI tend to fall within the purview of discrete psychological paradigms, including psychoanalytic, neo-analytic–psychodynamic, psychosomatic, behavioral, cognitive, and neurobiological approaches to psychopathology. Drawing on all these theories, the integrative macroparadigm of developmental psychopathology is a promising framework for conceptualizing and evaluating developmental pathways toward and away from NSSI in the aftermath of maltreatment (see Yates, 2004, for a discussion). The remainder of this chapter uses a developmental psychopathology framework to explicate three pathways toward NSSI in the aftermath of childhood maltreatment through representations of self and others, regulation of affective experience, physiological reactivity, or a combination of these.

An Organizational View of Development and Psychopathology

A central feature of a developmental psychopathology framework is a recognition that development proceeds through successive cycles of differentiation and hierarchical integration within and across the behavioral and biological systems of the individual (Werner & Kaplan, 1964). Within this organizational model of development, adaptation reflects the quality of integration within and across systems as it influences the individual's capacity to negotiate salient developmental issues. Whereas positive adaptation promotes the flexible and effective negotiation of developmental issues, maladaptation (i.e., psychopathology) occurs when a developmental deviation from normal patterns of adaptation constrains or compromises their negotiation (Sroufe & Rutter, 1984). It is important to note that the relations among successive adaptations follow probabilistic rather than deterministic pathways, such that there is a tendency for development to stay the same, but there is always a potential for change. Moreover, as a product of dynamic transactions across multiple systems, developmental pathways evidence structural and meaningful heterogeneity toward and away from disorder. However, early experience lies at the root of all pathways as the foundation on which subsequent adaptations are formed (Gottlieb & Willoughby, 2006; Sroufe, Egeland, & Kreutzer, 1990).

Developmental pathways take their prototypic patterning from early exchanges in the caregiving milieu. Recurrent patterns of exchange in the caregiving milieu guide processes of differentiation and integration across cognitive, emotional, social, and neurobiological systems, such that the dyadic organization of the infant–caregiver relationship (i.e., attachment) gives rise to self-organization (Sroufe, 1995; Stern, 1985). A secure attachment organization develops in the context of a sensitive and responsive caregiving environment from which the child can actively engage and explore the world and to which she or he can turn when frightened, threatened, or fatigued (Ainsworth, Blehar, Waters, & Wall, 1978; Bowlby, 1969/1982). In the context of insensitive care, however, children adopt nonoptimal balances between exploration and proximity-seeking behaviors, tending to favor exploration in the context of a rejecting caregiver (i.e., avoidant) and proximity seeking in the context of an inconsistent caregiver (i.e., resistant). In both patterns of insecure attachment, the child develops a strategy that allows her or him to self-regulate and maintain a functional relationship with the caregiver despite her or his limitations. Yet insecure strategies are costly because either the child is not able to engage in behaviors that will elicit comfort (i.e., avoidant), or the child's need for comfort cannot be gratified (i.e., resistant; Sroufe, 1990). Nevertheless, insecure patterns of attachment are coherent and organized, although somewhat less effective, strategies to regulate proximity to the caregiver under stress.

The maintenance of an organized attachment strategy, whether secure or insecure, may not be possible in cases in which the parent has repeatedly operated as a source of alarm. In the face of a frightening caregiver, the child is confronted with "the simultaneous needs to approach, and take flight from, the parent" (Hesse & Main, 2000, p. 1118). The child who encounters repeated situations of "fright without solution" in the caregiving milieu cannot develop an organized strategy for satisfying her or his attachment needs. When faced with attachment needs, these children exhibit an array of odd, fearful, disjointed, or contradictory behaviors that reflect a collapse in attentional and behavioral strategies for coping with distress and suggest a fundamental disorganization of the attachment system (Hesse & Main, 2000; Main & Solomon, 1990). As a profound disturbance of the caregiving milieu, maltreatment is likely to have enduring and negative ramifications for attachment and the developing self (Carlson, Yates, & Sroufe, in press; Harter, 1999). Relative to their nonmaltreated peers, maltreated children are more likely to be insecurely attached, evidencing particularly high rates of disorganized attachment (Cicchetti & Barnett, 1991; Egeland & Sroufe, 1981; van Ijzendoorn, Scheungel, & Bakermanns-Kranenburg, 1999).

Despite suggestions that a lack of secure attachments may contribute to NSSI (Farber, 2000; van der Kolk et al., 1991; Zlotnick, Mattia, & Zimmerman, 1999), research has yet to examine relations between infant attachment quality and NSSI. A prospective analysis of the relation between attachment quality and NSSI revealed a modest relation between insecure attachment organization in infancy and self-injurious outcomes in young adulthood. However, disorganized attachment was significantly overrepresented in the developmental histories of individuals who self-injure, with a history of disorganization increasing the odds of engaging in NSSI more than threefold (Yates, 2005). Not surprisingly, participants with a history of disorganized attachment were more likely to have experienced maltreatment. These data point to the salience of the caregiving milieu, and of deviations in that milieu, for understanding NSSI.

In the context of the caregiving milieu, the child internalizes a sense of the caregiving other as reliable or unreliable, as protective or threatening, and a complementary self-representation as deserving or undeserving of care, as effective or inept at eliciting adequate nurturance, support, and protection (Bowlby, 1969/1982; Sroufe, 1990). At the representational level, these exchanges form the basis of working models of the self, of others, and of the self-with-others that guide future behavior and shape subsequent experiences in the interpersonal milieu (Carlson, Sroufe, & Egeland, 2004). Regulatory processes are similarly influenced by early relational patterns that lay the foundation for cognitive and affective processing, the integration of thinking with feeling, and the capacity to share self and feeling states with important others in the psychosocial milieu (Fonagy, Gergely, Jurist, & Target, 2002; Sroufe, 1995). Finally, early exchanges in the caregiving environment directly regulate the child's psychobiological reactivity by entraining excitatory and inhibitory neural processes that form the foundation for basic patterns of reactivity and resources for arousal modulation and state integration (Gunnar, Brodersen, Nachmias, Buss, & Rigatuso, 1996; Hofer, 1994; Schore, 1994; Spangler & Grossmann, 1999). Acting in isolation from, or interacting with, attachment history, child maltreatment may undermine development in one or more of these domains, thereby initiating representational, regulatory, or reactive pathways toward self-injurious outcomes (see Table 7.1).

The Representational Path: Self and Other in Self-Injury

A representational pathway toward NSSI holds that maltreatment causes or exacerbates negative representations of the self, of others, and of the self in relation to others that, in turn, contribute to self-injurious outcomes. As described previously, exchanges in the early caregiving relationship lay the foundation for children's core beliefs about self-worth and self-efficacy, expectations of others' responsiveness and care, and general schemas of relationships as safe and nurturing or dangerous and hurtful. Theoretical and empirical evidence converges to suggest that maltreatment contributes to a hostile and critical view of the self as defective, unlovable, or loathsome (Fischer & Ayoub, 1994; Toth, Cicchetti, Macfie, & Emde, 1997). In the context of maltreatment, the child faces a conflict between internalizing the blame for the abuse, thereby yielding a representation of the self as bad, or externalizing the blame for the abuse, thereby yielding a representation of others as unsafe and of the self as unworthy of care (Fonagy et al., 2002; Murthi, Servaty-Seib, & Elliott, 2006). In this way, negative self-representations may be compounded by similar distortions in

TABLE 7.1
Possible Pathways Underlying Observed Associations
Between Child Maltreatment and Nonsuicidal Self-Injury

Developmental pathway	Core systems	Role of body
Representational	Representations of self as defective Representations of others as malevolent Representations of relationships as dangerous	Site for punishment and/or soothing in lieu of relationships
Regulatory	Thwarted integration of affect and cognition Reduced symbolization of affect through language Decreased capacity to reflect on feeling states of self and others	Medium for symbolizing affect, particularly in an impulsive way given the reduction of cognitive input
Reactive	Neurophysiological dysregulation in biochemical and neuroendocrine processes underlying stress reactivity and regulation	Tool to alter biological reactivity and arousal

representations of others such that, in anticipation of unavailable, critical, or ineffective soothing agents during times of distress, the maltreated child may behave in ways that preclude potentially restorative relational experiences (e.g., withdrawal, wariness, manipulation, aggression; Crittenden, 1990). Through representational processes, what was once external to the child becomes internalized and operational in actively shaping subsequent development.

Negative representational processes may eventuate in self-injurious outcomes as the individual turns to the body for self-punishment or absolution in the face of perceived infractions or as a tool for self-soothing and definition in the absence of positive relational resources. Evidence evaluating representational pathways in NSSI is scarce. Several studies have documented lower levels of self-esteem and self-efficacy among both maltreated youth (Egeland, Sroufe, & Erikson, 1983; Schneider-Rosen & Cicchetti, 1991; Toth et al., 1997) and persons who self-injure (Brown, Comtois, & Linehan, 2002; Haines & Williams, 1997; Low et al., 2000; Suyemoto, 1998). Similarly, both maltreated youth (Toth et al., 1997) and persons who self-injure often articulate a pervasive sense of distrust in their view of others (Levenkron, 1998; Simeon & Favazza, 2001). In a recent study of high school students, youth-reported feelings of alienation and mistrust toward their parents significantly explained the observed relation between parental criticism and self-injury (Yates, Tracy, & Luthar, 2008). However, the partial mediating effect of representational processes in this study points to the multidetermined nature of NSSI and the likelihood that multiple pathways and processes contribute to self-injurious outcomes.

The Regulatory Path: Integrative, Symbolic, and Reflective Capacities

Prominent theories of self and emotional development emphasize the importance of early caregiving for the child's emerging capacities for cognitive–affective integration, symbolization, reflection, and, ultimately, regulation (Bowlby, 1969/1982; Cicchetti & Beeghly, 1987a; Fonagy et al., 2002; Harter, 1999; Schore, 1994; Sroufe, 1995; Stern, 1985). The caregiver's sensitive and contained or containing response to the child's affective expression teaches her or him that emotion will not overwhelm the parent (and by extension the child) and that affect can be shareable, knowable, and tolerable (Bion, 1962; Sroufe, 1995). Over time and in the context of an empathic caregiving relationship, affects become increasingly differentiated, complex, and symbolized (Krystal, 1988; Sroufe, 1995). In the case of maltreatment, however, a deviation occurs such that increasingly sophisticated defensive processing of affect develops rather than the adaptive processing that typifies normative development. In this view, NSSI may constitute an action and bodily based emotion regulation strategy in the absence of adaptive integrative, symbolic, and reflective capacities.

Children with a history of sensitive care and a secure organization of attachment behavior have access to both affectively and cognitively generated information. These children possess a sense of safety and flexibility that enables them to know what they feel and to feel what they know. In contrast, children with a history of insensitive caregiving may learn to depend on cognitively generated information to the relative exclusion of affect (i.e., avoidant) or to operate on the basis of unmoderated affect that is not tempered or informed by cognition (i.e., resistant; Crittenden, 1994). In the case of aversive care (i.e., maltreatment), the disruption in this early organization (i.e., disorganization) reflects more than an imbalance between cognition and affect; it is a splitting such that affect may be separated from cognition. In these instances, a dissociation between thinking and feeling may arise. Thus, maltreatment, especially when it occurs in the context of an insecure or disorganized caregiving organization, may contribute to an enduring pattern of dissociative coping (Carlson et al., in press; Fischer & Ayoub, 1994).

Coupled with a disintegration between affect and cognition, maltreatment may subvert the child's normative progression toward the use of symbols, particularly language, to share emotional experiences with others. In this way, maltreatment may leave affect to be symbolized through the body rather than language and relationships (Farber, 2000; Miliora, 1998; van der Kolk et al., 1996). The typically developing child acquires increasing capacities for symbolization and reflection through fantasy, play, and language (Cicchetti & Beeghly, 1987a; Sroufe, 1990; Stern, 1985). Over time, language serves to contain affect, facilitating its transition from the body to the mind to the intersubjective space of relationships with others (Krystal, 1997). Mounting evidence suggests that insensitive caregiving and maltreatment undermine developing symbolic capacities (Allessandri, 1991), particularly the ability to process emotional experiences through language. Maltreated toddlers engage in lower levels of verbal dialogue and use less descriptive speech than their nonmaltreated peers (Coster, Gersten, Beeghly, & Cicchetti, 1989), particularly with respect to feeling states, such as hunger, anger, or fatigue (Cicchetti & Beeghly, 1987b).

Failure to organize experience linguistically leaves it to be symbolized on a somatosensory level through sensation, behavior, and somatization. Moreover, maltreated youth may remain psychologically and physiologically hyperresponsive to arousal cues because they move from perception (i.e., arousal) to action (i.e., fight or flight) without intervening moderation by cognition, symbolization, and, ultimately, reflection (Crittenden, 1994; Fonagy et al., 2002; van der Kolk et al., 1996). It is not surprising, then, that deficits or distortions in reflective functioning and affective processing have been connected with violence and aggression broadly (Fonagy & Target, 1995) and with NSSI in particular (Paivio & McCulloch, 2004; van der Kolk et al., 1996; Zlotnick et al., 1996).

A regulatory perspective on NSSI holds that children must resolve the challenge of affective processing through alternative methods when maltreatment has stymied or distorted the development of normative integrative, symbolic, and reflective capacities. Compensatory strategies may entail separating what one feels from what one thinks (i.e., dissociation) or processing affect through the body somatization rather than in relationships. In this view, dissociation and somatization may reflect deficits in affective processing and distortions in the developing self that follow from maltreatment and contribute to NSSI. In support of this hypothesis, evidence suggests that dissociation and somatization follow from antecedent risks (e.g., disorganized attachment, child maltreatment) that preclude normative affective processing (Atlas, Wolfson, & Lipschitz, 1995). Furthermore, both dissociation and somatization have been connected to deficits in affective processing (e.g., alexithymia; Berenbaum & James, 1994; Krystal, 1988), to one another (Saxe et al., 1994; van der Kolk et al., 1996), and to NSSI (van der Kolk et al., 1996; Yates, Carlson, & Egeland, 2008).

The Reactive Path: Trauma, Neurobiology, and Arousal Modulation

In addition to representational or regulatory processes, adverse experience in the caregiving milieu may alter core systems underlying physiological reactivity, thereby activating or changing biological systems that may contribute to self-injurious outcomes. Growing evidence indicates that maltreatment influences the structure, organization, and function of neurobiological stress response systems (De Bellis, 2001; Gunnar, 2000; Perry & Pollard, 1998; Yates, 2007). At the same time, physiological processes underlying NSSI have become a central focus of examination (Schroeder, Oster-Granite, & Thompson, 2002). Although NSSI is multiply determined at both behavioral and physiological levels, the current literature points to the influence of maltreatment on physiological reactivity as a potentially salient process underlying self-injurious pathways.

As discussed previously, safe and predictable exchanges in early caregiving lay the groundwork for patterns and processes of biological reactivity (Gunnar et al., 1996; Hofer, 1994; Schore, 1994; Spangler & Grossmann, 1999). Among these systems, the limbic–hypothalamic–pituitary–adrenal (L-HPA) axis, which regulates long-term stress responses, and the norepinephrine–sympathetic–adrenal–medullary (NE-SAM) system, which regulates acute stress responses, evidence significant alterations in the wake of child maltreatment (Cicchetti, 2003; Gunnar, 2000; Yates, 2007). Under normal circumstances, reciprocal connections within and between the L-HPA and NE-SAM systems serve to modulate behavioral, emotional, cognitive, metabolic, immunological, autonomic, and endocrine responses to stressful stimuli (C. A. Nelson & Carver, 1998; Vasquez, 1998). However, maltreatment may induce alterations in these systems that contribute to indiscriminate flight–fight reactions, depression, anxiety, suicidal behavior, and other symptoms of pathology (see Cicchetti & Walker, 2003, for a review). With respect to NSSI, preliminary evidence suggests that trauma-induced alterations in the L-HPA, NE-SAM, or both systems may contribute to NSSI (Novak, 2003; Sachsse, von der Hyde, & Huether, 2002). Moreover, interactions between these systems and other biological processes known to underlie NSSI (e.g., opioid and serotonergic functioning; see van der Kolk, 1987) strongly suggest that maltreatment may instantiate a reactive path toward NSSI, in part through alterations in L-HPA or NE-SAM stress responses.

The endogenous opioid system (EOS) has received considerable attention from researchers interested in NSSI (see Symons, 2002, for a review; see also chap. 6, this volume), although empirical studies of its role in NSSI have yielded mixed results (Russ et al., 1992; Russ, Roth, Kakuma, Harrison, & Hull, 1994). Given its integral role in the formation and maintenance of primary attachment relationships, the EOS is a likely target of maltreatment-induced alterations in neurobiological reactivity (E. E. Nelson & Panksepp, 1998; Panksepp, Herman, & Conner, 1978; van der Kolk, 1987). Yet the EOS has been largely ignored in the extant maltreatment literature. Alterations in EOS functioning as a consequence of maltreatment may contribute to NSSI by alleviating feelings of isolation and alienation (Panksepp et al., 1978), providing positive physiological reinforcement for self-injury (Grossman & Siever, 2001) or inducing states (e.g., dissociation) that, in turn, precipitate NSSI (Saxe, Chawla, & van der Kolk, 2002).

In addition to core stress response systems, recent findings from genetically informed studies suggest that gene–environment interactions influence individual trajectories toward and away from specific pathological outcomes, including antisocial behavior and violence (Caspi et al., 2002; Jaffee et al., 2005) and depression and suicidality (Caspi et al., 2003; Gibb, McGeary, Beevers, & Miller, 2006). For example, genetic variants of serotonergic genes have been connected to low levels of serotonin and impulsivity, depressed mood, and self-harming behavior (Meyer et al., 2003; Pooley, Houston, Hawton, & Harrison, 2003). Serotonergic genes have also been implicated in the developmental sequelae of child maltreatment (Kaufman et al., 2004). Although interactions between serotonergic genes and maltreating environments may contribute to self-injurious outcomes, research suggests that the relation between serotonergic function and NSSI is complex, likely involves other systems (e.g., dopaminergic, noradrenergic), and requires further empirical evaluation (Rujescu, Thalmeier, Moller, Bronisch, & Giegling, 2007).

As described in chapter 6, efforts to identify pathophysiological processes underlying pathways between maltreatment and NSSI join a new wave of research that aims to elucidate neurodevelopmental mechanisms in the pathophysiology of mental disorders (see Cicchetti & Walker, 2003, for a review), including NSSI (Grossman & Siever, 2001; Schroeder et al., 2002). Yet the processes by which trauma-induced alterations in neurobiological reactivity contribute to NSSI remain to be determined. In all likelihood, reactive processes contribute to NSSI directly at a physiological level, as well as indirectly by increasing subjective states of distress and arousal that may, in turn, magnify representational or regulatory pathways toward NSSI.

FUTURE DIRECTIONS

In the context of the caregiving milieu, prototypic representations of self, of others, and of self-with-others are laid down; core capacities for the integration, symbolization, and reflection of cognitive and affective states develop to enable self-regulation; and basic physiological reactivity is entrained. In isolation or in combination, maltreatment-induced alterations in representational, regulatory, and reactive processes shape pathways toward NSSI. These pathways are important foci for future research that aims to clarify the relation between child maltreatment and NSSI. With its emphasis on multiple levels of analysis, patterns of continuity and discontinuity, and transactional exchanges between the individual and her or his environment over time, the framework of developmental psychopathology will inform innovative research initiatives aimed at furthering our understanding of child maltreatment, NSSI, and the relations between them.

A Multidimensional Perspective

Specific types of maltreatment (e.g., sexual, physical, emotional) evidence different relations with pathological outcomes (Briere & Elliott, 2003; Mullen et al., 1996; Trickett & McBride-Chang, 1995). Moreover, a variety of factors within maltreatment subtypes (e.g., sexual abuse) moderate pathways toward such outcomes (Trickett et al., 2001). Thus, specific types of maltreatment likely contribute to NSSI in qualitatively or quantitatively different ways. For example, child sexual abuse appears especially prominent in etiological paths toward NSSI. One hypothesis for why NSSI is associated with sexual abuse is that this form of violation tends to elicit dissociative defenses and posttraumatic symptoms that, in turn, motivate or enable tension-reducing behaviors such as self-injury (Briere & Gil, 1998). Furthermore, sexual abuse localizes trauma squarely in the domain of the body, which later serves as the target of self-harm. Future research should examine whether (a) different kinds of maltreatment contribute to NSSI through different pathways (e.g., see Gibb et al., 2006), (b) whether some kinds of maltreatment contribute to NSSI whereas others relate to other pathological outcomes (e.g., see Dubo et al., 1997), and (c) whether specific forms of maltreatment contribute to different types of NSSI (Yates, Carlson, & Egeland, 2008).

Researchers typically conceptualize NSSI as a homogeneous phenomenon that is either present or absent. However, research points to meaningful variation within the broad domain of NSSI as a function of its severity, frequency, age of onset, and motivations for injury in both clinical (Brodsky, Cliotre, & Dulit, 1995; Zlotnick et al., 1999) and community settings (Cyr, McDuff, Wright, Theriault, & Cinq-Mars, 2005; Whitlock, Eckenrode, & Silverman, 2006). As discussed previously, recent findings suggest that child sexual abuse contributes to recurrent NSSI, whereas child physical abuse may be more salient for intermittent NSSI. Moreover, recurrent and intermittent NSSI appeared to be motivated by different factors (Yates, Carlson, & Egeland, 2008). Similarly, a recent study by Nock and Prinstein (2005) revealed predictable variation in psychiatric correlates of NSSI as a function of the motivational processes underlying it. Thus, a profitable direction for future research lies in studies that examine whether and how different forms of maltreatment or specific features of the maltreating environment explain variation in the form, function, or frequency of NSSI.

Sensitivity and Specificity

Given evidence that both maltreatment and NSSI are more heterogeneous than originally thought, pathways between maltreatment and NSSI may be similarly variable. Beyond normative developmental patterns, developmental psychopathology strives to identify and explain individual differences in developmental outcomes and pathways. Efforts to ascertain the sensitivity and specificity of maltreatment experiences leading to NSSI, as well as of the developmental pathways underlying these relations, are important for understanding the development of NSSI.

Child maltreatment is a powerful player in the etiology of NSSI, but it is neither necessary nor sufficient for self-injurious outcomes. There is a need to clarify the factors that differentiate among maltreated individuals who engage in NSSI, maltreated individuals who do not engage in NSSI, and persons who engage in NSSI but do not have a history of maltreatment. Similarly, research must examine the sensitivity and specificity of self-injurious pathways to understand how and when representational, regulatory, or reactive processes contribute to NSSI versus other forms of psychopathology. Finally, there is a need to determine whether observed relations between maltreatment and NSSI reflect a specific association or merely a broader relation between multiple risk environments and NSSI. To this end, preliminary data point to the unique contribution of child maltreatment to NSSI above and beyond a host of potential comorbid risks, including child cognitive ability, child temperament, exposure to partner violence in the home, familial instability, economic status, and maternal life stress (Yates, Carlson, & Egeland, 2008). Moreover, relatively little work has been done to understand when and why particular developmental processes may be activated in pathways between maltreatment and self-injurious outcomes.

Along similar lines, developmental psychopathology encourages and informs investigations of factors associated with the initiation, persistence, and desistance of adaptational pathways, recognizing that there may be meaningful variation across these factors. For example, the initiating conditions for NSSI may be distinct from those that underlie its persistence over time (e.g., see Suyemoto, 1998). In one study, social contagion effects contributed to the initiation of NSSI, but other factors emerged as more salient for determining its course over time (Yates, Carlson, & Egeland, 2008). With respect to the process-level pathways discussed here, representational processes may render individuals vulnerable to peer influence as a function of a heightened desire to belong and need for external validation, whereas reactivity processes may underlie continuity over time, particularly as reactive systems become stronger with repeated injury. Clarifying issues of sensitivity and specificity is essential to inform appropriate practice.

Translating Process to Practice

Overwhelming evidence points to robust relations between child maltreatment and NSSI. As discussed here, representational, regulatory, or reactive processes may underlie these relations to varying degrees. The application of process models to practice will increase practitioners' understanding of how best to intervene with persons who self-injure and of how best to prevent self-injurious pathways in the aftermath of maltreatment. At the representational level, efforts to foster positive representational processes and to challenge negative beliefs and expectations of self and others may prove important for treatment. Regulatory processes are central to many contemporary approaches to treatment that focus on self-reflection, distress tolerance, and affect regulation (Bateman & Fonagy, 2004; Linehan, 1993). However, resources to help child victims express their experiences through symbol (e.g., play, art) and language may be especially salient for efforts to stymie self-injurious pathways in the aftermath of maltreatment. Finally, at the level of reactivity, both pharmacotherapeutic interventions and bodily based interventions that lend coherence within and across neurobiological systems will likely prove to be effective. In sum, the extant literature suggests that NSSI is multiply determined such that successful prevention and intervention efforts must be multifaceted and flexible to permit their tailoring to the specific process or processes that are relevant for understanding, and by extension intervening with, any single self-injurious pathway.

REFERENCES

Ainsworth, M. D. S., Blehar, M. C., Waters, E., & Wall, S. (1978). *Patterns of attachment: A psychological study of the strange situation.* Hillsdale, NJ: Erlbaum.

Albach, F., & Everaerd, W. (1992). Posttraumatic stress symptoms in victims of childhood incest. *Psychotherapy and Psychosomatics, 57,* 143–151.

Allessandri, S. M. (1991). Play and social behaviors in maltreated preschoolers. *Developmental Psychopathology, 3,* 191–206.

Atlas, J. A., Wolfson, M. A., & Lipschitz, D. S. (1995). Dissociation and somatization in adolescent inpatients with and without history of abuse. *Psychological Reports, 76,* 1101–1102.

Bateman, A., & Fonagy, P. (2004). *Psychotherapy for borderline personality disorder: Mentalization-based treatment.* Oxford, England: Oxford University Press.

Berenbaum, H., & James, T. (1994). Correlates and retrospectively reported antecedents of alexithymia. *Psychosomatic Medicine, 56,* 353–359.

Bion, W. R. (1962). *Learning from experience.* New York: Basic Books.

Boudewyn, A. C., & Huser Liem, J. (1995). Childhood sexual abuse as a precursor to depression and self-destructive behavior in adulthood. *Journal of Traumatic Stress, 8,* 445–459.

Bowlby, J. (1982). *Attachment.* New York: Basic Books. (Original work published 1969)

Briere, J., & Elliott, D. M. (2003). Prevalence and psychological sequelae of self-reported childhood physical and sexual abuse in a general population sample of men and women. *Child Abuse & Neglect, 27,* 1205–1222.

Briere, J., & Gil, E. (1998). Self-mutilation in clinical and general population samples: Prevalence, correlates, and functions. *American Journal of Orthopsychiatry, 68,* 609–620.

Briere, J., & Zaidi, L. (1989). Sexual abuse histories and sequelae in female psychiatric emergency room patients. *The American Journal of Psychiatry, 146,* 1602–1606.

Brodsky, B. S., Cliotre, M., & Dulit, R. A. (1995). Relationship of dissociation to self-mutilation and childhood abuse in borderline personality disorder. *The American Journal of Psychiatry, 152,* 1788–1792.

Brown, M. Z., Comtois, K. A., & Linehan, M. M. (2002). Reasons for suicide attempts and nonsuicidal self-injury in women with borderline personality disorder. *Journal of Abnormal Psychology, 111,* 198–202.

Carlson, E. A., Sroufe, L. A., & Egeland, B. (2004). The construction of experience: A longitudinal study of representation and behavior. *Child Development, 75,* 66–83.

Carlson, E. A., Yates, T. M., & Sroufe, L. A. (in press). Development of dissociation and development of the self. In P. F. Dell & J. O'Neil (Eds.), *Dissociation and the dissociative disorders: DSM–V and beyond.* New York: Routledge.

Carroll, J., Schaffer, C., Spensley, J., & Abramowitz, S. I. (1980). Family experiences of self-mutilating patients. *American Journal of Psychiatry, 137,* 852–853.

Caspi, A., McClay, J., Moffitt, T. E., Mill, J., Martin, J., Craig, I. W., et al. (2002, August 2). Role of genotype in the cycle of violence in maltreated children. *Science, 297,* 851–853.

Caspi, A., Sugden, K., Moffitt, T. E., Taylor, A., Craig, I. W., Harrington, H., et al. (2003, July 18). Influence of life stress on depression: Moderation by a polymorphism in the 5-HTT gene. *Science, 301,* 386–389.

Cicchetti, D. (2003). Neuroendocrine functioning in maltreated children. In D. Cicchetti & E. F. Walker (Eds.), *Neurodevelopmental mechanisms in psychopathology* (pp. 345–365). New York: Cambridge University Press.

Cicchetti, D., & Barnett, D. (1991). Attachment organization in maltreated preschoolers. *Development and Psychopathology, 3,* 397–411.

Cicchetti, D., & Beeghly, M. (Eds.). (1987a). *Atypical symbolic development.* San Francisco: Jossey-Bass.

Cicchetti, D., & Beeghly, M. (1987b). Symbolic development in maltreated youngsters: An organizational perspective. In D. Cicchetti & M. Beeghly (Eds.), *Atypical symbolic development* (pp. 31–45). San Francisco: Jossey-Bass.

Cicchetti, D., & Valentino, K. (2006). An ecological–transactional perspective on child maltreatment: Failure of the average expectable environment and its influence on child development. In D. Cicchetti & D. Cohen (Eds.), *Handbook of developmental psychopathology* (2nd ed., Vol. 1, pp. 129–201). Hoboken, NJ: Wiley.

Cicchetti, D., & Walker, M. (Eds.). (2003). *Neurodevelopmental mechanisms in psychopathology.* New York: Cambridge University Press.

Coster, W., Gersten, M., Beeghly, M., & Cicchetti, D. (1989). Communicative functioning in maltreated toddlers. *Developmental Psychology, 25,* 1020–1027.

Crittenden, P. M. (1990). Internal representational models of attachment relationships. *Infant Mental Health Journal, 11,* 259–277.

Crittenden, P. M. (1994). Peering into the black box: An experimental treatise on the development of self in young children. In D. Cicchetti & S. L. Toth (Eds.), *Rochester Symposium on Developmental Psychopathology: Disorders and dysfunctions of the self* (Vol. 5, pp. 79–148). Rochester, NY: University of Rochester Press.

Cyr, M., McDuff, P., Wright, J., Theriault, C., & Cinq-Mars, C. (2005). Clinical correlates and repetition of self-harming behaviors among female adolescent victims of sexual abuse. *Journal of Child Sexual Abuse, 14,* 49–68.

De Bellis, M. D. (2001). Developmental traumatology: The psychobiological development of maltreated children and its implications for research, treatment, and policy. *Development and Psychopathology, 13,* 539–564.

de Young, M. (1982). Self-injurious behavior in incest victims: A research note. *Child Welfare, 61,* 577–584.

Dubo, E. D., Zanarini, M. C., Lewis, R. E., & Williams, A. A. (1997). Childhood antecedents of self-destructiveness in borderline personality disorder. *Canadian Journal of Psychiatry, 42,* 63–69.

Egeland, B., & Sroufe, L. A. (1981). Attachment and early maltreatment. *Child Development, 52,* 44–52.

Egeland, B., Sroufe, L. A., & Erikson, M. (1983). The developmental consequences of different patterns of maltreatment. *Child Abuse & Neglect, 7,* 155–157.

Farber, S. K. (2000). *When the body is the target: Self-harm, pain, and traumatic attachments.* Northvale, NJ: Jason Aronson.

Favazza, A. R., & Conteiro, K. (1989). Female habitual self-mutilators. *Acta Psychiatrica Scandinavica, 1129,* 78–84.

Fischer, K. W., & Ayoub, C. (1994). Affective splitting and dissociation in normal and maltreated children: Developmental pathways for self in relationships. In D. Cicchetti & S. L. Toth (Eds.), *Rochester Symposium on Developmental Psychopathology: Disorders and dysfunctions of the self* (Vol. 5, pp. 149–222). Rochester, NY: University of Rochester Press.

Fonagy, P., Gergely, G., Jurist, E. L., & Target, M. (2002). *Affect regulation, mentalization, and the development of the self.* New York: Other Press.

Fonagy, P., & Target, M. (1995). Understanding the violent patient: The use of the body and the role of the father. *The International Journal of Psychoanalysis, 76,* 487–501.

Gibb, B. E., McGeary, J. E., Beevers, C. G., & Miller, I. W. (2006). Serotonin transporter (5-HTTLPR) genotype, childhood abuse, and suicide attempts in adult psychiatric inpatients. *Suicide and Life-Threatening Behavior, 36,* 687–693.

Gottlieb, G., & Willoughby, M. T. (2006). Probabilistic epigenesis of psychopathology. In D. Cicchetti & D. Cohen (Eds.), *Handbook of developmental psychopathology* (2nd ed., Vol. 1, pp. 673–700). Hoboken, NJ: Wiley.

Green, A. H. (1978). Self-destructive behavior in battered children. *The American Journal of Psychiatry, 135,* 579–582.

Grossman, R., & Siever, L. (2001). Impulsive self-injurious behavior: Neurobiology and psychopharmacology. In D. Simeon & E. Hollander (Eds.), *Self-injurious behaviors: Assessment and treatment* (pp. 117–148). Washington, DC: American Psychiatric Publishing.

Gunnar, M. R. (2000). Early adversity and the development of stress reactivity and regulation. In C. A. Nelson (Ed.), *The Minnesota symposia on child psychology: The effects of early adversity on neurobehavioral development* (Vol. 31, pp. 163–200). Mahwah, NJ: Erlbaum.

Gunnar, M. R., Brodersen, L., Nachmias, M., Buss, K., & Rigatuso, J. (1996). Stress reactivity and attachment security. *Developmental Psychobiology, 29,* 191–204.

Haines, J., & Williams, C. L. (1997). Coping and problem solving of self-mutilators. *Journal of Clinical Psychology, 53,* 177–186.

Harter, S. (1999). *The construction of the self: A developmental perspective.* New York: Guilford Press.

Hesse, E., & Main, M. (2000). Disorganized infant, child, and adult attachment: Collapse in behavioral and attentional strategies. *Journal of the American Psychoanalytic Association, 48,* 1097–1127.

Hofer, M. A. (1994). Early relationships as regulators of infant physiology and behavior. *Acta Pediatrica Supplements, 397,* 9–18.

Jaffee, S. R., Caspi, A., Moffitt, T. E., Dodge, K. A., Rutter, M., Taylor, A., & Tully, L. A. (2005). Nature × nurture: Genetic vulnerabilities interact with physical maltreatment to promote conduct problems. *Development and Psychopathology, 17,* 67–84.

Kaufman, J., Yang, B. Z., Douglas-Palumberi, H., Houshyar, S., Lipschitz, D., Krystal, J. H., & Gelernter, J. (2004). Social supports and serotonin transporter gene moderate depression in maltreated children. *Proceedings of the National Academy of Sciences, 101,* 17316–17321.

Krystal, J. H. (1988). *Integration and self-healing: Affect, trauma, and alexithymia.* Hillsdale, NJ: Analytic Press.

Krystal, J. H. (1997). Desomatization and the consequences of infantile psychic trauma. *Psychoanalytic Inquiry, 17,* 126–150.

Levenkron, S. (1998). *Cutting: Understanding and overcoming self-mutilation.* New York: Norton.

Linehan, M. M. (1993). *Cognitive behavioral treatment of borderline personality disorder.* New York: Guilford Press.

Lipschitz, D. S., Winegar, R. K., Nicolaou, A. L., Hartnick, E., Wolfson, M., & Sowthwick, S. M. (1999). Perceived abuse and neglect as risk factors for suicidal behavior in adolescent inpatients. *The Journal of Nervous and Mental Disease, 187,* 32–39.

Low, G., Jones, D., MacLeod, A., Power, M., & Duggan, C. (2000). Childhood trauma, dissociation and self-harming behaviour: A pilot study. *British Journal of Medical Psychology, 73,* 269–278.

Main, M., & Solomon, J. (1990). Procedures for identifying infants as disorganized/disoriented in the Ainsworth Strange Situation. In M. Greenberg, D. Cicchetti, & E. M. Cummings (Eds.), *Attachment in the preschool years* (pp. 121–160). Chicago: University of Chicago Press.

Meyer, J. H., McMain, S., Kennedy, S. H., Korman, L., Brown, G. M., DaSilva, J. N., et al. (2003). Dysfunctional attitudes and 5-HT2 receptors during depression and self-harm. *The American Journal of Psychiatry, 160,* 90–99.

Miliora, M. T. (1998). Trauma, dissociation, and somatization: A self-psychological perspective. *The Journal of the American Academy of Psychoanalysis and Dynamic Psychiatry, 26,* 273–293.

Mullen, P. E., Martin, J. L., Anderson, J. C., Romans, S. E., & Herbison, G. P. (1996). The long-term impact of the physical, emotional, and sexual abuse of children: A community study. *Child Abuse & Neglect, 20,* 7–21.

Murthi, M., Servaty-Seib, H. L., & Elliott, A. N. (2006). Childhood sexual abuse and multiple dimensions of self-concept. *Journal of Interpersonal Violence, 21,* 982–999.

Nelson, C. A., & Carver, L. J. (1998). The effects of stress and trauma on brain and memory: A view from developmental cognitive neuroscience. *Development and Psychopathology, 10,* 793–810.

Nelson, E. E., & Panksepp, J. (1998). Brain substrates of infant–mother attachment: Contributions of opioids, oxytocin, and norepinephrine. *Neuroscience Biobehavioral Review, 22,* 437–452.

Nock, M. K., & Prinstein, M. J. (2005). Contextual features and behavioral functions of self-mutilation among adolescents. *Journal of Abnormal Psychology, 114,* 140–146.

Noll, J. G., Horowitz, L. A., Bonanno, G. A., Trickett, P. K., & Putnam, F. W. (2003). Revictimization and self-harm in females who experienced childhood sexual abuse. *Journal of Interpersonal Violence, 18,* 1452–1471.

Novak, M. A. (2003). Self-injurious behavior in rhesus monkeys: New insights into its etiology, physiology, and treatment. *American Journal of Primatology, 59,* 3–19.

Paivio, S. C., & McCulloch, C. R. (2004). Alexithymia as a mediator between childhood trauma and self-injurious behaviors. *Child Abuse & Neglect, 28,* 339–354.

Panksepp, J., Herman, B., & Conner, R. (1978). The biology of social attachment: Opiates alleviate separation distress. *Biological Psychiatry, 13,* 607–618.

Perry, B. D., & Pollard, R. A. (1998). Homeostasis, stress, trauma, and adaptation: A neurodevelopmental view of childhood trauma. *Child and Adolescent Psychiatric Clinics of North America, 7,* 33–51.

Pooley, E. C., Houston, K., Hawton, K., & Harrison, P. J. (2003). Deliberate self-harm is associated with allelic variation in the tryptophan hydroxylase gene (TPH A779C), but not with polymorphisms in five other serotonergic genes. *Psychological Medicine, 33,* 775–783.

Rujescu, D., Thalmeier, A., Moller, H.-J., Bronisch, T., & Giegling, I. (2007). Molecular genetic findings in suicidal behavior: What is beyond the serotonergic system? *Archives of Suicide Research, 11,* 17–40.

Russ, M. J., Roth, S. D., Kakuma, T., Harrison, K., & Hull, J. W. (1994). Pain perception in self-injurious borderline patients: Naloxone effects. *Biological Psychiatry, 35,* 207–209.

Russ, M. J., Roth, S. D., Lerman, A., Kakuma, T., Harrison, K., Shidledecker, J. H., et al. (1992). Pain perception in self-injurious patients with borderline personality disorder. *Biological Psychiatry, 32,* 501–511.

Sachsse, U., von der Hyde, S., & Huether, G. (2002). Stress regulation and self-mutilation. *The American Journal of Psychiatry, 159,* 672.

Santa Mina, E. E., & Gallop, R. M. (1998). Childhood sexual and physical abuse and adult self-harm and suicidal behavior: A literature review. *Canadian Journal of Psychiatry, 43,* 793–800.

Saxe, G. N., Chawla, N., & van der Kolk, B. A. (2002). Self-destructive behavior in patients with dissociative disorders. *Suicide and Life-Threatening Behavior, 32,* 313–320.

Saxe, G. N., Chinman, G., Berkowitz, M. D., Hall, K., Lieberg, G., Schwartz, J., & van der Kolk, B. A. (1994). Somatization in patients with dissociative disorders. *The American Journal of Psychiatry, 151,* 1329–1334.

Schneider-Rosen, K., & Cicchetti, D. (1991). Early self-knowledge and emotional development: Visual self-recognition and affective reactions to mirror self-images in maltreated and nonmaltreated toddlers. *Developmental Psychology, 27,* 471–478.

Schore, A. N. (1994). *Affect regulation and the origin of the self: The neurobiology of emotional development*. Hillsdale, NJ: Erlbaum.

Schroeder, S. R., Oster-Granite, M. L., & Thompson, T. (Eds.). (2002). *Self-injurious behavior: Gene–brain–behavior relationships*. Washington, DC: American Psychological Association.

Simeon, D., & Favazza, A. R. (2001). Self-injurious behaviors: Phenomenology and assessment. In D. Simeon & E. Hollander (Eds.), *Self-injurious behaviors: Assessment and treatment* (pp. 1–28). Washington, DC: American Psychiatric Publishing.

Spangler, G., & Grossmann, K. E. (1999). Individual and physiological correlates of attachment disorganization in infancy. In J. Solomon & C. George (Eds.), *Attachment disorganization*. New York: Guilford Press.

Sroufe, L. A. (1990). An organizational perspective on the self. In D. Cicchetti & M. Beeghly (Eds.), *The self in transition: Infancy to childhood* (pp. 281–307). Chicago: University of Chicago Press.

Sroufe, L. A. (1995). *Emotional development: The organization of emotional life in the early years*. New York: Cambridge University Press.

Sroufe, L. A., Egeland, B., & Kreutzer, T. (1990). The fate of early experience following developmental change: Longitudinal approaches to individual adaptation in childhood. *Child Development, 61,* 1363–1373.

Sroufe, L. A., & Rutter, M. (1984). The domain of developmental psychopathology. *Child Development, 55,* 17–29.

Stern, D. N. (1985). *The interpersonal world of the infant*. New York: Basic Books.

Suyemoto, K. L. (1998). The functions of self-mutilation. *Clinical Psychology Review, 18,* 531–554.

Symons, F. S. (2002). Self-injury and pain: Models and mechanisms. In S. R. Schroeder, M. L. Oster-Granite, & T. Thompson (Eds.), *Self-injurious behavior: Gene–brain–behavior relationships* (pp. 223–234). Washington, DC: American Psychological Association.

Toth, S. L., Cicchetti, D., Macfie, J., & Emde, R. N. (1997). Representations of self and other in the narratives of neglected, physically abused, and sexually abused preschoolers. *Development and Psychopathology, 9,* 781–796.

Trickett, P. K., & McBride-Chang, C. (1995). The developmental impact of different forms of child abuse and neglect. *Developmental Review, 15,* 311–337.

Trickett, P. K., Noll, J. G., Reiffman, A., & Putnam, F. W. (2001). Variants of intrafamilial sexual abuse experience: Implications for short- and long-term development. *Development and Psychopathology, 13,* 1001–10019.

van der Kolk, B. A. (1987). The separation cry and the trauma response: Developmental issues in the psychobiology of attachment and separation. In B. A. van der Kolk (Ed.), *Psychological trauma* (pp. 31–62). Washington, DC: American Psychiatric Press.

van der Kolk, B. A., Pelcovitz, D., Roth, S., Mandel, F. S., McFarlane, A., & Herman, J. (1996). Dissociation, somatization, and affect dysregulation: The complexity of adaptation to trauma. *The American Journal of Psychiatry: Festschrift Supplement, 153,* 83–93.

van der Kolk, B. A., Perry, J. C., & Herman, J. L. (1991). Childhood origins of self-destructive behaviour. *The American Journal of Psychiatry, 148,* 1665–1676.

van Ijzendoorn, M. H., Scheungel, C., & Bakermanns-Kranenburg, M. J. (1999). Disorganized attachment in early childhood: Meta-analysis of precursors, concomitants and sequelae. *Development and Psychopathology, 11,* 225–249.

Vasquez, D. M. (1998). Stress and the developing limbic–hypothalamic–pituitary–adrenal axis. *Psychoneuroendocrinology, 23,* 663–700.

Wedig, M. M., & Nock, M. K. (2007). Parental expressed emotion and adolescent self-injury. *Journal of the American Academy of Child & Adolescent Psychiatry, 46,* 1171–1178.

Werner, H., & Kaplan, B. (1964). *Symbol formation: An organismic-developmental approach to language and the expression of thought.* New York: Wiley.

Whitlock, J. L., Eckenrode, J., & Silverman, D. (2006). Self-injurious behaviors in a college population. *Pediatrics, 117,* 1939–1948.

Wiederman, M. W., Sansone, R. A., & Sansone, L. A. (1999). Bodily self-harm and its relationship to childhood abuse among women in a primary care setting. *Violence Against Women, 5,* 155–163.

Yates, T. M. (2004). The developmental psychopathology of self-injurious behavior: Compensatory regulation in posttraumatic adaptation. *Clinical Psychology Review, 24,* 35–74.

Yates, T. M. (2005). *A longitudinal study of self-injurious behavior in a community sample.* Unpublished doctoral dissertation, University of Minnesota, Minneapolis.

Yates, T. M. (2007). The developmental consequences of child emotional abuse: A neurodevelopmental perspective. *Journal of Emotional Abuse, 7,* 19–34.

Yates, T. M., Carlson, E. A., & Egeland, B. (2008). A prospective study of child maltreatment and self-injurious behavior in a community sample. *Development and Psychopathology, 20,* 651–671.

Yates, T. M., Tracy, A. J., & Luthar, S. S. (2008). Nonsuicidal self-injury among "privileged" youth: Longitudinal and cross-sectional approaches to developmental process. *Journal of Consulting and Clinical Psychology, 76,* 52–62.

Zlotnick, C., Mattia, J. I., & Zimmerman, M. (1999). Clinical correlates of self-mutilation in a sample of general psychiatric patients. *The Journal of Nervous and Mental Disease, 187,* 296–301.

Zlotnick, C., Shea, M. T., & Pearlstein, T. (1996). The relationship between dissociative symptoms, alexithymia, impulsivity, sexual abuse and self-mutilation. *Comprehensive Psychiatry, 37,* 12–16.

8

MEDIA, THE INTERNET, AND NONSUICIDAL SELF-INJURY

JANIS WHITLOCK, AMANDA PURINGTON,
AND MARINA GERSHKOVICH

Tracy struggles with her emotions, visibly frustrated and angered by the contentious interactions with her mother and her best friend. She lives with her single but warm and attentive mother and brother in a working-class California neighborhood. At 13, Tracy is the epitome of a junior high schooler—worried about fitting in, growing up, and reconciling a somewhat turbulent past with the promise of future independence. One night, after a particularly volatile exchange with her mother followed by a disappointing experience with her best friend, Tracy's agitation is palpable. At the pinnacle of her distress, Tracy makes her way to the bathroom and reaches for a pair of small scissors stored in the vanity. Although a typical part of bathroom paraphernalia, the scissors serve a particular and unusual function for Tracy. Sinking to the floor, she slides the sharp edge across her wrist—lightly enough to avoid serious injury, but deep enough to cause blood to well up as it slowly passes over the delicate skin. On her wrist lie the telltale signs of other, similar moments. After one long cut, she lets the blades fall drunkenly from her hand as she covers her wounds with her shirtsleeve—already stained with dried blood. As Tracy sits crumpled on the floor, the camera zooms out and the scene assumes a slightly fuzzy focus. Sirens wail low and distant in the

139

background. Viewers may or may not realize that the shot is patterned after a typical drug scene in which an addict shoots up and nods off in the middle of an inner-city slum. No viewer, however, will miss the effect of the act—Tracy is now very calm; her anxiety soothed by a "drug" she has not had to buy, steal, or imbibe.

Tracy's story, the central narrative of the film *Thirteen* (Beva, Chasin, Fellner, Hunter, & Hardwick, 2003), is important for many reasons. One of these is that her self-injurious response to stress is reflective of what some have called a new "epidemic" among youth (Brumberg, 2006; Galley, 2003; Welsh, 2004). Although lack of baseline data prohibits empirical validation of this assumption, there is a reasonably high degree of consensus about the likelihood of its validity among youth-focused service providers (N. L. Heath, Toste, & Beettam, 2006; Whitlock, Eells, Cummings, & Purington, in press). The second reason Tracy's story is important is because the public display of her self-injury, available to millions of viewers, has become an increasingly common scene in movies, television shows, and Web-based video media. At least 14 pop icons publicly revealed self-injurious habits from 1993 to 2004 (Beller, 1998; Conroy et al., 1998; Diamond, 1999; C. Heath, 1993, 1998a, 1998b, 2001, 2004; "Holmes reveals," 2005; Maerz, 2001; Ro, 2000; Villa 65, 1995; Weiss, 1998; Wurtzel, 1994). Although not all possessed widespread popular appeal, celebrities such as Princess Diana, Johnny Depp, Angelina Jolie, and Christina Ricci all publicly admitted to nonsuicidal self-injury (NSSI) and shared detailed information about how and why it worked for them. Although not intended to promote self-injury, such high-profile disclosures do serve as avenues for dissemination of ideas that in epidemiological terms may serve as vectors for contagion. Scenes and themes of self-injurious behaviors have also appeared in popular television shows such as *Seventh Heaven, Degrassi, House M.D., Grey's Anatomy, Nip/Tuck,* and *Will and Grace.* Although Tracy's practice of NSSI is a behavior foreign to most adults, it is anything but novel to most contemporary adolescents—in part because self-injury is now firmly part of the media landscape.

The remainder of this chapter is dedicated to a review of literature, theories, and a nascent empirical study germane to the role of the media on NSSI. We begin with a review of the forms of mass communication available daily to most individuals within and outside of the United States followed by a brief discussion of empirical linkages between media exposure and NSSI, aggression, and suicide. We then present preliminary findings from our study of the links between self-injury and media and examine several of the key theoretical mechanisms through which media and the Internet may influence youth behavior. Finally, we discuss implications for clinical practice and community-based intervention.

VECTORS FOR COMMUNICATION . . . AND CONTAGION

In 1975, most American families owned or had access to a television, a radio, a phone, and a mailbox. Some received newspapers. By 2006, media routes into and out of the average American home had nearly tripled. Not only had technologies for these basic 1975 media modalities expanded considerably with the advent of cable, satellite, home message recorders, VHS and DVD, and "express" mail deliveries, but wholly novel technologies were developing as well. Personal computers, iPods, handheld camcorders, wireless technology, smart phones, and the Internet are just some of the common fixtures of the contemporary American home media ecology. In the span of less than one generation, opportunities for receiving and sending communications have fundamentally transformed the way individuals connect with information and others outside their proximal environments.

One result of these changes is that today's children and adolescents live media-saturated lives. The sheer multiplicity and pervasiveness of opportunities to both receive and send information has rendered the diffusion of ideas easily accomplished. In a nationally representative study of 8- to 18-year-olds (Roberts, Foehr, & Rideout, 2005), researchers found that 99% of American homes possess at least one television, and 60% of children ages 2 to 18 live in a home with three televisions. More than 70% of children ages 2 to 18 have in-home access to video game consoles, and 86% of youth ages 8 to 18 report at least one computer; 74% live in homes with an Internet connection. On average, a typical U.S. child between 8 and 18 years of age is likely to live in a home equipped with three televisions that probably receive a cable or satellite signal, three VCRs or DVD players, three radios, three CD–tape players, two video game consoles, and a personal computer. In all likelihood, the computer is connected to the Internet and supports instant messaging. Despite the popularity of interactive media, however, older forms of screen media still dominate young people's media exposure. Indeed, more than two thirds (68%) of youth ages 11 to 14 have televisions in their bedrooms, where parental oversight of use is limited. Although the average youth reports spending nearly 6.5 hours per day using media (including the Internet), he or she is exposed to more than 8.5 hours per day of media messages. Referred to as *media multitasking*, this seeming paradox arises as a by-product of the fact that for one quarter of the time in which youth use media, they report using two or more simultaneously (Roberts et al., 2005).

In 1979, well before the media revolution, the much revered psychologist Urie Bronfenbrenner articulated what has become foundational work on the ecology of human development (Bronfenbrenner, 1979). In his reckoning, the media was regarded as a distal influence with developmental leverage far secondary to that of the real people and institutions in children's lives—parents, peers, schools, and other important adults and institutions linked to them geographically or through extended family networks. Today, however, peers and even adults who live hundreds or thousands of miles away and without connection to an individual's local family or peer network can assume a pivotal and influential role in a person's life with the mere click of a mouse.

It is not surprising that well-articulated theory and investigation about the full spectrum and magnitude of these changes on human interaction, development, behavior, and life trajectory has not paralleled the rapidity of the media revolution. Most research to date has been conducted on the effects of screen (i.e., what is often thought of as unidirectional) media in which audiovisual systems that deliver content that does not depend on directive responses from the viewer (e.g., television, cinema and movies, music, print news). The Internet, however, provides an array of interactive, or bidirectional, media in which communications functions are built into traditional screen systems (e.g., Internet, telephone, satellite-based telecommunications such as cell phones and smart phones).

Empirical study of the role that bidirectional or interactive media plays in real-life behavior is less than a decade old. Most commonly, these studies target the Internet, broadly conceived. As with unidirectional media, most of the studies do find effects, although these vary greatly in magnitude and nature. In large part this is because bidirectional media forms allow for much more nuanced types of exchange and effect because users may actually be interacting with real individuals through a virtual medium. For example, studies show that Internet use permits the development of positive bonding through formation of social ties which some individuals find difficult to construct offline (Hampton & Wellman, 2003; Kavanaugh & Patterson, 2001). They also suggest, however, that Internet use may increase isolation in real life, expose and reinforce maladaptive self-narratives, or permit the networking of individuals with offline agendas that are dangerous to society (Becker, Mayer, Nagenborg, El-Faddagh, & Schmidt, 2004; Norris, Boydell, Pinhas, & Katzman, 2006; Whitlock, Powers, & Eckenrode, 2006; Ybarra & Mitchell, 2005). Similarly, access to information unavailable locally facilitates information gathering and resources otherwise inaccessible (Borzekowski, Fobil, & Asante, 2006) that can advance educational objectives, and thus academic performance, in children with less reliable access to high-quality education (Jackson et al., 2006). It may also, however, permit vulnerable individuals to readily identify and view potentially damaging content (Ybarra & Mitchell, 2005).

In contrast, unidirectional media is both better researched and easier to understand, in large part because it does not permit exchange or message coconstruction as do the Internet and other bidirectional media modalities. Three decades worth of experience with unidirectional media affirms the potency of influence—especially for adolescents and children (Brown et al., 2006; Escobar-Chaves et al., 2005; Gould, 2001; Huesmann, Moise-Titus,

Podolski, & Eron, 2003; Johnson, Cohen, Smailes, Kasen, & Brook, 2002; Paik & Comstock, 1994). For example, every study included in a 2006 special issue of *Archives of Pediatrics & Adolescent Medicine* found significant main effects for media on all child and adolescent behaviors examined. Such findings are not unique. Virtually every media study on the relationship between media and aggression, for example, shows a strong, direct relationship. Indeed, the relationship is so consistently documented that in July 2000, six major professional societies, including the American Psychological Association, the American Medical Association, and the American Academy of Pediatrics, issued a joint statement about its effects. Grounded in a review of more than 1,000 studies, the statement acknowledged as fact the now well-documented empirical link between on-screen violence and child and adolescent behavior and called for coordinated policy responses (Cook et al., 2000).

The mechanisms behind such influence are complex. Although it would be naive to assume that media causes behavior, such as self-injury, research overwhelmingly shows that media plays an important role in disseminating behavioral innovations, in normalizing novel behaviors, and in "priming" through the creation of scripts, which may slowly prepare viewers, particularly young viewers, to try or adopt behaviors they may never have considered. Most scholars attribute the well-documented relationship between media and aggression to the sheer volume of images young media viewers absorb. For example, the 3-year National Television Violence Study (NTVS) analyzing more than 10,000 hours of programming in the United States found that 61% of all programs and nearly 67% of children's programs contained violence. On average, the authors concluded, children view about 10,000 acts of violence per year, a figure that exceeds the amount and severity of violence that actually occurs in the United States (Center for Communication and Social Policy, 1998).

Image prevalence, however, is not the only empirical link to real-life behavior; mere suggestion seems to matter as well. The power of media suggestion was first documented in the 18th century when Goethe penned *The Sorrows of Young Werther*, a novel in which the main character dies by suicide. Following publication of the book in 1774, a rash of suicides prompted several regions to ban it for fear of more (Marsden, 1998). The possible association between media messages and behavior went uninvestigated until Émile Durkheim (1897/1997), well known for his work on suicide, went in pursuit of the answer. His study found no conclusive evidence that social factors, such as imitation, influenced suicide rates. Durkheim's proclamation effectively ended the scholarship in this area until 1974, when another empirical study of the same question documented a link. Phillips's (1974) study reviewed suicides publicized in *The New York Times*, the *New York Daily News*, the *Chicago Tribune*, and the *London Daily Mirror* and showed a clear association between published stories about suicide and subsequent completed suicides in the area in which the story was published. More recent studies found similarly that the magnitude of the increase in suicides and suicide attempts following a suicide story is proportional to the amount, duration, and prominence of media coverage (Gould, Jamieson, & Romer, 2003; Stack, 2000).

How a character or scene is portrayed matters as well. For example, in the vast majority of the programs reviewed as part of the NTVS, violent perpetrators were portrayed as heroes of the stories, and victims rarely suffered pain (Center for Communication and Social Policy, 1998). Similarly, in a review of suicide contagion studies, Stack (2000) found that reports based on newspaper accounts, celebrity suicides, real rather than fictional suicides, and suicide attempts rather than suicide deaths are more likely to inspire copycat effects. Not all groups are at the same risk of media effects. Research consistently shows adolescents and young to be particularly vulnerable to reports and depictions of suicide and aggression in the mass media (Bushman & Huesmann, 2006; Gould et al., 2003).

EMPIRICAL STUDY OF SELF-INJURY AND THE MEDIA

Because it is likely that many of the same factors critical in linking media and aggression or suicide may be at work with self-injury (with or without suicidal intent), we set out to examine the extent and characterization of self-injury in unidirectional media, bidirectional media, and on the Internet. The study objectives were modest and aimed primarily at documenting the quantity, form, and characterization of self-injury available in contemporary media outlets, with particular attention to Internet message boards and movies, music, and news articles. The Internet message board–focused component of this work found that self-injury Internet message boards are numerous, very easily accessed, and highly frequented; 406 were identified in January 2005, and there were more than 500 a year later. We also found that once online, individuals do much of what they do—namely, seek and provide support and information—offline. They also exchange and share strategies for ceasing the behavior, finding help, avoiding detection, treating severe wounds, and even for injuring in new or different ways (Whitlock et al., 2006). Like the complex story emerging from Internet-focused research, the findings hold hope and caution for those interested in understanding and addressing the role the Internet plays in self-injury (Whitlock et al., 2006; Whitlock, Lader, & Conterio, 2007) and clearly signal the need for additional research in this area.

Our investigation of the role the media plays in disseminating self-injury is less well developed but merits consideration of the findings to date. Although identifying the point at which self-injury began to surface in community populations in more than isolated pockets is impossible, we have endeavored to estimate and track the entry and spread of self-injury images and stories in movies, songs, and print news. We have also conducted content analyses of movies in which self-injury is depicted. The method, results, and interpretation of our findings follow.

Method

Study of the link between self-injury and media is fraught with limitations. The primary limitation is that there exists no standardized mechanism for identifying media forms, such as movies, television shows, and music, in which self-injury appears. The only exception to this limitation is print news, in which search engines such as LexisNexis and Factiva do permit systematic search of current and archived print news by keyword. With these limitations in mind, we began building a database of movies, songs, and print news in which self-injury appears in early 2004. Our first task was to simply document frequency of each by year. The second task, particular to movies, was to code for specific content with attention paid to the way characters were portrayed. What follows is a preliminary summary of our findings to date.

We identified movies and songs featuring self-injury content by sending out regular inquiries to personal and professional networks about whether they had seen a movie with NSSI scenes or knew of songs with NSSI lyrics; through regular visits to NSSI message boards and YouTube sites, where members often discuss music, movies, and television shows with NSSI content; and by visiting two Web sites that include specific references for NSSI media and literature (http://anthology.self-injury.net/section/nonfictional_literature.php and http://imdb.com). Self-injury news stories were identified in a far more systematic fashion through querying of the LexisNexis search engine using multiple terms including *self-injury* and *self-mutilation*. All news articles identified were counted, even if they originated from the same story (such as an Associated Press article) because including all provides a snapshot of the degree of market penetration. Coding of movie content was accomplished through independent viewing, and coding was done by trained student coders. As shown in Table 8.1, movies were coded to capture (a) sex, race, age, and socioeconomic status of the self-injurious characters; (b) self-injury form; (c) presence of comorbid mental illness and degree of suicidal intent; and (d) extent to which self-injurious characters were portrayed as strong (vs. weak) and appealing (e.g., likely to be someone with whom viewers would identify). Character strength and appeal were coded dichotomously. To establish intercoder reliability, coding for all movies was compared across coder dyads. Agreement was assessed by calculating the proportion of codes each individual in the pair coded the same. Intercoder agreement across all pairs was 90%, and discrepancies were discussed until agreement was reached.

TABLE 8.1
Nonsuicidal Self-Injury (NSSI) Characters

Variables	Self-injurious characters, % (n) (N = 43)
NSSI character profile	
Sex	
Male	41.9 (18)
Female	58.1 (25)
Age	
Under 12	2.4 (1)
12–20	28.6 (12)
21–30	31.0 (13)
31–40	23.8 (10)
Over 40	14.0 (6)
Race	
Caucasian	100% (44)
Socioeconomic status	
Low	21.4 (9)
Middle	47.6 (20)
High	31.0 (13)
Character appeal	
Strength	
Strong	61.5 (26)
Weak	39.5 (17)
Character Appeal	
High	79.5 (34)
Low	20.9 (9)
NSSI form	
Form	
Cutting	61.5 (24)
Bruising	12.8 (5)
Other	15.4 (6)
Burn	7.7 (3)
Stab	2.6 (1)
Comorbidity with mental illness and suicide	
Presence of comorbid mental illness	
Overt (diagnosed)	23.1 (10)
Implied	46.2 (20)
None	30.2 (13)
Suicidality	
Attempt	17.9 (7)
Completion	17.9 (7)
None	67.4 (29)
Intervention	
Mental health treatment	25.6 (11)
Physical health treatment	7.7 (3)
Both mental and physical health treatment	5.1 (2)
No formal treatment	61.5 (26)

Results

As of spring 2007, a total of 47 movies that feature unambiguous NSSI scenes or characters had been identified. Examples included *Thirteen*, *A Lion in Winter*, *Secretary*, *Sid and Nancy*, and *The Scarlet Letter*. Of these, 11 included scenes suggestive of NSSI behavior but not overtly referenced, so they were excluded in these analyses. Of the remaining 36, all but 1 were coded as "drama," 16% ($n = 6$) "horror," 11% ($n = 4$) "biography," 11% ($n = 4$) "action," and 5.5% ($n = 2$) "romance"; movies could fall into more than one genre category. Most, 72.2% ($n = 26$), were rated R, 22.2% ($n = 8$) were rated PG-13, and the remaining 2 were unrated.

Eighty-nine songs with self-injury references had been identified by the same date. Although song genre is difficult to quantify, the vast majority (86.7%) could be classified as some type of rock (e.g., alternative, emotional, gothic, heavy metal, punk), 4.8% as pop, and 6.0% as rap.

Figure 8.1 shows the publication date ranges of both movies and songs over time. The upward trend in both categories is striking. Only 2 movies with unambiguous self-injury references or scenes prior to 1980 were identified. In contrast, between 2000 and 2005, we identified more than 50 songs and 20 movies. Extreme caution in interpreting this trend is warranted because it may be largely due to an artifact of the methodology used to identify data sources. However, self-injury news stories exhibit a similar trend, as shown in Figure 8.2. Because one can systematically search for news stories by keyword, the validity of these data is far more certain.

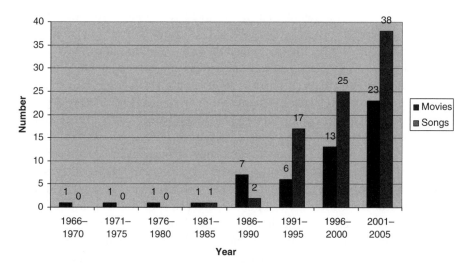

Figure 8.1. Movies and songs with self-injury referenced by year. NSSI = nonsuicidal self-injury.

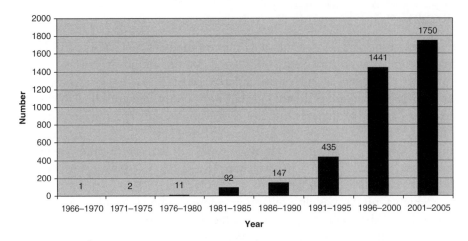

Figure 8.2. Self-injury-focused print news stories by year. NSSI = nonsuicidal self-injury.

As shown with movies and music, there exists a clear upward linear trend over time. Evidence of self-injury in print news media prior to 1990 was quite rare—we identified only 253 stories between 1966 and 1990. In contrast, from 2000 to 2005, we identified 1,750 stories alone, with a steady increase each year.

Analysis of movies with self-injury scenes reveals interesting trends across characters. The 36 movies coded featured 43 characters with explicit self-injury experience. As is evident in Table 8.1, the majority, although not by a large margin, were female (58.1%) and in their teens (28.6%), 20s (31%), or 30s (23.8%). Only one was depicted as less than 12 years of age, and the remainder (14%) were portrayed as over 40. All of the self-injurious characters were identified as White, and the majority (78.6%) as of middle to high socioeconomic status. Most (61.5%) were portrayed as strong characters likely to elicit empathy from viewers (79.5%). Most cut (61.5%) and had overt or implied mental illness (69.3%), but only about one third (35.8%) were depicted as having attempted or completed suicide. The majority (61.5%) received no mental or physical treatment for their self-injury during the course of the movie.

In general, the trends observed across time, movie, and character are quite consistent with mainstream perception of the behavior and those who practice it. Considered together, the evidence suggests that media may serve as at least one source of the contemporary public perception of the "self-injurer" as a White female "cutter"—of the 36 movies coded, nearly half (46.6%) included a White female shown cutting; all but 2 of these were featured in movies made since 1995. Furthermore, although definitive evidence about changes in the prevalence of self-injury in media over time will forever be lacking, our data show, with certainty, that it is quite prevalent now. The extent to which increasing media coverage of self-injury, as part of narrative, news stories, and focused conversation (e.g., on Internet message boards), spreads or reinforces the behavior is beyond the purview of research to date. However, in light of well-established research on the effect of uni- and bidirectional media on behavior, it is likely that future studies of this relationship will demonstrate a link. To what, however, can one attribute such a link? How do media leverage influence? To these questions one must turn to theory for answers.

THEORETICAL EXPLANATIONS FOR THE EFFECT OF MEDIA AND THE INTERNET ON SELF-INJURY

No single theory is sufficient to explain human behavior. Human beings are dynamic; the human mind acts as an associative network in which concepts, emotions, and ideas may become activated by related stimuli in ways impossible to predict or model. For example, viewing a violent scene, whether self- or other-directed, may prime individuals for aggressive thoughts, emotions, and scripts. Such priming and its subsequent effects may occur outside of awareness and through cues only remotely connected to aggression. How does this happen? Sociocultural theories are those designed to explain how the external world affects internal developmental processes. The external social worlds in which individuals grow, through engagement in activities, which require cognitive and communicative functions, promote and shape developmental options and trajectories (Kublin, Wetherby, Crais, & Prizant, 1998; Vygotsky, 1934/1986). A subset of these theories goes far in helping to explain the effect media has on behavior.

Convergence and Emergent Norm Theories

Convergence theory, first described by Turner and Killian (1972), holds that individuals will seek out and converge around a set of mutual interests. Such impulses, for example, are likely to dictate the media content and virtual communities to which individuals become attracted. *Emergent norm theory* adds to this the idea that although individuals in a group will consciously or unconsciously alter their behavior to conform to what they perceive to be group norms, groups are also dynamic in that, once established, they give rise to new and novel norms as they progress (Turner, 1964). The tendency to form groups and to generate new norms may be particularly salient for adolescents and young adults because by middle childhood peers occupy a primary role in development.

Emergent norm theory is most applicable to bidirectional media modalities. The role of the virtual world, such as Internet message boards, blogs, or YouTube, in permitting self-injury groups to form around a shared behavior is an example of these theories and, in particular, of the way they work in tandem. In these contexts, individuals converge around a set of shared behaviors out of which new norms may arise. For example, virtual communities are formed through convergence, through shared interest in self-injury. Once founded, through small acts of support, censure, and sharing, members establish a set of expectations to guide exchange. Depictions of self-injury posted by members may become attractive or normalized to others over time simply because of the perceived commonalities shared by the group. These online experiences may subsequently shape offline expectations and, ultimately, behavior. Similar processes may be at work in unidirectional media as well, where the "group" in which one comes to belong, at least symbolically, may consist of a character or set of characters with whom one interacts through identification, such as through a movie or television series. This may be especially true if the behavior helps the character achieve an attractive goal, such as easing distress, gaining the attention of others, or gaining status within their peer group.

Social Learning Theory

Social learning theory, most commonly associated with Albert Bandura (1977), suggests that when presented with an ambiguous situation, individuals imitate actions they have witnessed others perform in the past. The classic example, based on Bandura's early experimental tests, showed that after watching a more mature person engage in violent behavior toward a doll, children in the experimental group were significantly more likely to subsequently behave aggressively toward the doll, even if the reason for the model's behavior was unclear or the aggression was unprovoked. Media, social learning theory holds, is a particularly potent force in behavior because merely observing what others do, particularly when the others are similar to the observer, can affect later behavioral choices. The ability to visualize and carry out actions that one has witnessed others engage in may ultimately determine behavior, particularly in situations in which behavioral options are ambiguous, such as while experiencing affective distress. This is true even when the original purpose for engaging in the viewed behavior is unclear because it is the contextual, visceral similarities between the observed and observer that forge the behavioral association.

Disinhibition and Script Theories

Disinhibition theory (Freedman, 1982) suggests that behaviors are spread because seeing another individual perform a considered action reduces the inhibition to perform it. Like social learning theory, disinhibition theory suggests that observing others engage in a behavior renders it more possible or conceivable. This is particularly true if an individual is conflicted about performing a certain behavior but sees another complete it successfully or with positive results. For example, in the scene from *Thirteen* described at the beginning of this chapter, observing NSSI as both painless and an effective means of quickly reducing anxiety may lower viewer inhibitions to trying the behavior in similar circumstances. The staging of the scene as one likening self-injury to an effective drug—even if its effectiveness is only temporarily— may contribute to the disinhibition effect.

Similarly, *script theory* dictates that individuals are more likely to repeat a behavior, or script, when a previous use of the behavior was successful (Albeson, 1976). Scripts represent actions, participants, and physical objects that come to represent a narrative to explain perceptions and behaviors. Script theory would predict that individuals adopt behaviors not only from observed models but also from storylines. Although applicable to unidirectional media experiences, such as viewing, reading, or listening to narratives inclusive of self-injury, script theory holds tremendous promise in explaining the effects of online bidirectional exchanges on offline behavior because participants may engage in *narrative reinforcement* (Whitlock et al., 2007), which evolves out of coconstruction of stories that essentially explain and justify self-injury linked behavioral choices—for better and worse—through interaction with others using similar scripts. Both disinhibition and script theories help to explain the desensitization and normalization of behavior that empirical studies of aggression document. Similarly, they suggest that when self-injury is depicted as painless, effective, and common, inhibition may be lowered and scripts which support its value adopted.

CONCLUSION

The evidence reviewed in this chapter suggests that individuals vulnerable to the acquisition and maintenance of NSSI are likely to encounter both a means of exposure and multiple opportunities to experience self-injury-related images, symbols, or stories, by either self-selection or chance. Uni- and bidirectional forms of media may serve as vectors for the introduction and contagion of self-injury. Indeed, the empirical data presented, although methodologically limited, support this assumption. These same processes may reinforce the behavior among those already engaging in NSSI. In light of the many mechanisms through which media influences behavior, the existence of both means and likelihood of exposure is concerning and has important implications for clinicians and researchers.

Clinical Implications

The perception that a behavior is common and rational may ultimately render treatment or intervention more difficult. Similarly, identification with individuals known or believed to engage in NSSI through social modeling or actual exchange, such as that provided through the Internet, may couple the need for belonging to a community of like-minded others who engage in NSSI. Even among individuals committed to ceasing the behavior, consistent and easy access to self-injury scripts and images in media may interfere with recovery. There are several clinical implications that follow from this review.

First, media- and Internet-use histories should be taken as part of intake and risk assessment procedures. When high use of either is detected, integration of periodic assessment and behavioral impact question routes similar to those described for the Internet (Whitlock et al., 2007) may be warranted. Lines of questioning will be most germane to treatment when they assess the degree and nature of media exposure or participation, as in the case of Internet communities, as well as the nature and magnitude of the impact on behavior.

Second, media and Internet use may introduce and reinforce self-injurious behavior through a variety of mechanisms: (a) identification of and fraternization with like-minded others; (b) behavior modeling; and (c) inclusion of scripts, sounds, or images that introduce or reinforce personal self-injury narratives. As evident in empirical studies linking media to aggression and suicide, the impact of uni- and bidirectional media is likely to be amplified when images are both plentiful and associated with high-profile individuals, such as celebrities. Assessing the mechanisms through which clients are influenced by media will assist in deciding appropriate therapeutic approaches and media-use recommendations.

Empirical Implications

Research on the relationship between media and self-injury behavior is scant. However, because uni- and bidirectional media modalities are potent vectors for the spread of ideas and behaviors, it is critical to advance understanding of the means through which they may be encouraging adoption or maintenance of the behavior. Although we present here empirical evidence that media representations of self-injury are increasingly available, it is not clear to what extent these representations influence self-injurious behavior of viewers and participants. Nor is it clear how interventions designed to moderate the relationship between media or Internet use and self-injury might most effectively do so. Well-designed empirical studies aimed at investigating the nature and magnitude of the relationship between media exposure to self-injury are needed. Such studies would focus on the effects of media and Internet use on NSSI and the extent to which these effects vary by media type and exposure.

REFERENCES

Abelson, R. P. (1976). Script processing in attitude formation and decision-making. In J. S. Carroll & J. W. Payne (Eds.), *Cognition and social behavior* (pp. 35–45). Oxford, England: Erlbaum.

Bandura, A. (1977). *Social learning theory*. Englewood Cliffs, NJ: Prentice-Hall.

Becker, K., Mayer, M., Nagenborg, M., El-Faddagh, M., & Schmidt, M. H. (2004). Parasuicide online: Can suicide websites trigger suicidal behaviour in predisposed adolescents? *Nordic Journal of Psychiatry, 58,* 111–114.

Beller, T. (1998, August). Hollywood's freaky it girl and hello, nasty? *SPIN, 14,* 78–82, 149.

Beva, T., Chasin, L., Fellner, L. Hunter, H. (Producer), & Hardwick, C. (Director). (2003). *Thirteen* [Motion picture]. United States: Michael London Productions.

Borzekowski, D. L. G., Fobil, J. N., & Asante, K. O. (2006). Online access by adolescents in Accra: Ghanaian teens' use of the Internet for health information. *Developmental Psychology, 42,* 450–458.

Bronfenbrenner, U. (1979). *The ecology of human development.* Cambridge, MA: Harvard University Press.

Brown, J. D., L'Engle, K. L., Pardun, C. J., Guo, G., Kenneavy, K., & Jackson, C. (2006). Sexy media matter: Exposure to sexual content in music, movies, television, and magazines predicts Black and White adolescents' sexual behavior. *Pediatrics, 117,* 1018–1027.

Brumberg, J. J. (2006, December). Are we facing an epidemic of self-injury? *The Chronicle Review.* Retrieved February 4, 2007, from http://chronicle.com/cgi-bin/printable.cgi?article=http://chronicle.com/weekly/v53/i16/16b00601.htm

Bushman, B. J., & Huesmann, L. R. (2006). Short-term and long-term effects of violent media on aggression in children and adults. *Archives of Pediatrics & Adolescent Medicine, 160,* 348–352.

Center for Communication and Social Policy. (1998). *National Television Violence Study 3.* Thousand Oaks, CA: Sage.

Conroy, T., Sheffield, R., Touré, Lipsky, D., Goodell, J., Healy, M., et al. (1998, August 20). Hot actress: Christina Ricci. *Rolling Stone, 793,* 74–75.

Cook, D. E., Kestenbaum, C., Honaker, L. M., Ratcliffe Anderson, E., American Academy of Family Physicians, & American Psychiatric Association. (2000, July 26). *Joint statement on the impact of entertainment violence on children: Congressional Public Health Summit.* Retrieved April 5, 2008, from http://www.aap.org/advocacy/releases/jstmtevc.htm

Diamond, J. (1999, January). Behind the scenes with Christina Ricci. *Mademoiselle,* 100–101, 128.

Durkheim E. (1997). *Suicide.* New York: The Free Press. (Original work published 1897)

Escobar-Chaves, S. L., Tortolero, S. R., Markham, C. M., Low, B. J., Eitel, P., & Thickstun, P. (2005). Impact of the media on adolescent sexual attitudes and behaviors. *Pediatrics, 116,* 303–326.

Freedman, J. L. (1982). Theories of contagion as they relate to mass psychogenic illness. In M. J. Colligan, J. W. Pennebaker, & L. R. Murphy (Eds.), *Mass psychogenic illness* (pp. 171–182). Hillsdale, NJ: Erlbaum.

Galley, M. (2003). Student self-harm: Silent school crisis. *Education Week, 3*, 2.

Gould, M. S. (2001). Suicide and the media. *Annals of the New York Academy of Sciences, 932*, 200–221.

Gould, M. S., Jamieson, P., & Romer, D. (2003). Media contagion and suicide among the young. *American Behavioral Scientist, 46*, 1269–1284.

Hampton, K. N., & Wellman, D. (2003). Neighboring in Netville: How the Internet supports community and social capital in a wired suburb. *City & Community, 2*, 277–311.

Heath, C. (1993, May). Johnny Depp—Portrait of the oddest as a young man. *Details*, 88–95, 166, 168.

Heath, C. (1998a, January 22). Fiona, the caged bird sings. *Rolling Stone*. Retrieved July 1, 2007, from http://sites.uol.com.br/diogohenriques/artigos/rs01-98.html

Heath, C. (1998b, November). The love song of Marilyn Manson. *Guitar School*. Retrieved July 1, 2007, from http://www.basetendencies.com/press/Rolling Stone98.html

Heath, C. (2001, July 5). Blood sugar sex magic. *Rolling Stone, 872*, 68–79, 156.

Heath, C. (2004, October). The wild one. GQ. Retrieved July 1, 2007, from http://www.colinfarrellfansite.com/gallery/thumbnails.php?album=128&page=1

Heath, N. L., Toste, J. R., & Beettam, E. (2006). "I am not well-equipped": High school teachers' perceptions of self-injury. *Canadian Journal of School Psychology, 21*, 73–92.

Holmes reveals self-harm ordeal. (2005, May 29). *BBC Sport*. Retrieved July 1, 2007, from http://news.bbc.co.uk/sport1/hi/athletics/4590655.stm

Huesmann, L. R., Moise-Titus, J., Podolski, C.-L., & Eron, L. D. (2003). Longitudinal relations between children's exposure to TV violence and their aggressive and violent behavior in young adult: 1977–1992. *Developmental Psychology, 39*, 201–221.

Jackson, L. A., vonEye, A., Biocca, F. A., Barbatsis, G., Zhao, Y., & Fitzgerald, H. E. (2006). How does home Internet use influence the academic performance of low-income children? *Developmental Psychology, 42*, 429–435.

Johnson, J. G., Cohen, P., Smailes, E. M., Kasen, S., & Brook, J. S. (2002, March 29). Television viewing and aggressive behavior during adolescence and adulthood. *Science, 295*, 2468–2471.

Kavanaugh, A., & Patterson, S. J. (2001). The impact of community computer networks on social capital and community involvement. *American Behavioral Scientist, 45*, 496–509.

Kublin, K. S., Wetherby, A. M., Crais, E. R., & Prizant, B. M. (1998). Using dynamic assessment within collaborative contexts: The transition from intentional to symbolic communication. In A. M. Wetherby, S. F. Warren, & J. Reichle (Eds.), *Transitions in prelinguistic communication: Preintentional to intentional and presymbolic to symbolic* (pp. 285–312). Baltimore: Brookes Publishing.

Maerz, J. (2001, October 31). Appetite for resurrection. *SF Weekly*. Retrieved July 1, 2007, from http://www.sfweekly.com/2001-10-31/music/appetite-for-resurrection

Marsden, P. (1998). Memetics and social contagion: Two sides of the same coin? *Journal of Memetics, 2*, 68–86.

Norris, M. L., Boydell, K. M., Pinhas, L., & Katzman, D. K. (2006). Ana and the Internet: A review of pro-anorexia websites. *International Journal of Eating Disorders, 39*, 443–447.

Paik, H., & Comstock, G. (1994). The effects of television violence on anti-social behavior: A meta-analysis. *Communication Research, 21*, 516–546.

Phillips, D. (1974). The influence of suggestion on suicide: Substantive and theoretical implication of the Werther effect. *American Sociological Review, 39*, 340–354.

Ro, R. (2000, May 30). *Garbage's Shirley Manson admits to "cutting."* Retrieved July 1, 2007, from http://www.mtv.com/news/articles/1429321/20000530/nullgarbage.jhtml

Roberts, D. F., Foehr, U. G., & Rideout, V. (2005). *Generation M: Media in the lives of 8–18 year-olds*. Washington, DC: Henry J. Kaiser Family Foundation.

Stack, S. (2000). Media impacts on suicide: A quantitative review of 293 findings. *Social Science Quarterly, 81*, 957–971.

Turner, R. H. (1964). Collective behavior. In R. E. L. Faris (Ed.), *Handbook of modern sociology* (pp. 382–425). Chicago: Rand McNally.

Turner, R. H., & Killian, L. M. (1972). *Collective behavior*. Englewood Cliffs, NY: Prentice-Hall.

Villa 65. (1995, November). *Radio interview with Richey Edward*. Retrieved July 1, 2007, from http://articles.richeyedwards.net/dutchradionov94.html

Vygotsky, L. (1986). *Thought and language*. Cambridge, MA: MIT Press. (Original work published 1934)

Weiss, P. (1998, October). The Love issue. *SPIN*. Retrieved July 1, 2007, from http://www.angelfire.com/hi/barbiesdead/spin98.html

Welsh, P. (June 28, 2004). Students' scars point to emotional pain. *USA Today*, p. 11a.

Whitlock, J. L., Eells, G., Cummings, N., & Purington, A. (in press). Non-suicidal self-injury on college campuses: Mental health provider assessment of prevalence and need. *Journal of College Student Psychotherapy*.

Whitlock, J. L., Lader, W., & Conterio, K. (2007). The role of virtual communities in self-injury treatment: Clinical considerations. *Journal of Clinical Psychology: In Session, 63*, 1135–1143.

Whitlock, J. L., Powers, J. L., & Eckenrode, J. (2006). The virtual cutting edge: The Internet and adolescent self-injury. *Developmental Psychology, 42*, 407–417.

Wurtzel, E. (1994). *Prozac nation*. New York: Berkley.

Ybarra, M. L., & Mitchell, K. J. (2005). Exposure to Internet pornography among children and adolescents: A national survey. *CyberPsychology & Behavior, 8*, 473–486.

9

NONSUICIDAL SELF-INJURY AMONG PEOPLE WITH DEVELOPMENTAL DISABILITIES

JAMES K. LUISELLI

Nonsuicidal self-injury (NSSI) has been a longstanding clinical problem in the field of developmental disabilities (Luiselli, Matson, & Singh, 1992; Tate & Baroff, 1966). Prevalence studies estimate that between 10% and 20% of people who have developmental disabilities engage in NSSI (Oliver, Murphy, & Corbett, 1987; Schroeder, Schroeder, Smith, & Dalldorf, 1978). As summarized by Richman and Lindauer (2005), NSSI is frequently associated with individuals who have profound intellectual disability, sensory or physical handicaps, and certain genetic conditions, such as Cornelia de Lange syndrome and Lesch–Nyhan disease (Cataldo & Harris, 1982).

Self-injurious topography among people with developmental disabilities includes banging the head and body against objects; striking the face and body with the hands; scratching, biting, and excoriating the skin; pressing the fingers against the eyes; and pulling the hair. Many children and adults perform multiple NSSI responses and remain treatment resistant for many years. The chronic display of NSSI produces tissue damage, body disfigurement, and increased risk of infection because of open wounds. Furthermore, high-frequency and persistent NSSI interferes with educational and habilitation programming, which are so vital in the lives of people who have learning and behavior challenges. NSSI also is socially stigmatizing and often requires treatment within restrictive service settings.

Professionals representing the discipline of applied behavior analysis (ABA) have a lengthy history of treating NSSI within the developmental disabilities population (Kahng, Iwata, & Lewin, 2002). The past 4 decades of ABA research have increased psychologists' knowledge about the causes of NSSI and how to intervene effectively. This chapter describes and summarizes the evolution of ABA methodology and practice as it applies to NSSI among people with developmental disabilities. It begins with a review of functional behavior assessment (FBA) and functional analysis (FA) as first steps toward treatment formulation. Next, I discuss treatment implementation that is guided by FBA and FA results. The chapter concludes with clinical and research recommendations.

FUNCTIONAL BEHAVIOR ASSESSMENT AND FUNCTIONAL ANALYSIS

E. G. Carr (1977) published a conceptual model that was instrumental in understanding the operant mechanisms responsible for NSSI. One source of control is social positive reinforcement in the form of verbal comments, eye contact, and physical interaction that occurs as a consequence for NSSI. To illustrate, a teacher might reprimand a student by stating, "No, don't hit yourself," following a self-inflicted slap to the face. Although the teacher's reaction is intended to stop the NSSI, in fact it will maintain the behavior if the student enjoys adult social attention. NSSI in this case is attention eliciting because the consequence imposed by the teacher is positively reinforcing.

A tangible-eliciting function of NSSI also is categorized as social positive reinforcement. Here, the reinforcing consequence is giving a person a preferred object contingent on NSSI. Food, toys, and activities are common tangible stimuli.

A second source of control posited by E. G. Carr (1977) is social negative reinforcement. This influence is apparent when NSSI results in the termination of a situation or condition that a person dislikes. For example, direct instruction with children and adults who have developmental disabilities can be unpleasant for them if it is too demanding, effortful, or confusing. Should a teacher terminate instruction when the person performs NSSI, the behavior will be negatively reinforced because it effectively produces an "escape" from the nonpreferred situation.

A third influence on NSSI is automatic reinforcement, in which behavior is maintained by its own sensory consequences. Automatic positive reinforcement operates when, for example, a person displays self-injurious eye pressing to produce photic stimulation. Automatic negative reinforcement operates when, for example, a person who has an ear infection strikes the side of her or his head because it briefly alleviates discomfort. As seen in these examples, automatically reinforced NSSI occurs independent of social contingencies.

The functional influences on NSSI can operate in several ways. It is possible, for example, for a person to have more than one topography of NSSI, each under the control of a different reinforcing consequence. Thus, head hitting by a man who has intellectual disability could be reinforced by contingent social attention, whereas hair pulling could be reinforced (automatically) by pleasurable sensory stimulation. Furthermore, a single topography of NSSI—say, skin-picking—could be attention eliciting under some conditions and escape motivated at other times. Finally, the function of NSSI can change over time. In illustration, a child may push forcefully against her or his abdomen in response to stomach pain. When the physical discomfort abates, the NSSI may continue if the solicitous caring and attention by adults has become socially pleasurable.

As E. G. Carr's (1977) conceptual model of NSSI gained acceptance from the professional community, clinicians and researchers designed measurement methodologies to isolate behavior function. There are two methods in this regard. FBA is a correlational approach that evaluates conditions associated with NSSI to form hypotheses about controlling variables. The second method, FA, is an experimental strategy that measures NSSI in response to direct manipulation of controlling variables.

Functional Behavior Assessment

One type of FBA is classified as an indirect approach that relies on informant-generated impressions and reports. Essentially, people familiar with the person who has NSSI (e.g., teachers, parents, therapists, peers) are asked their opinion about possible controlling variables. An instrument such as the Motivation Assessment Scale (MAS; Durand & Crimmins, 1988) includes 16 questions that are posed to an informant with the objective of identifying attention, tangible, escape, and automatic reinforcement functions. Based on a Likert-type scale, ratings for each question range from 0 (never) to 6 (always). Item 3, for example, asks, "Does this behavior occur when you are talking to other people in the room?" A strong affirmative rating to this question would suggest an attention eliciting (i.e., social positive reinforcement) function for NSSI. In total, each of the four behavior functions addressed by the MAS includes four questions—the ratings to which are computed as an average score per function. High average scores suggest clinically relevant sources of control.

The Functional Assessment Interview (FAI; O'Neill et al., 1997) is another informant-driven protocol. The FAI has 11 sections that sample information about problem behaviors. During an interview conducted by a responsible professional, an informant is asked questions about antecedent and consequence events often associated with behavior such as NSSI. It is important to note that the FAI gathers information about when a problem behavior is not likely to occur. The FAI examines a variety of ecological events (e.g., medical status, sleep patterns, mealtime routines) and interpersonal contacts, thereby producing a comprehensive formulation that guides intervention planning.

Descriptive methods are a second type of FBA characterized by direct observation of a person under naturalistic conditions. Bijou, Peterson, and Ault (1968) pioneered this approach with their presentation of antecedent–behavior–consequence data collection. While watching a person who engages in NSSI participate in a variety of activities, an observer records each occurrence of NSSI and notes particular events that immediately precede (i.e., antecedents) and follow (i.e., consequences) the behavior. The resulting data are then evaluated to determine whether specific situations reliably predict NSSI or its absence. In doing so, hypotheses about behavior could be generated.

As noted, certain antecedent events can set the occasion for NSSI through established stimulus control (Luiselli, 2005). Touchette, MacDonald, and Langer (1985) presented a scatter-plot analysis as a first step toward confirming stimulus control over problem behaviors. The recording protocol requires a practitioner to indicate whether a person's problem behavior did not occur, occurred one time, or occurred two or more times during successive 30-minute intervals within the day. By reviewing data over several days, "problem behavior may be correlated with a time of day, the presence or absence of certain people, a social setting, a class of activities, a contingency of reinforcement, a physical environment, and combinations of these and other variables" (p. 345). Accordingly, intervention can proceed by modifying one or more of these behavior–environment relationships.

Both indirect and descriptive FBA have the advantage of being easily administered by practitioners. From a clinical perspective, it is important to gather information from individuals who are knowledgeable about the person with NSSI and to document objectively how often the behavior occurs and under what conditions. Typically, both assessment methods are performed together, for example, by obtaining informant-produced impressions about behavior function, followed by direct observation and data collection. To reiterate, FBA enables one to form a working hypothesis (e.g., "The child's NSSI appears to be escape motivated") but not a confirmatory cause-and-effect relationship.

Functional Analysis

In contrast to FBA, an FA measures NSSI during experimentally manipulated conditions. In the seminal publication on this topic, Iwata, Dorsey,

Slifer, Bauman, and Richman (1982) constructed conditions to represent social positive reinforcement, social negative reinforcement, and automatic reinforcement functions. Iwata, Dorsey, Slifer, Bauman, and Richman (1982) studied nine children who had developmental disabilities and NSSI during daily 15-minute sessions, with each session featuring one of the following conditions:

- *Social disapproval.* A therapist sat in a room and allowed the child access to toys. The therapist sat away from the child, reading a book or magazine. When the child displayed NSSI, the therapist disapproved by stating, "Don't do that; you're going to hurt yourself." This condition provided social attention contingent on NSSI (i.e., social positive reinforcement).
- *Academic demand.* A therapist sat in a room with the child and presented her or him with instructional tasks that were difficult to complete. When the child displayed NSSI, the therapist removed the task, turned away for 30 seconds, and then resumed instruction. This condition provided escape from social demands contingent on NSSI (i.e., social negative reinforcement).
- *Unstructured play.* A therapist sat in a room and allowed the child access to toys. There were no consequences for NSSI. Instead, the therapist presented the child with social praise and brief physical contact (i.e., hand on shoulder) every 30 seconds without NSSI. "This condition served as a control procedure for the presence of an experimenter, the availability of potentially stimulating materials, the absence of demands, the delivery of social approval for appropriate behavior, and the lack of approval for self-injury" (Iwata et al., 1982, p. 203).
- *Alone.* The child was present in the room without the therapist or access to toys or other potentially stimulating materials. This condition tested for automatic (sensory) reinforcement as a source of control over NSSI.

Iwata et al. (1982) found that for six of the nine children, higher frequencies of NSSI were associated with a specific experimental condition. Their results were the first to document that NSSI could be a function of different sources of reinforcement. When the data from an FA are graphed, the response differentiation among conditions isolates controlling variables. Figure 9.1 shows how such data might appear within the experimental methodology designed by Iwata et al. (1982). These hypothetical data verify that the person's NSSI was consistently higher in the academic demand condition. Given this finding, an intervention to decrease and possibly eliminate NSSI would have to consider that the behavior is reinforced by escape from demands.

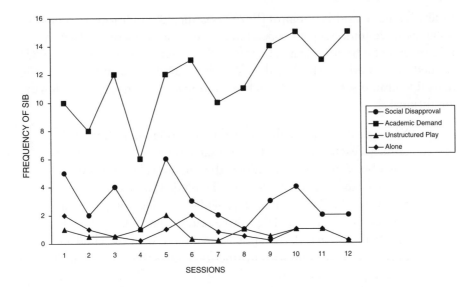

Figure 9.1. Example of functional analysis data in a hypothetical case of self-injurious behavior (SIB).

Further analysis would be required to confirm the aversive elements of the academic demand condition.

FA has gained widespread application within the professional community. An experimental–epidemiological evaluation conducted by Iwata et al. (1994) summarized data from 152 single-participant analyses with people who had developmental disabilities and engaged in NSSI over an 11-year period. The data comprised approximately 1,000 hours of experimental sessions and revealed conclusive outcomes (i.e., differential or uniformly high-frequency responding) in 95.4% of the analyses. Regarding the identified behavior function, the sample proportions were 38.1% for social negative reinforcement, 26.3% for social positive reinforcement (i.e., attention and tangible), 25.7% for automatic reinforcement, and 5.3% for multiple controlling variables. These results support FA as a highly effective methodology for verifying person-specific (i.e., idiographic) environmental determinants of NSSI.

The advantages of FA notwithstanding, this methodology requires greater sophistication than a typical FBA. Another concern is the ecological validity of an FA—namely, the fact that it is conducted under simulated (i.e., analogue) conditions that are removed from the natural environment. In an exhaustive review of the published literature about the FA of problem behaviors, Hanley, Iwata, and McCord (2003) concluded that there has been "systematic growth in the use of functional analysis methodology as a primary method of behavior assessment and, more generally, as a means of studying environment–behavior relations" (p. 178). Furthermore, many FAs have been performed in applied settings such as schools, and it appears that the time commitment is no greater than that required for an FBA (Iwata et al., 2000). Recent research also has shown that practitioners can be taught the skills to independently conduct an FA (Moore et al., 2002; Moore & Fisher, 2007). In summary, FA methodologies continue to be refined, adapted to clinical exigencies, and represent the experimental standard in cases of NSSI and other problem behaviors.

Biological Basis of Nonsuicidal Self-Injury

Beyond FBA and FA approaches considering the operant mechanisms responsible for NSSI, there are biological influences that must be considered and have been shown to interact with environmental contingencies (E. G. Carr & Smith, 1995; Cataldo & Harris, 1982; Kennedy & Becker, 2006). Infection or inflammation of the middle ear (i.e., otitis media; Luiselli, Cochran, & Huber, 2005; O'Reilly, 1997), constipation (E. G. Carr & Smith, 1995), and premenstrual syndrome (E. G. Carr, Smith, Giacin, Whelan, & Pancari, 2003) are just some of the representative maladies. E. G. Carr and Smith (1995) used the term *biological setting events* to explain the interaction between a person's physical state and environmental contingencies. Thus, Kennedy and Meyer (1996) found that escape-maintained problem behaviors of three students during instruction were frequent when one student had allergy symptoms and two students had poor sleep the night before. When the students were allergy-free and had slept soundly, problem behaviors during instruction were less frequent. In this example, the presence and absence of specific physical conditions increased or decreased (respectively) each student's motivation to perform escape behaviors.

Figure 9.2 depicts data from a clinical case study in which NSSI was affected by a medical problem. Reported by Luiselli et al. (2005), the study involved a 5-year-old boy with autism who had episodes of NSSI consisting of head hitting, body punching, face pinching, hair pulling, and skin scratching. The frequency and duration of NSSI episodes decreased subsequent to a treatment plan implemented at school. However, NSSI episodes increased unexpectedly on two occasions during intervention, and both times the elevated self-injury was correlated with physician-diagnosed otitis media. On these occasions, the boy received antibiotic medication, intervention remained in effect, and NSSI episodes decreased again. By assessing and analyzing biological influences on NSSI, preventive and health care regimens can be prescribed in conjunction with function-based behavior supports (E. G. Carr & Blakeley-Smith, 2006).

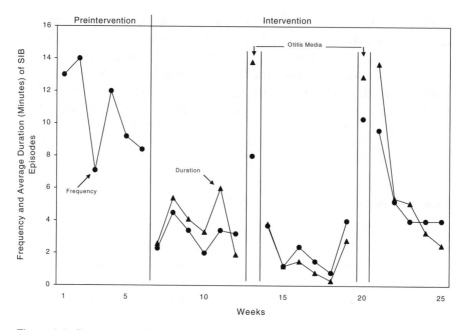

Figure 9.2. Frequency and duration of self-injurious episodes displayed by a child with autism with and without the presence of otitis media. SIB = self-injurious behavior. From "Effects of otitis media on a child with autism receiving behavioral intervention for self-injury," by J. K. Luiselli, M. L. Cochran, and S. A. Huber, 2005, *Child & Family Behavior Therapy, 27,* p. 54. Copyright 2005 by Taylor & Francis Ltd. Reprinted with permission.

BEHAVIORAL TREATMENT OF NONSUICIDAL SELF-INJURY

The earliest behavioral treatment of NSSI in people with developmental disabilities, reported during the 1960s and 1970s, differed dramatically from contemporary approaches. One distinction is that first-generation studies did not include functional assessment and analysis to inform treatment selection. Indeed, clinicians and researchers did not consistently adopt FBA and FA methods in earnest until Iwata et al.'s (1982) publication. A second notable change is that behavioral treatment of self-injurious behavior 30 to 40 years ago was dominated by punishment or aversive procedures—that is, intervention that emphasized negative consequences such as overcorrection, physical restraint, and electric shock (Forehand & Baumeister, 1976). By contrast, current philosophy is dominated by assessment-derived treatment, matched to behavior function, with a focus on preventive, positive reinforcement, and skill-building methods (Luiselli, 2004). Finally, much of the early research on NSSI was conducted in simulated or analogue settings. These contexts provided desirable experimental rigor but did not approximate naturalistic environments or typical social situations. Present-day behavioral treatment with people who have developmental disabilities and engage in NSSI is more likely to be applied and evaluated in school, home, and community locations.

This section describes behavioral treatment procedures that have been effective in decreasing and eliminating NSSI. The procedures are categorized by social positive reinforcement, social negative reinforcement, and automatic reinforcement functions. In some cases, a particular procedure (with slight variation) is applicable with each function. Other procedures have relevance to only a specific function. Although the bulk of research presented here applies to NSSI, I include demonstrations with other problem behaviors when they help exemplify treatment formulation and implementation.

Social and Tangible Positive Reinforcement

Several treatment procedures are available for social and tangible positive reinforcement of NSSI. It should be noted that such intervention must be preceded by a preference assessment (Pace, Ivancic, Edwards, Iwata, & Page, 1985) that identifies the social and tangible stimuli that are pleasurable for the person.

Differential reinforcement (DR) refers to presentation of a pleasurable stimulus when problem behaviors do not occur and to withholding the stimulus when a problem behavior is demonstrated. This is a relatively straightforward procedure that can be implemented in several ways. For example, with the DR of other behavior (DRO), a practitioner gives the person a pleasurable stimulus when she or he does not display NSSI for a specified amount of time. Another alternative is the DR of alternative behavior (DRA), in which the pleasurable stimulus follows behavior that is physically incompatible with NSSI. Numerous studies have shown that treatment of NSSI with DRO and DRA procedures can sometimes be effective when applied in isolation, but more commonly, they are effective when combined with antecedent–control manipulations and NSSI-contingent consequences (Kern & Kokina, in press).

Behavior reduction also can be achieved by presenting reinforcement on a noncontingent or fixed-time (FT) schedule. Noncontingent reinforcement (NCR), in fact, is a misnomer because *reinforcement*, by definition, is a contingent event that increases behavior (Skinner, 1948). However, NCR has become the conventional terminology accepted by behavior analysts. In one of the first evaluations of NCR, Vollmer, Iwata, Zarcone, Smith, and Mazaleski (1993) treated attention-maintained NSSI of three adults who had intellectual disability. The NCR intervention involved a therapist providing brief social attention to the adults every few seconds on an FT schedule, whether or not they displayed NSSI. Over successive days, the FT schedule was increased gradually to a terminal criterion of 5 minutes. The results of this study were that NCR was as effective as DRO in reducing each adult's NSSI to near-zero frequency. NCR continues to be a popular intervention procedure for attention and tangible-maintained problem behaviors (J. E. Carr & LeBlanc, 2006).

NCR has several advantages, principally that it is relatively easy to implement because it is not behavior dependent. That is, presentation of reinforcement is based on the passage of time and not the occurrence of NSSI, as is customary with DRO and DRA procedures. NCR also maximizes a person's exposure to reinforcement that otherwise can be delayed with DR methods (Vollmer, Iwata, Zarcone, Smith, & Mazaleski, 1993). As a decelerative intervention, it appears that NCR operates by reducing one's motivation to perform problem behaviors. In the case of attention and tangible-maintained NSSI, delivering pleasurable stimuli noncontingently serves as an abolishing operation (Friman & Hawkins, 2006), in effect giving a person frequent and response-independent reinforcement so that seeking desirable consequences through NSSI is diminished.

If NSSI is maintained by attention and tangible items, then teaching a person to access these stimuli using functionally equivalent but more acceptable behavior could be therapeutic. This strategy is the basis of functional communication training (FCT), initially reported by E. G. Carr and Durand (1985). FCT entails building language responses as a substitute for problem behaviors. For example, a child who engages in NSSI to elicit adult attention might be taught to ask, "Am I doing good work?" or "Can I talk to you?" Similarly, tangible-maintained NSSI would be approached by having the child make requests for preferred objects (e.g., "I want to play with that toy"). Like DRO and DRA procedures, research supports FCT as an effective intervention for attention and tangible maintained NSSI by itself and when combined with other methods (E. G. Carr & Durand, 1985; Durand & Carr, 1991; Peterson et al., 2005).

Because many people with developmental disabilities do not acquire speech, is FCT successful if a child or adult is nonverbal? Numerous applications confirm that various augmentative and alternative communication systems can be incorporated in an intervention plan that targets problem behaviors including NSSI (O'Reilly, Cannella, Sigafoos, & Lancioni, 2006). Some of the FCT responses have been activating vocal output communication aids (Sigafoos, Arthur, & O'Reilly, 2003) and making requests with visual materials such as the Picture Exchange Communication System (Charlop-Christy, Carpenter, Le, LeBlanc, & Kellet, 2002).

Social Negative Reinforcement

Recall that social negative reinforcement operates when NSSI produces escape from a nonpreferred situation. One consequence-focused intervention is to prevent escape, otherwise known as escape extinction (E. G. Carr, Newsom, & Binkoff, 1980). Essentially, escape is not permitted by prompting a person to perform alternative behavior, blocking self-injurious responses, or restraining movement. Note that these procedures properly address behavior function, but they are not easy to implement, may provoke other problem behaviors, and necessitate at least initially, negative physical contact between the person performing NSSI and the person intervening.

A more preventive approach to escape-maintained NSSI is to manipulate conditions that provoke or set the occasion for the behavior (Luiselli, 2008; Miltenberger, 2006). Consider as an example a student's NSSI that is associated with difficult instruction in a school setting and is motivated by escape. NSSI in this context can be treated effectively by first confirming the demand features of instruction and then reducing task difficulty by presenting (a) preferred tasks (Foster-Johnson, Ferno, & Dunlap, 1994), (b) shorter duration tasks (Dunlap, Kern-Dunlap, Clarke, & Robbins, 1991), or (c) easy tasks interspersed with more difficult tasks (Kennedy, Itkonen, & Lindquist, 1995). It is also possible to decrease NSSI by altering the pace of instruction and gradually increasing the frequency of requests (instructional fading; Butler & Luiselli, 2007; Dunlap, Dyer, & Koegel, 1983; Zarcone et al., 1993). One additional strategy is to allow a student to make choices about the tasks and sequence of instruction (Romaniuk et al., 2002).

Similar to NCR described previously, noncontingent escape (NCE) has been used as an intervention for escape-maintained problem behaviors including NSSI (Butler & Luiselli, 2007; Kodak, Miltenberger, & Romaniuk, 2003; Vollmer, Marcus, & Ringdahl, 1995). NCE often begins by allowing a continuous break from low or no-demand interactions. With NSSI absent under such conditions, the duration of time before taking a break is increased progressively. Thus, an adult with NSSI in a habilitation service setting might start with a noncontingent break from vocational training sessions every 60 seconds, then every 90 seconds, 120 seconds, and so on until an acceptable break schedule is achieved. Again, like NCR, NCE is a relatively easy procedure to implement, making it attractive to practitioners in a variety of applied settings.

Most applications of NCE require a practitioner to acknowledge when a break is permitted, usually on an FT schedule. A person also can request a break from nonpreferred situations through FCT by teaching a response such as, "Can we stop now?" Person-initiated break requests typically are honored continuously and, similar to NCE, gradually delayed to promote intervention fading. For example, a child or adult accustomed to taking a break every time the request is made might be required to complete several tasks or receive instruction for a longer amount of time before a break is permitted.

Automatic Reinforcement

NSSI that is automatically reinforced occurs independent of social contingencies. Although there are several plausible explanations for high-frequency and undifferentiated NSSI within all conditions of an FA, this pattern usually suggests automatic reinforcement as the maintaining variable (Hanley et al., 2003). To address this source of control, treatment research has concentrated on procedures that either block the sensory-reinforcing effects from NSSI or provide alternative and equally preferred sensory stimulation.

Sensory extinction was introduced by Rincover and associates to eliminate automatic reinforcement produced by stereotypy and NSSI (Rincover, 1978; Rincover, Cook, Peoples, & Packard, 1979). The procedure is applied through continuous wearing of protective equipment. Relative to NSSI, examples of sensory extinction include having children with developmental disabilities wear padded helmets for head banging (Rincover & Devany, 1982), various textured gloves for skin scratching (Rincover & Devany, 1982) and eye touching (Luiselli & Waldstein, 1994), pliable plastic cuffs for wrist biting (Luiselli, 1988), and goggles for eye gouging (Tang, Patterson, & Kennedy, 2003). Although sensory extinction was piloted as a treatment procedure, it can be used in a preintervention FA to isolate the controlling effects of automatic reinforcement. Clinicians contemplating sensory extinction for NSSI should note that it may be difficult to block some types of stimulation and that wearing protective equipment could be stigmatizing and interfere with instruction. Accordingly, sensory extinction interventions must be systematically faded with the objective of gradually eliminating protective equipment while maintaining decreased NSSI (Luiselli, 1991).

Sensory extinction should not be confused with mechanical restraint in which protective equipment physically prevents a person from performing NSSI (Luiselli, 1992a). Treatment with restraint usually is reserved for intractable NSSI in which there is a high risk of tissue damage. Inducing restraint has been accomplished with devices such as a wrist immobilizer (Obi, 1997) and arm splints (Oliver, Hall, Hales, Murphy, & Watts, 1998; Zhou, Goff, & Iwata, 2000). Like sensory extinction, mechanical restraint eventually must be faded and ideally eliminated so that a person has purposeful movement and can participate meaningfully during instruction (Moore, Fisher, & Pennington, 2004; Wallace, Iwata, Zhou, & Goff, 1999). Unlike sensory extinction, mechanical restraint exerts control by preventing NSSI from occurring without purposefully attenuating sources of automatic reinforcement.

Response-blocking is another procedure that can decrease automatically reinforced NSSI (Hagopian & Adelinis, 2001; Lerman, Kelley, Vorndran, & Van Camp, 2003; Luiselli, 1992b). It consists of physically preventing a person from completing the behavior and contacting the reinforcing sensory stimulation. As an illustration, a practitioner responsible for intervention would position her or his arms in front of a person with hand-to-face slapping to stop the behavior. Although this procedure removes the purported source of reinforcement (i.e., hand-to-face tactile contact), it is possible that it is simply an aversive consequence that reduces NSSI through punishment.

Response blocking also requires continuous monitoring so that all attempts at engaging in NSSI can be prevented.

NCR treatment, reviewed with other behavior functions, also has been evaluated with automatically reinforced problem behaviors including NSSI. Treatment can be implemented by allowing a person continuous access to sensory events that are similar to the stimulation produced by the NSSI. Alternatively, stimuli can be presented noncontingently on an FT schedule. Regardless of method, it appears that treatment is most effective when NCR is matched to the identified automatic reinforcement (Piazza, Adelinis, Hanley, Goh, & Delia, 2000; Rapp, 2006; Simmons, Smith, & Kliethermes, 2003). So, if the target NSSI topography were hair pulling and the maintaining sensory consequence were manipulating hair between the fingers, a possible NCR procedure might be allowing the person to play with sensory materials that mimic strands of hair.

Problem behaviors maintained by automatic reinforcement also have been treated effectively with environmental enrichment or simply giving a person access to unmatched sensory stimuli (Ahearn, Clark, DeBar, & Florentino, 2005; Lindberg, Iwata, & Kahng, 1999; Ringdahl, Vollmer, Marcus, & Roane, 1997). Consistent with an analysis of sensory-focused NCR posited by Rapp (2007), research needs to clarify "whether reductions in automatically reinforcement behavior are attributable to stimulus competition (i.e., alternative sensory reinforcement temporarily displaces the automatic sensory reinforcer) or stimulus substitution (i.e., the preferred item generates similar or identical stimulation)" (p. 74).

CONCLUSION

This chapter reviewed NSSI among people with developmental disabilities, focusing on the discipline of ABA and the evolution of contemporary treatment procedures. Although considerable advancements in knowledge and practice have been made, much remains to be learned about NSSI and its treatment. Furthermore, intervention must continue to be informed by experimentally rigorous research that is disseminated to practitioners and service providers. This summary section considers several clinical and research recommendations.

Clinical Recommendations

First, the treatment of NSSI among people who have developmental disabilities must be implemented by natural care providers such as teachers, parents, and staff within specialized service settings. Although functional analyses and intensive treatment evaluations may be conducted initially by highly credentialed professionals having extensive clinical expertise, intervention ultimately becomes the responsibility of individuals who interact routinely with a child or adult at home, school, and the community. For this reason, treatment procedures must be practical, easily understood, and capable of being implemented with integrity. In the majority of cases, treatment is never discontinued but instead is applied for many years, often with modification, or possibly is lifelong. Despite this concern about long-term behavior support, little information is available on the course of NSSI multiple years after treatment (Bird & Luiselli, 2000; Foxx, 2003; Luiselli, Sperry, & Connolly, 2002). Put simply, it is incumbent on professionals to ensure that intervention effects on NSSI persist and sustain an improved quality of life.

Second, successful treatment of NSSI depends on FBA and FA outcomes. The design of methodologies to isolate behavior function has had a profound influence on how psychologists treat NSSI by allowing procedures to be matched to antecedent and consequence-controlling variables. Absent such assessment and analysis, treatment cannot be properly formulated. The challenge for professionals providing services to people who have developmental disabilities is to ensure that there always is preintervention FBA and FA, which can be completed efficiently within the relevant contexts in which NSSI is encountered.

Third, the social validity of behavioral treatment is another determinant of clinical success. Social validity asks whether intervention procedures and outcomes are judged to be acceptable by the people who implement them. Many treatment plans for NSSI feature multiple procedures, continuous monitoring, and detailed data collection. If these plans are too complex and difficult to apply, practitioners will view them unfavorably, possibly affecting intervention integrity. Furthermore, the desired result from treatment for NSSI must be either elimination of the behavior or significant reduction that is correlated with improved health status, skill acquisition, and personal happiness. Treatment outcome that is considered inadequate by practitioners or procedures that cannot be supported are not socially valid (Kennedy, 2002).

Fourth, some young children with developmental disabilities display "proto-injurious behavior" (Berkson & Tupa, 2002), or nonclinical topographies of NSSI that can potentially evolve into more serious disorders. Low-intensity behaviors such as stereotypic head banging, eye poking, and body hitting, which are similar to NSSI but do not produce bodily damage, are evident in children who are under age 5 and sensitive to FA manipulations (Berkson, 2002; Berkson & Tupa, 2002; Kurtz et al., 2003; Richman & Lindauer, 2005; Roane, Ringdahl, Vollmer, Whitmarsh, & Marcus, 2006). As a measure of secondary prevention, professionals should continue to evaluate procedures for identifying proto-injurious behavior in children with developmental disabilities and instituting early intervention services at critical periods.

Fifth and finally, can treatment of NSSI with people who have developmental disabilities contribute to practice guidelines with nondisabled individuals? Noteworthy are studies by Nock and Prinstein (2004, 2005) targeting NSSI among adolescent psychiatric inpatients and the association with behavior function (e.g., social positive reinforcement, social negative reinforcement, automatic reinforcement) and contextual features (e.g., thinking about hurting oneself, presence of pain, use of alcohol or drugs). Their findings revealed definitive influences on NSSI that suggest diverse treatments. For example, NSSI maintained by automatic reinforcement could be treated through affect-regulation skills training. When social positive and negative reinforcements are the source of control, therapy is directed at interpersonal and communication skills. This research demonstrates the relationship of functional assessment and analysis to treatment formulation, so much a component of behavioral intervention in the developmental disabilities, translated cogently to a different clinical population and type of NSSI. These and other collaborations between disciplines surely will advance one's knowledge about why people injure themselves and how best to care for them.

Research Recommendations

There are several research recommendations for improving evidence-based treatment of NSSI. First, most of the research reviewed in this chapter was treatment focused and conducted by behavioral psychologists using single-case experimental methodology (Barlow, Nock, & Hersen, 2008). This approach toward evaluation should continue given the unique presentation of NSSI often seen in people with developmental disabilities, the need to isolate behavior function, and the many person-specific clinical decisions that must be made to affect therapeutic change. Group comparison (nomethetic) research is less suited to these clinical foci.

Second, it has been shown that NSSI can be controlled by multiple influences (Iwata et al., 1994). NSSI that has more than one source of reinforcement can be the most difficult to treat and usually poses a more complex clinical dilemma compared with single-source control. By far, most of the current treatment research has centered on social positive reinforcement, social negative reinforcement (i.e., escape), and automatic reinforcement of NSSI. More definitive research on the treatment of multiply determined NSSI has yet to accumulate. Also, research comparing different intervention procedures would be of value.

Third, relative to treatment emphasizing the consequences of NSSI, there is less research on the effectiveness of antecedent intervention. Several of the studies cited in this chapter found that NSSI could be prevented or greatly diminished by manipulating behavior-provoking conditions. The directions for future research in this area are many. For example, are there valid and user-friendly assessment instruments that isolate antecedent contextual variables so that preventive intervention can be derived (McAtee, Carr, & Schulte, 2004)? Are various antecedent procedures successful when implemented as the only intervention, or do they have to be combined with consequence methods to be maximally effective? Finally, does antecedent intervention work best for some types of NSSI but not others?

Fourth, nonbehavioral treatment of NSSI through pharmacotherapy has increased productively in past years. Good research support exists documenting that psychotropic medications can reduce NSSI in people with developmental disabilities when prescribed properly and frequently, in conjunction with behavioral intervention (Luiselli, Blew, & Thibadeau, 2001; Sperry, Luiselli, Hauser, MaGee, & Magnifico, 2003; Stigler, Posey, & McDougle, 2002; Zarcone et al., 2001). I suggest that behavioral psychopharmacology represents fertile ground for clinical researchers. Recommended directions for such research include evaluating the comparative effects from different medications, the relationship of medication dosage to treatment outcome, and the influence of medication on FA results, as reported recently (Valdovinos, Ellringer, & Alexander, 2007; Zarcone et al., 2004).

A fifth and final recommendation is that to the extent possible, research on NSSI should be carried out under naturalistic conditions. Simulated or analogue studies are well represented in the extant literature and have been instrumental in defining experimental protocol for evaluating behavioral treatment of NSSI. However, the antecedent and consequence variables maintaining a person's NSSI may not be replicated or controlled adequately during simulated sessions. In addition, the contexts in which intervention must be implemented by practitioners and caregivers can also differ significantly from those arranged in a more artificial environment. Research will advance practice by conducting it in the real-world settings where people who have developmental disabilities live, attend school, work, and access their community.

REFERENCES

Ahearn, W. H., Clark, K. M., DeBar, R., & Florentino, C. (2005). On the role of preference in response competition. *Journal of Applied Behavior Analysis, 38,* 247–250.

Barlow, D. H., Nock, M. K., & Hersen, M. (2008). *Single-case experimental designs: Strategies for studying behavior change* (3rd ed.). Boston: Allyn & Bacon.

Berkson, G. (2002). Early development of stereotyped and self-injurious behaviors: Age trends. *American Journal on Mental Retardation, 107,* 468–477.

Berkson, G., & Tupa, M. (2002). Incidence of self-injurious behavior: Birth to 3 years. In S. R. Schroeder, M. L. Oster-Granite, & T. Thompson (Eds.), *Self-injurious behavior: Gene–brain–behavior relationships* (pp. 1–19). Washington, DC: American Psychological Association.

Bijou, S. W., Peterson, R. F., & Ault, M. H. (1968). A method to integrate descriptive and experimental field studies at the level of data and empirical concepts. *Journal of Applied Behavior Analysis, 1*, 175–191.

Bird, F., & Luiselli, J. K. (2000). Positive behavioral support of adults with developmental disabilities: Assessment of long-term adjustment and habilitation following restrictive treatment histories. *Journal of Behavior Therapy and Experimental Psychiatry, 31*, 5–19.

Butler, L. R., & Luiselli, J. K. (2007). Escape maintained problem behavior in a child with autism: Antecedent functional analysis and intervention evaluation of noncontingent escape (NCE) and instructional fading. *Journal of Positive Behavior Interventions, 9*, 195–202.

Carr, E. G. (1977). The motivation of self-injurious behavior: A review of some hypotheses. *Psychological Bulletin, 84*, 800–816.

Carr, E. G., & Blakeley-Smith, A. (2006). Classroom intervention for illness-related problem behavior in children with developmental disabilities. *Behavior Modification, 30*, 901–924.

Carr, E. G., & Durand, V. M. (1985). Reducing behavior problems through functional communication training. *Journal of Applied Behavior Analysis, 18*, 111–126.

Carr, E. G., Newsom, C. D., & Binkoff, J. A. (1980). Escape as a factor in the aggressive behavior of two retarded children. *Journal of Applied Behavior Analysis, 13*, 101–117.

Carr, E. G., & Smith, C. E. (1995). Biological setting events for self-injury. *Mental Retardation and Developmental Disabilities Research Reviews, 1*, 94–98.

Carr, E. G., Smith, C. E., Giacin, T. A., Whelan, B. M., & Pancari, J. (2003). Menstrual discomfort as a biological setting event for severe problem behavior: Assessment and intervention. *American Journal on Mental Retardation, 108*, 117–133.

Carr, J. E., & LeBlanc, L. A. (2006). Noncontingent reinforcement as antecedent behavior support. In J. K. Luiselli (Ed.), *Antecedent control: Innovative approaches to behavior support* (pp. 147–164). Baltimore: Brookes Publishing.

Cataldo, M. F., & Harris, J. C. (1982). The biological basis for self-injury in the mentally retarded. *Analysis and Intervention in Developmental Disabilities, 2*, 21–39.

Charlop-Christy, M. H., Carpenter, M., Le, L., LeBlanc, L. A., & Kellet, K. (2002). Using the Picture Exchange Communication System (PECS) with children with autism: Assessment of PECS acquisition, speech, social-communication behavior, and problem behavior. *Journal of Applied Behavior Analysis, 35*, 213–231.

Dunlap, G., Dyer, K., & Koegel, R. L. (1983). Autistic self-stimulation and inter-trial interval duration. *American Journal on Mental Deficiency, 88*, 194–202.

Dunlap, G., Kern-Dunlap, L., Clarke, S., & Robbins, F. R. (1991). Functional assessment, curricular revision, and severe problem behavior. *Journal of Applied Behavior Analysis, 24*, 387–397.

Durand, V. M., & Carr, E. G. (1991). Functional communication training to reduce challenging behavior: Maintenance and application in new settings. *Journal of Applied Behavior Analysis, 24*, 251–264.

Durand, V. M., & Crimmins, D. B. (1988). Identifying the variables maintaining self-injurious behavior. *Journal of Autism and Developmental Disorders, 18*, 99–117.

Forehand, R., & Baumeister, A. A. (1976). Deceleration of aberrant behavior among retarded individuals. In M. Hersen, R. M. Eisler, & P. M. Miller (Eds.), *Progress in behavior modification* (Vol. 2, pp. 223–278). New York: Academic Press.

Foster-Johnson, L., Ferro, J., & Dunlap, G. (1994). Preferred curricular activities and reduced problem behaviors in students with intellectual disabilities. *Journal of Applied Behavior Analysis, 27*, 493–504.

Foxx, R. M. (2003). The treatment of dangerous behavior. *Behavioral Interventions, 18*, 1–21.

Friman, P. C., & Hawkins, R. O. (2006). Contribution of establishing operations to antecedent intervention. In J. K. Luiselli (Ed.), *Antecedent control: Innovative approaches to behavior support* (pp. 31–52). Baltimore: Brookes Publishing.

Hagopian, L. P., & Adelinis, J. D. (2001). Response blocking with and without redirection for the treatment of pica. *Journal of Applied Behavior Analysis, 34*, 527–530.

Hanley, G. P., Iwata, B. A., & McCord, B. E. (2003). Functional analysis of problem behavior: A review. *Journal of Applied Behavior Analysis, 36*, 147–185.

Iwata, B. A., Dorsey, M. F., Slifer, K. J., Bauman, K. E., & Richman, G. S. (1982). Toward a functional analysis of self-injury. *Analysis and Intervention in Developmental Disabilities, 2*, 3–20.

Iwata, B. A., Pace, G. M., Dorsey, M. F., Zarcone, J. R., Vollmer, T. R., Smith, R. G., et al. (1994). The functions of self-injurious behavior: An experimental–epidemiological analysis. *Journal of Applied Behavior Analysis, 27*, 215–240.

Iwata, B. A., Wallace, M. D., Kahng, S., Lindeberg, J. S., Roscoe, E. M., Conners, J., et al. (2000). Skill acquisition in the implementation of functional analysis methodology. *Journal of Applied Behavior Analysis, 33*, 181–194.

Kahng, S., Iwata, B. A., & Lewis, A. B. (2002). Behavioral treatment of self-injury, 1964–2000. *American Journal on Mental Retardation, 107*, 212–221.

Kennedy, C. H. (2002). The maintenance of behavior change as an indicator of social validity. *Behavior Modification, 26*, 594–604.

Kennedy, C. H., & Becker, A. (2006). Health conditions in antecedent assessment and intervention of problem behavior. In J. K. Luiselli (Ed.), *Antecedent control: Innovative approaches to behavior support* (pp. 73–97). Baltimore: Brookes Publishing.

Kennedy, C. H., Itkonen, T., & Lindquist, K. (1995). Comparing interspersed requests and social comments as antecedents for increasing student compliance. *Journal of Applied Behavior Analysis, 28*, 97–98.

Kennedy, C. H., & Meyer, K. A. (1996). Sleep deprivation, allergy symptoms, and negatively reinforced problem behavior. *Journal of Applied Behavior Analysis, 29*, 133–135.

Kern, L., & Kokina, A. (in press). Using positive reinforcement to decrease challenging behavior. In J. K. Luiselli, D. C. Russo, W. P. Christian, & S. M. Wilczynski (Eds.),

Effective practices for children with autism: Educational and behavior support interventions that work. New York: Oxford University Press.

Kodak, T., Miltenberger, R. G., & Romaniuk, C. (2003). The effects of differential negative reinforcement of other behavior and noncontingent escape on compliance. *Journal of Applied Behavior Analysis, 36,* 379–382.

Kurtz, P. F., Chin, M. D., Huete, J. M., Tarbox, R. S. F., O'Connor, J. T., Paclwskji, T. R., & Rush, K. S. (2003). Functional analysis and treatment of self-injurious behavior in young children: A summary of 30 cases. *Journal of Applied Behavior Analysis, 36,* 205–219.

Lerman, D. C., Kelley, M. E., Vorndran, C. M., & Van Camp, C. M. (2003). Collateral effects of response blocking during the treatment of stereotypic behavior. *Journal of Applied Behavior Analysis, 36,* 119–123.

Lindberg, J. S., Iwata, B. A., & Kahng, S. W. (1999). On the relation between object manipulation and stereotypic self-injurious behavior. *Journal of Applied Behavior Analysis, 32,* 51–62.

Luiselli, J. K. (1988). Comparative analysis of sensory extinction treatments for self-injury. *Education and Treatment of Children, 11,* 149–156.

Luiselli, J. K. (1991). Functional assessment and treatment of self-injury in a pediatric nursing care resident. *Behavioral Residential Treatment, 6,* 311–320.

Luiselli, J. K. (1992a). Assessment and treatment of self-injury in a deaf-blind child. *Journal of Developmental and Physical Disabilities, 4,* 219–226.

Luiselli, J. K. (1992b). Protective equipment. In J. K. Luiselli, J. L. Matson, & N. N. Singh (Eds.), *Self-injurious behavior: Assessment, analysis, and treatment* (pp. 235–268). New York: Springer-Verlag.

Luiselli, J. K. (2004). Behavior support and intervention: Current issues and practices in developmental disabilities. In J. L. Matson, R. B. Laud, & M. L. Matson (Eds.), *Behavior modification for persons with developmental disabilities: Treatments and supports* (pp. 33–54). Kingston, NY: National Association for the Dually Diagnosed.

Luiselli, J. K. (2005). Stimulus control. In G. Sugai & R. Horner (Eds.), *Encyclopedia of behavior modification and cognitive behavior therapy* (pp. 1548–1552). Newbury Park, CA: Sage.

Luiselli, J. K. (2008). Antecedent (preventive) intervention for challenging behavior. In J. K. Luiselli, D. C. Russo, W. P. Christian, & S. M. Wilczynski (Eds.), *Effective practices for children with autism: Educational and behavior support interventions that work* (pp. 393–412). New York: Oxford University Press.

Luiselli, J. K., Blew, P., & Thibadeau, S. (2001). Therapeutic effects and long-term efficacy of antidepressant medication for persons with developmental disabilities. *Behavior Modification, 25,* 62–78.

Luiselli, J. K., Cochran, M. L., & Huber, S. A. (2005). Effects of otitis media on a child with autism receiving behavioral intervention for self-injury. *Child & Family Behavior Therapy, 27,* 51–56.

Luiselli, J. K., Matson, J. L., & Singh, N. N. (Eds.). (1992). *Self-injurious behavior: Assessment, analysis, and treatment.* New York: Springer-Verlag.

Luiselli, J. K., Sperry, J. M., & Connolly, N. M. (2002). Elimination of mechanical restraint, community-based behavior support, and seven-year maintenance evaluation in the treatment of a woman with mental retardation and multiple psychiatric disorders. *Mental Health Aspects of Developmental Disabilities, 5,* 69–77.

Luiselli, J. K., & Waldstein, N. (1994). Evaluation of restraint elimination interventions for students with multiple disabilities in a pediatric nursing care facility. *Behavior Modification, 18,* 352–365.

McAtee, M., Carr, E. G., & Schulte, C. (2004). A contextual assessment inventory for problem behavior. *Journal of Positive Behavior Interventions, 6,* 148–165.

Miltenberger, R. G. (2006). Antecedent interventions for challenging behaviors maintained by escape from instructional activities. In J. K. Luiselli (Ed.), *Antecedent control: Innovative approaches to behavior support* (pp. 101–124). Baltimore: Brookes Publishing.

Moore, J. W., Edwards, R. P., Sterling-Turner, H. E., Riley, J., DuBard, M., & McGeorge, A. (2002). Teacher acquisition of functional analysis methodology. *Journal of Applied Behavior Analysis, 35,* 73–77.

Moore, J. W., & Fisher, W. W. (2007). The effects of videotape modeling on staff acquisition of functional analysis methodology. *Journal of Applied Behavior Analysis, 40,* 197–202.

Moore, J. W., Fisher, W. W., & Pennington, A. (2004). Systematic application and removal of protective equipment in the assessment of multiple topographies of self-injury. *Journal of Applied Behavior Analysis, 37,* 73–77.

Nock, M. K., & Prinstein, M. J. (2004). A functional approach to the assessment of self-mutilative behavior. *Journal of Consulting and Clinical Psychology, 72,* 885–890.

Nock, M. K., & Prinstein, M. J. (2005). Contextual features and behavior functions of self-mutilation among adolescents. *Journal of Abnormal Psychology, 114,* 140–146.

Obi, C. (1997). Restraint fading and alternative management strategies to treat a man with Lesch–Nyhan syndrome over a two-year period. *Behavioral Interventions, 12,* 195–202.

Oliver, C., Hall, S., Hales, J., Murphy, G., & Watts, D. (1998). The treatment of self-injurious behavior by the systematic fading of restraints: Effects on self-injury, self-restraint, adaptive behavior, and behavioral correlates of affect. *Research in Developmental Disabilities, 19,* 143–165.

Oliver, C., Murphy, G. H., & Corbett, J. A. (1987). Self-injurious behavior in people with mental handicap: A total population study. *Journal of Mental Deficiency Research, 31,* 147–162.

O'Neill, R. E., Horner, R. H., Albin, R. W., Sprague, J. R., Storey, K., & Newton, J. S. (1997). *Functional assessment and program development for problem behavior: A practical handbook.* Pacific Grove, CA: Brooks/Cole.

O'Reilly, M. F. (1997). Functional analysis of episodic self-injury correlated with recurrent otitis media. *Journal of Applied Behavior Analysis, 30,* 165–167.

O'Reilly, M. F., Cannella, H. I., Sigafoos, J., & Lancioni, G. (2006). Communication and social skills interventions. In J. K. Luiselli (Ed.), *Antecedent control: Innovative approaches to behavior support* (pp. 187–206). Baltimore: Brookes Publishing.

Pace, G. M., Ivancic, M. T., Edwards, G. L., Iwata, B. A., & Page, T. J. (1985). Assessment of stimulus preference and reinforcer value with profoundly retarded individuals. *Journal of Applied Behavior Analysis, 18,* 249–255.

Peterson, S. M., Caniglia, C., Royster, A. J., Macfarlane, E., Plowman, K., Baird, S. J., & Wu, N. (2005). Blending functional communication training and choice making to improve task engagement and decrease problem behavior. *Educational Psychology, 25,* 257–274.

Piazza, C. C., Adelinis, J. D., Hanley, G. P., Goh, H. L., & Delia, M. D. (2000). An evaluation of the effects of matched stimuli on behaviors maintained by automatic reinforcement. *Journal of Applied Behavior Analysis, 33,* 13–27.

Rapp, J. T. (2006). Toward an empirical method for identifying matched stimulation: A preliminary investigation. *Journal of Applied Behavior Analysis, 39,* 137–140.

Rapp, J. T. (2007). Further evaluation of methods to identify matched stimulation. *Journal of Applied Behavior Analysis, 40,* 73–88.

Richman, D. M., & Lindauer, S. E. (2005). Longitudinal assessment of stereotypic, proto-injurious, and self-injurious behavior exhibited by young children with developmental delays. *American Journal of Mental Retardation, 110,* 439–450.

Rincover, A. (1978). Sensory extinction: A procedure for eliminating self-stimulatory behavior in developmentally disabled children. *Journal of Abnormal Child Psychology, 6,* 299–310.

Rincover, A., Cook, A. R., Peoples, A., & Packard, D. (1979). Sensory extinction and sensory reinforcement principles for programming multiple adaptive behavior change. *Journal of Applied Behavior Analysis, 12,* 221–233.

Rincover, A., & Devany, J. (1982). The application of sensory extinction to self-injury. *Analysis and Intervention in Developmental Disabilities, 2,* 67–82.

Ringdahl, J. E., Vollmer, T. R., Marcus, B. A., & Roane, H. S. (1997). An analogue evaluation of environmental enrichment: The role of stimulus preference. *Journal of Applied Behavior Analysis, 30,* 203–216.

Roane, H. S., Ringdahl, J. E., Vollmer, T. R., Whitmarsh, E. L., & Marcus, B. A. (2006). A preliminary description of the occurrence of proto-injurious behavior in typically developing children. *Journal of Early Intensive Behavior Intervention, 3,* 334–347.

Romaniuk, C., Miltenberger, R. G., Conyers, C., Jenner, N., Jurgens, M., & Rigenberg, C. (2002). The influence of activity choice on behavior problems maintained by escape versus attention. *Journal of Applied Behavior Analysis, 35,* 349–362.

Schroeder, S. R., Schroeder, C. S., Smith, B., & Dalldorf, J. (1978). Prevalence of self-injurious behaviors in a large state facility for the retarded: A three-year follow-up study. *Journal of Autism and Childhood Schizophrenia, 8,* 261–269.

Sigafoos, J., Arthur, M., & O'Reilly, M. F. (2003). Effects of speech output on maintenance of requesting and frequency of vocalizations in three children with developmental disabilities. *Augmentative and Alternative Communication, 19*, 37–47.

Simmons, J. N., Smith, R. G., & Kliethermes, L. (2003). A multiple-schedule evaluation of immediate and subsequent effects of fixed-time food presentation on automatically maintained mouthing. *Journal of Applied Behavior Analysis, 36*, 541–544.

Skinner, B. F. (1948). "Superstition" in the pigeon. *Journal of Experimental Psychology, 38*, 168–172.

Sperry, J. M., Luiselli, J. K., Hauser, M. J., MaGee, C. M., & Magnifico, M. (2003). Treatment effects of paroxetine on disruptive and self-harming behaviors associated with polyuria in an adult with mental retardation, autism, and obsessive compulsive disorder. *NADD Bulletin, 6*, 47–52.

Stigler, K. A., Posey, D. J., & McDougle, C. J. (2002). Recent advances in the pharmacotherapy of autism. *Expert Review of Neurotherapeutics, 2*, 499–510.

Tang, J., Patterson, T. G., & Kennedy, C. H. (2003). Identifying specific sensory modalities maintaining the stereotypy of students with multiple profound disabilities. *Research in Developmental Disabilities, 24*, 433–451.

Tate, B. G., & Baroff, G. S. (1966). Aversive control of self-injurious behavior in a psychotic boy. *Behaviour Research and Therapy, 4*, 281–287.

Touchette, P. E., MacDonald, R. F., & Langer, S. N. (1985). A scatter plot for identifying stimulus control of problem behavior. *Journal of Applied Behavior Analysis, 18*, 343–351.

Valdovinos, M. G., Ellringer, N. P., & Alexander, M. L. (2007). Changes in the rate of problem behavior associated with the discontinuation of the antipsychotic medication quetiapine. *Mental Health Aspects of Developmental Disabilities, 10*, 64–67.

Vollmer, T. R., Iwata, B. A., Zarcone, J. R., Smith, R. G., & Mazaleski, J. L. (1993). The role of attention in the treatment of attention-maintained self-injurious behavior: Noncontingent reinforcement and differential reinforcement of other behavior. *Journal of Applied Behavioral Analysis, 26*, 9–21.

Vollmer, T. R., Iwata, B. A., Zarcone, J. R., Smith, R. G., & Mazaleski, J. L. (2002). Within-session patterns of self-injury as indicators of behavioral function. *Research in Developmental Disabilities, 14*, 479–492.

Vollmer, T. R., Marcus, B. A., & Ringdahl, J. E. (1995). Noncontingent escape as treatment for self-injurious behavior maintained by negative reinforcement. *Journal of Applied Behavior Analysis, 28*, 15–26.

Wallace, M. D., Iwata, B. A., Zhou, L., & Goff, G. A. (1999). Rapid assessment of the effects of restraint on self-injury and adaptive behavior. *Journal of Applied Behavior Analysis, 32*, 525–528.

Zarcone, J. R., Hellings, J. A., Crandall, K., Reese, R. M., Marquis, J., Fleming, K., et al. (2001). Effects of risperidone on aberrant behavior of persons with developmental disabilities: I. Double-blind crossover study using multiple measures. *American Journal on Mental Retardation, 106*, 525–538.

Zarcone, J. R., Iwata, B. A., Vollmer, T. A., Jagtiani, S., Smith, R. G., & Mazaleski, J. L. (1993). Extinction of self-injurious escape behavior with and without instructional fading. *Journal of Applied Behavior Analysis, 26*, 353–360.

Zarcone, J. R., Lindauer, S. E., Morse, P. S., Crosland, K. A., Valdovinos, M. G., McKerchar, T. L., et al. (2004). Effects of risperidone on destructive behavior of persons with developmental disabilities: III. Functional analysis. *American Journal of Mental Retardation, 109*, 310–321.

Zhou, L., Goff, G. A., & Iwata, B. A. (2000). Effects of increased response effort on self-injury and object manipulation as competing responses. *Journal of Applied Behavior Analysis, 33*, 29–40.

III

WHAT ARE THE MOST EFFECTIVE WAYS TO ASSESS AND TREAT NONSUICIDAL SELF-INJURY?

10

ASSESSMENT OF NONSUICIDAL SELF-INJURY

E. DAVID KLONSKY AND ANNA WEINBERG

Accurate and thorough assessment is important in both clinical and research settings. Clinically, assessments are the basis for case conceptualization and treatment planning. In research contexts, assessments are necessary to determine the prevalence, correlates, longitudinal trajectory, or other features of the variables being studied. In this chapter, we address the assessment of nonsuicidal self-injury (NSSI). We present recommendations for interacting with individuals being assessed, identify the domains that should be targeted for assessment, and describe the properties of questionnaires and interviews that have been developed to assess NSSI.

THE ASSESSOR'S DEMEANOR

Assessing NSSI presents unique challenges. Many who are unfamiliar with NSSI may experience negative reactions to the behavior, such as shock, disgust, or blame. Some may therefore have to manage their own reactions while conducting the assessment. In addition, many who engage in NSSI are aware that the behavior can elicit negative reactions and attributions from others. Thus, establishing and maintaining a good rapport is essential for a thorough and accurate assessment. Otherwise, the individual being assessed may withhold or alter information about NSSI.

Barry Walsh (2007), a leading figure in the study and treatment of NSSI, has suggested using a "low-key, dispassionate demeanor" (p. 1060) when assessing and treating NSSI. An interview style that indicates negative feelings about NSSI, or perhaps even a heightened interest in the behavior, may be off-putting to the individual being assessed. Conversely, expressions of support might be taken to condone or encourage the behavior. A low-key, dispassionate stance may represent a useful middle ground. Kettlewell (1999) recommended a tone that conveys a "respectful curiosity," a sentiment echoed by Walsh (2006, 2007). From this perspective, the assessor conveys a genuine interest in understanding an individual's history and experience of NSSI while maintaining a nonjudgmental, deferential demeanor.

DOMAINS OF INTEREST

Nonsuicidal self injury is a complex and multidimensional construct. In order to fully understand it, it is important to assess multiple domains, including but not limited to the history of NSSI, the context, and the functions. Information about each of these domains should prove useful in case conceptualization and treatment planning.

History of Nonsuicidal Self-Injury

Many aspects of NSSI are useful to assess for clinical or research purposes. Most assessments begin with a history of NSSI. This includes methods of NSSI used (e.g., cutting, burning, scratching, hitting), the frequency of the behavior, the locations of the injuries on the body (e.g., arms, shoulders, thighs, stomach), age of onset, and time of most recent instance. It is also important to asses the medical severity of the injuries, such as the extent of bleeding or bruising (if any), how often the injuries have to be bandaged, how often professional medical attention has been required (e.g., stitches, burn treatment), and how often NSSI caused more tissue damage than intended. In addition, questions can address the duration and number of wounds per NSSI episode. As with all domains, it is useful to inquire about both "typical" instances of NSSI and "recent" instances.

Context

A second domain of interest is the context in which NSSI occurs. There are many types of contextual variables: environmental, cognitive, affective, and biological. Understanding the context in which NSSI occurs can help identify the variables that prompt and encourage the behavior.

Environment

Environmental factors refer to events in the individual's environment that precede, accompany, or follow NSSI. Events related to friends, family, significant others, work, and school can all relate to NSSI in important ways. For example, NSSI may follow poor performance on an exam or in a fight with a close friend or romantic partner; NSSI may be performed alone and in secret, or by two or more friends together in the school bathroom; NSSI may be followed by either positive or negative reactions by loved ones. A thorough assessment of the environmental context is important for understanding how NSSI operates for a given individual.

Cognitions

Cognitions refer to thoughts one might have before, during, or after NSSI. As for environmental variables, there are an infinite number of cognitions that may be part of the context in which NSSI occurs. Examples include "Nobody likes me"; "Nothing will help me feel better except NSSI"; "If I self-injure my boyfriend/girlfriend won't leave me"; "NSSI will show my parents that my problems are real"; "If I self-injure, I won't have to do my homework"; and "I wonder whether this will hurt?" The thoughts one has about NSSI influence the likelihood that the behavior will continue.

Affect

Affect refers to the emotions or feelings one might have before, during, or after NSSI. Understanding these feelings is vital for understanding one's motivations for NSSI (Klonsky, 2007). Key feelings to assess include anger (at both oneself and others), anxiety, sadness, frustration, guilt, shame, disgust, emptiness, hopelessness, and loneliness. At least some of these are likely to accompany NSSI. Some feelings, such as shame and guilt, may both prompt and result from NSSI. It is also important to assess feelings such as calm, relief, and satisfaction, because these may occur after or as a result of NSSI. Finally, some individuals may feel suicidal before or after NSSI, and it is important to determine the extent to which NSSI occurs in the context of suicidal thoughts.

Biological Factors

Many types of biological variables help form the context for NSSI. Substances such as alcohol, marijuana, heroin, cocaine, and MDMA (i.e.,

3,4-methylenedioxy-*N*-methylamphetamine)—among many others—may lower one's inhibitions for NSSI and mask the pain of NSSI, potentially leading to greater tissue damage. Other biological variables to consider include insomnia, fatigue, illness, and premenstrual syndrome. These factors may increase vulnerability to stress and thereby increase the likelihood that NSSI will occur.

Functions

Although contextual variables help illuminate the functions served by NSSI, it is also important to assess functions directly. Broadly speaking, there are two types of functions to assess: automatic and social (Glenn & Klonsky, 2007; Nock & Prinstein, 2004, 2005). *Automatic* refers to reinforcement by oneself (e.g., NSSI is performed to stop bad feelings). *Social* refers to reinforcement by others (e.g., NSSI is performed to influence and elicit desired behaviors from others).

Many discrete functions have also been identified that are worthy of assessment (Klonsky, 2007). Functions that might fall within the category of automatic reinforcement include affect regulation (i.e., alleviating acute negative emotions or emotional pressure), self-punishment (i.e., directing anger or punishment at oneself), antidissociation (i.e., interrupting periods of depersonalization or dissociation), and antisuicide (i.e., avoiding or coping with suicidal thoughts). Functions that might fall within the category of social reinforcement include interpersonal influence (i.e., shaping others' behavior), peer bonding (i.e., developing or strengthening attachments with friends), and autonomy (i.e., asserting one's independence from others). In clinical contexts, accurate assessment of functions is extremely useful for case conceptualization and treatment planning. Measures useful for assessing functions are described later in the chapter.

Other Domains of Interest

Other features of NSSI also warrant assessment. Individuals vary in how much pain is experienced during NSSI. Those who experience little pain may be at risk of causing more severe tissue damage and of attempting suicide (Nock, Joiner, Gordon, Lloyd-Richardson, & Prinstein, 2006). In addition, individuals vary in how much time elapses between the urge to self-injure and the actual NSSI. Some self-injure almost immediately following the urge, whereas others may typically wait more than an hour (Klonsky & Olino, 2007). This variable might be especially relevant to assess in treatment contexts because more time between NSSI urges and episodes affords more opportunities to implement strategies to avoid NSSI. Finally, it is useful to assess the implement with which NSSI is performed. Some individuals use the same implement each time (e.g., a pocket knife kept in the top drawer of a nightstand), whereas others may use whatever happens to be accessible (e.g., paper clip, scissors, fingernail, kitchen knife). This information, too, may be particularly useful in treatment contexts because removing access to the means of NSSI can help reduce the occurrence of NSSI (Klonsky & Glenn, 2008).

ASSESSMENT INSTRUMENTS

Although there is general agreement regarding the importance of assessing the domains described in the previous section, methods of conducting the assessment are less straightforward. Only a handful of NSSI measures have been developed, and their psychometric properties are not as well established as those for measures of suicidality. We describe four types of instruments: omnibus, functional, behavioral, and brief. The psychometric properties of each instrument are presented in Table 10.1, and the scope of assessment of each instrument appears in Table 10.2.

Omnibus Measures

We first describe omnibus measures of NSSI. These instruments assess a variety of NSSI domains and are the most comprehensive instruments available, although they do not necessarily assess each and every domain relevant to NSSI. Two instruments stand out in terms of comprehensiveness and psychometric properties.

The first is the Suicide Attempt Self-Injury Interview (SASII; Linehan, Comtois, Brown, Heard, & Wagner, 2006), a 31-item structured interview. Although the SASII assesses all nonfatal acts in which an individual deliberately causes self-injury, it makes a clear distinction between acts with and without suicidal intent and includes good coverage of NSSI. For each separate self-injurious episode endorsed by the respondent, the SASII evaluates the context, frequency, lethality, topography, intent and outcome expectations, resulting physical condition, medical treatment received, antecedent events, planning and preparation, contextual and behavioral factors, and functional outcomes.

Among the strengths of the SASII is the detailed account of each self-injurious act endorsed by the respondent. This level of detail, however, can also render the measure time-consuming in individuals with an extensive history of self-injurious behaviors, and in instances in which economy is a factor, a standard short form is available, as is a computerized scoring version. The SASII was developed on psychiatric inpatients, emergency room admits, and women meeting assessment criteria for borderline personality disorder

TABLE 10.1
Psychometric Properties of Instruments for Assessing Nonsuicidal Self-Injury

Instrument	Internal consistency	Interrater reliability	Test–retest reliability	Content validity	Construct validity	Validity generalization	Treatment sensitivity	Clinical utility	Highly recommended
Omnibus									
SASII	G	E	E	G	G	A	G	G	X
SITBI	N/A	E	A	G	G	G	U	A	X
SBQ	G	N/A	A	U	G	A	A	G	
SHBQ	G	N/A	A	A	G	I	U	A	
Functional									
FASM	A	N/A	U	A	A	G	U	A	
ISAS	E	N/A	U	G	A	U	U	A	
SIQ	G	N/A	A	A	G	A	U	A	
SIMS	G	N/A	U	A	A	A	U	A	
FAST	E	N/A	G	A	G	G	U	A	
Behavioral									
DSHI	G	N/A	G	A	A	A	U	A	
SHI	A	N/A	U	A	G	A	U	A	
Brief									
SNAP	G	N/A	N/A	A	G	G	U	G	
TSI	G	N/A	U	A	G	G	U	G	
SCID-OCSD	G	U	U	U	U	U	U	G	

Note. Some information in this table is derived from Nock, Wedig, Janis, and Deliberto (2008). SASII = Suicide Attempt Self-Injury Interview; G = good; E = excellent; A = adequate; SITBI = Self-Injurious Thoughts and Behaviors Interview; U = unavailable; SBQ = Suicidal Behaviors Questionnaire; SHBQ = Self-Harm Behavior Questionnaire; I = inadequate; FASM = Functional Assessment of Self-Mutilation; ISAS = Inventory of Statements About Self-Injury; SIQ = Self-Injury Questionnaire; SIMS = Self-Injury Motivation Scale; FAST = Firestone Assessment of Self-Destructive Thoughts; DSHI = Deliberate Self-Harm Inventory; SHI = Self-Harm Inventory; SNAP = Schedule for Nonadaptive and Adaptive Personality; TSI = Trauma Symptom Inventory; SCID-OCSD = Structured Clinical Interview for Obsessive–Compulsive Spectrum Disorders.

TABLE 10.2

Scope of Instruments for Assessing Nonsuicidal Self-Injury (NSSI)

Instrument	Type	No. items	Topography	Frequency	Lethality	Intent/ functions	History of NSSI	History of suicidality
				Omnibus				
SASII	SI	31	Y	Y	Y	Y	Y	Y
SITBI	SI	169	Y	Y	Y	Y	Y	Y
SBQ	SR	90	Y	Y	N	Y	Y	Y
SHBQ	SR	32	Y	Y	Y	N	Y	Y
				Functional				
FASM	SR	22	Y	Y	Y	Y	Y	N
ISAS	SR	39	Y	Y	N	Y	Y	N
SIQ	SR	30	Y	Y	Y	Y	Y	Y
SIMS	SR	35	N	N	N	Y	N	N
FAST	SR	84	N	N	N	Y	N	N
				Behavioral				
DSHI	SR	17	Y	Y	Y	N	Y	N
SHI	SR	22	Y	Y	Y	N	Y	N
				Brief				
SNAP	SR	375	N	N	N	N	Y	Y
TSI	SR	100	N	Y	N	N	Y	N
SCID-OCSD	SI	U	Y	Y	N	N	Y	N

Note. SASII = Suicide Attempt Self-Injury Interview; SI = structured interview; Y = yes; SITBI = Self-Injurious Thoughts and Behaviors Interview; SBQ = Suicidal Behaviors Questionnaire; SR = self-report; N = no; SHBQ = Self-Harm Behavior Questionnaire; FASM = Functional Assessment of Self-Mutilation; ISAS = Inventory of Statements About Self-Injury; SIQ = Self-Injury Questionnaire; SIMS = Self-Injury Motivation Scale; FAST = Firestone Assessment of Self-Destructive Thoughts; DSHI = Deliberate Self-Harm Inventory; SHI = Self-Harm Inventory; SNAP = Schedule for Nonadaptive and Adaptive Personality; TSI = Trauma Symptom Inventory; SCID-OCSD = Structured Clinical Interview for Obsessive–Compulsive Spectrum Disorders; U = unknown.

(BPD; Linehan et al., 2006) and has primarily been used among female BPD populations (Brown, Comtois, & Linehan, 2002; Koons et al., 2001; Linehan, Armstrong, Suarez, Allmon, & Heard, 1991; Linehan, Heard, & Armstrong, 1993). The measure has excellent interrater reliability and adequate validity (Linehan et al., 2006). The scale is not intended, however, to predict future behavior or assess risk but rather to evaluate past behaviors.

The second highly recommended instrument is the Self-Injurious Thoughts and Behaviors Interview (SITBI; Nock, Holmberg, Photos, & Michel, 2006). The SITBI is a 169-item (short form = 72 items) structured interview that assesses the topography, frequency and presence of suicide plans, ideation, gestures and attempts, as well as both thoughts of NSSI and instances of NSSI. The SITBI defines *NSSI* as any deliberate self-harm without the desire to die and, like the SASII, devotes separate and detailed modules to assessment of these behaviors. The instrument evaluates methods, age of onset, frequency, functions, severity, precipitants, concurrent consumption of drugs or alcohol, medical treatment, social influences, impulsivity, and respondent's estimated likelihood of future occurrence of NSSI. The SITBI can be administered by well-trained and well-supervised bachelor's-level personnel and can be completed within 3 to 15 minutes.

In addition to the standard version, the SITBI is also available in a parental-report version. Although the SITBI is currently being used in clinical and research settings, it has thus far been evaluated on only a single sample of adolescents and young adults and so requires further examination in other populations. In the initial study, interrater reliability was excellent, and test–retest reliability was good to excellent depending on the domain assessed. Construct validity was verified by demonstrating convergence between the SITBI and several other measures of NSSI and suicidality.

Two other omnibus measures of NSSI also warrant mention. The Suicidal Behaviors Questionnaire (SBQ; Linehan, 1981), is a 90-item self-report measure that, in addition to past and predicted future instances of NSSI (defined as intentional self-harm with no intent to die), assesses past and future suicide ideation, attempts, and gestures. Along with method, frequency, and intent of each self-injurious act, the SBQ also includes 55 items assessing the individual's understood reasons for self-injurious behaviors and as such is an excellent measure for assessing the functional value of NSSI. The SBQ has demonstrated reliability and validity in hospital settings (Linehan, Camper, Chiles, Strosahl, & Shearin, 1987; Linehan, Chiles, Egan, Devine, & Laffaw, 1986). Two abbreviated versions of the SBQ (Cole, 1988; Linehan, 1996) and one interview-administered version (Suicidal Behaviors Interview; Ivanoff & Jang, 1991) have also been used among psychiatric outpatients, college students, nonclinical populations, and prison inmates (Addis & Linehan, 1989; Cotton, Peters, & Range, 1995; Ivanoff & Jang, 1991; Sabo, Gunderson, Najavits, Chauncey, & Kisiel, 1995).

The Self-Harm Behavior Questionnaire (SHBQ; Gutierrez, Osman, Barrois, & Kopper, 2001) is a 32-item self-report questionnaire that examines suicidal behaviors, ideation, attempts, and gestures, as well as risk-taking behaviors and NSSI. In the SHBQ, NSSI is defined as intentional self-harm lacking suicidal intent (i.e., "non-lethal suicide-related behavior"; Gutierrez, Osman, Barrois, & Kopper, 2001, p. 477), but NSSI is considered primarily as a precursor to and predictor of future suicidal ideation and attempts. Within the NSSI module of the SHBQ, method, frequency, age of onset, most recent occurrence, lethality, and medical outcome of self-injury are also assessed. The SHBQ has good interrater reliability, internal consistency, and convergent validity with other measures of suicide-related behaviors and has been translated into German (Fliege et al., 2006); however, it has yet to be tested on English-speaking clinical populations.

Functional Measures

Some measures have been developed specifically to assess functions of or motivations for NSSI. The Functional Assessment of Self-Mutilation (FASM; Lloyd, Kelley, & Hope, 1997) is a self-report measure that defines NSSI as deliberate damage to body tissue that is not suicidal in its intent and assesses the presence of NSSI such as cutting/carving, burning, scraping skin to draw blood, hitting self on purpose, and pulling out hair. In addition to method, frequency, age-of-onset, and history of NSSI are also assessed. The FASM is distinctive among these measures in the attention paid to functions of self-injury: The measure captures 22 possible reasons for self-injurious behaviors (e.g., "to stop bad feelings," "to punish yourself," "to feel relaxed," "to be like someone you respect") and provides additional free-response space for unlisted reasons. These reasons can be understood within a four-factor functional model: automatic negative reinforcement, automatic positive reinforcement, social negative reinforcement, and social positive reinforcement (Lloyd-Richardson, Perrine, Dierker, & Kelley, 2007; Nock & Prinstein, 2004, 2005). The FASM has adequate internal consistency (Lloyd et al., 1997) and has been tested in normative samples (Lloyd et al., 1997), clinical samples (Guertin, Lloyd-Richardson, Spirito, Donaldson, & Boergers, 2001), incarcerated youth (Penn, Esposito, Schaeffer, Fritz, & Spirito, 2003), and adolescents (Lloyd-Richardson et al., 2007; Nock & Prinstein, 2004, 2005).

The Inventory of Statements About Self-Injury (ISAS; Glenn & Klonsky, 2007; Klonsky & Glenn, in press; Klonsky & Olino, 2008) is a newer measure designed to assess motivations as comprehensively as possible. It was developed on the basis of a comprehensive literature review on NSSI functions (Klonsky, 2007). It measures each of the functions identified in the review (e.g., affect regulation, self-punishment, interpersonal influence) plus several others (e.g., peer bonding). Each function on the ISAS is assessed by three items. Participants rate how well items complete the phrase, "When I harm myself, I am. . . ." Examples of items and the functions they assess are the following: "calming myself down" (i.e., affect regulation), "punishing myself" (i.e., self-punishment), "seeking care or help from others" (i.e., interpersonal influence), and "fitting in with others" (i.e., peer bonding). Participants rate each item on a 3-point scale as *very relevant, somewhat relevant,* or *not relevant.* The questionnaire takes approximately 8 minutes to complete.

An exploratory factor analysis with promax rotation revealed two superordinate factors that were consistent with previous research (Nock & Prinstein, 2004). The first factor (eigenvalue = 3.5) represents socially reinforcing functions (i.e., interpersonal influence, peer bonding, sensation seeking, and interpersonal boundaries). The second factor (eigenvalue = 1.4) represents automatically reinforcing functions (i.e., affect regulation, self-punishment, antisuicide, and antidissociation). These were the only two factors with eigenvalues greater than 1. Inspection of the scree plot also indicated that two factors should be retained. The two-factor solution accounted for 61% of the variance and displayed excellent internal consistency (Klonsky & Glenn, in press). Regarding construct validity, the two factors correlated in expected ways with key clinical variables (Glenn & Klonsky, 2007; Klonsky & Glenn, in press). We recommend this questionnaire because it is comprehensive and has a robust, theoretically sound factor structure; however, because its psychometric properties are based on a single, large college sample, further work is necessary to ensure the validity and utility of the ISAS for other populations.

The Self-Injury Questionnaire (SIQ; Santa Mina et al., 2006) is a 30-item self-report instrument designed specifically to capture the varying intentions underlying self-injurious behaviors (both suicidal and nonsuicidal in nature). The SIQ measures intentions for each method of self-injury across four subscales: "Body Alterations, Indirect Self-Harm, Failure to Care for Self, and Overt Self-Injury" (Santa Mina et al., 2006, p. 222). Each instance of self-injurious behavior is also measured by frequency, type, and function, as well as its association to childhood trauma history. The SIQ was developed with a nonclinical population and shows strong internal consistency and good construct validity.

The Self-Injury Motivation Scale (SIMS; Osuch, Noll, & Putnam, 1999) is a 35-item self-report questionnaire assessing motivations for NSSI. A factor analysis yielded six motivation factors: modulating affect (e.g., "to decrease feelings of rage"), inflicting self-punishment (e.g., "to remind myself that I deserve to be hurt or punished"), influencing others (e.g., "to seek support or caring from others"), self-stimulation (e.g., "to experience a 'high' that feels like a drug high"), and two less interpretable factors labeled by the authors as "desolation" and "magical control." The SIMS demonstrated good reliability and validity in the original study sample of 99 psychiatric patients, as well as in a sample of adolescents who cut their skin (Kumar, Pepe, & Steer, 2004).

The Firestone Assessment of Self-Destructive Thoughts (FAST; Firestone & Firestone, 1996) is an 84-item self-report questionnaire that assesses 11 levels of self-destructive thoughts, although it does not capture behaviors. Thought subtypes include "self-denial," "self-contempt," "suicide plan," and "suicide injunction," and the frequency of each is measured. The FAST does not assess functions as explicitly as other measures in this section but does illuminate some of the thoughts that could motivate NSSI. The FAST has been used in clinical and nonclinical populations (Firestone & Firestone, 1996) and shows high test–retest reliability, internal consistency, and internal reliability (Firestone & Firestone, 1998).

Behavioral Measures

Behavioral measures are those that assess a history of various NSSI behaviors with little additional detail. Such measures are most useful for determining which and how often NSSI behaviors have been performed.

Gratz's (2001) Deliberate Self-Harm Inventory (DSHI) is a 17-item self-report behaviorally based measure designed to capture exclusively NSSI, in which NSSI is defined as "deliberate, direct destruction or alteration of body tissue without conscious suicidal intent, but resulting in injury severe enough for tissue damage to occur" (p. 253). The DSHI assesses 16 specific NSSI behaviors (and one "Other" category specified by respondent) for history, age of onset, frequency and severity, and includes commonly occurring behaviors such as skin cutting, skin carving, and intentional bruising. Two newer versions are also in development to allow for assessment of change in behaviors over time. The DSHI was developed in a population of college students (Gratz, 2001) and has shown high internal consistency; adequate convergent, construct, and discriminant validity; and adequate test–retest reliability over a maximum period of 4 weeks. A German version (Fliege et al., 2006) has also shown good internal consistency and high test–retest reliability. A slightly modified Swedish version of this measure (Lundh, Karim, & Quilisch, 2007) has also been developed.

The Self-Harm Inventory (SHI; Sansone, Wiederman, & Sansone, 1998), a 22-item yes–no self-report questionnaire, takes as its definition of self-harm intentionally self-destructive behaviors. Because the SHI does not assess intent to die, however, it is difficult to distinguish suicide-related self-injury from NSSI. However, the 22 items on the measure assess history, frequency, and method of commonly occurring self-injurious behaviors in questions such as, "Have you ever, intentionally, or on purpose: Cut yourself on purpose? Burned yourself on purpose? Set yourself up in a relationship to be rejected?" A single open-ended response at the end provides coverage for any forms of self-injury not captured by the 22 items assessed.

The SHI was developed for use in both clinical (Sansone, Fine, & Nunn, 1994; Sansone, Gage, & Wiederman, 1998; Sansone, Sansone, &

Morris, 1996) and nonclinical (Sansone, Wiederman, & Sansone, 1998; Sansone, Wiederman, Sansone, & Touchet, 1998; Wiederman, Sansone, & Sansone, 1998) populations and has been translated into German and Dutch. The measure demonstrates adequate convergent validity with measures of depression (Sansone, Wiederman, Sansone, & Touchet, 1998), BPD (Sansone, Gage, & Wiederman, 1998), and history of childhood abuse (Sansone, Wiederman, & Sansone, 1996).

Brief Measures

The measures in this section are those developed to measure constructs other than NSSI but that include items that may be useful for a brief assessment or screening. The Schedule for Nonadaptive and Adaptive Personality (Clark, 1996) is a clinically validated 375-item self-report questionnaire intended primarily to assess trait dimensions in personality pathology. Two items in the instrument (i.e., "When I get very tense, hurting myself physically somehow calms me down" and "I have hurt myself on purpose several times") capture self-injurious behavior. Neither item, however, discriminates between suicidal and NSSI.

The Trauma Symptom Inventory (Briere, 1995), a 100-item self-report questionnaire, with demonstrated reliability and validity in clinical samples, was designed initially to measure specific symptoms of trauma. A single item (asking respondents to rate the frequency with which they have engaged in "intentionally hurting yourself [e.g., by scratching, cutting or burning] even though you weren't trying to commit suicide") captures nonspecific NSSI, but clinicians and researchers seeking to clarify relationships between childhood trauma and occurrence of self-injury may find this scale of interest.

Finally, the Structured Clinical Interview for Obsessive–Compulsive Spectrum Disorders (SCID-OCSD; du Toit, van Kradenburg, Niehaus, & Stein, 2001), a clinician-administered interview consisting of nine modular subscales, captures compulsive self-injurious behaviors (i.e., skin picking, trichotillomania) in the context of obsessive–compulsive spectrum disorders. Although the SCID-OCSD has been used for clinical assessment and research purposes and has demonstrated high internal consistency, its other psychometric properties have yet to be verified.

CONCLUSION

Accurate and thorough assessment of NSSI is important in both research and treatment contexts. Questions about NSSI should be communicated with respectful curiosity and in a low-key, dispassionate demeanor. The assessment should target the history of NSSI (including methods, frequency, age of onset, most recent episode, and medical severity), the context in which NSSI occurs (including environmental, cognitive, affective, and biological factors), and the functions of NSSI (including both automatic and social functions). Relatively few instruments of NSSI have been developed. Two psychometrically sound and comprehensive options are the SASII (Linehan et al., 2006) and the SITBI (Nock et al., 2006). Regarding functions of NSSI, the FASM offers the most established psychometric properties; however, the ISAS (Glenn & Klonsky, 2007; Klonsky & Glenn, 2008; Klonsky & Olino, 2007) may represent the most comprehensive instrument. The field would benefit from the continued development and validation of NSSI measures.

Clinical Recommendations

When assessing NSSI, it is advised that the clinician maintain a nonjudgmental, dispassionate demeanor while conveying respectful curiosity about the individual's history and experience of NSSI. In addition, it is important to determine the individual's history of NSSI, including the methods, contexts, environments, thoughts, emotions, biological factors, and functions associated with behavior. Two omnibus assessment measures are particularly helpful for both clinical and research purposes and are therefore highly recommended: Linehan's SASII (Linehan et al., 2006) and Nock's SITBI (Nock et al., 2006).

Research Recommendations

For instances in which NSSI rather than suicide is a primary interest, it will be useful to develop more measures or refine existing measures such that nonfatal acts with an intent to die are more explicitly discriminated from those in which no such intent is present. The development of assessment measures that better capture change over time (and as a result of therapy) is also recommended. Finally, many of the existing assessment measures have as yet been tested on only a few populations. For the purposes of greater generalizability, further research using these tools with a broader spectrum of populations is recommended.

REFERENCES

Addis, M., & Linehan, M. M. (1989, November). *Predicting suicidal behavior: Psychometric properties of the suicidal behaviors questionnaire*. Poster presented at the Association for the Advancement of Behavior Therapy Annual Meeting, Washington, DC.

Briere, J. (1995). *Trauma Symptom Inventory (TSI) professional manual*. Lutz, FL: Psychological Assessment Resources.

Brown, M. Z., Comtois, K. A., & Linehan, M. M. (2002). Reasons for suicide attempts and nonsuicidal self-injury in women with borderline personality disorder. *Journal of Abnormal Psychology, 111,* 198–202.

Clark, L. A. (1996). *Schedule for Adaptive and Nonadaptive Personality: Manual for administration, scoring, and interpretation.* Minneapolis: University of Minnesota Press.

Cole, D. A. (1988). Hopelessness, social desirability, depression, and parasuicide in two college student samples. *Journal of Consulting and Clinical Psychology, 56,* 131–136.

Cotton C. R., Peters, D. K., & Range, L. M. (1995). Psychometric properties of the Suicidal Behaviors Questionnaire. *Death Studies, 19,* 391–397.

du Toit, P. L., van Kradenburg, J., Niehaus, D., & Stein, D. J. (2001). Comparison of obsessive–compulsive disorder patients with and without comorbid putative obsessive–compulsive spectrum disorders using a structured clinical interview. *Comprehensive Psychiatry, 42,* 291–300.

Firestone, R. W., & Firestone, L. A. (1996). *Firestone Assessment of Self-Destructive Thoughts.* San Antonio, TX: Psychological Corporation.

Firestone, R. W., & Firestone, L. A. (1998). Voices in suicide: The relationship between self-destructive thought processes, maladaptive behavior, and self-destructive manifestations. *Death Studies, 22,* 411–433.

Fliege, H., Kocalevent, R., Walter, O. B., Beck, S., Gratz, K. L., Gutierrez, P. M., & Klapp, B. F. (2006). Three assessment tools for deliberate self-harm and suicide behavior: Evaluation and psychopathological correlates. *Journal of Psychosomatic Research, 61,* 113–121.

Glenn, C. R., & Klonsky, E. D. (2007, May). *The functions of non-suicidal self-injury: Measurement and structure.* Presented at the annual meeting of the Association of Psychological Science, Washington, DC.

Gratz, K. L. (2001). Measurement of deliberate self-harm: Preliminary data on the Deliberate Self-Harm Inventory. *Journal of Psychopathology and Behavioral Assessment, 23,* 253–263.

Guertin, T., Lloyd-Richardson, E., Spirito, A., Donaldson, D., & Boergers, J. (2001). Self-mutilative behavior in adolescents who attempt suicide by overdose. *Journal of the American Academy of Child & Adolescent Psychiatry, 40,* 1062–1069.

Gutierrez, P. M, Osman, A., Barrois, F. X., & Kopper, B. A. (2001). Development and initial validation of the Self-Harm Behavior Questionnaire. *Journal of Personality Assessment, 77,* 475–490.

Ivanoff, A., & Jang, S. J. (1991). The role of hopelessness and social desirability in predicting suicidal behavior: A study of prison inmates. *Journal of Consulting and Clinical Psychology, 59,* 394–399.

Kettlewell, C. (1999). *Skin game: A cutter's memoir.* New York: St. Martin's.

Klonsky, E. D. (2007). The functions of deliberate self-injury: A review of the evidence. *Clinical Psychology Review, 27,* 226–239.

Klonsky, E. D., & Glenn, C. R. (2008). Resisting urges to self-injure. *Behavioural and Cognitive Psychotherapy, 36*, 211–220.

Klonsky, E. D., & Glenn, C. R. (in press). Assessing the functions of non-suicidal self-injury: Psychometric properties of the Inventory of Statements about Self-Injury (ISAS). *Journal of Psychopathology and Behavioral Assessment*.

Klonsky, E. D., & Olino, T. M. (2008). Identifying clinically distinct subgroups of self-injurers: A latent class analysis. *Journal of Consulting and Clinical Psychology, 76*, 22–27.

Koons, C. R., Robins, C. I., Tweed, J. L., Lynch, T. R., Gonzalez, A. M., Morse, J. Q., et al. (2001). Efficacy of dialectical behavior therapy in women veterans with borderline personality disorder. *Behavior Therapy, 32*, 371–390.

Kumar, G., Pepe, D., & Steer, R. A. (2004). Adolescent psychiatric inpatients' self-reported reasons for cutting themselves. *The Journal of Nervous and Mental Disease, 192*, 830–836.

Linehan, M. M. (1981). *Suicide Behaviors Questionnaire*. Unpublished manuscript, University of Washington, Seattle.

Linehan M. M. (1996). *Suicidal Behaviors Questionnaire (SBQ)*. Unpublished manuscript, University of Washington, Seattle.

Linehan, M. M., Armstrong, H. E., Suarez, A., Allmon, D., & Heard, H. L. (1991). Cognitive–behavioral treatment of chronically parasuicidal borderline patients. *Archives of General Psychiatry, 48*, 1060–1064.

Linehan, M. M., Camper, P., Chiles, J. A., Strosahl, K., & Shearin, E. (1987). Interpersonal problem solving and parasuicide. *Cognitive Therapy and Research, 11*, 1–12.

Linehan, M. M., Chiles, J. A., Egan, K. J., Devine, R. H., & Laffaw, J. A. (1986). Presenting problems of parasuicides versus suicide ideators and nonsuicidal psychiatric patients. *Journal of Consulting and Clinical Psychology, 54*, 880–881.

Linehan, M. M., Comtois, K. A., Brown, M. Z., Heard, H. L., & Wagner, A. (2006). Suicide attempt self-injury interview (SASII): Development, reliability, and validity of a scale to assess suicide attempts and intentional self-injury. *Psychological Assessment, 18*, 302–312.

Linehan, M. M., Heard, H. L., & Armstrong, H. E. (1993). Naturalistic follow-up of a behavioral treatment for chronically parasuicidal borderline patients. *Archives of General Psychiatry, 50*, 971–974.

Lloyd, E. E., Kelley, M. L., & Hope, T. (1997, March). *Self-mutilation in a community sample of adolescents: Descriptive characteristics and provisional prevalence rates.* Poster presented at the annual meeting of the Society for Behavioral Medicine, New Orleans, LA.

Lloyd-Richardson, E., Perrine, N., Dierker, L., & Kelley, M. L. (2007). Characteristics and functions of non-suicidal self-injury in a community sample of adolescents. *Psychological Medicine, 37*, 1183–1192.

Lundh, L. G., Karim, J., & Quilisch, E. (2007). Deliberate self-harm in 15-year-old adolescents: A pilot study with a modified version of the Deliberate Self-Harm Inventory. *Scandinavian Journal of Psychology, 48*, 33–41.

Nock, M. K., Holmberg, E. B., Photos, V. I., & Michel, B. D. (2007). The Self-Injurious Thoughts and Behaviors Interview: Development, reliability, and validity in an adolescent sample measure. *Psychological Assessment, 19*, 309–317.

Nock, M. K., Joiner, T. E., Gordon, K. H., Lloyd-Richardson, E., & Prinstein, M. J. (2006). Non-suicidal self-injury among adolescents: Diagnostic correlates and relation to suicide attempts. *Psychiatry Research, 144*, 65–72.

Nock, M. K., & Prinstein, M. J. (2004). A functional approach to the assessment of self-mutilative behavior. *Journal of Consulting and Clinical Psychology, 72*, 885–890.

Nock, M. K., & Prinstein, M. J. (2005). Contextual features and behavioral functions of self-mutilation among adolescents. *Journal of Abnormal Psychology, 114*, 140–146.

Nock, M. K., Wedig, M. M., Janis, I. B., & Deliberto, T. L. (2008). Self-injurious thoughts and behaviors. In J. Hunsley & E. Mash (Eds.), *A guide to assessments that work* (pp. 158–177). New York: Oxford University Press.

Osuch, E. A., Noll, J. G., & Putnam, F. W. (1999). The motivations for self-injury in psychiatric patients. *Psychiatry, 62*, 334–346.

Penn, J. V., Esposito, C. L., Schaeffer, L. E., Fritz, G. K., & Spirito, A. (2003). Suicide attempts and self-mutilative behavior in a juvenile correctional facility. *Journal of the Academy of Child & Adolescent Psychiatry, 42*, 762–769.

Sabo, A. N., Gunderson, J. G., Najavits, L. M., Chauncey, D., & Kisiel, C. (1995) Changes in self-destructiveness of borderline patients in psychotherapy. *The Journal of Nervous Mental Disorders, 183*, 370–376.

Sansone, R. A., Fine, M. A., & Nunn, J. L. (1994). A comparison of borderline personality symptomatology and self-destructive behavior in women with eating, substance abuse, and both eating and substance abuse disorders. *Journal of Personality Disorders, 8*, 219–228.

Sansone, R. A., Gage, M. D., & Wiederman, M. W. (1998). Investigation of borderline personality disorder among non-psychotic, involuntarily hospitalized clients. *Journal of Mental Health Counseling, 20*,133–140.

Sansone, R. A., Sansone, L. A., & Morris, D. (1996). Prevalence of borderline personality symptoms in two groups of obese subjects. *The American Journal of Psychiatry, 153*, 117–118.

Sansone, R. A., Wiederman, M. W., & Sansone, L. A. (1996). The relationship between borderline personality symptomatology and healthcare utilization among women in an HMO setting. *Journal of Managed Care, 2*, 515–518.

Sansone, R. A., Wiederman, M. W., & Sansone, L. A. (1998). The Self-Harm Inventory: Development of a scale for identifying self-destructive behaviors and borderline personality disorder. *Journal of Clinical Psychology, 54*, 973–983.

Sansone, R. A., Wiederman, M. W., Sansone, L. A., & Touchet, B. (1998). An investigation of primary care patients on extended treatment with selective serotonin reuptake inhibitors. *American Journal of Managed Care, 4*, 1721–1723.

Santa Mina, E. E., Gallop, R., Links, P., Heslegrave, R., Pringle, D., Wekerle, C., & Grewal, P. (2006). The Self-Injury Questionnaire: Evaluation of the psychometric properties in a clinical population. *Journal of Psychiatric and Mental Health Nursing, 13*, 221–227.

Walsh, B. (2006). *Treating self-injury: A practical guide.* New York: Guildford Press.

Walsh, B. (2007). Clinical assessment of self-injury: A practical guide. *Journal of Clinical Psychology, 63*, 1057–1068.

Wiederman, M. W., Sansone, R. A., & Sansone, L. A. (1998). History of trauma and attempted suicide among women in a primary care setting. *Violence and Victims, 13*, 3–9.

11

COGNITIVE THERAPY FOR NONSUICIDAL SELF-INJURY

CORY F. NEWMAN

In assessing and treating clients who exhibit nonsuicidal self-injury (NSSI), cognitive therapists pay special attention to the maladaptive beliefs that underlie the clients' problematic behaviors. These beliefs shed light on the idiosyncratic logic that clients use in choosing to engage in behavior that appears to the outside observer to be incomprehensibly self-defeating. Cognitive therapists do not adopt the conceptual viewpoint that clients who self-harm are expressing an inherent "need to suffer" or masochism. Instead, NSSI is conceptualized as a faulty coping mechanism—an attempt at self-help gone awry, maintained by a variety of internal and environmental consequences that reinforce the behavior.

By definition, NSSI represents behavior in which the client has no intent to die, along with a low level of lethality in terms of the method(s) used (see chap. 1, this volume). A typical example is the person who makes superficial cuts on his arms, just enough to draw blood, an act that gives him a subjective sense of control and "relief" from emotional suffering and obsessive rumination. Nonetheless, clinicians would do well to bear in mind that even persons who typically demonstrate behavior that is low on the dimensions of intent and lethality may in fact still be at risk of suicide.

NSSI and frank suicidality are not mutually exclusive (M. Z. Brown, Comtois, & Linehan, 2002; Nock, Joiner, Gordon, Lloyd-Richardson, & Prinstein, 2006). A client who is using NSSI to distract herself from her sense of profound shame in one instance may be the same client who believes that she truly does not deserve to live in another instance. Thus, it is clinically prudent to continue to assess clients' subjective level of suicidal intent and the means with which they plan to harm themselves (i.e., lethality), even when it has been established that the primary and customary problem is NSSI. Additionally, even when the clients' self-harming behavior is consistently in the "low intent–low lethality" category, it is possible that they may accidentally take highly lethal action against themselves. For example, one client with a long history of cutting herself nearly died after she engaged in self-harming while impaired on alcohol and other drugs. She reported having been amused at how little pain she felt while inebriated, so she continued to cut deeper out of a sense of morbid curiosity. In this condition, the client also had poor motor control over the razor, thereby inflicting more damage to her arm than she had intended. The result was a dangerous loss of blood and the necessity of calling for emergency assistance. Thus, therapists would do well to let it be known that they take their clients' self-harming behavior seriously, including recognizing the potential for inadvertent suicide. In sum, the destructiveness of NSSI is not to be underestimated in therapy, even if the client insists that "it's no big deal."

COGNITIVE ASSESSMENT OF NONSUICIDIAL SELF-INJURY

There are a number of formal assessment measures that examine clients' reasons for their NSSI behaviors as well the environmental factors that maintain or otherwise support the behavior. For example, the Functional Assessment of Self-Mutilation (FASM; Lloyd, Kelley, & Hope, 1997; Nock & Prinstein, 2004) asks clients to report the methods, frequency, and reasons for their self-harming behaviors. Among these reasons are to "stop bad feelings," "relieve feeling numb or empty," "let others know how desperate you are," and many others. Clients' responses can help therapists formulate hypotheses about clients' faulty beliefs that support the NSSI. A related measure is the Suicide Attempt Self-Injury Interview (SASII; Linehan, Comtois, Brown, Heard, & Wagner, 2006), which assesses factors pertinent to both intentional injury and nonfatal suicidal attempts, including clients' motivations for their actions. For example, the interpersonal influence factor contains the item "Get back at or hurt someone," whereas the emotional relief factor includes the item "Stop feeling self-hatred/shame."

These questionnaires may provide the clinician with a rich source of hypotheses about their clients' thinking styles. Consequently, clients' problematic beliefs pertinent to NSSI and their relationship with NSSI become important targets for intervention in cognitive therapy. In addition, it is vital to assess the behavioral aspects of NSSI, such as the method(s) chosen, the frequency of acts of NSSI, and the settings in which they occur. These data help clinicians and clients alike to understand the scope of the problem, as well as the context in which it occurs (i.e., triggers and consequences; Nock & Prinstein, 2004).

Clients' Maladaptive Beliefs About Nonsuicidal Self-Injury

Even in the absence of the use of the formal measures noted earlier, therapists can be alert to signs of clients' distorted beliefs about NSSI. Clients do not always express their beliefs overtly, but they often give clues while describing their experiences with NSSI. The astute cognitive therapist frequently asks open-ended questions that will elicit such clues, which may then be pursued. For example, the therapist may ask clients to describe their "relationship with their bodies" (Walsh, 2006, p. 172). Such an unexpected and provocative question may then lead clients to reveal their negative body attitudes, the likes of which may potentiate the risk of NSSI. The following sample dialogue serves to illustrate the use of open-ending questioning:

> Client: I was in one of those "places" again where I just couldn't cope. . . . I just couldn't deal. I just had to cut myself. I didn't know what else to do with myself.

> Therapist: What were some of the things that were running through your mind at the time?

> Client: Just the usual stuff.

> Therapist: Such as . . . ?

> Client: I don't know. You know . . . stuff like, "I have to pull myself together. How am I gonna get through this day?"

> Therapist: At what point in your thinking did the option of cutting yourself come to mind?

> Client: [emphatically and defiantly] It's always an option.

> Therapist: What I meant was when did you come to a decision about cutting yourself, and how did you arrive at that decision?

> Client: It's what calms me down, and I had too many things to do. I couldn't afford to wig out all day. I had to pull myself together.

> Therapist: My goodness, that's so ironic . . . that you cut yourself apart to pull yourself together. [pause] How much do you believe that cutting yourself actually is a useful way to cope? Give it a rating, from 0 to 100.

In this example, the therapist essentially reflects what the client has said but puts it in the form of a belief. The therapist also poses a question in such a way that the client is encouraged to rate the degree to which she believes that cutting herself is an effective way to cope. This enables the client to express some degree of ambivalence about her view of the cutting, without feeling pressure to retract her statement. It also shows that one's beliefs are not necessarily all-or-none phenomena. One of the ways in which therapists can lessen potential power struggles is by acknowledging that the clients do not necessarily have to relinquish their beliefs entirely. It may be sufficient to lower their degree of belief or to find alternative beliefs that may supersede the original beliefs, such as, "Cutting myself makes me feel that I am coping, but getting some exercise, doing something constructive, and working on some therapy homework are better ways to cope."

The following are some of the implicit, maladaptive beliefs that clients have reported in support of their NSSI behaviors. Although on the basis of clinical anecdote, the following examples are largely consistent with the formal, empirical assessment literature as noted earlier. Therapists can keep these hypothesized client beliefs in mind, so as to be prepared to detect them when clients express these beliefs obliquely or indirectly and to provide clients with accurate empathy, rather than the expected admonishments. The generic term *NSSI* is used in the examples that follow as a substitute for whatever specific self-harming behaviors are referred to in any given case.

- "Doing NSSI behaviors gives me a sense of control and coping that I don't have anywhere or anytime else." (This belief is associated with helplessness, low self-efficacy, and difficulties in normal affect regulation; see Chapman, Specht, & Cellucci, 2005.)
- "If I don't act on my urge to do NSSI behaviors, I am going to feel like I want to explode and *really* do something crazy!" (This is seen in clients who believe that NSSI is a small price to pay for quelling their rage; see M. Z. Brown et al., 2002.)
- "I hate my body, and it is my enemy." (This type of statement is typical of clients who experience poor body image and high alienation from their physical selves; see Alderman, 1997.)
- "Nobody notices or believes how badly I feel until I start doing NSSI behavior." (Such a statement reflects clients' sense of helplessness in communicating their feelings or their lack of faith in other people understanding unless they do something dramatic and harmful; see Nock & Prinstein, 2004.)
- "I am generally empty and numb, but NSSI reminds me that I am real and that I can feel something." (This belief is encountered in clients who dissociate and who may especially be likely to have had histories of trauma; see Nock & Prinstein, 2005.)

When therapists notice that clients seem to maintain one or more of these beliefs (or additional beliefs not exhaustively mentioned here), they can give the clients direct feedback, educating them about the power of personal beliefs, and documenting the beliefs collaboratively as part of the ongoing assessment process. It is generally inadvisable to dispute clients' beliefs head on without first taking time to learn how the clients came to develop such beliefs over time and to explore how the beliefs are maintained. Instead, the therapist opts to express accurate empathy while highlighting the role of the client's beliefs and beginning the process of examining how these beliefs function in his or her everyday life. The following is a sample dialogue that demonstrates the early stages of trying to address the client's belief that her NSSI is "the only way" she can cope.

Client: What I do to my body is *my* private business. I don't understand why everybody has to be so concerned. Just leave me alone!

Therapist: Well, part of what you're saying makes sense to me. Most people want their privacy. They don't want people interfering in their personal business. So if that's the way you feel, I can understand that. [*Client looks down in silence, so therapist takes the opportunity to say more.*] I have some mixed feelings about that subject. Part of me really wants to respect your privacy. I mean, even in therapy, you have a right to privacy. At the same time, I think I owe you some clinical attention. If you are endangering yourself in any way, that really concerns me, and I want to help. I wonder if other people in your life feel the same way.

Client: But I'm *not* endangering myself. I'm trying to cope. When I cut myself, it calms me down, that is until other people start freaking out over it like I'm gonna kill myself or something.

Therapist: You've hit on something important there. You believe that your NSSI behavior is helpful to you, but those who care about you think you're at risk for harm, and they get very concerned. It's also very hard to keep your NSSI totally private. There are telltale signs, and then you *really* lose your privacy because those who care about you jump to the conclusion that you have major psychological issues and that you might want to kill yourself. So, unfortunately, your NSSI behavior actually contributes to your *loss* of privacy. What's your opinion about what I just said? [*Client remains silent, not making eye contact.*] I would really value your feedback right now. Where do *you* stand?

Client: [*anguished*] Well what else am I supposed to do? The cutting is the only way I know how to cope! What do people want from me?

Therapist: Well, those are two separate issues; very important issues. You want to know how *else* you are supposed to cope with your strong, painful emotions. That's a reasonable question, and we can begin to get into that right now if you want to. The other thing you are asking is what other people want from you. We can explore that, too. I can start by telling you what it is that *I* am asking from you as your partner in therapy, and you can tell me what you want from me. I'm open to discussion. How about you?

Notice that the therapist does not risk invalidating the client by contradicting the client's beliefs. Instead, the therapist tries to frame the issues for further discussion, which will lead to an evaluation of the client's beliefs pertinent to her NSSI behavior. The intended result, over time, is for the client to remodel her beliefs, such that new, more adaptive considerations are incorporated that will lessen her motivation to engage in the NSSI behavior. For example, with regard to her right to privacy, the revised, more therapeutic viewpoint might take the following form: "It is important to maintain my privacy, and one of the best ways to do this is to take care of myself so that people who care about me will not be alarmed by what I am doing to myself."

The client's beliefs about NSSI need to be assessed in the greater context of the client's more general beliefs about self, world, and future (i.e., the *cognitive triad;* see A. T. Beck, 1976). For example, many clients demonstrating NSSI also meet diagnostic criteria for borderline personality disorder (Chapman et al., 2005; Nock et al., 2006). Such clients may maintain a maladaptive schema of personal "badness" (or the related concepts of "defectiveness" or "social exclusion"; see Layden, Newman, Freeman, & Morse, 1993; Young, 1999). In this context, clients may believe that they do not deserve to get well and that their NSSI behavior is fitting and proper punishment for a person as "bad" as they are. In such a case, therapists may encounter seemingly inexplicable roadblocks in trying to help the client overcome the urge to commit acts of NSSI, because they will have missed ascertaining the greater context of a client who believes that she warrants self-punishment. Similarly, a client with posttraumatic stress disorder may believe that she is "irreparably damaged" from the trauma(s) and thus conclude that stopping her NSSI behavior will have no remedial effect anyway. The therapists of such clients have the double duty of assessing (and ultimately trying to modify) the general maladaptive beliefs associated with the relevant diagnosed disorder, as well as the specific beliefs pertinent to the NSSI behavior per se.

Faulty Assumptions About Nonsuicidal Self-Injury Maintained by Therapists

It goes without saying that therapists will be in the best position to help their clients reduce and, it is hoped, eliminate their NSSI if they have established a good therapeutic relationship and if they have formulated a thorough case conceptualization that explains the contingencies and maladaptive beliefs that maintain the NSSI. To do this, therapists have to approach clients who self-harm with an open mind toward understanding their idiosyncratic beliefs about the role of NSSI in their lives. If clients ascertain that their therapists are headstrong about stopping the NSSI behavior without trying to understand why they do it, the likelihood of there being good therapeutic collaboration will diminish. With this in mind, it behooves therapists to be aware of their own faulty beliefs about treating clients with NSSI. A nonexhaustive list, with brief explanations, follows:

- *Clients understand that NSSI is harmful and must be stopped.* Many clients are ambivalent about their NSSI and have come to view it as playing a helpful role in their lives. They may fear that without the NSSI, they will have no way to cope or regulate their heightened emotionality. Therefore, clients will feel even greater levels of distress and hopelessness. Thus, therapists should openly express a willingness to understand the appeal of NSSI to clients, even as they set a therapeutic agenda that includes the reduction and ultimate elimination of the need for self-harm.

- *Clients will bring up the subject of NSSI if it has occurred this week.* As with many behaviors that are associated with impulse control problems, shame, and stigma (e.g., use of illicit drugs, sexual addictions), NSSI is a topic that is not easy to discuss but very easy to avoid. Therapists should not assume that their clients will automatically discuss their NSSI behaviors since the previous session. Instead, therapists can explain that NSSI will be a topic in each and every session—an automatic part of the agenda—and that although it is ideal if the clients bring it up first (e.g., as part of the self-monitoring homework review), the therapist will always ask.

- *Clients' self-report about their NSSI must be 100% accurate for it to be useful.* Ideally, self-monitoring should produce accurate data. However, therapists would be engaging in the distortion of all-or-none thinking if they maintain that clients' under-reporting of their NSSI renders the process of self-monitoring useless. Therapists can bear in mind that many clients feel ashamed to admit the extent of their NSSI. They may fear being scolded, rejected, controlled, or abandoned by their therapists if they reveal the true extent of their self-harming behaviors. The process of self-monitoring is useful in its own right because it counteracts the clients' minimization, dismissal, and dissociation associated with NSSI. If the client says that there were no incidents this week but the therapist believes that this may not be true, the therapist can still ask about "close calls" the client may have had. This is similar to how therapists handle drug-abusing clients who claim not to have used (see A. T. Beck, Wright, Newman, & Liese, 1993). Therapists can ask, "Did you have any urges to hurt yourself?"; "What triggers started these urges?"; and "How did you coach yourself through the situation so that you did not act on the urge?" In this sense, even when clients deny that they have engaged in NSSI, the task of self-monitoring leads nicely into the sorts of therapeutic questions discussed earlier and therefore is a useful part of treatment regardless of the veracity of the subjectively reported data.

■ *NSSI merely represents attention-seeking and exercising control over others*. Although there is indeed evidence that some clients use NSSI as a form of interpersonal communication (Nock & Prinstein, 2004; Rudd, Joiner, & Rajab, 2001), this therapist assumption is usually associated with negative feelings toward the client. Perhaps the therapist feels frustrated because the client's NSSI is not abating or is escalating in response to the therapist's setting of limits and goals. Perhaps people (and other mental health care professionals) in the client's life have used the word *manipulative* to describe the patient, and this label is influencing the therapist's conceptualization of the problem. When therapists maintain this assumption, it signifies that healthy communication is in short supply and needs to be facilitated. Therapists can say to the client,

> When you harm yourself, you are communicating distress. Can we work together so that you can communicate this distress in words? Even if you do not wish to share these words with others at first, would you consider writing down the words for yourself, perhaps in a journal, and we can decide later how to make good use of those words?

INTERVENTIONS

Cognitive therapy is best known for targeting and modifying the maladaptive automatic thoughts and core beliefs of clients who habitually experience undue emotional distress. However, cognitive therapy also addresses problematic behaviors to reduce harm and build skills. In cases of NSSI, cognitive therapy interventions aim to teach clients alternative, more adaptive ways to cope with emotional distress, to use positive self-instruction to delay acting on urges to self-harm, to think about themselves and their relationship to their bodies in ways that are not conducive to NSSI, and to be more hopeful and self-efficacious.

The following is a nonexhaustive sampling of such interventions. Because there is a dearth of empirical literature on cognitive therapy for NSSI per se, the majority of interventions are derived from cognitive therapy protocols for treating clients with frank suicidality (e.g., see Berk, Henriques, Warman, Brown, & Beck, 2004; G. K. Brown et al., 2005) or severe personality disorders (e.g., see G. K. Brown, Newman, Charlesworth, Crits-Christoph, & Beck, 2004).

Utilizing Less Damaging Alternative Behaviors

Although it would be ideal for clients to be able to transition from full self-harming mode to zero self-harming behaviors in one therapeutic leap, this is usually unrealistic. As with most behavioral pattern changes, the clients must be "shaped" toward a goal. There are at least three intermediary steps that clients can take on the path from self-harming to relinquishing such behavior. One step is transitioning to behaviors that cause subjective pain but little or no damage to body tissue, and another step is the use of gestures that are merely symbolic of self-harm but actually cause neither pain nor damage. An example of the former is the *ice-cube method* (see Layden et al., 1993; Linehan, 1993) in which clients who wish to inflict pain on themselves hold ice cubes in their hands (or one in their mouth, or both) until the ice cube is melted. This causes physical pain but does no damage, nor does it violate the clients' physical self. An example of the latter is drawing on oneself with a water-soluble red marker, as if to symbolize drawing blood from cutting. Yet another step is the use of imagery of self-harm, which has been shown to reduce physiological signs of stress in a population of prison inmates who engaged in self-injuring behavior (Haines, Williams, Brian, & Wilson, 1995). Again, the purpose of such interventions is not to reinforce NSSI behavior in any way but rather to help wean clients from their NSSI behaviors in graded stages.

Rehabilitative Self-Punishment

For those clients who maintain that their NSSI represents an attempt to punish themselves (e.g., out of a sense of being bad and deserving of pain), the following intervention may be introduced as a way to work therapeutically within this system of self-reproach. The technique of *rehabilitative self-punishment* asks the client to list and describe those behaviors that are normatively considered to be healthy and productive but that the clients believe are too difficult and aversive for them to do. Such actions may include increasing exercise, decreasing or stopping smoking, doing basic upkeep around one's household, paying bills, returning phone calls, and other similar acts of responsibility and delay of gratification. Clients who are low in self-efficacy often will lament that it is too hard to do such things—that delaying gratification and doing responsible things is actually painful for them. At this point, the therapist can suggest that this may be just the sort of "pain" that the clients can choose to inflict on themselves as a substitute for their typical NSSI. Unlike the NSSI, the activities that comprise rehabilitative self-punishment are not destructive and in fact can improve health and self-efficacy over time. At the very least, the sort of productive behaviors mentioned here can break vicious cycles of self-neglect, self-harm, and downward spiraling. If the clients balk at doing the behaviors of rehabilitative self-punishment, this can open up the discussion about how the clients actively decide that some self-punishments are preferred over others. Usually, what emerges is the finding that clients find NSSI "easier" to do, which fits their sense of low efficacy.

Modifying Maladaptive Beliefs About Nonsuicidal Self-Injury

One of the central tasks of cognitive therapy is to identify clients' problematic beliefs about themselves, their lives, and their use of NSSI. These then become important targets for intervention, both in session and for homework. For example, the therapist can directly address the client's stated belief that cutting herself is "the only way" to alleviate her rage. Of course, the first step is for the therapist to offer sincere empathy for the client's predicament. However, the therapist then gently offers that perhaps the client is needlessly and erroneously reaching a conclusion about her options for coping and that perhaps there may be other, less harmful ways to manage anger. Together, therapist and client examine the latter's history for concrete, objective evidence of times when the client has been successful in calming herself without resorting to NSSI. At first, the client may simply state that no such examples exist, but the tendency for such clients to exhibit poor autobiographical recall should be taken into account before abandoning this intervention. The following is a sample dialogue, in which the therapist uses *guided-discovery* questioning (see J. S. Beck, 1995) to begin to modify the client's biased belief:

> Client: I don't know any other way! I have *never* been able to handle anger other than cutting myself.

> Therapist: Well, I believe that it may be very difficult to think about times when you coped with your rage in a nonharmful way, but I have to think that there have been exceptions to your "rule," somewhere along the way, and perhaps we can use such exceptions to provide clues about coping skills that are dormant within you and that can be reawakened. What do you think?

Client:	[long pause] I just don't know. It just seems that cutting myself is the only way. I can't remember dealing with my anger any other way. I once stuck a fork in my hand under the table.
Therapist:	I know this is difficult, but it's really important. There may be untapped coping skills within you, based on past experience. These experiences might provide you with evidence that harming yourself does *not* have to be the only way. Would you be willing to spend some time right now discussing this possibility and then perhaps extending it into a homework assignment?
Client:	I'm getting a little angry right now, just talking about this.
Therapist:	What is going through your mind?
Client:	You're making me do something I can't do!
Therapist:	[*Takes a moment to offer a sympathetic glance and to formulate a sensitive and constructive response.*] I can see how you might look at it that way. [*pause*] What is it about this situation that makes you think things that increase your anger?
Client:	This is just too much pressure.
Therapist:	It's not my intention to pressure you, so I am truly sorry if it comes across that way. I actually have respect and hope for you, and that's why I make assumptions about your being able to cope with anger more effectively. [*pause*] Like right now, for instance. How are you coping with your anger right now, without cutting yourself?
Client:	I'm not *that* angry.
Therapist:	Good. You kept the anger in check. You didn't let it escalate. I would be very interested to study how you did that. It might give us some evidence that cutting yourself does not have to be the only way, as you typically believe. What are you saying to yourself so that you are succeeding in modifying your anger about the pressure you feel from me right now?

On the basis of dialogues such as this, therapists can give their clients homework assignments designed to improve their skills in using cognitive restructuring so that they are not held as emotional hostages to their worst thoughts and beliefs.

Another way to assist clients in responding rationally to their maladaptive beliefs is to create flash cards containing their most promising rational responses in anticipation of thoughts that ordinarily would trigger high levels of negative affect or a heightened risk of self-harm (Berk et al., 2004). The rationale for this procedure is that it is often difficult for clients to generate rational responses from scratch while they are emotionally dysregulated, but it may be much more reasonable for them to recognize and respond favorably to positive self-statements if they are already written and easily accessed. The following are examples of what the flash cards might say:

- "Reserve judgment. There's no need to rush to punish yourself. Give yourself the benefit of the doubt, just as you do for others. This is being more fair to yourself."
- "Preserve your privacy by being safe and well. If you hurt yourself, it risks calling attention to yourself in a negative way. Write down your thoughts in your private journal instead of hurting yourself."
- "Do something physical and healthy. Take a walk. Do some stretching. Feel pain through sensible exercise (if you must feel pain)."
- "Tell someone how you feel, rather than turning against yourself. Let them know that you are talking to them to be constructive and to connect with them positively."

The skills of rational responding and belief modification require ongoing practice and represent a gradual process. The effort and time involved in teaching clients to be skilled in this particular self-help method are small prices to pay to help them use higher order executive functioning to overcome old, harmful beliefs that otherwise reinforce NSSI.

Improving Communication and Problem-Solving Skills

As noted, some persons use NSSI to communicate their anger, despair, loneliness, and other negative emotions to others. They sometimes believe that NSSI represents the best way—perhaps the only way—to make their point. It is unfortunate, and predictable, that such clients often fail to achieve their intended goal. More than soliciting understanding, they alienate themselves from others, cause disruptions in their own lives, and lower both their self-efficacy and their credibility as well-functioning people in the eyes of others.

In a related vein, by choosing to engage in NSSI behavior, clients demonstrate poor problem-solving skills. They may believe that by harming themselves they are indeed handling a problem (such as by combating dissociative symptoms to feel something), but in fact they are making their life problems worse. Not only is their original problem (e.g., loneliness, self-loathing, panic over their overwhelming life stressors) not solved, but clients also have now introduced yet another noxious element into their personal lives and put their health at further risk.

Thus, cognitive therapists include communication and problem-solving skills training on their list of interventions with the NSSI population. Regarding the former, direct therapist feedback, role-playing exercises, simulated letter writing, and journaling play important roles in teaching clients to verbalize their distress in appropriate ways. Regardless of the specific technique used, the strategy is the same: to practice using well-chosen words to communicate with others, especially when negative affect is heightened.

With regard to problem solving, therapist and client can work on a written, well-specified *crisis plan* (Berk et al., 2004) to prepare for scenarios when they are experiencing severe dysphoria and hopelessness. Although this method was developed to prevent actual suicidal behavior, it can be readily applied to NSSI as well. By making use of the crisis plan, clients break the vicious cycle of distress—self-harm—negative consequences—exacerbation of distress. As such, the crisis plan represents a fundamental first step in solving problems by reducing impulsivity and harm. When clients learn the principles of damage control, they are then in a better position to begin to solve the bigger, ongoing difficulties of their lives (e.g., relational rifts, pressures or failures at school or work, financial issues, health problems, housing difficulties).

The written crisis plan ideally should be collaboratively composed early in treatment. Copies of the crisis plan should be placed in convenient locations (e.g., small notebook in a handbag, top drawer of a bedside table, medicine cabinet, a flash drive on a key ring for immediate use at any computer). The contents of the plan typically involve a variety of interventions, including the use of flashcards; *delay and distraction* techniques such as taking a walk, calling a friend, watching a film, doing yoga or other forms of relaxation and exercise; and using self-soothing stimuli (e.g., soft blanket, warm bath, fragrances, music or nature sounds on CDs, interacting with a pet).

A particularly powerful way to delay acting on the urge to engage in NSSI is the use of the *hope kit* (Berk et al., 2004; see also Ellis & Newman, 1996). This is literally a container of accumulated reminders of clients' reasons to take better care of themselves and not to hurt themselves. For example, a client may be instructed to use an old, empty shoebox to store the following items: birthday and holiday greeting cards received from loved ones in the past, photos of important people in their lives, old letters, mementos of successes, and lists of future goals (e.g., brochures of places where the client would like to travel). The client is instructed to look through the contents of the hope kit when his or her thoughts turn toward pessimism and self-dislike. The purpose is to remind the clients that they are important, that they have positive worldly ties, that they have things to be proud of and to look forward to, and that harming themselves is incompatible with these important markers in their lives.

SPECIAL ISSUES

Issues sometimes arise in the course of treating NSSI that go outside the usual agenda of outpatient cognitive therapy. Nevertheless, the prepared clinician would do well to be aware of the some of the following phenomena, so that they may become incorporated into the treatment plan.

Time Misperceptions

There is some evidence that persons who engage in impulsive self-harming behavior demonstrate anomalies in their sense of time perception (Berlin & Rolls, 2004). Although still in its early stages, this line of research has important implications for treatment. Anecdotally, clients who hurt themselves often talk about their urgent need to take action to stop their emotional pain by any means. Their focus is entirely in the moment but not in the positive way associated with mindfulness exercises. Rather, their sense of pain (and the corresponding desire to get rid of it) becomes all-consuming, as if the full extent, scope, and meaning of their life are reducible to the question, "How can I stop my suffering right this second?" The past, with all its stories and experiences that comprise the client's life and identity, is a distant blur. The future, with all its possibilities for a better life, is not even considered. All that matters is eliminating a highly uncomfortable feeling, right now. This is the time when many people with impulse-control disorders, such as those who engage in NSSI, are most vulnerable.

This phenomenon may be related to the data on deficits in autobiographical recall and future imaging in clients with mood disorders (Williams, Barnhofer, Crane, & Duggan, 2005) and the linkage between hopelessness and suicidality (A. T. Beck, Brown, Berchick, Stewart, & Steer, 1990; A. T. Beck, Brown, Steer, Dahlsgaard, & Grisham, 1999). If so, these findings suggest that an important intervention and homework assignment may involve the client responding to an urge to do self-harming behavior by writing a brief narrative about a past experience, as well as a short note about a specific activity that the client expects to do within the next few days. After completion of this thoughtful task, the client would then monitor changes in his or her level of urge to follow through with the originally intended NSSI, ending with a decision about whether this behavior still seems like a pressing need. Although the nuts and bolts of this intervention (along with the methods by which to elicit cooperation) are beyond the scope of this chapter (see Ellis & Newman, 1996, for details), it suffices to say that teaching clients to be more focused on the specifics of their life experiences—past, present, and future—works against the seemingly overpowering temptations of the moment to engage in NSSI.

Peer-Group Support for Nonsuicidal Self-Injury

One of the more disturbing findings in the field of suicidology is the *contagion effect*, whereby a highly conspicuous suicide (e.g., a popular student) can influence others to attempt suicide, leading to epidemiologic suicide clusters (see Joiner, 2003). Similarly, Nock and Prinstein (2005) found that self-injurious behavior in adolescents tended to occur more frequently among friends, especially when these behaviors were perceived to be successful in eliciting attention or other desired consequences.

The cognitive therapist must therefore bear in mind that what may seem to be a blatantly dysfunctional belief in an individual (out of context) may actually be seen as approved and normative within the client's inner-circle peer group. As such, the client may take pride in his or her NSSI and thus be particularly at odds with a therapist who does not acknowledge this social "upside" to the phenomenon. These social influences pose a great challenge to the cognitive therapist, but they can be managed with a combination of validation, collaboration on agreed-on goals of treatment, and by focusing on additional, healthier social contexts in the client's life from which to draw inspiration.

Nonsuicidal Self-Injury as a "Hidden Agenda" in Therapy

There are clients who present with dysphoria, anxiety, or any number of standard, common problems but who neglect to mention that they are engaging in NSSI. This may occur because the clients genuinely do not view the NSSI as a problem or perhaps because they are ashamed or deliberately secretive about it. Signs of NSSI as a hidden agenda in therapy include the use of benign euphemisms (e.g., *scratching, picking*) to minimize the degree of self-damage, the habitual wearing of clothing that leaves very little skin exposed (even in hot weather), and comments that indicate that the clients feel alienated from their own bodies (e.g., they recoil from being touched because they feel "disgusting"). Walsh (2006) hypothesized that signs such as these increase the probability that the client has suffered trauma such as sexual assault or abuse and thus recommended that the treatment involve the sorts of exposures and rational restructuring appropriate for clients with posttraumatic stress disorder.

Although a thorough description of the assessment and treatment for body dysmorphia and posttraumatic stress disorder goes beyond the scope of this chapter, the reader is referred to Walsh (2006) for a comprehensive description of these issues in the context of NSSI. The upshot is that clinicians need to be mindful of the possibility of NSSI in clients who have been physically traumatized or who have exaggerated negative reactions to their own bodies, even if they do not mention NSSI as a perceived problem in their lives. Sometimes a seemingly simple question such as, "Could you describe your relationship to your own body?" can open the door to a discussion of self-harming actions that heretofore had been kept secret from the therapist.

CONCLUSION

The empirical literature on cognitive therapy for NSSI is lacking. However, given the confirmed linkage between NSSI and risk of actual suicide, it is reasonable to hypothesize that the empirically supported methods used to address and reduce suicidal ideation and behaviors may be highly applicable to cases of NSSI. The recent findings of the efficacy of a short-term outpatient cognitive therapy protocol in the prevention of suicide attempts in a highly at-risk population (Berk et al., 2004; G. K. Brown et al., 2005) provide hope that NSSI may be similarly amenable to reduction through treatment.

Likewise, the growing literature on the cognitive vulnerabilities and deficits of suicidal clients (see Ellis, 2006, for a comprehensive review) sheds light on the types of assessment and intervention that may bolster NSSI clients' coping skills. For example, a cognitive therapy research protocol for NSSI can place special emphasis on such issues as autobiographical recall, future imaging and planning, problem solving, hopelessness, morbid perfectionism and related distortions in body image, communication skills, dysfunctional beliefs about self-harm and its consequences, exposure and rational responding to trauma memories, and reconstruing the urge to self-punish as providing opportunities for self-rehabilitation. In the same way that G. K. Brown et al. (2005) treated clients who had just been hospitalized for a suicide attempt (without specific focus on their formal diagnosis), future cognitive therapy research programs for NSSI could target clients whose symptom profile involves self-harming actions, regardless of their official diagnoses.

As is the case with any treatment study, it will be extremely important to determine the degree to which treatment effects endure, such that a reduction or cessation of NSSI is apparent at follow-up. Likewise, given the globally harmful effects of NSSI on those who engage in it, it will be necessary to assess the full range of clients' adaptive functioning as a result of treatment, not simply the status of the NSSI. Clients who experience psychological gains over a wide range of domains not only have a better chance of maintaining their improvements in NSSI but also will benefit from a higher quality of life overall, as well as a stronger sense of self-efficacy. These goals are an inherent part of the method and spirit of cognitive therapy.

Research Recommendations

Effective cognitive therapy should be reflected not only in a reduction of self-harming behaviors but also in durable changes in corresponding maladaptive beliefs that otherwise support the NSSI. Thus, outcome measures should ideally include the currently validated assessment measures for NSSI (e.g., FASM, SASII) to assess therapeutic changes in the clients' beliefs.

In terms of a specific treatment protocol, the promising cognitive therapy manual for those who recently attempted suicide (Berk et al., 2004; G. K. Brown et al., 2005) can be adapted for use with populations who engage in NSSI. Although the client recruitment strategy would have to undergo significant changes, the basic treatment protocol could be used as a stand-alone module or as a component to be added to other cognitive therapy treatment packages (e.g., for major depression, borderline personality disorder, posttraumatic stress disorder).

The treatment methods described here can be strengthened further by adding interventions that address the empirical findings on cognitive deficits in clients with self-harming or suicidal tendencies (or both). For example, cognitive therapy for NSSI could explicitly target clients' problems with problem solving, body image distortions, helplessness, hopelessness, autobiographical recall, time perception, and self-punitive perfectionism.

Clinical Recommendations

Of central importance in the cognitive therapy of NSSI is the assessment and exploration of the clients' beliefs that support their NSSI. Therapists can express empathic understanding while soliciting the clients' collaboration in reevaluating their beliefs. To maximize compliance and steady progress, therapists should try to shape clients' behavior away from NSSI through graded tasks because an all-or-none demand for abstinence may not elicit optimal levels of collaboration, hope, or frank disclosure.

Additionally, it is important for therapists to pay special attention to building clients' direct, healthy communication skills, as expressed in session and in everyday life. The better that clients can express themselves verbally, the less compelling will be their belief in the need to communicate through NSSI.

REFERENCES

Alderman, T. (1997). *The scarred soul: Understanding and ending self-inflicted violence*. Oakland, CA: New Harbinger.

Beck, A. T. (1976). *Cognitive therapy and the emotional disorders*. New York: International Universities Press.

Beck, A. T., Brown, G. K., Berchick, R. J., Stewart, B. L., & Steer, R. A. (1990). Relationship between hopelessness and ultimate suicide: A replication with psychiatric outpatients. *The American Journal of Psychiatry, 147*, 190–195.

Beck, A. T., Brown, G. K., Steer, R. A., Dahlsgaard, K. K., & Grisham, J. R. (1999). Suicide ideation at its worst point: A predictor of eventual suicide in psychiatric outpatients. *Suicide and Life-Threatening Behavior, 29*, 1–9.

Beck, A. T., Wright, F. D., Newman, C. F., & Liese, B. S. (1993). *Cognitive therapy of substance abuse*. New York: Guilford Press.

Beck, J. S. (1995). *Cognitive therapy: Basics and beyond*. New York: Guilford Press.

Berk, M. S., Henriques, G. R., Warman, D. M., Brown, G. K., & Beck, A. T. (2004). A cognitive therapy intervention for suicide attempters: An overview of the treatment and case examples. *Cognitive and Behavioral Practice, 11*, 265–277.

Berlin, H. A., & Rolls, E. T. (2004). Time perception, impulsivity, emotionality, and personality in self-harming borderline personality disorder patients. *Journal of Personality Disorders, 18*, 358–378.

Brown, G. K., Newman, C. F., Charlesworth, S. E., Crits-Christoph, P., & Beck, A. T. (2004). A open clinical trial of cognitive therapy for borderline personality disorder. *Journal of Personality Disorders, 18*, 257–271.

Brown, G. K., Ten Have, T., Henriques, G. R., Xie, S. X., Hollander, J. D., & Beck, A. T. (2005). Cognitive therapy for the prevention of suicide attempts: A randomized controlled trial. *The Journal of the American Medical Association, 294*, 563–570.

Brown, M. Z., Comtois, K. A., & Linehan, M. M. (2002). Reasons for suicide attempts and non-suicidal self-injury in women with borderline personality disorder. *Journal of Abnormal Psychology, 111*, 198–202.

Chapman, A. L., Specht, M. W., & Cellucci, T. (2005). Borderline personality disorder and deliberate self-harm: Does experiential avoidance play a role? *Suicide and Life-Threatening Behavior, 35*, 388–399.

Ellis, T. E. (Ed.). (2006). *Cognition and suicide: Theory, research, and therapy*. Washington, DC: American Psychological Association.

Ellis, T. E., & Newman, C. F. (1996). *Choosing to live: How to defeat suicide through cognitive therapy*. Oakland, CA: New Harbinger.

Haines, J., Williams, C. L., Brian, K. L., & Wilson, G. V. (1995). The psychophysiology of self-mutilation. *Journal of Abnormal Psychology, 104*, 471–489.

Joiner, T. E. (2003). Contagion of suicidal symptoms as a function of assortative relating and shared relationship stress in college roommates. *Journal of Adolescence, 26*, 495–504.

Layden, M. A., Newman, C. F., Freeman, A., & Morse, S. B. (1993). *Cognitive therapy of borderline personality disorder*. Needham Heights, MA: Allyn & Bacon.

Linehan, M. M. (1993). *Cognitive–behavioral treatment of borderline personality disorder*. New York: Guilford Press.

Linehan, M. M., Comtois, K. A., Brown, M. Z., Heard, H. L., & Wagner, A. (2006). Suicide attempt self-injury interview (SASII): Development, reliability, and validity of a scale to assess suicide attempts and intentional self-injury. *Psychological Assessment, 18*, 303–312.

Lloyd, E. E., Kelley, M. L., & Hope, T. (1997, April). *Self-mutilation in a community sample of adolescents: Descriptive characteristics and provisional relapse rates*. Poster session presented at the annual meeting of the Society for Behavioral Medicine, New Orleans, LA.

Nock, M. K., Joiner, T. E., Jr., Gordon, K. H., Lloyd-Richardson, E., & Prinstein, M. J. (2006). Nonsuicidal injury among adolescents: Diagnostic correlates and relation to suicide attempts. *Psychiatry Research, 144,* 65–72.

Nock, M. K., & Prinstein, M. J. (2004). A functional approach to the assessment of self-mutilative behavior. *Journal of Consulting and Clinical Psychology, 72,* 885–890.

Nock, M. K., & Prinstein, M. J. (2005). Contextual features and behavioral functions of self-mutilation among adolescents. *Journal of Abnormal Psychology, 114,* 140–146.

Rudd, M. D., Joiner, T., & Rajab, M. H. (2001). *Treating suicidal behavior: An effective, time-limited approach.* New York: Guilford Press.

Walsh, B. W. (2006). *Treating self-injury: A practical guide.* New York: Guilford Press.

Williams, J. M. G., Barnhofer, T., Crane, C., & Duggan, D. S. (2006). The role of overgeneral memory in suicidality. In T. E. Ellis (Ed.), *Cognition and suicide: Theory, research, and therapy* (pp. 173–192). Washington, DC: American Psychological Association.

Young, J. (1999). *Cognitive therapy for personality disorders: A schema-focused approach* (3rd edition). Sarasota, FL: Professional Resource Exchange.

12

BEHAVIOR THERAPY FOR NONSUICIDAL SELF-INJURY

THOMAS R. LYNCH AND CAROLINE COZZA

The primary aim of this chapter is to examine nonsuicidal self-injury (NSSI) from a modern behavioral perspective, influenced by a prominent behavioral theory that considers negative emotions as the primary proximal cause of NSSI (Linehan, 1993a). First, we briefly define what we mean by *modern behaviorism*. Second, we outline our theoretical perspective and review behavioral domains that we consider important when conducting a functional analysis of NSSI, including (a) biological, establishing, and stimulus control operations; (b) consequential operations; (c) a special form of consequential operation—self-punishment; and (d) rule-governed operations. Next, we review interventions that have been used to treat NSSI, focusing primarily on dialectical behavior therapy (DBT) because it is the only behavioral treatment with empirical support. Finally, we outline the hypothesized mechanisms of change unique to DBT. We do not attempt to discuss all potential mechanisms that could be associated with change in patient outcomes, nor do we believe it is possible to do so at this stage of treatment development. Instead, we focus on hypothesized mechanisms that we believe to be particularly salient in the treatment of NSSI.

BEHAVIORISM: "IT'S MORE THAN YOU MIGHT THINK"

Although commonly and mistakenly relegated to the study of overt or public behavioral responses, behavioral theory and methods have evolved considerably since the early writings of John B. Watson (1913). Currently, three distinct developmental periods have been identified in behavior therapy representing increasingly sophisticated empirical research and differences with regard to the ways in which behavioral treatments have been conceptualized (Hayes, Masuda, Bissett, Luoma, & Guerrero, 2004). The first wave focused primarily on the techniques associated with operant and classical conditioning principles. Influenced heavily by Watson (1924), the first wave essentially claimed metaphysically that the "mind" did not exist (e.g., thinking was subvocal speech), and consequently, the only relevant unit of analysis was overt behavior. In addition, from this perspective, even if mind existed, Watson argued that it was methodologically impossible to study with any scientifically approved approach (Hayes, Follette, & Follette, 1995). Thus, the first wave would analyze self-injury as respondent (i.e., behavior controlled by antecedent external stimuli) and/or operant (i.e., behavior controlled by the external reinforcing or punishing contingencies) and would consider mediators such as cognition irrelevant.

The second wave of behavior therapy reacted to what was considered a lack of cognitive mediational accounts and attempted to use behavioristic empirical methods to study the functioning of the mind on the basis of computer metaphors (Hayes et al., 1995). This, according to the proponents of the second wave, added to the unit of analysis the idea that behavior could be caused by private events (e.g., cognition, appraisals). Consistent with the previous wave, direct change efforts were used; now, however, social learning and cognitive principles were included in the therapy, and cognitions were added to the list of potentially relevant clinical targets to be addressed during treatment (Bandura, 1969; Beck, Rush, Shaw, & Emery, 1979). Thus, the second wave of behavioral therapy not only would have examined self-injury from a respondent–operant perspective but also would have accounted for the influence of modeling, cognition, beliefs, schemas, or a combination of these.

The burgeoning of the third wave began when critics started to evaluate the extent to which the newer second wave cognitive techniques were supported by the types of experimental and empirical methods that had solidified the scientific significance of behavioral approaches from the outset (Corrigan, 2001). For example, third-wave proponents argued that a psychological act in context could never be fully explained solely by the actions of the various parts the organism (e.g., cognitions, neural substrates), and all explanations that give causal priority to one form of behavior over another were viewed as incomplete (Hayes et al., 1995). From this perspective, cognition and feelings are behaviors that are not qualitatively different from overt behavior, and assigning them a special causal or mediational status reifies one type of behavior over another while placing undue emphasis on changing private experience. In addition, using a contextualistic approach, behavior was understood in terms not of its topography but of its function. Thus, acts of intentional self-injury may appear similar but functionally be quite different. For example, cutting behavior might function to elicit nurturance for one person, reduce aversive emotions in another, and self-punish in a third, or these functions may all be within the behavioral repertoire of the same person. As such, the third wave challenged the fundamental first- and second-wave principles that focused primarily on changing the form or frequency of problematic behavior (e.g., changing dysfunctional schemas, behavior, sensations, emotions) by empirically testing therapeutic methods that altered the function of a behavior without altering their form (Hayes, 2004). This resulted in the development of a number of new treatments emphasizing acceptance and contact with the present moment. Examples of these treatments include DBT (Linehan, 1993a), acceptance and commitment therapy (ACT; Hayes, Strosahl, & Wilson, 1999), functional analytic psychotherapy (Kohlenberg & Tsai, 1991), integrative behavioral couples therapy (Christensen, Jacobson, & Babcock, 1995), and mindfulness-based cognitive therapy (Segal, Williams, & Teasdale, 2002). In acceptance-based strategies, patients' aim of controlling their private experience (e.g., thoughts, feelings, sensations), not the private experience itself, is targeted for change (Hayes, Wilson, Gifford, Follette, & Strosahl, 1996). From this perspective, trying willfully to change, suppress, or inhibit unwanted suicidal or self-injurious thoughts may actually exacerbate the problem (e.g., see Cukrowicz, Ekblad, Cheavens, Rosenthal, & Lynch, 2008; Lynch, Chapman, Rosenthal, Kuo, & Linehan, 2006; Lynch, Cheavens, Morse, & Rosenthal, 2004; Lynch, Robins, Morse, & Karuse, 2001; Lynch, Schneider, Rosenthal, & Cheavens, 2007).

A FUNCTIONAL APPROACH TO NONSUICIDAL SELF-INJURY

Many of the definitions used by behaviorists to define NSSI have been confounded by an inability to measure behavioral intent or motivation. In other words, determining whether self-injurious behaviors are intended solely for self-injury or more elaborately as a means to suicide is difficult given that the intentions motivating these behaviors are not always clear to those executing them. For instance, one may be thinking about suicide while engaging in self-injurious behaviors, but not expecting to die. This matter may be complicated when unreliable and invalid measures are used to assess behavioral intent. As such, research by Linehan, Heard, Wagner, and Brown (1997) suggested that for suicidal intent to be reliably assessed, it must be measured by well-trained interviewers, using a structural interview format.

A BIOSOCIAL THEORY

Our theoretical perspective is heavily influenced by a biosocial theory that conceptualizes NSSI as an operant response that is reinforced by the immediate benefits of temporary emotional distraction and relief from intense negative affect, despite a variety of long-term consequences (Linehan, 1993a; Wagner & Linehan, 1997). This theory was formulated to explain the development and maintenance of criterion behaviors (e.g., NSSI) associated with borderline personality disorder (BPD), a disorder with high rates of self-injury and suicidal behavior. The theory proposes that a biological or genetic predisposition for emotional vulnerability and a pervasive invalidating environment transact to produce the extreme emotion dysregulation and impulsivity that is commonly associated with NSSI (Linehan, 1993a). Using this model as a basis, we consider *urges to engage* in self-harm and the *aversive emotions* that precede self-harm most often to be classically conditioned events; whereas *actual self-injury* (e.g., cutting) is an operant response reinforced by reductions in negative arousal, verification of self-constructs, or social interactions. In addition, this perspective accounts for the impact of NSSI on the individual's sense of self (see Kohlenberg & Tsai, 1991, for a behavioral formulation of self), and as such, NSSI is hypothesized to function as both an escape from and an attack on the self, usually within a context of extreme shame or humiliation (Brown, Comtois, & Linehan, 2002; Ivanoff, Brown, & Linehan, 2001).

The empirical research on the relationship between emotion dysregulation and NSSI has focused primarily on individuals with BPD. Although self-injurious behaviors are associated with various Axis I and Axis II disorders, including major depression and substance abuse, research has suggested that factors such as hopelessness with regard to the former and dysregulated impulsivity for the latter are more closely associated with self-injurious behaviors in these instances than is emotion dysregulation per se (Joiner, Brown, & Wingate, 2005). However, research examining emotional links to NSSI has consistently identified anger, anxiety, and shame as being the emotions most highly correlated with self-injury. With regard to anger, findings show that many individuals who engage in NSSI report that they do so as a means to regulate anger (Brown et al., 2002). Although anxiety disorders in general have been found to increase the risk for suicide attempts (Gould et al., 1998; Kessler et al., 2001), comorbid anxiety and depression appear particularly troubling in the context of NSSI. Studies suggest that patients with both anxiety and depressive disorders report higher incidents of NSSI compared with those with either one or the other (Bakish, 1999; Noyes, 1991; Rudd, Dahm, & Rajab, 1993). Finally, as we have discussed, shame appears to be a particularly deleterious emotion with regard to NSSI. The relationship between emotions of shame or guilt and NSSI is fairly well established (Anderson, 1981; Leibenluft, Gardner, & Cowdry, 1987; Linehan, 1993a; Shapiro, 1987;

Walsh & Rosen, 1988), and current research suggests that high levels of shame predict increases in the urge to self-injure (Brown & Linehan, 1996). Collectively, these findings provide some support for the theory that emotion regulation is among the functions that NSSI serves. Using this emotion-based theory as a framework, we organize our discussion into four overlapping domains: (a) biological, establishing, and stimulus control operations; (b) consequential operations; (c) a special form of consequential operation—self-punishment; and (d) rule-governed operations.

Biological, Establishing, and Stimulus Control Operations

According to Linehan's (e.g., 1993a) behavioral conceptualization, (a) NSSI always occurs within the context of emotional experience (biological vulnerabilities and establishing operations), (b) NSSI is always secondary to some type of cue (stimulus control operations), and (c) NSSI becomes habitual because of reinforcing consequences (consequential operations). Contextual factors associated with NSSI are those that make the production of intense negative emotions (e.g., shame, anger, contempt) more likely and consequently exacerbate urges to self-harm or self-punish, increase desires to hide or disappear, or interfere with problem solving and emotional processing (Brown et al., 2002; Ivanoff et al., 2001). These factors include biological vulnerabilities for increased sensitivity and reactivity to emotional cues, factors that momentarily enhance the reinforcement salience of particular emotional cues (i.e., establishing operations), and ideographic discriminant stimuli (S^Ds) that trigger intense negative emotional states.

Biological vulnerabilities refer to the individual variations in physiological reactivity to emotional stimuli (Boyce & Ellis, 2005). This vulnerability in BPD is hypothesized to consist of greater emotional sensitivity (i.e., low threshold for recognition of emotional stimuli), greater emotional reactivity (i.e., high amplitude of emotional responses), and a slower return to baseline arousal (i.e., long duration of emotional responses), all of which exacerbate difficulties in regulating emotion and increase the likelihood of NSSI (Linehan, 1993a). The authors of a recent review of the literature in this area (Rosenthal et al., 2008) concluded that studies using self-report methods consistently find that individuals with BPD report being more emotionally intense and reactive to emotional stimuli relative to control participants and that neuroimaging studies suggest that individuals with BPD can be characterized by neurological vulnerabilities. However, Rosenthal et al. (2008) reported that findings are inconclusive when examining behavioral and psychophysiological indices of emotional responding. It is interesting to note that the unique preponderance of both self-injurious behaviors and an inability to regulate emotions among patients with BPD were what led researchers to consider the dynamic between the two (Linehan, 1993a).

Establishing operations are motivational factors that influence the evocative functions and reinforcement salience of certain stimuli and the probability that behaviors associated with those stimuli may be elicited (Dougher, Perkins, Greenway, Koons, & Chiasson, 2002; Michel, Valach, & Waeber, 1994). For example, food deprivation is an establishing operation that momentarily increases the salience of food as a form of reinforcement (e.g., "My croissant tastes better when I'm hungry"). Because DBT for NSSI is based on the premise that self-injury occurs in the context of emotional experience, establishing operations are referred to as emotion vulnerability factors. Emotion vulnerabilities or NSSI-establishing operations can include a wide variety of events, including lack of sleep or food, a recent loss of a loved one or recent argument, physical fatigue, alcohol or drug use, physical pain, or other related stressors.

From a *stimulus control* operations perspective, the aversive emotions associated with self-harm or urges to self-harm are a direct consequence of the preceding stimulus. Stimulus control operations refer to the presentation of stimuli that signal other stimuli (stimulus–stimulus relations). This is referred to as *classically conditioned* or *respondent* behavior and is defined as learned behavior under the control of the antecedent (the preceding stimulus). Any place, person, object, sensation, emotion, or verbal or temporal event that in the past has been repeatedly paired with positive stimuli associated with self-injury can serve as a salient cue for NSSI. One of the most common respondent cues are urges for self-harm. For example, a neutral stimulus (e.g., razor blade) automatically elicits an urge to self-harm because it has repeatedly been associated with (i.e., it preceded) a positive stimulus (e.g., nurturance, relief following reductions in aversive arousal). It is important to note that classically conditioned urges for self-harm are not cognitively mediated, and conscious cognition is not necessary for the elicitation of conditioned associations (Ohman & Mineka, 2001). In addition, the acquisition of a classically conditioned relationship between two stimuli (e.g., time of day and urge to cut with a razor) can occur independent of conscious awareness; therefore, these associations can form regardless of whether an individual "wants" them or is consciously aware of them. Ohman and Mineka (2001) argued that resistance to cognitive influences has an evolutionary advantage because of the defensive value of rapid responding, which would be compromised if responding depended on detailed cognitive analyses. In addition, research suggests that some disorders (e.g., anxiety and trauma-related disorders) are more likely to acquire classically conditioned associations relative to other clinical populations or normal control participants (see Mineka & Zinbarg, 1995; Orr et al., 2000). Although, to our knowledge, this has yet to be examined specifically among those who self-injure, it is clear that respondent behavior must be accounted for when conducting an assessment of the factors that influence the production of NSSI (see Nock & Banaji, 2007).

Stimulus control operations also involve the presentation of stimuli that make it possible for actions to have consequences (i.e., stimulus–response–consequence relations). This is called *instrumental* or *operant* conditioning and is defined as learned behavior under the control of reinforcing or punishing consequences. *Discriminant stimuli* (S^Ds) refers to stimuli that signify the availability of reinforcement. Thus, each episode of self-injury has antecedent stimuli that signal the likelihood of reinforcement. As mentioned earlier, our behavioral perspective accounts for three types of reinforcers that are commonly associated with NSSI: reductions in aversive arousal, self-verification, and positive reinforcement (e.g., nurturance). However, S^Ds are also under contextual control, meaning that contextual stimuli influence the reinforcement potential of any given stimuli. For example, a hospitalized client may learn that self-injury is more likely to be followed by increased attention and nurturance (i.e., positive reinforcement) when it occurs on days when the nursing staff appears well rested but not on days when the unit is understaffed or providers appear tired. Thus, despite the presence of a number of antecedents associated with self-injury on any given day, the client is most likely to engage in self-injury on the days when staff members are in a positive mood.

Consequential Operations

A functional analytic approach needs to account for not only relevant antecedents but also reinforcing consequences. NSSI provides a means by which one can escape the negative experience of shame or other extremely aversive emotions through (a) the reduction of depersonalization that it induces (Wagner & Linehan, 1997), (b) physiological and psychological relief secondary to reductions in aversive arousal (Haines, Williams, Brian, & Wilson, 1995), or (c) the loss of consciousness that may result from a drug overdose or blood loss. Retrospective self-reports suggest that more than 60% of the time NSSI, functions to reduce aversive emotional arousal, and psychophysiological arousal have been shown to be immediately and significantly reduced following self-injury imagery (Haines et al., 1995). In this sense, self-injurious behaviors are negatively reinforced in that they provide a momentarily efficient means of reducing arousal and removing negative emotions (e.g., see Gardner & Cowdry, 1985). However, the mechanisms accounting for the apparent reinforcing nature of seemingly painful self-harm behavior (e.g., cutting) have yet to be determined. Indeed, self-injurious behavior is often correlated with reduced pain perception. For example, in patients with BPD, reduced pain perception as well as higher pain thresholds were found (Russ et al., 1992). In addition, research has shown that pain thresholds in BPD patients who engage in self-injurious behavior tend to be significantly higher compared with healthy control participants and to be positively correlated with symptoms of stress (i.e., dissociation and aversive arousal compared with healthy control participants; Ludäscher et al., 2007). Thus, it is possible that those engaging in self-harm do not experience the injury itself as physically painful, yet exactly how lowered pain perception is related or leads to self-reported emotional relief following NSSI is unknown.

In addition, as an expression of emotional distress, NSSI can function to influence and control other people's behaviors. Prior research shows that distressed behavior prompts both negative and solicitous emotions but deters hostile reactions (Biglan, Rothlind, Hops, & Sherman, 1989), and NSSI has been shown to reduce aggressive or hostile actions by family members and increase nurturance (Hilt, Nock, Lloyd-Richardson, & Prinstein, 2008). Thus, social responses likely function to reinforce the probability of NSSI. Indeed, Linehan (1993a) hypothesized that some social environments will tend to intermittently reinforce emotional escalation and threats of self-harm. For example, when requests for emotional caretaking are ignored or invalidated, children may learn that if they escalate their demands (i.e., threaten self-injury), then suddenly attention and nurturance are forthcoming.

Self-Punishment as a Consequential Operation

Behaviorism considers all behavior that becomes part of a behavioral repertoire to be adaptive or functional (i.e., the behavior is reinforced or reinforcing). One of the more perplexing motivations associated with NSSI for many behaviorists are self-reported reasons for engaging in self-injury as a means to punish oneself. Indeed, punishment by definition should reduce the probability of a particular behavior, and at least on the surface "causing oneself pain" does not sound particularly reinforcing. Thus, the question becomes, What is reinforcing about self-punishment?

Linehan et al. (1993a) proposed a potential answer; essentially, intense experiences of shame and humiliation were hypothesized to be associated with extreme self-incriminations, and these extremely negative self-judgments resulted in strong urges to punish the self (Brown et al., 2002; Ivanoff et al., 2001). On the basis of Swann's self-verification theory (Swann, 1983), NSSI is considered to self-verify a sense of self that one is "bad" or "evil" and deserving of punishment. Indeed, self-verification is considered a general reinforcer, even if it means enduring pain and discomfort (Swann, Rentfrow, & Gosling, 2003). Research confirms this perspective, showing that individuals favor information that confirms their self-view over other available reinforcers, particularly if that self-view is extreme (Giesler, Josephs, & Swann, 1996; Pelham & Swann, 1994; Swann, 1997; Swann, de la Ronde, & Hixon, 1994). Research has also demonstrated that when self-constructs are disconfirmed, people tend to experience negative emotional arousal (Gellatly & Meyer, 1992). Thus, acts of self-punishment through self-injury are reinforced because they verify or confirm the individual's pathological sense of self, theoretically resulting in reductions of aversive arousal (i.e., negative reinforcement). This can develop into a vicious self-confirming cycle, leading to rigid rule-governed behavior. For example, a person who self-injures may think, "Since, I am hurting myself, then it must be true that I am evil; therefore, I must be punished by continuing to injure myself."

Rule-Governed Behavior

A common class of operant antecedents includes verbal stimuli or behaviors that take on societal or self-rules (Zettle & Hayes, 1982). This type of rule-governed behavior specifies a relationship between a behavior (e.g., cutting my wrists) and a consequence (e.g., more attention, less aversive emotion). Because the behavior is based on rules (i.e., historical experiences or societal expectations), it can become problematic precisely because the rule-governed behavior is less responsive to current contingencies (i.e., what is occurring in the present moment). For example, studies have demonstrated that individuals who are verbally instructed on a task do not change strategies when contingencies change. Rather, they persist in a given strategy because it is consistent with a rule that verbally specifies contingencies (e.g., see Hayes, Brownstein, Haas, & Greenway, 1986). When NSSI is under the control of a verbal rule (e.g., "If I do not cut myself, then the emotional distress I am feeling will be intolerable"), the natural contingencies associated with the transitory nature of aversive emotional experience may rarely be encountered because the person follows the "rule" and self-injures before the emotion passes. Consequently the individual never learns that he or she can tolerate emotional distress without having to self-injure. In addition, literal belief in rules may lead to beliefs that thoughts or emotions are dangerous (i.e., "If I think X, then a very bad thing will happen") and that certain thoughts are in themselves "bad" or equivalent to an unwanted action (e.g., see Rachman, 1997). As a consequence, individuals may come to believe that they must punish themselves through self-injury whenever they experience certain taboo thoughts or emotions, or they may try to suppress emotional thoughts, which research has shown to be a particularly ineffective strategy (e.g., see Lynch et al., 2001, 2004, 2007).

BEHAVIORAL INTERVENTIONS
FOR NONSUICIDAL SELF-INJURY

Overall, there is a paucity of empirical research on the treatment of NSSI; this observation is consistent with that of other investigators in the field who have noted that research on suicidal behaviors has not been a priority for those in the clinical research community (e.g., see Linehan,

1997). Our initial search of the Medline, PsychLit, and Google Scholar data-bases, included the combined key terms *behavior therapy* and *self-injury*, result-ing in 67 potential articles or books. We then did a combined search for *parasuicide* and *behavior therapy*, which yielded 30 hits. Not surprisingly, our review revealed that there have not been any randomized controlled trials (RCTs) examining the effects of behavioral treatment on NSSI, other than DBT. Consequently, our review that follows is limited to published empir-ical findings from RCTs and quasi-experimental studies using DBT. In clos-ing, we briefly discuss other behavior therapies that, although currently lacking in data, have been discussed theoretically by developers or researchers to possibly have utility in treating NSSI.

Dialectical Behavior Therapy

Of the behavioral treatments for NSSI, DBT has garnered the most empirical evidence for its efficacy in treating BPD, a disorder with high rates of NSSI, relative to any other psychotherapy or pharmacological interven-tion. At this time, DBT has been evaluated and found to be efficacious for the treatment of BPD in seven well-designed RCTs conducted across four inde-pendent research teams (Koons et al., 2001; Linehan, Armstrong, Suarez, Allmon, & Heard, 1991; Linehan, Comtois, et al., 2006; Linehan et al., 1999, 2002; Linehan, Heard, & Armstrong, 1993; Linehan, Tutek, Heard, & Armstrong, 1994; Turner, 2000; Verheul et al., 2003). In addition, it has demonstrated efficacy in RCTs for chronically depressed older adults (Lynch, Morse, Mendelson, & Robins, 2003), older depressed adults with comorbid personality disorder (Lynch et al., 2007), and individuals with eating disor-ders (Safer, Telch, & Agras, 2001; Telch, Agras, & Linehan, 2001).

DBT was developed as a treatment for people with BPD, particularly those who are highly suicidal. DBT draws its principles from behavioral sci-ence, dialectical philosophy, and Zen practice. It emphasizes the balance of acceptance and change, with the overall goal of helping patients build a life worth living. In addition, DBT helps therapists avoid the burnout often expe-rienced by those treating the behaviors associated with BPD and NSSI.

DBT therapists use behavioral principles such as conditioning, rein-forcement, and shaping to conceptualize patients' behavior. As such, they focus on factors that maintain dysfunctional behaviors, such as reinforcers of self-injurious behavior. Although behavioral principles inform our models for how to change ineffective behaviors, a great challenge faced by DBT thera-pists in treating patients with BPD is to balance efforts directed toward change with acceptance and validation. For example, in conducting a chain analysis of NSSI, a DBT therapist radically emphasizes that a client is doing his or her best, while simultaneously working with the client to explore options for change. Thus, the chain analysis provides a means through which not only the client's desires and impulses may be validated but also skills to change the behavior may be discussed. In the case of BPD, a common dialectical tension is that a behavior, such as NSSI, may be functional in the short term in helping to alleviate distress but dysfunctional in the long term by causing negative effects on health, interpersonal functioning, and an increased risk of suicide. As suggested earlier, this dialectical tension is resolved by synthesizing the thesis with the antithesis—in this case validating the need to alleviate distress while highlighting the utility of skills that help to maximize both short- and long-term gains. This "middle path" approach of dialectics is an inherent feature of Zen, which DBT uses in an effort to help clients behave more effectively and live more balanced lives.

Functions and Modes of Dialectical Behavior Therapy

DBT is a comprehensive treatment designed to function through various interventions delivered in four modes of therapy. Individual DBT therapy is organized around a hierarchy of target goals that aim to eliminate (a) NSSI and suicidal behaviors; (b) therapy interfering behaviors such as nonattendance or not doing homework; and (c) factors leading to decreased quality of life, including homelessness and drug dependence. Thus, built within the framework of the treatment design is the goal of targeting self-injurious behaviors directly and specifically. Unlike most behavioral treatments that consider NSSI as a peripheral symptom or consequence of psychopathology, DBT addresses NSSI in its own right and gives priority to reducing its frequency in the hierarchy of treatment goals.

In DBT, skills training teaches clients mindfulness, distress tolerance, emotion regulation, and interpersonal effectiveness—four primary skill sets for managing psychological distress. Mindfulness focuses on the quality of awareness that an individual brings to the present moment. Mindfulness practice emphasizes letting go of attachments and becoming "one" with current experience, without judgment or any effort to change "what is." With regard to NSSI, mindfulness practice provides a means through which one can learn to let go of negative feelings directed at the self that culminate in the motivation to self-injure. Likewise, in emphasizing the significance of the present moment, experiences and mistakes from the past become less threatening and directive. Distress tolerance training aims to equip clients with a range of specific methods designed to improve the client's capacity to tolerate aversive situations, feelings, or thoughts; to survive crises; and to radically accept what they cannot change. Emotion regulation training is generally more change focused and includes methods designed to identify the emotion being experienced, decide whether the emotion is justified, and then develop ways for modulating the emotion if the client so desires. Finally, interpersonal effectiveness training is designed to help clients interact with others to improve relationships while simultaneously maintaining their personal values and self-respect.

A third mode of therapy in DBT typically involves a skills generalization component that often translates into telephone contact outside of normal therapy hours (i.e., *coaching calls*) to assist clients in integrating the skills and principles taught in DBT into real-life situations. The fourth and final mode of therapy is a consultation team designed to support the therapists in working with difficult clients.

Randomized Controlled Trials of Dialectical Behavior Therapy for Patients With Nonsuicidal Self-Injury

Although a number of outcome variables were measured in the RCTs of DBT, this section focuses solely on the findings pertaining to NSSI. The first major RCT of DBT was conducted by Linehan et al. (1991, 1993, 1994) at the University of Washington. This study included 44 participants with BPD and a history of recent and repeated intentional self-injury, suicide attempts, or both who were randomized to either DBT ($n = 22$) or treatment as usual (TAU) in the community ($n = 22$). Although the results should be viewed in light of some methodological limitations typical of early efficacy studies, the data revealed substantially greater reductions in intentional self-injury rate and associated medical risk for the participants receiving DBT (Linehan et al., 1991, 1993, 1994). Although improvements were seen for individuals in both conditions, no significant advantage for DBT was found on measures of psychopathology including suicidal ideation and depression.

An independent research team at Duke University (Koons et al., 2001) compared outpatient DBT with TAU for women veterans with BPD at the Durham Veterans Administration Medical Center. This study was intended to replicate Linehan and colleagues' (1991) original findings and to examine DBT's efficacy with a less severely afflicted group of patients. Twenty patients were randomized to either DBT ($n = 10$) or TAU ($n = 10$). Alterations were made to Linehan's original inclusion criteria such that a history of intentional self-injury was not required. In accounting for the lower acuity of these participants, the length of treatment was reduced from 12 to 6 months, and weekly group skills-training sessions were reduced from 180 to 90 minutes; apart from these modifications, standard DBT was delivered in accordance with Linehan's original (1993, 1993b) protocol. Results indicate that DBT was statistically superior to TAU on outcome measures of suicidal ideation as measured by group by time interaction over the treatment period. Moreover, results point to a trend toward improvement in NSSI for individuals in the DBT condition but not for those in TAU.

A second independent research team compared standard DBT with TAU for the treatment of women with BPD attending community psychiatry and substance abuse clinics in Amsterdam (van den Bosch, Koeter, Stijnen, Verheul, & van den Brink, 2005; van den Bosch, Verheul, Schippers, van den Brink, 2002; Verheul et al., 2003). This study represents the first large-scale RCT of "standard" DBT undertaken in a nonacademic setting. Sixty-four participants were ultimately randomized to either DBT ($n = 31$) or TAU ($n = 33$). Results indicate that participants assigned to DBT engaged in significantly less NSSI and self-damaging impulsive behaviors and were significantly more likely to stay in treatment than TAU participants. Although fewer DBT participants attempted suicide (2 of 27 vs. 8 of 31), this difference was not statistically significant. Post hoc analyses revealed that DBT had a more stark advantage over TAU for treating suicide attempts and NSSI among severely afflicted participants. A follow-up assessment 6 months after the conclusion of treatment revealed that the superior gains associated with DBT were maintained, although the advantages were less pronounced than at immediate posttreatment.

In the largest and most rigorously controlled RCT of DBT to date, Linehan, Comtois, et al. (2006) compared standard DBT with community treatment by experts (CTBE). This study aimed to replicate the results of the original study while controlling for a wide range of potential confounds not specifically addressed therein, such as matching groups on variables that included the total number of lifetime suicide attempts and nonsuicidal self-injuries, number of psychiatric hospitalizations, history of bona fide suicide attempts versus NSSI only, age, and presence of negative prognostic factors (i.e., severe depression and severely impaired interviewer-assessed global functioning).

The final sample consisted of 101 (52 DBT, 49 CTBE) participants, who met *Diagnostic and Statistical Manual of Mental Disorders* (4th ed.; American Psychiatric Association, 1994) diagnostic criteria for BPD and who had attempted suicide or self-injured (or both) at least once in the previous 8 weeks and twice in the previous 5 years. Although participants in both conditions showed substantial improvements, the DBT group generally exhibited better treatment response, particularly on outcomes related to behaviors specifically targeted by treatment including suicidal ideation and suicide attempts. Participants assigned to DBT were half as likely to attempt suicide as those assigned to CTBE (23.1% with at least one suicide attempt in DBT vs. 46% in CTBE). Similarly, although not statistically significant, those receiving DBT engaged in fewer "nonambivalent" suicide attempts (5.8% in DBT vs. 13.3% in CTBE). Moreover, ratings of medical risk associated with self-injurious or suicidal behaviors were significantly lower in the DBT group. Participants receiving DBT also used significantly fewer crisis services (e.g., psychiatric emergency department [ED] visits and inpatient admissions) than participants assigned to CTBE. Although a significant difference was seen for all psychiatric ED visits and admissions in general, it was particularly evident in the case of ED visits and admissions solely for suicidal ideation. During the treatment year, those in CTBE were twice as likely as DBT participants to visit the ED for suicidal ideation (33.3% CTBE vs. 15.7% DBT) and 3 times as likely to be admitted for suicidal ideation (35.6% CTBE vs. 9.8% DBT; Linehan, Comtois, et al., 2006). Consistent with prior studies, participants in DBT were also significantly less likely to drop out of treatment. No measured outcomes favored CTBE.

Quasi-Experimental Studies of Dialectical Behavior Therapy

In addition to the RCTs just discussed, a number of nonrandomized, quasi-experimental studies have measured the effects of DBT on NSSI. These results suggest that adaptations of DBT for adult inpatients have been beneficial. Specifically, one investigation found that the implementation of DBT resulted in a significant reduction in the mean monthly rate of suicidal and nonsuicidal self-injurious behaviors for individuals in a psychiatric unit (Barley et al., 1993); another study of inpatients revealed a similar finding in which the number of suicidal and nonsuicidal self-injurious behaviors for adult women with BPD was significantly decreased following the administration of DBT (Bohus et al., 2000). Results from a follow-up study of the latter investigation revealed that following discharge from an inpatient unit, participants who had received 3 months of DBT showed significant reductions in the frequency of self-injurious behaviors 1 month after treatment cessation. Moreover, when compared with individuals in a waitlist condition, those who underwent the inpatient DBT program had more significant clinical improvements including greater reductions in NSSI (Bohus et al., 2004). Although the lack of randomization in these quasi-experiments must be taken into consideration when interpreting these results, they nonetheless support the pursuit of future research of this treatment for NSSI.

Behavioral Activation and Acceptance Commitment Therapy

Behavioral activation therapy for depression (BATD) incorporates many of the theoretical principles of DBT (Lejuez, Hopko, LePage, Hopko, & McNeil, 2002). BATD operates on the premise that increased activity is a necessary precursor to changes in self-injurious behaviors. As such, patients in BATD are confronted with the paradigm of emotion validation in the context of behavioral change that is emblematic of DBT: Patients are told that although treatment requires a significant commitment, the probability that they will overcome NSSI is high. However, unlike DBT in which direct skill enhancement functions as the proposed mechanism of change, BATD is mediated through an increase in positive affective experiences gained by a direct increase in exposure to rewarding and healthy behaviors. Thus, rather than emphasizing skill acquisition, BATD focuses on positive changes in the environment in an effort to decrease NSSI and increase the salience and proportion of experiences that empower the patient with a sense that theirs is a life worth living (Hopko, Lejuez, Ruggiero, & Eifert, 2003).

ACT (Hayes et al., 1999) is predicated on the philosophies of functional contextualism (Biglan & Hayes, 1996; Hayes, 1993) and relational frame theory. It emphasizes the significance of language and cognitions in affecting human experience; yet unlike cognitive therapy approaches, ACT considers private experience (e.g., emotion, thoughts, sensations) not to require effort to change but instead acknowledgment or acceptance. From an ACT perspective, psychological difficulties are the result of the way in which verbal processes interact with direct contingencies (i.e., what is occurring in the present moment) to generate narrow and inflexible behavioral repertoires. The primary targets for intervention are behaviors that interfere with an individual's ability to participate fully in valued life domains.

Combining the approaches just described, DBT emphasizes change and acceptance as the core dialectic; directing change efforts toward current environmental or behavioral responses that can be altered (e.g., cutting a wrist, yelling obscenities, an alcoholic raising his or her hand to take a sip of a drink) and acceptance efforts toward behaviors that are less amenable or impossible to change (e.g., rumination, sensations associated with an emotion) and for which change efforts (e.g., suppression) may function to exacerbate. Thus, DBT more explicitly emphasizes acceptance-based strategies relative to BATD. Although similar to ACT, DBT emphasizes acceptance of emotional experience; it is unlike ACT in its providing a caveat that change strategies (e.g., opposite action) may be necessary when the magnitude of the emotional experience is extreme (Linehan, Bohus, & Lynch, 2007).

DIALECTICAL BEHAVIORAL THERAPY: HYPOTHESIZED MECHANISMS OF ACTION

As noted earlier, the only behavioral treatment that has been empirically tested and established as an efficacious treatment for NSSI is DBT, and as a consequence, this section focuses on hypothesized mechanisms of change associated with DBT for NSSI. The essential question is how and why DBT works or, more specifically, "the processes through which therapeutic change occurs" (Kazdin & Nock, 2003, p. 1117). *Mechanisms of change* are mediators (Baron & Kenny, 1986) of treatment outcome, or those variables that account for the relationship between the treatment intervention and the outcome. Beyond functioning as a mediator, researchers have suggested that in order to demonstrate that a particular variable constitutes a mechanism of change, the proposed mechanism must (a) be specific and uniquely related to treatment change; (b) precede changes in the relevant outcome variable or variables; (c) be replicable and generalizable, demonstrated through experimental methodology; and (d) be situated within and supported by a broader knowledge base. However, despite considerable research support for treatment packages, there exists a gaping disconnect between the treatment outcome research and the theories of therapeutic change on which these treatments are based.

Enhancing Motivation to Change

Tyrer, Mitchard, Methuen, and Ranger (2003) noted the importance of accounting for issues associated with willingness or desire to change when classifying personality disorders. This can be extended to issues of treatment associated with any maladaptive behavior, including NSSI and suicidal behaviors (e.g., see Spirito, Plummer, Gispert, & Levy, 1992). From the outset, DBT assumes that attachment to the therapist and the development of a therapeutic alliance may be difficult, and that willingness to change a behavior such as NSSI that has likely been intermittently reinforced (e.g., reduced negative emotions) or self-confirming (e.g., client believes he or she deserves to be punished) is not necessarily a given. From the first session, the DBT therapist targets willingness on the client's part to eliminate NSSI from his or her behavioral repertoire. This includes educating the client regarding behavioral principles (e.g., reinforcement principles) and also pointing out the negative consequences of NSSI (e.g., maintains sense of self as flawed or pathological, may increase risk for inadvertent death). A variety of strategies to accomplish this is well articulated in the manual (see Linehan, 1993a). For example, the dialectical strategy of devil's advocate is used to strengthen a patient's commitment to treatment by providing a somewhat outlandish argument against committing, leading the patient to argue for commitment (Lynch et al., 2006). The mechanism behind devil's advocate may be based on prior research showing that public proclamation regarding intentions to modify a behavior enhances the likelihood that such changes will be made, in part because the public proclamation is seen to reflect how a person really feels (e.g., see Rollnick & Miller, 1995). In addition, although DBT is necessarily focused on changing NSSI, DBT also focuses considerable dialectic therapeutic energy on accepting and validating the patient's current condition as it is in the moment. From a behavioral perspective, validation may enhance the patient's motivation to remain in therapy by reducing the negative emotional arousal associated with blocking goals or disconfirming self-constructs (Lynch et al., 2006) and by providing a self-confirmatory environment (e.g., see Lynch et al., 2006; McCall & Simmons, 1966; Swann, 1983; Wachtel, 1977).

Controlling Eliciting Stimuli

One of the most important and primary principles associated with DBT treatment for NSSI pertains to stimulus control. Situation selection, situation modification, and attention toward or away from emotional stimuli (e.g., avoiding bars if alcoholic) have been shown to significantly modify emotional experience (see Gross, 1998). For NSSI, identifying the contextual cues associated with high urges for self-harm (e.g., temporal, environmental, emotional, social, preferred method of self-harm) begins this process. The therapist works with the patient on eliminating these triggers (e.g., discarding a favorite knife that is used for cutting, not being alone at a certain time of the day). The hypothesized mechanism of this approach is based on the DBT emotion-based conceptualization of NSSI. That is, self-injury is operant behavior that occurs in the context of extreme aversive arousal. Consequently, controlling the proximal antecedents (S^Ds) that serve as cues for NSSI reduces the likelihood that the behavior will occur. S^Ds refer to discriminative stimuli that influence the occurrence of an operant response by virtue of the schedules of enforcement that have been associated with that specific response. It is important to note that removing all relevant S^Ds is not possible, nor would this necessarily be considered a goal in treatment. Typically, stimulus control is used earlier in therapy to help the client gain some success with reducing the frequency of NSSI and over time, as relevant skills are acquired, the therapist is more likely to increasingly use behavioral exposure principles (discussed later).

Extinction and Extinction Bursts

Because NSSI is considered operant behavior, one relatively straightforward way to reduce the probability of NSSI is to control or eliminate the reinforcing consequences of self-injury (reinforcing stimuli [S^Rs]). The behavior principle associated with this approach is called *extinction*. However, this process can be extremely difficult, particularly if the reinforcing consequences occur on an intermittent basis (i.e., not every NSSI event is reinforced) or are automatic in nature (i.e., within the individual; e.g., see Nock & Prinstein, 2004, 2005). Research shows that intermittently reinforced behavior is much more difficult to extinguish (e.g., gambling; Petry & Roll, 2001). In addition, once the reinforcing consequences are removed, instead of immediately reducing the probability of the operant behavior, it is more likely that the frequency of the behavior will actually increase dramatically for a period of time; this is called an *extinction burst*. For example, attention by a therapist (e.g., extra phone contact or therapy sessions) following an episode of self-injury may reinforce NSSI; it can be expected that NSSI will temporarily increase once extinction is implemented. What is often not understood is that if the reinforcing consequence is reinstated during an extinction burst (e.g., therapist soothes), the behavior then becomes intermittently reinforced and reinforced at a higher intensity—and as a result may subsequently be more resistant to extinction. In addition, the behavior of the therapist is negatively reinforced; that is, extinction bursts are experienced as aversive by those around the behavior (e.g., think of a temper tantrum). Thus, by giving in and soothing the client, the hostility or emotional arousal exhibited by the client temporarily stops (e.g., tantrum stops because the candy is given), and the therapist's palpable relief reinforces future soothing. Thus, therapists can be reinforced by their clients to engage in iatrogenic behaviors. DBT approaches this by instituting what is called the *24-hour rule*, which states that a therapist informs the client that no therapist–client contact will occur for 24 hours after a client self-injures (see Linehan, 1993a, for exceptions to this rule). Instead, the client is told to make contact with the therapist before engaging in NSSI to use the therapist's attention to reinforce adaptive behavior (i.e., use of skills).

In DBT, the skill of evaluating the pros and cons of engaging in NSSI is also used to help the client bring into present awareness both short- and long-term negative consequences of self-injury and likely positive consequences of engaging in alternative behaviors. Poor problem-solving skills (i.e., defining and formulating the problem and generating alternative solutions) have been shown to predict higher suicidality, hopelessness, and depression in a suicidal psychiatric sample and to be moderately predictive of the same variables in a college student sample (D'Zurilla, Chang, Nottingham, & Faccini, 1998).

Targeting Nonsuicidal Self-Injury

A key strategy in DBT with suicidal individuals is for therapists to monitor NSSI and suicidal behavior on a daily basis with diary cards, to assess precipitants and consequences, and to apply problem-solving strategies to develop alternative responses to distress or urges to self-harm. Thus, DBT targets self-injurious behaviors directly, not hypothesized disorders thought to result in a greater likelihood for self-injurious behavior (e.g., depression).

The specificity and thoroughness with which DBT evaluates NSSI in session can be experienced as aversive, particularly when discussed in excruciating detail as is the case for a behavioral chain analysis. From this perspective, the mechanism of change associated with this type of scrutiny can be seen as the application of a mild aversive contingency. Thus, a chain analysis may function as a punisher for engaging in NSSI, and with repeated use, the client learns that if he or she engages in self-injury, the next therapy session will involve a lengthy discussion of the behavior and the surrounding context (Lynch et al., 2006). Indeed, clinically we have observed, on multiple occasions, clients indicating that they thought of hurting themselves but then remembered that they would have to talk about it in session and so decided to use a different method to regulate their emotion.

In addition, discussing the chain of events that led to NSSI may increase the likelihood that the patient will recognize future patterns and implement skillful behavior when needed, and as such another mechanism of action may be related to an enhanced ability for stimulus discrimination or episodic memory (Lynch et al., 2006). Research has suggested that BPD is associated with a tendency for overly generalized nonspecific memory for personally relevant events (Startup et al., 2001). For example, consider a client who recently felt extreme anger and despair following a request by her to her partner for help in making dinner for their three small children. A behavioral chain analysis revealed that her partner ignored her request, exacerbating her emotional vulnerability. On analysis, the precipitating event for NSSI occurred when one of the children spilled a full glass of milk over the entire table, leading to the client isolating herself in a bathroom and banging her head repeatedly against the wall. The consequence of this behavior was that her partner opens the bathroom door, sees blood, behaves more nurturing (i.e., positively reinforces self-injury), and the client cries and feels intense shame. By reviewing in detail the chain of events leading to NSSI, it is hypothesized that this rehearsal of events may enhance the client's episodic memory for the pattern of events that precipitates NSSI. Repeated and detailed accounting of the antecedent vulnerability factors, behaviors, and consequences associated with self-injury then enhance the ability of the client to recognize the warning signs of an impending episode of NSSI, consciously apply newly learned emotion regulation, and develop new associations that alter the signaling strength of the antecedents that in the past were associated with self-injury (through behavioral exposure). Over time, stimuli that previously elicited overwhelming emotional responding and related problem behaviors (i.e., self-injury) become conditioned stimuli for skillful behavior, and therapist reinforcement of newly acquired skills strengthen these associations (Lynch et al., 2006).

Changing Vulnerability to Emotional Cues and Urges for Self-Harm

Changing emotional vulnerability changes the establishing operation or reinforcing effects of particular events and the subsequent behavior of the individual. Two sets of processes are needed here: biological change and context change. Although there are a wide range of individual variations in physiological reactivity to emotional stimuli (Boyce & Ellis, 2005), it remains possible even when highly influenced by immutable genetic dispositions or early developmental experiences for individuals to influence their vulnerability to react to emotional stimuli (Linehan et al., 2007). As such, DBT focuses on teaching skills that target behaviors that contribute to biological homeostasis and emotional reactivity. These include physical illness, balanced nutrition, avoiding mood-altering drugs, sufficient sleep, and adequate exercise (Linehan, 1993a). Other skills target high emotional arousal. An example is using cold, icy water on the face, a method derived from research on the human dive reflex that is elicited by a combination of breath holding and face immersion with cold water (Linehan et al., 2007). The dive reflex involves both branches of the autonomic nervous system: parasympathetic activation (bradycardia) and concurrent sympathetic activation (vasoconstriction; Hurwitz & Furedy, 1986). In addition, when emotional arousal is high, acute bouts of intense exercise or progressive muscle relaxation are also recommended (Linehan et al., 2007). All of these DBT techniques focus on changing the biological vulnerability to emotional cues and in theory reduce the likelihood that urges or acts of self-harm will occur.

Mindfulness and Deliteralization

A core skill in DBT is mindfulness training. Mindfulness involves learning to control the focus of attention, not the object being observed, and may help modulate emotional experience by enhancing the ability to turn focus attention away from that which is not useful and attend to what is (Lynch et al., 2006). Indeed, research has shown that being able to disengage from emotional stimuli may reduce the tendency to experience negative affect (Ellenbogen, Schwartzman, Stewart, & Walker, 2002). Thus, being able mindfully to turn attention away from stimuli that in the past elicited emotions or urges to self-harm is hypothesized to reduce the likelihood of NSSI. In addition, mindfulness teaches clients to observe thoughts as "only thoughts" that are not necessarily true (Lynch et al., 2006). This may deliteralize (e.g., see Hayes, Kohlenberg, & Melancon, 1989) or remove literal belief in cognitions associated with NSSI that in the past were considered valid interpretations of events (e.g., "I deserve to be punished"). In addition, mindfulness may change classically conditioned associations by teaching clients to observe without judgment emotional action urges or response tendencies rather than automatically responding to them (e.g., fear elicits an action urge of escape, anger elicits an action urge to attack). Thus, without deliberate effort (i.e., by simply observing without judgment), mindfulness may create new benign associations to classically conditioned stimuli, and as such alter the appraisal associated with the stimuli. For example, the transitory sensations, thoughts, and urging components of fear are simply observed without the assumption that the experience requires down-regulation, avoidance, or change strategies. So, too, urges for self-harm and its attendant thoughts and emotions can simply be observed without judgment as a transitory painful sensation or experience. By changing the response tendency associated with the urge (i.e., from approach–avoid to observe), new associations are acquired. With repeated practice, these new benign associations become increasingly dominant, and the individual learns that they do not have to respond to every action urge or response tendency that is associated with emotion or NSSI. With repeated practice over time, it is hypothesized that mindfulness influences the individual's sense of self from malignant to benign or neutral; therefore, the desire to self-punish (i.e., verify their sense of self) through self-injury is reduced.

Behavioral Exposure

Discussing antecedent emotional responses, as well as urges and acts of self-harm, promotes nonreinforced exposure to stimuli associated with these behaviors (i.e., changes classically conditioned stimulus–stimulus relations). Behavioral chain analyses of episodes of self-injury are particularly helpful in changing the automatic elicitation of shame. Discussing shameful events in detail (i.e., an episode of self-injury) is hypothesized to work precisely because the new learning (i.e., the therapist's benign rather than malignant response to the client's shame) changes the association between the stimulus and the respondent (i.e., shame), thereby facilitating engagement in problem solving (Lynch et al., 2006).

Skills Generalization

In DBT, clients are encouraged to contact therapists by telephone throughout treatment as a means to reduce suicidal and NSSI crises, increase problem solving, learn how to ask appropriately for help from others, and facilitate repair of recent ruptures in the therapeutic relationship. Telephone consultation may enhance generalization through the application of contingencies and coaching and shaping behavior in vivo. In addition, telephone consultation may reduce the reemergence of problem behavior by functioning as an extinction or learning reminder. This is hypothesized to occur through principles of learning (Bouton, 1993; Bouton & Brooks, 1993). Essentially, in-clinic therapy can be conceptualized as an extinction-training context for problem behaviors. For example, urges to engage in NSSI during the session are not reinforced; thus, self-harm attempts in session extinguish over time, and telephone calls between sessions may serve as cues for the retrieval of extinction memories from therapy sessions and memories of effective behavior learned in treatment.

CONCLUSION

Our behavioral conceptualization considers NSSI as an operant response that is reinforced by the immediate benefits of temporary emotional distraction and relief from intense negative affect, despite a variety of long-term consequences. Urges to engage in self-harm and the aversive emotions that precede self-harm are considered classically conditioned events, whereas actual self-injury (e.g., cutting) is seen as an operant response reinforced through reductions in negative arousal, verification of self-constructs, or social interactions. Units of analyses are functionally and contextually based and include eliciting operations (e.g., biological vulnerabilities, establishing vulnerabilities, S^Ds), consequential operations (e.g., negative reinforcement, self-punishment), and rule-governed operations (e.g., thoughts, beliefs). The only behavioral treatment that has demonstrated treatment advantages in reducing NSSI and suicidal behavior over some type of active treatment control has been DBT. As such, the clinical recommendations that follow are based on this approach, but it is important to note that these suggestions are not intended to be comprehensive (see Linehan, 1993a, 1993b; Linehan, Davison, Lynch, & Sanderson, 2006, for detailed protocols and principles).

Clinical Recommendations

First, the therapist should strike a balance between empathy and acceptance on the one hand, and structured specific behavior-changing efforts on the other hand. Second, both client and therapist should specify and agree to the goals, the format, the modalities, and the treatment strategies of the therapy before it formally begins. Third, NSSI and suicidal behavior should in general always be considered at the top of the treatment hierarchy with regard to priority. Monitoring should occur on a daily basis (e.g., through use of diary cards), and a functional ideographic chain and solution analysis of NSSI or suicidal events, increases in urges to self-harm or attempt suicide, or both should ideally be conducted following each occurrence. Fourth, the client's motivation for treatment is enhanced and therapeutic change is most likely if the therapist can address therapeutic impasses with nonconfrontational strategies and if the individual therapist is flexible in his or her limits, being more available to the client during period of crisis. However, therapists treating clients engaging in NSSI and suicidal behavior should be both honest and explicit about their limits. Fifth, focus in treatment for NSSI and suicidal behavior should be present-oriented, and exploration of the past should not occur until the client has solidly established behavioral and emotional control. Sixth, treatment of NSSI and suicidal behavior is best when designed to be comprehensive; that is, it aims to enhance client capabilities and behavioral skills as well as motivation and attends specifically to generalization from the therapeutic setting to the client's ordinary life. Seventh, particularly early in treatment, stimulus control procedures should be used (e.g., removing razor blades from the client's home if they cut). Eighth, treatment should progress toward using exposure to the cues setting off maladaptive emotions and urges that are linked with NSSI and suicidal behavior combined with blocking escape behaviors (i.e., self-injury) while reinforcing skillful, opposite-to-emotion responses. Ninth, specific protocols should be developed that provide therapist availability for crisis intervention and coaching of skills outside the time frame of scheduled therapy appointments. Tenth, and finally, therapists treating clients with NSSI or suicidal behavior require emotional support for this type of work and should also receive ongoing consultation and supervision.

Research Recommendations

Although across studies DBT as a treatment package has resulted in significant reductions in self-injurious behavior, suicide attempts, and suicidal ideation, further research is desperately needed. If the field is to progress, research must explicitly begin to focus on understanding how, why, when, and for whom DBT interventions are effective. This includes mechanism and dismantling studies designed to determine the essential components of DBT, as well as the degree of fidelity to the DBT manual required to obtain effective results. Clinical trials of DBT or other behavioral treatments should define and measure hypothesized mechanisms of action that stand up to tests of plausibility and coherence. Clinical trials should also use multiple measurement points to determine a gradient (i.e., dosage effect) with the understanding that changes in a hypothesized mechanism of action precede changes in outcome. Finally, development and testing of novel time-limited interventions (e.g., telephone coaching, problem-solving and solution analysis, brief training in deliteralization techniques) that can be delivered by health care providers with relatively little mental health training or within nontertiary-based treatment centers (e.g., EDs, primary care offices) have enormous potential.

In conclusion, research should continue to focus on improving empirically supported behavioral interventions (e.g., DBT) through the conduct of component and process-analytic studies, dismantling studies, studies designed to analyze response predictors, and large-sample effectiveness research in community settings; at the same time, researchers should be encouraged to develop new and more time-limited approaches. We hope that this chapter provides the impetus for others to expand research efforts into these new domains and continue a tradition based on empirical observation to mitigate the human suffering associated with NSSI and suicidal behavior.

REFERENCES

American Psychiatric Association. (1994). *Diagnostic and statistical manual of mental disorders* (4th ed.). Washington, DC: Author.

Anderson, N. H. (1981). *Foundations of information integration theory*. New York: Academic Press.

Bakish, D. (1999). The patient with comorbid depression and anxiety: The unmet need. *The Journal of Clinical Psychiatry, 60,* 20–24.

Bandura, A. (1969). *Principles of behavior modification.* New York: Holt, Rinehart, & Winston.

Barley, W. D., Buie, S. E., Peterson, E. W., Hollingsworth, A. S., Griva, M., Hickerson, S. C., et al. (1993). Development of an inpatient cognitive–behavioral treatment program for borderline personality disorder. *Journal of Personality Disorders, 7,* 232–240.

Baron, R. M., & Kenny, D. A. (1986). The moderator–mediator variable distinction in social psychological research: Conceptual, strategic, and statistical considerations. *Journal of Personality and Social Psychology, 51,* 1173–1182.

Beck, A. T., Rush, A. J., Shaw, F. F., & Emery, G. (1979). *Cognitive therapy of depression.* New York: Guilford Press.

Biglan, A., & Hayes, S. C. (1996). Should the behavioral sciences become more pragmatic? The case for functional contextualism in research on human behavior. *Applied and Preventive Psychology: Current Scientific Perspectives, 5,* 47–57.

Biglan, A., Rothlind, J., Hops, H., & Sherman, L. (1989). Impact of distressed and aggressive behavior. *Journal of Abnormal Psychology, 98,* 218–228.

Bohus, M., Haaf, B., Simms, T., Limberger, M. F., Schmahl, C., Unckel, C., et al. (2004). Effectiveness of inpatient dialectical behavioral therapy for borderline personality disorder: A controlled trial. *Behaviour Research and Therapy, 42,* 487–499.

Bohus, M., Haaf, B., Stiglmayr, C., Pohl, U., Bohme, R., & Linehan, M. M. (2000). Evaluation of inpatient dialectical-behavioral therapy for borderline personality disorder: A prospective study. *Behaviour Research and Therapy, 38,* 875–887.

Bouton, M. E. (1993). Context, time, and memory retrieval in the interference paradigms of Pavlovian learning. *Psychological Bulletin, 114,* 80–90.

Bouton, M. E., & Brooks, D. C. (1993). Time and context effects on performance in a Pavlovian discrimination reversal. *Journal of Experimental Psychology: Animal Behavior Processes, 19,* 165–179.

Boyce, W. T., & Ellis, B. J. (2005). Biological sensitivity to context: I. An evolutionary–developmental theory of the origins and functions of stress reactivity. *Development and Psychopathology, 17,* 271–301.

Brown, M. Z., Comtois, K. A., & Linehan, M. M. (2002). Reasons for suicide attempts and nonsuicidal self-injury in women with borderline personality disorder. *Journal of Abnormal Psychology, 111,* 198–202.

Brown, M. Z., & Linehan, M. M. (1996, November). *The relationship between negative emotions and parasuicide in borderline personality disorder.* Poster presented at the Association for Advancement of Behavior Therapy, New York

Christensen, A., Jacobson, N. S., & Babock, J. C. (1995). Integrative behavioral couple therapy. In N. S. Jacobson & A. S. Gurman (Eds.), *Clinical handbook of couples therapy* (pp. 31–64). New York: Guilford Press.

Corrigan, P. W. (2001). Getting ahead of the data: A threat to some behavior therapies. *The Behavior Therapist, 24,* 189–193.

Cukrowicz, K. C., Ekblad, A., Cheavens, J. S., Rosenthal, M. Z., & Lynch, T. R. (2008). Coping and thought suppression as predictors of suicidal ideation in depressed older adults with personality disorders. *Aging & Mental Health, 12,* 149–157.

Dougher, M. J., Perkins, D. R., Greenway, D., Koons, A., & Chiasson, C. (2002). Contextual control of equivalence-based transformation of functions. *Journal of the Experimental Analysis of Behavior, 78,* 78–63.

D'Zurilla, T. J., Chang, E. C., Nottingham, E. J., & Faccini, L. (1998). Social problem-solving deficits and hopelessness, depression, and suicidal risk in college students and psychiatric inpatients. *Journal of Clinical Psychology, 54,* 1091–1107.

Ellenbogen, M. A., Schwartzmann, A. E., Stewart, J., & Walker, C. D. (2002). Stress and selective attention: The interplay of mood, cortisol levels, and emotion information processing. *Psychophysiology, 39,* 723–732.

Gardner, D. L., & Cowdry, R. W. (1985). Suicidal and parasuicidal behavior in borderline personality. *Psychiatric Clinic North America, 8,* 389–403.

Gellatly, I., & Meyer, J. (1992). The effects of goal difficulty on physiological arousal, cognition, and task performance. *Journal of Applied Psychology, 77,* 694–704.

Giesler, R. B., Josephs, R. A., & Swann, W. B., Jr. (1996). Self-verification in clinical depression. *Journal of Abnormal Psychology, 105,* 358–368.

Gould, M. S., King, R., Greenwald, S., Fisher, P., Schwab-Stone, M., Kramer, R., et al. (1998). Psychopathology associated with suicidal ideation and attempts among children and adolescents. *Journal of the American Academy of Child and Adolescent Psychiatry, 37,* 915–923.

Gross, J. J. (1998). Antecedent- and response-focused emotion regulation: Divergent consequences for experience, expression, and physiology. *Journal of Personality and Social Psychology, 74,* 224–237.

Haines, J., Williams, C., Brian, K., & Wilson, G. (1996). The psychophysiology of self-mutilation. *Journal of Abnormal Psychology, 104,* 479–489.

Hayes, S. C. (1993). Analytic goals and the varieties of scientific contextualism. In S. C. Hayes, L. J. Hayes, H. W. Reese, & T. R. Sardin (Eds.), *Varieties of scientific contextualism* (pp. 11–27). Reno, NV: Context Press.

Hayes, S. C. (2004). Acceptance and commitment therapy and the new behavior therapies: Mindfulness, acceptance and relationship. In S. C. Hayes, V. M. Follette, & M. M. Linehan (Eds.), *Mindfulness and acceptance: Expanding the cognitive behavioral tradition* (pp. 1–29). New York: Guilford Press.

Hayes, S. C., Brownstein, A. J., Haas, J. R., & Greenway, D. E. (1986). Instructions, multiple schedules, and extinction: Distinguishing rule-governed from schedule-controlled behavior. *Journal of the Experimental Analysis of Behavior, 46,* 137–147.

Hayes, S. C., Follette, W. C., & Follette, V. M. (1995). Behavior therapy: A contextual approach. In A. S. Gunman & S. B. Messer (Eds.), *Essential psychotherapies: Theory and practice* (pp. 128–181). New York: Guilford Press.

Hayes, S. C., Kohlenberg, B., & Melancon, S. (1989). Avoiding and altering rule-control as a strategy of clinical intervention. In S. C. Hayes (Ed.), *Rule-governed behavior: Cognition, contingencies, and instructional control* (pp. 359–385). New York: Plenum Press.

Hayes, S. C., Masuda, A., Bissett, R., Luoma, J., & Guerrero, L. F. (2004). DBT, FAP, and ACT: How empirically oriented are the new behavior therapy technologies? *Behavior Therapy. 35*, 35–54.

Hayes, S. C., Strosahl, K. D., & Wilson, K. G. (1999). *Acceptance and commitment therapy: An experiential approach to behavior change.* New York: Guilford Press.

Hayes, S. C., Wilson, K. G., Gifford, E. V., Follette, V. M., & Strosahl, K. (1996). Experiential avoidance and behavioral disorders: A functional dimensional approach to diagnosis and treatment. *Journal of Consulting and Clinical Psychology, 64*, 1152–1168.

Hilt, L. M., Nock, M. K., Lloyd-Richardson, E., & Prinstein, M. J. (2008). Longitudinal study of nonsuicidal self-injury among young adolescents: Rates, correlates, and preliminary test of an interpersonal model. *Journal of Early Adolescence, 28*, 455–469.

Hopko, D. R., Lejuez, C. W., Ruggiero, K. J., & Eifert, G. H. (2003). Contemporary behavioral activation treatments for depression: Procedures, principles, and progress. *Clinical Psychology Review, 23*, 699–717.

Hurwitz, B. E., & Furedy, J. J. (1986). The human dive reflex: An experimental, topographical and physiological analysis. *Physiology & Behavior, 36*, 287–294.

Ivanoff, A., Brown, M. Z., & Linehan, M. M. (2001). Dialectical behavior therapy for impulsive self-injurious behaviors. In D. Simeon & E. Hollander (Eds.), *Self-injurious behaviors: Assessment and treatment* (pp. 149–174). Washington, DC: American Psychiatric Press.

Joiner, T. E., Brown, J. S., & Wingate, L. R. (2005). The psychology of neurobiology of suicidal behavior. *Annual Review of Psychology, 56*, 287–314.

Kazdin, A. E., & Nock, M. K. (2003). Delineating mechanisms of change in child and adolescent therapy: Methodological issues and research recommendations. *Journal of Child Psychology and Psychiatry, 44*, 1116–1129.

Kessler, R. C., Berglund, P. A., Bruce, M. L., Koch, J. R., Laska, E. M., Leaf, P. J., et al. (2001). The prevalence and correlates of untreated serious mental illness. *Health Services Research, 36*, 987–1007.

Kohlenberg, R. J., & Tasi, M. (1991). *Functional analytic psychotherapy: Creating intense and curative therapeutic relationships.* New York: Plenum Press.

Koons, C. R., Robins, C. L., Tweed, J. L., Lynch, T. R., Gonzalez, A. M., & Morse, J. Q. (2001). Efficacy of dialectical behavior therapy in women veterans with borderline personality disorder. *Behavior Therapy, 32*, 371–390.

Leibenluft, E., Gardner, D. L., & Cowdry, R. W. (1987). The inner experience of the borderline self-mutilator. *Journal of Personality Disorders, 1*, 317–324.

Lejuez, C. W., Hopko, D. R., LePage, J. P., Hopko, S. D., & McNeil, D. W. (2002). A brief behavioral activation treatment for depression. *Cognitive and Behavioral Practice, 8*, 164–175.

Linehan, M. M. (1993a). *Cognitive–behavioral treatment for borderline personality disorder.* New York: Guilford Press.

Linehan, M. M. (1993b). *Skills training manual for treating borderline personality disorder*. New York: Guilford Press.

Linehan, M. M. (1997). Behavioral treatments of suicidal behaviors: Definitional obfuscation and treatment outcomes. *Annals of the New York Academy of Sciences, 836,* 302–328.

Linehan, M. M., Armstrong, H. E., Suarez, A., Allmon, D., & Heard, H. L. (1991). A cognitive–behavioral treatment of chronically parasuicidal borderline patients. *Archives of General Psychiatry, 48,* 1060–1064.

Linehan, M. M., Bohus, M., & Lynch, T. R. (2007). Dialectical behavior therapy for pervasive emotion dysregulation: Theoretical and practical underpinnings. In J. Gross (Ed.), *Handbook of emotion regulation* (pp. 581–605). New York: Guilford Press.

Linehan, M. M., Comtois, K. A., Murray, A. M., Brown, M. Z., Gallop, R. J., & Heard, H. L. (2006). Two-year randomized trial and follow-up of dialectical behavior vs therapy by experts for suicidal behaviors and borderline personality disorder. *Archives of General Psychiatry, 63,* 757–766.

Linehan, M. M., Davison, G., Lynch, T. R., & Sanderson, C. (2006). Principles of therapeutic change in the treatment of personality disorders. In L. Castonguay & L. Beutler (Eds.), *Principles of therapeutic change that work* (pp. 239–252). New York: Oxford University Press.

Linehan, M. M., Dimeff, L. A., Reynolds, S. K., Comtois, K. A., Shaw-Welch, S., & Heagerty, P. (2002). Dialectical behavior therapy versus comprehensive validation plus 12-step for the treatment of opioid dependent women meeting criteria for borderline personality disorder. *Drug and Alcohol Dependence, 67,* 13–26.

Linehan, M. M., Heard, H. L., & Armstrong, H. E. (1993). Naturalistic follow-up of a behavioral treatment for chronically parasuicidal borderline patients. *Archives of General Psychiatry, 50,* 971–974.

Linehan, M. M., Heard, H. L., Wagner, A. M., & Brown, M. Z. (1997). *Parasuicide history interview: Development of validity and reliability.* Unpublished manuscript. University of Washington, Seattle.

Linehan, M. M., Schmidt, H., Dimeff, L. A., Craft, J. C., Kanter, J., & Comtois, K. A. (1999). Dialectical behavior therapy for patients with borderline personality disorder and drug-dependence. *The American Journal on Addictions, 8,* 279–292.

Linehan, M. M., Tutek, D. A., Heard, H. L., & Armstrong, H. E. (1994). Interpersonal outcome of cognitive behavioral treatment of chronically suicidal borderline patients. *The American Journal of Psychiatry, 151,* 1771–1776.

Ludäscher, P., Bohus, M., Lieb, K., Philipsen, A., Jochims, A., & Schmahl, C. (2007). Elevated pain thresholds correlate with dissociation and aversive arousal in patients with borderline personality disorder. *Psychiatry Research, 149,* 291–296.

Lynch, T. R., Chapman, A. L., Rosenthal, Z. M., Kuo, J. R., & Linehan, M. M. (2006). Mechanisms of change in dialectical behavior therapy: Theoretical and empirical observations. *Journal of Clinical Psychology, 62,* 459–480.

Lynch, T. R., Cheavens, J. S., Cukrowicz, K. C., Thorp., S., Bronner, L., & Beyer, J. (2007). Treatment of older adults with co-morbid personality disorder and depression: A dialectical behavior therapy approach. *International Journal of Geriatric Psychiatry, 22*, 131–143.

Lynch, T. R., Cheavens, J. S., Morse, J. Q., & Rosenthal, M. Z. (2004). A model predicting suicidal ideation and hopelessness in depressed older adults: The impact of emotion inhibition and affect intensity. *Aging & Mental Health, 8*, 1–12.

Lynch, T. R., Morse, J. Q., Mendelson, T., & Robins, C. J. (2003). Dialectical behavior therapy for depressed older adults: A randomized pilot study. *The American Journal of Geriatric Psychiatry, 11*, 1–13.

Lynch, T. R., Robins, C. J., Morse, J. Q., & Krause, E. D. (2001). A mediational model of relating affect intensity, emotion, inhibition, and psychological distress. *Behavior Therapy, 32*, 519–536.

Lynch, T. R., Schneider, K. G., Rosenthal, M. Z., & Cheavens, J. S. (2007). A mediational model of trait negative affectivity, dispositional thought suppression, and intrusive thoughts following laboratory stressors. *Behaviour Research and Therapy, 45*, 749–761.

McCall, G. J., & Simmons, J. L. (1966). *Identities and interactions: An examination of human associations in everyday life*. New York: Free Press.

Michel, K., Valach, L., & Waeber, V. (1994). Understanding deliberate self-harm: The patients' views. *Crisis, 15*, 172–178.

Mineka, S., & Zinbarg, R. (1995). Conditioning and etiological models of anxiety disorders: Stress-in-dynamic context anxiety models. In D. A. Hope (Ed.), *Nebraska Symposium on Motivation: Vol. 43. Perspectives on anxiety, panic, and fear* (pp. 135–210). Lincoln: University of Nebraska Press.

Nock, M. K., & Banaji, M. R. (2007). Assessment of self-injurious thoughts using a behavioral test. *The American Journal of Psychiatry, 164*, 820–823.

Nock, M. K., & Prinstein, M. J. (2004). A functional approach to the assessment of self-mutilative behavior. *Journal of Consulting and Clinical Psychology, 72*, 885–890.

Nock, M. K., & Prinstein, M. J. (2005). Contextual features and behavioral functions of self-mutilation among adolescents. *Journal of Abnormal Psychology, 114*, 140–146.

Noyes, R. (1991). Suicide and panic disorder: A review. *Journal of Affective Disorders, 1*, 1–11.

Ohman, A., & Mineka, S. (2001). Fears, phobias, and preparedness: Toward an evolved module of fear and fear learning. *Psychological Review, 108*, 483–522.

Orr, S. P., Metzger, L. J., Lasko, N. B., Macklin, M. L., Peri, T., & Pitman, R. K. (2000). De novo conditioning in trauma-exposed individual with and without posttraumatic stress disorder. *Journal of Abnormal Psychology, 109*, 290–298.

Pelham, B. W., & Swann, W. B., Jr. (1994). The juncture of intrapersonal and interpersonal knowledge: Self-certainty and interpersonal congruence. *Personality and Social Psychology Bulletin, 20*, 349–357.

Petry, N. M., & Roll, J. M. (2001). A behavioral approach to understanding and treating pathological gambling. *Seminars in Neuropsychiatry, 6*, 177–183.

Rachman, S. (1997). A cognitive theory of obsessions. *Behaviour Research and Therapy, 35*, 793–802.

Rollnick, S., & Miller, W. R. (1995). What is motivational interviewing? *Behavioural and Cognitive Psychotherapy, 23*, 325–334.

Rosenthal, M. Z., Gratz, K., Kosson, D. S., Lejuez, C. W., Cheavens, J. S., & Lynch, T. R. (2008). Borderline personality disorder and emotional functioning: A review of the research literature. *Clinical Psychology Review, 28*, 75–91.

Rudd, M. D., Dahm, P. F., & Rajab, M. H. (1993). Diagnostic comorbidity in persons with suicidal ideation. *The American Journal of Psychiatry, 150*, 928–934.

Russ, M. J., Roth, S. D., Lerman, A., Kakuma, T., Harrison, K., Shindledecker, R. D., et al. (1992). Pain perception in self-injurious patients with borderline personality disorder. *Biological Psychiatry, 32*, 501–511.

Safer, D. L., Telch, C. F., & Agras, W. (2001). Dialectical behavior therapy for bulimia nervosa. *The American Journal of Psychiatry, 158*, 632–634.

Segal, Z. V., Williams, J. M. G., & Teasdale, J. D. (2002). *Mindfulness-based cognitive therapy for depression: A new approach to preventing relapse*. New York: Guilford Press.

Shapiro, S. (1987). Self-mutilation and self-blame in incest. *American Journal of Psychotherapy, 41*, 46–54.

Spirito, A., Plummer, B., Gispert, M., & Levy, M. (1992). Adolescent suicide attempts: Outcomes at follow-up. *American Journal of Orthopsychiatry, 62*, 464–468.

Startup, M., Heard, H., Swales, M., Jones, B., Williams, J. M. G., & Jones, R. S. P. (2001). Autobiographical memory and parasuicide in borderline personality disorder. *British Journal of Clinical Psychology, 40*, 113–120.

Swann, W. B., Jr. (1983). Self-verification: Bringing social reality into harmony with the self. In J. Suls & A. G. Greenwald (Eds.), *Social psychological perspectives on the self* (pp. 33–66). Hillsdale, NJ: Erlbaum.

Swann, W. B., Jr. (1997). The trouble with change: Self-verification and allegiance to the self. *Psychological Science, 8*, 177–180.

Swann, W. B., Jr., de la Ronde, C., & Hixon, J. G. (1994). Authenticity and positivity strivings in marriage and courtship. *Journal of Personality and Social Psychology, 66*, 857–869.

Swann, W. B., Jr., Rentfrow, P. J., & Gosling, S. D. (2003). The precarious couple effect: Verbally inhibited men + critical, disinhibited women = bad chemistry. *Journal of Personality and Social Psychology, 85*, 1095–1105.

Telch, C. F., Agras, W., & Linehan M. M. (2001). Dialectical behavior therapy for binge eating disorder. *Journal of Consulting and Clinical Psychology, 69*, 1061–1065.

Turner, R. M. (2000). Understanding dialectical behavior therapy. *Clinical Psychiatry, 7*, 95–98.

Tyrer, P., Mitchard, S., Methuen, C., & Ranger, M. (2003). Treatment rejecting and treatment seeking personality disorders: Type R and Type S. *Journal of Personality Disorders, 17*, 263–267.

van den Bosch, L. M., Koeter, M. W. J., Stijnen, T., Verheul, R., & van den Brink, W. (2005). Sustained efficacy of dialectical behavior therapy for borderline personality disorder. *Behaviour Research and Therapy, 43*, 1231–1241.

van den Bosch, L. M., Verheul, R., Schippers, G. M., & van den Brink, W. (2002). Dialectical behavior therapy of borderline patients with and without substance use problems: Implementation and long-term effects. *Additive Behavior, 27*, 911–923.

Verheul, R., van den Bosch, L. M. C., Koeter, M. W. J., De Ridder, M. A. J., Stijnen, T., & van den Brink, W. (2003). Dialectical behavior therapy for women with borderline personality disorder: 12-month, randomized clinical trial in the Netherlands. *The British Journal of Psychiatry, 182*, 135–140.

Wachtel, P. (1977). *Psychoanalysis and behavior therapy: Toward an integration.* New York: Basic Books.

Wagner, A. W., & Linehan, M. M. (1997). The relationship between childhood sexual abuse and suicidal behaviors in borderline patients. In M. Zanarini (Ed.), *The role of sexual abuse in the etiology of borderline personality disorder* (pp. 203–223). Washington, DC: American Psychiatric Association.

Walsh, B. W., & Rosen, P. M. (1988). *Self-mutilation: Theory, research, and treatment.* New York: Guilford Press.

Watson, J. B. (1913). Psychology as the behaviorist views it. *Psychological Review, 20*, 158–177.

Watson, J. B. (1924). *Behaviorism.* New York: Norton.

Zettle, R. D., & Hayes, S. C. (1982). Rule governed behavior: A potential theoretical framework for cognitive–behavioral therapy. In P. C. Kendall (Ed.), *Advances in cognitive behavioral research and therapy* (pp. 73–118). New York: Academy Press.

13

SPECIAL ISSUES IN TREATING ADOLESCENT NONSUICIDAL SELF-INJURY

ALEC L. MILLER, JENNIFER J. MUEHLENKAMP,
AND COLLEEN M. JACOBSON

This chapter addresses special issues in evaluating and treating adolescents who engage in nonsuicidal self-injury (NSSI). We begin by briefly reviewing the limited epidemiological data for this age group. Second, we briefly review the assessment strategies and interventions used with this population. Third, we discuss the unique features of dialectical behavior therapy (DBT) for adolescents who engage in NSSI. This entails a discussion of the various modes and functions of DBT, including working with affected families. We conclude with a discussion of how to manage contagion within a group-treatment milieu.

NONSUICIDAL SELF-INJURY AMONG ADOLESCENTS: THE SCOPE OF THE PROBLEM

Clinicians and researchers alike are all too aware that NSSI among adolescents is a serious, widespread, and growing problem. However, because epidemiological research that specifically addresses adolescent NSSI as distinct from suicidal behaviors is relatively nascent, the information available is somewhat scarce. Nonetheless, the studies that have addressed NSSI provide valuable information that will directly inform clinical intervention and prevention. In this section we provide a brief overview of the epidemiological research on NSSI, and then we comment briefly on the assessment of NSSI to provide a foundation for the discussion of treatment (see chaps. 3 and 7 for more on epidemiology and assessment).

Estimates of lifetime prevalence of NSSI based on high school samples range from 13.0% to 23.2% (Muehlenkamp & Gutierrez, 2004, 2007; Ross & Heath, 2002; Zoroglu et al., 2003). Further, the 12-month prevalence of NSSI ranges from 2.5% to 12.5% (Garrison et al., 1993; Muehlenkamp & Gutierrez, 2007), indicating that as many as 2.1 million high school students may engage in NSSI each year. The age of onset of NSSI typically falls between 12 and 14 years (Kumar, Pepe, & Steer, 2004; Muehlenkamp & Gutierrez, 2004, 2007; Nixon, Cloutier, & Aggarwi, 2002; Nock & Prinstein, 2004; Ross & Heath, 2002).

Despite popular belief, it is unclear whether NSSI is more common among girls than boys, as only two (Muehlenkamp & Gutierrez, 2007; Ross & Heath, 2002) of five (Garrison et al., 1993; Muehlenkamp & Gutierrez, 2004; Zoroglu et al., 2003) community-based studies concluded that girls were significantly more likely to engage in NSSI. The other three studies found no gender difference.

It is likely that the majority of adolescents who engage in NSSI have a psychiatric disorder. However, only one community-based study (Garrison et al., 1993) has included a formal assessment of both NSSI and psychiatric disorders; the researchers concluded that having a diagnosis of major depressive disorder (MDD), specific phobia, obsessive–compulsive disorder (8.3 times, 8.5 times, and 5.3 times, respectively), or a combination of these was associated with an elevated risk of engaging in NSSI. Studies that have included clinical samples of youth have identified elevated rates of MDD, externalizing disorders, substance use, and borderline personality disorder (BPD) among those who have engaged in NSSI compared with those who do not self-injure (Jacobson, Muehlenkamp, Miller, & Turner, 2008; Kumar et al., 2004; Nock, Joiner, Gordon, Lloyd-Richardson, & Prinstein, 2006).

In addition to psychiatric disorders, most notably depressive disorders, adolescents who have engaged in NSSI display elevated levels of hostility (Ross & Heath, 2003; Zoroglu et al., 2003), alexithymia (Kisiel & Lyons, 2001; Zlotnick, Shea, Perstein, Costello, & Begin, 1996), emotional reactivity (Nock, Wedig, Holmberg, & Hooley, 2008), and dissociation (Kisiel & Lyons, 2001; Zlotnick, Donaldson, Spirito, & Pearlstein, 1997) compared with their non-self-injuring peers. In addition, research indicates that experiencing stressful life events (Garrison et al., 1993), including interpersonal loss (Rosen, Walsh, & Rode, 1990), increases one's odds of engaging in NSSI.

ASSESSMENT CONSIDERATIONS

As indicated earlier, epidemiological research regarding NSSI among adolescents is a fairly new endeavor and, unfortunately, is hampered by limitations. Accurate interpretation of the research and execution of clinical assessment of NSSI requires an understanding of the classification and assessment schemes used in the field.

There are at least two important issues to consider when assessing NSSI among adolescents. The first is whether to use self-report instruments or a clinical interview. Self-report instruments may begin with a question such as, "Have you ever hurt yourself on purpose without wanting to die?" thus relying on the participant to decipher the meaning of the question on his or her own. Clinical interviews allow for further clarification of an act and the intent of it through dialogue between the interviewer and the interviewee. A strength of the self-report approach is that it may lead to more honest responding, whereas a strength of the clinician interview may be more accurate classification of the self-injurious behavior. Regardless of the type of approach (i.e., self-report or clinician interview) used, it is important to gather specific information about the behavior, including number of episodes of NSSI, number of injuries per episode, methods used, and access to instruments of implementation (Walsh, 2006). Research suggests that the greater the number of methods used to engage in NSSI, the greater the likelihood of making a suicide attempt (Nock et al., 2006; Zlotnick et al., 1997).

The second important issue to consider is how to integrate adolescent and parent reports, which often differ in the case of NSSI. In a clinical research setting, semistructured diagnostic interviews and self-report measures are often given to the adolescent and parent, and separate time is allotted for both parties. This can often take upward of 3 hours. In most clinical settings, including private practice settings, we recommend the following 90-minute consultation format to obtain valid information. The first 10 to 15 minutes is devoted to spending time with the adolescent and parent(s) and inviting each member to share his or her impression of the presenting problem and what they expect and want from this consultation or evaluation. The next 20 to 30 minutes is devoted to meeting with the parent(s) to provide an opportunity for the often distressed parent to share all the relevant family history and details of the adolescent's current NSSI and other associated maladaptive behaviors that might not otherwise be shared in the presence of the adolescent. Meeting with the parent(s) first allows the therapist to obtain data to inquire about whether the adolescent, who comes in alone subsequently for 30 to 45 minutes, denies any NSSI. It is important for the adolescent to have time alone to share his or her version of what brought the family in for the consultation and what behaviors are occurring. Some teens will completely deny or at least minimize the extent of the NSSI with parents in the room. After treatment is discussed and the therapist ascertains whether the adolescent is willing to consider stopping the NSSI, the therapist brings in the parent(s) to discuss the adolescent's intention to pursue treatment or not. A further rationale is provided for the various treatment options. Typically, at least in DBT, we encourage the parent(s) to participate in the therapy as well (as is discussed later in the chapter).

INTERVENTIONS

Despite growing concern about NSSI and the need to find effective treatments, few studies have focused on reducing this behavior (Miller & Glinski, 2000). Indeed, much of the current research has evaluated the efficacy of treatments for reducing suicidal behavior, and NSSI has been either subsumed under suicidal acts or ignored. Although the results from research on treatments for suicidal behavior are somewhat promising (e.g., see Brown et al., 2005; Linehan, Comtois, Murray, et al., 2006; Tryer et al., 2003; Verheul et al., 2003), they are mostly limited to adult populations, and their effectiveness within adolescent groups is unknown. Still, the positive findings suggest that there may be a range of potentially effective treatments available to practitioners.

Randomized controlled trials of therapy effectiveness for NSSI among adolescent samples are rare, and results are mixed. An additional problem is that many of the existing studies do not differentiate NSSI from suicide attempts, so interpretation of the findings warrants caution. For example, Harrington et al. (1998) examined the efficacy of adding a four-session family problem-solving therapy to routine care for adolescents who deliberately poisoned themselves. Results indicated that there were no significant differences between treatment groups on general outcomes or on acts of repeat self-poisoning, but within a subgroup of adolescents with MDD a significant reduction in suicidal ideation was found in the treatment group. Huey et al. (2004) reported more promising findings in their study, which emphasized working with families and systems as well. One hundred and fifty-six adolescents who presented to an emergency department following an act of self-harm (unclear whether suicidal or NSSI) were randomly assigned to receive either multisystemic family therapy (MST) or inpatient treatment as usual. The authors reported that MST resulted in significantly fewer suicide attempts and greater symptom reduction than treatment as usual over a 1-year follow-up. However, the findings are confounded by the fact that 44% of the MST sample also received inpatient care during the treatment period.

In addition to examining family interventions, some have evaluated the effectiveness of group-based interventions. In a sample of 105 adolescents discharged from an inpatient unit following a suicide attempt, Cotgrove et al. (1995) found no significant differences between their experimental treatment (i.e., group management plus readmission to inpatient treatment on demand) and treatment as usual (i.e., group management). More promising results were reported by Wood, Trainor, Rothwell, Moore, and Harrington (2001), who evaluated the effectiveness of treatment as usual versus treatment as usual plus group therapy. The group therapy intervention was described as being an integrated blend of multiple treatment modalities including problem-solving and cognitive–behavioral therapies, DBT, and psychodynamic interventions that were developmentally appropriate. Results indicated that adolescents in the group intervention were less likely to repeat their self-injury, although there was great within-group variability. The two groups did not differ on outcomes of depression, suicidality, or global functioning, which suggests the group may have a specific impact on self-injury. Replication of the findings is needed.

DIALECTICAL BEHAVIOR THERAPY

Although there are few empirical studies on treatments specifically for NSSI in adolescent populations, the preliminary findings are somewhat encouraging. On the basis of the large number of well-controlled randomized trials with adults in multiple settings by numerous research groups, DBT (Koons et al., 2001; Linehan, 1993a, 1993b; Linehan, Armstrong, Suarez, Allmon, & Heard, 1991; Linehan, Comtois, Brown, Heard, & Wagner, 2006) is considered the gold standard when it comes to treatment efficacy and effectiveness of reducing NSSI and suicidal behavior among outpatients diagnosed with BPD. DBT and its use in treating NSSI among adults are reviewed in detail in chapter 12 of this volume. Miller, Rathus, and Linehan (2007) published a book describing their adaptation of this well-established treatment for use with adolescents engaging in suicidal behavior and NSSI. Preliminary data find DBT with teens to be promising (Katz, Gunasekara, Cox, & Miller, 2004; Rathus & Miller, 2002; Trupin, Stewart, Beach, & Boesky, 2002). Using a quasi-experimental design, Rathus and Miller (2002) compared adolescent DBT with treatment as usual in a 12-week outpatient study. Adolescents referred to the clinic were assigned to either DBT ($n = 29$) or treatment as usual ($n = 84$). At the conclusion of the 12-week treatment, the DBT participants had fewer hospitalizations, lower suicidal ideation, and were more likely to have completed treatment. The two groups, however, did not differ on the number of suicide attempts, and it is unclear whether DBT led to improvements in NSSI, because this particular behavior was not formally assessed. The American Academy of Child & Adolescent Psychiatry (2001) suggested that DBT may be useful with this population. Randomized trials of DBT with this age group are now underway.

DBT for adolescents has been applied to adolescents with various psychological and behavioral problems in a wide range of treatment settings including outpatient, inpatient, residential, day treatment, and juvenile detention centers. DBT patients are also diverse in terms of ethnicities and socioeconomic levels and range from low-income, minority families living in the inner city to middle- and upper-middle-class, majority-group families from the suburbs. However, on the basis of numerous studies with various diagnostic groups and treatment centers, predominantly with adults and some older adolescents, DBT is uniquely effective at reducing NSSI and suicidal behaviors because they are the primary targets of treatment (Miller et al., 2007).

Dialectical Behavior Therapy Treatment Targets

In DBT with adolescents, the foci of therapy are pretreatment targets (i.e., agreement on goals and commitment to change) and first-stage targets (i.e., safety, stability, behavioral control of action, and enhancement of basic capabilities). In the first stage of DBT, the therapist structures each treatment interaction to address the following specific targets in a hierarchical order of importance:

- decreasing life-threatening and NSSI behaviors;
- decreasing behaviors that interfere with treatment, particularly noncompliance and premature dropout;
- decreasing behaviors that have a severe effect on quality of life, including substance abuse, school truancy, high-risk sex, and those that necessitate inpatient psychiatric care; and
- increasing behavioral skills.

As stated earlier, DBT targets suicide-related behaviors as the highest priority. Treating NSSI is placed among Stage 1 targets, above all other treatment targets (e.g., depression, substance use, family problems), because NSSI is highly comorbid with suicide attempts (Nock et al., 2006; Zlotnick et al., 1997) and may be a risk factor for suicide death.

The individual therapist applies the DBT strategies to the highest priority target relevant at the moment. For example, if a suicide attempt or NSSI episode occurred during the week, which should be noted on the patient's diary card, it is always treated first in the next session. The therapist takes an active stance early in treatment. Thus, the therapist sets the agenda collaboratively with the patient according to hierarchically ordered behavioral treatment targets and then uses this agenda to guide the session. Other treatment orientations may take a more passive stance at the start of treatment, allowing the patient to freely choose the session topic. In DBT, however, it is the extent of the disordered behavior (e.g., severity of dysfunction, complexity of other problems) that determines the focus of treatment both over the course of treatment as well as within a given treatment interaction. This adherence to predetermined behavioral targets must be balanced with letting the session unfold and skillfully weaving in the necessary components identified in this chapter. A common mistake by a beginning DBT individual therapist is to force the agenda on the patient; we call this error "following the manual instead of following the moment."

Comprehensive Multimodal Treatment Approach to Nonsuicidal Self-Injury

DBT for adolescents is a comprehensive treatment that requires the adolescent and family to commit to 16 weeks of at least twice-weekly therapy that addresses the five functions (Miller, 1999) across various modes of treatment. These functions and modes are outlined here and are elaborated later in this chapter. Function 1 is learning new skills delivered primarily in a psychoeducational multifamily skills training group. Five sets of skills are taught in the skills training group: (a) mindfulness skills to address the confusion about oneself, (b) emotion regulation skills to address emotional instability, (c) distress tolerance skills to target impulsivity, (d) interpersonal effectiveness skills to address interpersonal problems, and (e) "walking the middle path" skills to target adolescent family conflicts and dilemmas. Function 2 is working one-on-one with a therapist to reduce factors that interfere with the ability to use skills (i.e., increasing motivation) in both individual and family sessions. Function 3 is ensuring that skill generalization occurs through in vivo interventions (e.g., telephone consultation when in crisis; in vivo individual, group, or family therapy interactions). Function 4 is participating in a weekly therapist consultation meeting that provides both technical help and emotional support to assist them in performing DBT competently. Function 5 is structuring the environment, including collateral family sessions or meetings with other treatment providers or school personnel, so that the patient does not have to get worse to get additional help, and structuring the DBT program (e.g., time for supervision and consultation meetings) for therapists to deliver the treatment effectively and competently and so as not to burn out. In outpatient DBT with adolescents, these five functions are assigned to five concurrent modes of outpatient treatment including multifamily skills training group, individual therapy, telephone consultation, therapist consultation meetings, and family therapy. The primary therapist (i.e., the individual therapist) ensures that the system as a whole is providing each function.

Multifamily Skills Training Group

DBT's overarching goal is to build a life worth living. Thus, the therapist works to both reduce the aforementioned target behaviors and increase behavioral skills. The multifamily skills training group is the primary forum for the acquisition and strengthening of these skills, whereas the individual and family therapy sessions help clients generalize the skills to situations they encounter in their lives. This group allows teens to learn in the context of other teens as well as to have parents be exposed to other families struggling with similar issues. Typically, this "universality" experience promotes an atmosphere of connectedness and support while reducing anxiety.

The skills taught in DBT correspond directly to Linehan's reorganization of the *Diagnostic and Statistical Manual of Mental Disorders* (4th ed.; American Psychiatric Association, 1994) BPD symptoms (Linehan, 1993a). According to this reorganization, the symptoms fall into areas of dysregulation across five domains. DBT for adolescents maintains this conceptualization for multiproblem adolescents who engage in NSSI, even when full criteria for BPD are not met (Miller et al., 2007). The five areas of dysfunction and the corresponding skill modules are presented in Table 13.1.

Core mindfulness skills involve increased awareness of the present moment and of aspects of the self and environment. Specifically, the adolescent may have difficulty experiencing or identifying what she feels, why she feels the way she does, or identifying a stable sense of self. Moreover, the adolescent may report a pervasive sense of emptiness and have problems maintaining her feelings, opinions, or decisions around others. Teaching the teen who engages in self-injurious behavior how to nonjudgmentally observe and describe what she is feeling and thinking in the moment may be one of the most difficult, but also the most critical, skills for her to learn.

The interpersonal effectiveness skills address patients' difficulties in maintaining consistent and rewarding relationships. These adolescents typically have intense, unstable relationships and often experience panic-type anxiety and dread over relationships ending. In addition, they may stay in abusive relationships because of an intense fear of being alone. Interpersonal problems are common precipitating events for NSSI and suicidal behaviors among adolescents in general (Lewinsohn, Rohde, & Seeley, 1996).

TABLE 13.1
Five Areas of Dysfunction and Corresponding Dialectical
Behavior Therapy Skill Modules

Dysfunction	Skill module
Self dysregulation	Core mindfulness
Interpersonal dysregulation	Interpersonal effectiveness
Behavioral dysregulation	Distress tolerance
Emotional dysregulation	Emotion regulation
Cognitive dysregulation	Walking the middle path

The distress tolerance skills address impulsivity by teaching adolescents how to distract and soothe themselves effectively while considering pros and cons of their actions. These skills typically replace some of the following behaviors: self-inflicted cutting or burning, overdosing, engaging in physical fights, abusing alcohol or drugs, engaging in unprotected or promiscuous sex, cutting classes, and school truancy.

Emotion regulation skills address extreme emotional sensitivity; rapid, intense mood changes; and unmodulated emotional states characterized by chronic depression, anxiety, or problems with either overcontrolled or under-controlled anger. Identifying and labeling emotions, learning how to increase positive emotions, and reducing vulnerability to negative emotions are a few of the emotion regulation skills.

Walking the middle path skills address unbalanced thinking and behaviors among teens and family members. These skills involve learning about principles of behavior change, validation, and finding the middle path between common dialectical dilemmas in these families (e.g., authoritarian control vs. excessive leniency). Teaching dialectical thinking to adolescents requires a capacity to consider a situation having multiple truths (i.e., both–and) rather than maintaining an either–or (i.e., black-or-white) stance. For example, one teen needed help understanding that she could simultaneously love and hate her boyfriend. Or, another 15-year-old girl needed help moving to the middle path of "I have a right to be disappointed at my mother for saying no, and at the same time, I recognize her anxiety about my sleeping over at my new boyfriend's house for the first time when his parents are going to be out of town."

Individual Therapy

DBT individual outpatient therapy with adolescents consists of 16 weeks of 50- to 60-minute weekly sessions. The individual therapist is the primary therapist for that patient and oversees the entire treatment plan and all the providers. In individual therapy, adolescents learn to apply skills taught in the multifamily behavioral skills group to their own lives. The individual therapist balances problem-oriented change strategies (i.e., standard cognitive–behavioral techniques, including behavioral analyses, contingency management, cognitive modification, and exposure to emotional cues) and irreverent communication strategies, and provides consultation on patient strategies with environmental interventions and acceptance strategies (i.e., core validation strategies, reciprocal communication strategies) in session to "drag out" clients' more skillful responses in order to replace maladaptive responses.

The problem focus of each individual DBT session is determined jointly by the client's behavior since the last session and where the behavior falls on the target behavioral hierarchy. For example, if the adolescent has engaged in

NSSI since the last session, the first task in session is to conduct a behavioral and solution analysis of that target behavior. A behavioral analysis is a step-by-step examination of a problem behavior, including an exhaustive description of the moment-to-moment chain of environmental and behavioral events, including the antecedents and consequences of the target behavior. During the behavioral analysis, the therapist identifies emotions, cognitions, and skill deficits as well as behavioral and environmental factors that interfere with more adaptive solutions. The solution analysis identifies more effective behaviors the patient could have used and is encouraged to use next time.

During all sessions, the therapist actively teaches and reinforces adaptive behaviors, including those that occur within the therapeutic relationship, while consistently withholding reinforcement for maladaptive behaviors (i.e., those that are targeted for change). Between sessions, the client is strongly encouraged to use phone consultation with the individual therapist to help problem solve during crises, increase skills generalization, or repair the relationship with the therapist. In addition, by asking the adolescent to complete a diary card tracking self-injurious urges and actions each day, the therapist maintains a nonjudgmental yet persistent and demanding stance with the adolescent about disclosing NSSI. If the adolescent engages in NSSI and does not disclose it to the therapist and the therapist obtains the information from a third party, the therapist considers this therapy-interfering behavior that requires an extensive behavioral chain analysis to determine why the adolescent is withholding the information. It is surprising that none of us can recall the last time an adolescent consistently withheld information regarding NSSI and remained in DBT.

Commitment Strategies With Adolescents

At the initial stages of therapy, the individual therapist seeks an explicit, verbal commitment from the patient to participate in DBT for the length of the program and to reduce his or her maladaptive behaviors. Commitment strategies are critical both to obtain and to maintain a client's engagement in the treatment process. In our experience, inadequate commitment from the client, therapist, or both, can lead to therapy failures or early treatment terminations. The client may make an insufficient or glib commitment in the initial stages of the change process, or, more often, events within or outside of therapy may dissipate the client's previous commitments. This is particularly relevant to adolescents given that they usually reside in their environments experienced as invalidating and often feel hopeless about their situation improving. Adolescent commitment in DBT is both an important prerequisite for effective therapy and, in itself, a goal of the therapy. Therefore, DBT views the client's commitment to treatment and to change as a behavior itself, which can be elicited, learned, and reinforced. So, for example, rather than assuming that the adolescent is committed to implementing behavioral solutions to old problems, the therapist works collaboratively with the client to facilitate the patient's commitment to change. When working in a brief treatment model (16 weeks), the therapist must figure this out quickly.

In-session behaviors that are inconsistent with this initial degree of commitment and collaboration include refusing to work in therapy, avoiding or refusing to talk about feelings and events connected with target behaviors, and rejecting all input from the therapist or attempts to generate alternative solutions. It is important that the therapist actively targets these in-session problem behaviors. At these moments, the therapist should discuss the adolescent's commitment to therapy itself, with the goal of eliciting a recommitment.

Eliciting commitment necessitates a certain amount of salesmanship—the product being sold is new behavior and sometimes life itself. To obtain commitment to DBT, the therapist needs to be flexible and creative while using one or more commitment strategies. Linehan (1993a) identified eight commitment strategies: (a) selling commitment, evaluating pros and cons; (b) playing devil's advocate; (c) foot-in-the-door/door-in-the-face techniques; (d) connecting present commitments to prior commitment; (e) highlighting freedom to choose and absence of alternatives; (f) using principles of shaping; (g) cheerleading; and (h) agreeing on homework. Several examples are highlighted here.

In evaluating the pros and cons of proceeding with treatment, the therapist starts by laying out the counterarguments of pursuing treatment that the patient herself would likely consider. This is followed by a discussion of the advantages of participating in treatment. For example, the therapist might say,

> Now, thinking of the disadvantages of committing to treatment, it is going to take a huge effort, possibly too much effort, to change some of your long-standing behavioral patterns. The time commitment necessary for group and individual sessions, as well as therapy homework assignments, and phone consultations, may be too much for you right now. However, by making a commitment to treatment, we will work together to help you achieve your goals of reducing your self-cutting, keeping you out of the hospital, and helping you stay in school so that you can graduate. So we should weigh out the pros and cons before you make a final decision.

In the devil's advocate approach, the therapist argues against a commitment to treatment with the intent that the adolescent him or herself make the argument for participating in treatment. The therapist might say, "This treatment requires a huge time commitment, and I am not sure that you are up to it right now." This technique becomes quite useful with teenagers who are more likely to offer quick agreements without thinking through the consequences of those agreements, such as, "Oh yeah, I definitely want to do this therapy . . . and yes, I will never cut myself again."

Behavioral Analysis

In DBT, the first step in changing problematic behavior, such as NSSI, is to identify the variables that control the behavior. If more than one instance of NSSI occurred, then the most severe, best remembered instance is chosen. The therapist and the client then develop a complete account of the chain of events that led to and followed the NSSI, referred to as a *behavioral analysis*. During the behavioral analysis, the therapist looks for controlling antecedent and maintaining variables. He or she also tries to identify each point at which an alternative behavior could have kept the problem behavior from occurring. The detail obtained in an effective analysis is similar to that of a movie script. In other words, the description of the chain provides enough detail that one would be able to visualize it sufficiently to replicate and reenact the sequence of events. Included in this analysis is an assessment of vulnerability factors (e.g., sleep difficulties, pain, smoking marijuana), prompting events (e.g., boyfriend threatened to break up the relationship), and consequences (e.g., after she cut herself, the boyfriend agreed not to end the relationship) are also important factors to assess.

Problem Solving

Problem solving requires the therapist to weave in possible solutions to the behavioral analysis. The therapist and client must ask, "What solutions other than NSSI (the target behavior) could be applied to the problem at hand?" More specifically, the therapist looks for different points in the behavior chain to intervene, and there are many possible places to do so. For example, solutions can target any potential vulnerability factors (such as the sleep factor mentioned earlier); the precipitating event; key links such as specific cognitions, emotions, behaviors; and specific contingencies that may be maintaining dysfunctional behavior as well as extinguishing or punishing adaptive behavior. The therapist helps the client generate alternative solutions, encouraging the use of long- over short-term solutions (Miller et al., 2007).

Alternative solutions to the client's problem, and the tools to implement them, can usually be found among a variety of empirically validated technologies. The most common of these change procedures fall into four categories: skills training, exposure, contingency management, and cognitive modification. When conducting a solution analysis, the therapist must consider all change procedures available. One of the many challenges for the individual therapist is to prioritize these possible strategies quickly from most to least relevant to the target behavior.

Family Therapy

Just as it is important to assume a nonpejorative, nonblaming stance with teens engaging in NSSI, it is equally important to assume this stance with family members. Parents or caregivers often experience intense feelings of anxiety, shame, and failure, which may come across to their teens and therapists as only anger. It is important to validate the full range of the family members' emotions and help identify the primary emotions (typically not anger) that are easier for the adolescent to understand and even validate. Thus, family sessions need to target parental emotional vulnerability to not only increase treatment compliance but also strengthen parental capacity for learning new behavioral skills.

Family sessions might be indicated for various reasons: (a) orienting parents to DBT, including psychoeducation about NSSI; (b) working to facilitate communication between adolescent and family member(s) about an important issue; (c) conducting a behavioral analysis of a target behavior; or (d) handling a crisis (see Miller et al., 2007).

When a teen and therapist determine that specific family interactions are relevant to NSSI, the primary treatment target is to decrease family interactions that contribute to the context of the adolescent's NSSI. Conducting a family behavioral analysis typically involves first obtaining the adolescent's detailed report of the antecedents and consequences of NSSI and then obtaining the same information from the parent(s) in the subsequent family session. Data from these behavioral analyses help to identify the controlling variables (e.g., specific thoughts, emotions, skills deficits, or contingencies) that lead down the pathway to NSSI. After these variables are determined, a solution analysis is generated to help each family member identify a new behavior to use the next time a similar situation arises (see Miller et al., 2007).

DBT sessions also target reduction of family or parent behaviors that interfere with the treatment. To target only the adolescent's treatment-interfering behavior without considering such behavior in the parent(s) ignores the reality that parents often have a great deal of power over the adolescent's capacity to participate in treatment. For example, one of our adolescent clients was coming late and began canceling sessions. It turned out that it was not a matter of the adolescent's commitment to treatment; rather, it was the parent's variable commitment coupled with financial problems. Thus, this adolescent's mother was upset by what she perceived as "coddling of the adolescents" in group, and she stopped attending the group. She was also on welfare and ran out of money during certain portions of the month to pay for transportation to treatment.

The third target is to reduce family interactions that interfere with the family's quality of life. The focus is on helping the family, as a group, function in a more effective, respectful, and loving manner. One of the most common quality-of-life targets in family problems is communication. Over time, many families become chronically emotionally dysregulated. The family may present as continually angry or with the sense that members are always walking on eggshells. As a result, members tend to avoid direct communication with one another because of fear of aversive consequences. A DBT family therapy session often first addresses skills training in validation to set the stage for future behavioral and solution analyses regarding specific family problems. Often, family members are eager to start problem solving. Thus, it is important to orient families to the rationale for teaching validation and interpersonal effectiveness skills before problem solving begins (Miller et al., 2007).

Telephone Consultation

The individual therapist invites telephone calls or pages from the adolescent for (a) coaching skills during in vivo problematic situations, (b) repairing the relationship alliance, and (c) reporting good news. For example, if an adolescent is having urges to engage in NSSI and is unsure which DBT skills to use to avert the behavior, the adolescent is encouraged to page the therapist (24 hours a day, 7 days a week) to receive coaching as to how to manage his or her distress differently. This requires both a strong commitment on behalf of the adolescent to reduce this behavior and a sufficient therapeutic alliance that would foster such a call. Family members in the multifamily skills group are instructed to call the skills group leaders for telephone consultation as well for purposes of skills generalization. If the parent calls the adolescent's clinician for coaching related to a currently distressing situation with the teen, the therapist refers the parent back to the skills coach for coaching. If it is not acute and the parent wants to inform the therapist of some concerns, the therapist usually suggests having a family session within the next week or 2.

Therapist Consultation Meeting

The adolescent DBT therapist is required to attend a weekly 90-minute adolescent DBT consultation team meeting. The primary goals of the consultation meeting are to help therapists remain effective and motivated in delivering DBT. Furthermore, the treatment explicitly acknowledges and strives to address the stress and burnout that can occur when working with adolescents who engage in frequent NSSI. The team members accomplish this through remoralizing and reenergizing therapists and helping them to maintain a dialectical position in treatment. Overall, the consultation team "treats" the DBT therapists with the DBT treatment. As in treating patients, treating the therapist occurs in the context of balancing validation with problem-solving strategies.

Handling Issues of Confidentiality

Confidentiality can be broken when the therapist believes an adolescent is at serious risk. Defining what level of risk is serious enough to break confidentiality, however, may not always be clear when working with adolescents and their parents. Certainly, if the therapist determines there is high and imminent threat of suicide, the choice to notify another—typically the adolescent's parents—is straightforward. However, what about the case of self-injurious behaviors with no intent to die? Is self-injurious behavior, no matter how superficial, indicative of posing a serious danger to oneself when it is known that individuals who engage in self-injurious behaviors are more likely to eventually carry out a lethal suicide (e.g., see Brent et al., 1988)?

These complex decisions must be weighed against the fact that if confidentiality is ensured, the adolescent will likely have a higher level of disclosure to the therapist. Miller et al. (2007) suggested a number of guidelines to inform this decision making. It is critical to explain to adolescents and their parents the limits of confidentiality (i.e., if a therapist suspects or learns that the client is in imminent risk of killing him- or herself or another, or learns of ongoing child abuse) from treatment outset, to avoid later feelings of betrayal. In addition, the clinician must discuss how he or she will handle confidentiality regarding NSSI. In DBT, it is important to address the issue of NSSI with parents at the outset of treatment. The following example (Miller et al., 2007) depicts a common exchange between a parent and the DBT therapist:

> *Parent:*   I am worried that my daughter's cutting will get worse and she won't tell me, I won't see it, and now, in the name of confidentiality, you won't tell me either.
>
> *Therapist:*   I understand your concern. I want you to know that your daughter has agreed to track her self-harm on a diary card that we will review together each week, and as an aside, you know that the diary card is a private document that I would ask you not to view. Thus, I am going to be keeping careful track of her self-harm. Given that this behavior is frequent, and typically non-life-threatening, I believe it would not help your daughter or my therapeutic alliance with her if I contacted you each time she self-cut or even if I encouraged her to tell you herself each time she did it. So, I will say this: If I feel that her cutting is escalating in either frequency or medical dangerousness, I will break confidentiality. Otherwise, this behavior will be something that we will work on together, and I will not be contacting you each time she engages in it. Does that seem reasonable?

In the interest of the safety of adolescent patients, we suggest erring on a lower threshold for determining what level of threat merits breaking confidentiality—especially in the early stages of treatment. However, in the interest of maintaining a therapeutic alliance with the client, treating the client with respect, and following the principle of consulting to the client on handling the environment rather than consulting to the environment, we prefer to encourage clients to communicate to their caregivers about the issue of concern directly (Miller et al., 2007).

Contagion

One phenomenon clinicians need to pay attention to, particularly when running skills training groups, is contagion of NSSI. Contagion occurs when one person's self-injury leads another person(s) to engage in self-injury within a short time period from the original act. Although not widely studied, there is evidence suggesting that contagion occurs within group settings, particularly in the inpatient and residential milieu (Walsh & Rosen, 1985), and that it can easily be triggered within a group.

On the basis of clinical experience as well as the literature documenting triggers of contagion, Walsh (2006) provided a set of guidelines for managing or preventing contagion when working within a group setting that are consistent with the adolescent DBT skills group guidelines set forth by Miller et al. (2007). The first guideline is to reduce communication about acts of NSSI within the group. Group members need to be informed that discussing details of NSSI will not be permitted, primarily because such details can trigger self-injury in others. If an episode of self-injury surfaces in group, the individual should be reminded of the guideline and strongly encouraged to discuss the episode, in detail, with his or her individual therapist. Using individual therapy to address the behavior in detail is another suggested guideline, so that it is clearly established that DBT skills training group is designed to focus on skill acquisition and generalization, and not on acts of NSSI. We also support Walsh's (2006) third guideline, which is to reduce public display of scars, wounds, or bandages because they can be triggers for others.

Another recommendation to help reduce contagion is to assist adolescents with finding alternative ways to create a feeling of cohesion and belonging. Helping them identify other shared interests or experiences, similar personality characteristics, or engaging in mutually enjoyable activities are ways to create a feeling of connection and promote bonding. Including bonding activities as part of group therapy may be one way to facilitate intimacy among group members outside of their self-injury (see chap. 14 for a more detailed discussion of contagion).

CONCLUSION

Adolescent NSSI is a prevalent problem. Although DBT is a promising treatment for NSSI, researchers may find that a comprehensive treatment is not necessary to treat NSSI in adolescents who present with single disorders or for whom no BPD features exist. Further research is clearly indicated to examine risk factors for NSSI among adolescents as well as to determine the most effective and efficient psychosocial interventions for adolescent NSSI.

Research Recommendations

We propose two separate lines of research to advance understanding of NSSI among adolescents. First, research is needed to further develop, refine, and more universally administer psychometrically sound assessment measures of NSSI to clinical (e.g., inpatient, outpatient, residential, emergency room) and nonclinical samples (e.g., schools, pediatric practices) of adolescents to understand better current prevalence rates, methods, and functions. Second, we urge researchers to conduct a randomized controlled trial of DBT versus treatment by nonbehavioral experts, specifically targeting adolescents engaging in NSSI as the primary target behavior.

Clinical Recommendations

First, we propose the development of guidelines that inform a clinician as to what specific treatment strategies are indicated on the basis of the reported function of the adolescent's NSSI. Second, clinicians need to be better educated as to the common behavioral principles that maintain NSSI and the skills necessary to help alleviate such behaviors.

REFERENCES

American Academy of Child & Adolescent Psychiatry. (2001). *Child and Adolescent Level of Care Utilization System (CALOCUS) for psychiatric and addiction services*. Washington, DC: Author.

American Psychiatric Association. (1994). *Diagnostic and statistical manual of mental disorders* (4th ed.). Washington, DC: Author.

Brent, D. A., Perper, J. A., Goldstein, C. E., Kolko, D. J., Allan, M. J., Allman, C. J., & Zelenak, J. P. (1988). Risk factors for adolescent suicide: A comparison of adolescent suicide victim with suicidal inpatients. *Archives of General Psychiatry, 445*, 581–588.

Brown, G. K., Have, T. T., Henriques, G. R., Xie, S. X., Hollander, J. E., & Beck, A. T. (2005). Cognitive therapy for the prevention of suicide attempts: A randomized controlled trial. *The Journal of the American Medical Association, 294*, 563–570.

Cotgrove, A. J., Zirinsky, L., Black, D., & Weston, D. (1995). Secondary prevention of attempted suicide in adolescence. *Journal of Adolescence, 18*, 569–577.

Garrison, C. A., Cheryl, L. A., McKeown, R. E., Cuffe, S. P., Jackson, K. L., & Waller, J. L. (1993). Nonsuicidal physically self-damaging acts in adolescents. *Journal of Child and Family Studies, 2*, 339–352.

Harrington, R., Kerfoot, M., Dyer, E., McNiven, R., Gill, J., Harrington, V., et al. (1998). Randomized trial of a home-based family intervention for children who have deliberately poisoned themselves. *Journal of the American Academy of Child & Adolescent Psychiatry, 37*, 512–518.

Huey, S. J., Henggeler, S. W., Rowland, M. D., Halliday-Boykins, C. A., Cunningham, P. B., Pickrel, S. G., & Edwards, J. (2004). Multisystemic therapy effects on attempted suicide by youths presenting psychiatric emergencies. *Journal of the American Academy of Child & Adolescent Psychiatry, 43*, 183–190.

Jacobson, C. M., Muehlenkamp, J. J., & Miller, A. L., & Turner, J. B. (2008). Psychiatric impairment among adolescents engaging in different types of deliberate self-harm. *Journal of Clinical Child and Adolescent Psychology, 37*, 363–375.

Katz, L. Y., Gunasekara, S., Cox, B. J., & Miller, A. L. (2004). Feasibility of dialectical behavior therapy for parasuicidal adolescent inpatients. *Journal of the American Academy of Child & Adolescent Psychiatry, 43*, 276–282.

Kisiel, C. L., & Lyons, J. S. (2001). Dissociation as a mediator of psychopathology among sexually abused children and adolescents. *The American Journal of Psychiatry, 158*, 1034–1039.

Koons, C. R., Robins, C. J., Tweed, J. L., Lynch, T. R., Gonzalez, A. M., Morse, J. Q., et al. (2001). Efficacy of dialectical behavior therapy in women veterans with borderline personality disorder. *Behavior Therapy, 32*, 371–390.

Kumar, G., Pepe, D., & Steer, R. A. (2004). Adolescent psychiatric inpatients' self-reported reasons for cutting themselves. *The Journal of Nervous and Mental Disease, 192*, 830–836.

Lewinsohn, P. M., Rohde, P., & Seeley, J. R. (1996). Adolescent suicidal ideation and attempts: Prevalence, risk factors, and clinical implications. *Clinical Psychology: Science and Practice, 3*, 25–46.

Linehan, M. M. (1993a). *Cognitive–behavioral therapy of borderline personality disorder*. New York: Guilford Press.

Linehan, M. M. (1993b). *Skills training manual for treating borderline personality disorder*. New York: Guilford Press.

Linehan, M. M., Armstrong, H. E., Suarez, A., Allmon, D., & Heard, H. L. (1991). Cognitive–behavioral treatment of chronically parasuicidal borderline patients. *Archives of General Psychiatry, 48*, 1060–1064.

Linehan, M. M., Comtois, K. A., Brown, M. Z., Heard, H. L., & Wagner, A. W. (2006). Suicide attempt self-injury interview (SASII): Development, reliability, and validity of a scale to assess suicide attempts and intentional self-injury. *Psychological Assessment, 18*, 303–312.

Linehan, M. M., Comtois, K. A., Murray, A. M., Brown, M. Z., Gallop, R. J., Heard, H. L., et al. (2006). Two-year randomized trial and follow-up of dialectical behavior therapy vs. therapy by experts for suicidal behaviors and borderline personality disorder. *Archives of General Psychiatry, 63*, 757–766.

Miller, A. L. (1999). Dialectical behavior therapy: A new treatment approach for suicidal adolescents. *American Journal of Psychotherapy, 53*, 413–417.

Miller, A. L., & Glinski, J. (2000). Youth suicidal behavior: Assessment and intervention. *Journal of Clinical Psychology, 56*, 1131–1152.

Miller, A. L., Rathus, J. H., & Linehan, M. M. (2007). *Dialectical behavior therapy with suicidal adolescents*. New York: Guilford Press.

Muehlenkamp, J. J., & Gutierrez, P. M. (2004). An investigation of differences between self-injurious behavior and suicide attempts in a sample of adolescents. *Suicide and Life-Threatening Behavior, 34*, 12–23.

Muehlenkamp, J. J., & Gutierrez, P. M. (2007). Risk for suicide attempts among adolescents who engage in non-suicidal self-injury. *Archives of Suicide Research, 11*, 69–82.

Nixon, M. K., Cloutier, P. F., & Aggarwai, S. (2002). Affect regulation and addictive aspects of repetitive self-injury in hospitalized adolescents. *Journal of the American Academy of Child & Adolescent Psychiatry, 41*, 1333–1341.

Nock, M. K., Joiner, T. E., Jr., Gordon, K. H., Lloyd-Richardson, E., & Prinstein, M. J. (2006). Non-suicidal self-injury among adolescents: Diagnostic correlates and relation to suicide attempts. *Psychiatry Research, 144*, 65–72.

Nock, M. K., & Prinstein, M. J. (2004). A functional approach to the assessment of self-mutilative behavior. *Journal of Consulting and Clinical Psychology, 72*, 885–890.

Nock, M. K., Wedig, M. M., Holmberg, E. B., & Hooley, J. M. (2008). The Emotion Reactivity Scale: Development, evaluation, and relation to self-injurious thoughts and behaviors. *Behavior Therapy, 39*, 107–116.

Rathus, J. H., & Miller, A. L. (2002). Dialectical behavior therapy adapted for suicidal adolescents. *Suicide and Life-Threatening Behavior, 32*, 146–157.

Rosen, P., Walsh, B. W., & Rode, S. A. (1990). Interpersonal loss and self-mutilation. *Suicide and Life-Threatening Behavior, 20*, 177–184.

Ross, S., & Heath, N. (2002). A study of the frequency of self-mutilation in a community sample of adolescents. *Journal of Youth and Adolescence, 31*, 67–77.

Ross, S., & Heath, N. (2003). Two models of adolescent self-mutilation. *Suicide and Life-Threatening Behavior, 33*, 277–287.

Trupin, E. W., Stewart, D. G., Beach, B. & Boesky, L. (2002). Effectiveness of a dialectical behavior therapy program for incarcerated juvenile offenders. *Child and Adolescent Mental Health, 7*, 121–127.

Tryer, P., Thompson, S., Schmidt, U., Jones, V., Knapp, M., Davidson, K., et al. (2003). Randomized controlled trial of brief cognitive behavior therapy versus treatment as usual in recurrent deliberate self-harm: The POMPACT study. *Psychological Medicine, 33*, 969–976.

Verheul, R., van den Bosch, L. M., Koeter, M. W., de Ridder, M. A., Stijnen, T., & van den Brink, W. (2003). Dialectical behavior therapy for women with borderline personality disorder: 12-month, randomized clinical trial in the Netherlands. *The British Journal of Psychiatry, 182*, 135–140.

Walsh, B. W. (2006). *Treating self-injury: A practical guide*. New York: Guilford Press.

Walsh, B. W., & Rosen, P. (1985). Self-mutiliation and contagion: An empirical test. *The American Journal of Psychiatry, 142*, 119–120.

Wood, A., Trainor, G., Rothwell, J., Moore, A., & Harrington, R. (2001). Randomized trial of a group therapy for repeated deliberate self-harm in adolescents. *Journal of the American Academy of Child & Adolescent Psychiatry, 40*, 1246–1253.

Zlotnick, C., Donaldson, D., Spirito, A., & Pearlstein, T. (1997). Affect regulation and suicide attempts in adolescent inpatients. *Journal of the American Academy of Child & Adolescent Psychiatry, 36*, 793–798.

Zlotnick, C., Shea, M. T., Pearlstein, T. S. E., Costello, E., & Begin, A. (1996). The relationship between dissociative symptoms, alexithymia, impulsivity, sexual abuse, and self-mutilation. *Comprehensive Psychiatry, 37*, 12–16.

Zoroglu, S. S., Tuzun, U., Sar, V., Tutkin, H., Savas, H. A., Ozturk, M., et al. (2003). Suicide attempt and self-mutilation among Turkish high school students in relation with abuse, neglect, and dissociation. *Psychiatry and Clinical Neurosciences, 57*, 119–126.

14

RESIDENTIAL TREATMENT OF NONSUICIDAL SELF-INJURY

BARENT W. WALSH AND LEONARD A. DOERFLER

In this chapter, we focus on the residential treatment of nonsuicidal self-injury (NSSI). The term *residential* refers here to community-based group homes, special education boarding schools, and psychiatric inpatient settings. We do not discuss treatment of NSSI in forensic or correctional facilities.

It is not an easy task to write about residential treatment because it is among the most underresearched topics in the field of self-injury. Although we were able to locate a few studies on the inpatient treatment of self-injury, we found none whatsoever regarding group home or residential school settings. The absence of empirical research from group home and residential schools is regrettable because since the 1980s, the number of children and adolescents being served in such settings has increased substantially: "Analyses suggest that the growth in residential treatment has been accompanied by decreased access to inpatient treatment and that residential treatment centers increasingly serve as an alternative to inpatient psychiatric care" (Connor, Doerfler, Toscano, Volungis, & Steingard, 2004, p. 498). Some of the influences behind this increase have been the emergence of managed care and

---

Our profound thanks to Doug Watts, Ariana Millner-Hanley, Jennifer Eaton, Elizabeth Fessenden, and Carl Moran for their assistance in preparing this chapter.

related efforts to reduce expensive inpatient treatment. The view of managed care professionals is that residential treatment is a cost-effective alternative to inpatient care. Whether it is an effective treatment alternative has yet to be established.

LITERATURE ON RESIDENTIAL TREATMENT OF SELF-INJURY

Many of the earliest citations in the clinical literature regarding self-injury came from inpatient settings (e.g., see Offer & Barglow, 1960; Pao, 1969; Podvoll, 1969). Generally, these reports described the forms of the behavior and speculated as to motivations and psychodynamics. They did not discuss treatment at length. The 1970s and 1980s brought preliminary efforts to use empirical methods to study self-injury primarily in hospital or group home settings. For example, Ross and McKay (1979) studied the prevalence, clinical correlates, and relationship dynamics of self-injury in a large residential school for girls. They reported that in a sample of 136 an astonishing 86% of the girls had self-injured, representing one of the more dramatic social contagion episodes on record. Walsh and Rosen (1988) studied adolescents from both inpatient and group home settings and reported associations between histories of abuse, body alienation, and self-injury. Favazza, DeRosear, and Conterio (1989) also reported strong associations among NSSI, eating disorders, and traumatic experiences. Although Walsh and Rosen (1988) and Favazza et al. (1989) discussed the treatment of self-injury, they did not provide empirical assessment of treatment efficacy.

Only recently have researchers turned to the evaluation of treatment effectiveness related to self-injury. Muehlenkamp (2006) reviewed the empirically supported treatments of NSSI and concluded that two variants of cognitive–behavioral treatment have been evaluated most extensively in relation to NSSI: problem-solving therapy (PST; D'Zurilla & Goldfried, 1971; D'Zurilla & Nezu, 2001) and dialectical behavior therapy (DBT; Linehan, 1993a, 1993b; Miller, Rathus, & Linehan, 2007). Only a few inpatient applications of PST or DBT have been empirically evaluated; to date, none exist for group home or residential school applications.

Crowe and Bunclark (2000) evaluated a complex version of inpatient PST that included cognitive restructuring, medication, and group and family therapy. After treating 58 clients who self-injured over a 4-year period, they reported that 32 substantially decreased their NSSI, 23 stayed the same, and 3 got worse. Their study did not include a control group.

As noted in Muehlenkamp (2006), in a meta-analysis of 20 studies involving PST conducted by Hawton et al. (1998), the majority failed to produce reductions in self-injury (with or without suicidal intent) or failed to produce reductions that were superior to control groups. Therefore, Muehlenkamp

(2006) concluded that "overall, the research regarding the effectiveness of PST is inconclusive" (p. 170).

The findings regarding the residential treatment effectiveness of DBT appear somewhat more promising. DBT was originally presented as an outpatient treatment for suicidal women with borderline personality disorder. In the first randomized clinical trial, DBT was found to reduce significantly psychiatric hospitalizations, parasuicide attempts, medical severity of parasuicide, and treatment dropout compared with a treatment as usual (TAU) control group (Linehan, Armstrong, Suarez, Allmon, & Heard, 1991). (Note: In this and other DBT studies, the operational definition for *parasuicide* resembled but was not identical to the definition of *NSSI* used in this volume. Parasuicide included the common forms of NSSI but also such behaviors as nonfatal overdose.) Since this first evaluation of DBT, a number of additional randomized controlled trials (RCTs) have been conducted (see Miller et al., 2007), but none have involved inpatient or community residential settings.

We located three non-RCT studies that evaluated the effectiveness of DBT in treating NSSI on an inpatient basis. Barley et al. (1993) described an effort that transformed a psychodynamic inpatient unit to an inpatient DBT program. Drawing on a sample of 130 patients, they reported a significant decline in parasuicide compared with the previous treatment regimen. They also compared the new DBT service with another inpatient unit (without randomization) and found significantly lower rates of parasuicide on the DBT service.

Katz, Cox, Gunasekara, and Miller (2004) described a 2-week inpatient program for adolescents. They modified Miller et al.'s (2007) 16-week outpatient DBT protocol and provided individual DBT therapy twice per week, plus daily skills training groups, diary cards, and behavioral and solution analyses. Using standardized measures, they compared 26 adolescents receiving DBT with 27 adolescent receiving TAU on measures of depression, suicidal ideation, hopelessness, parasuicidal behavior, hospitalizations, and other variables. Results were that the DBT group had significantly fewer behavioral incidents on the ward than the TAU patients. At 1-year follow-up, both the DBT and TAU patients demonstrated significantly reduced parasuicidal behavior, depression, and suicidal ideation. Thus, results were equivocal as to any unique DBT effects.

Bohus et al. (2000) applied standard DBT in a 3-month inpatient program for adult women. A sample of 24 yielded significant reductions in NSSI at 1-month postdischarge. This study did not include a control group. Bohus et al. (2004) then performed a follow-up study comparing the DBT inpatients with a waitlist–TAU group. Participants were again evaluated 1-month postdischarge and showed significantly less NSSI than the control participants (31% vs. 62%). However, 31% still represents a substantial portion who were self-injuring.

On the basis of these findings from inpatient settings, Miller et al. (2007) concluded, "There are no data to suggest that inpatient treatments are effective in reducing suicidal behavior and non-suicidal self-injurious behavior" (p. 33). This conclusion seems to be more conservative than warranted. Granted, there are no RCTs in support of the effectiveness of inpatient DBT in treating NSSI, but there have been some encouraging findings that at least point in the right direction. This brings us to a discussion of the community-based residential treatment of NSSI.

COMMUNITY-BASED RESIDENTIAL TREATMENT OF NONSUICIDAL SELF-INJURY

As noted earlier, to date there are no empirical studies of the treatment of self-injury in group homes or residential schools. This is unfortunate in that such settings can provide treatment that is both intensive and extensive. Clients are in care many hours per day over extended periods of time. Such duration offers considerable opportunities for teaching and practicing new skills that may assist clients in learning to give up NSSI and other self-harm behaviors. Of course, the intensity of residential settings can also pose associated risks. Having multiple people live together who present with emotion dysregulation and dysfunctional behaviors can sometimes exacerbate these difficulties. One example is the social contagion of self-injury, which is discussed later in this chapter.

Connor et al. (2004) argued that "residential treatment needs to progress beyond the one size fits all approach and develop more specific and empirically proven treatments for the specific needs of [distinct] populations" (p. 497). Toward this end, in 1999 The Bridge of Central Massachusetts, a nonprofit human service agency for which the first author serves as executive director, implemented evidence-based practices in its group homes and support housing programs tailored to meet the needs of diverse clientele. One of the groups we serve has been adolescents who are suicidal or engage in self-injury. In reviewing the literature on the treatment of people with self-destructive behavior, we concluded that DBT was the most promising, empirically validated approach for the adolescents we serve. After being intensively trained in DBT, we took on the project of transforming a generic TAU group home for teens into a comprehensive DBT program. The components of this program are now briefly described, after which some preliminary outcome data are provided.

In May 2001, The Bridge opened Grove Street, a nine-bed program that serves males and females between the ages of 13 and 19. The program is located in a three-story, single-family-style home in a middle-class neighborhood. The adolescents served by Grove Street have had significant difficulties controlling their emotions and have displayed impulsive and self-destructive behaviors. They often are depressed, anxious, and aggressive and have had problems involving substance abuse, eating disorders, and attention deficits. Most have had multiple, extended psychiatric hospitalizations (see data in the section that follows). For an adolescent to be admitted to the residence, the severity of the disturbance must be expected to worsen without intensive clinical intervention, there must be a documented assessment that the adolescent or his or her family would be placed at risk if the adolescent were to live at home, and a less restrictive setting has to be ruled out as inappropriate or unavailable.

The Grove Street program offers the forms of DBT treatment summarized in Table 14.1. The table indicates how the provision of DBT at the Grove Street differs from Linehan's (1993a) original outpatient DBT formulation. There is a full-time, intensively trained, master's-level therapist who provides the individual DBT therapy and skills training in the program.

As the table indicates, a number of modifications have been made to standard outpatient DBT. These changes were made to accommodate the emotional and behavioral challenges and developmental abilities of the adolescent clientele. For example, adolescents with short attention spans tolerate groups of 1-hour duration much better than 2.5-hour sessions. Also, teaching skills using activity-based learning is generally more effective than more formal,

TABLE 14.1
Provision of Standard Outpatient Dialectical Behavior
Therapy (DBT) Versus Grove Street DBT

Treatment modality	Standard outpatient DBT	Grove Street
Individual therapy	Provided by outpatient clinician	Provided by clinician on site
Group skills training	Led by clinician and coleader; one 2.5-hour group/week	Led by clinician and several residential counselors; two 1-hour groups/week
Diary cards	Client self-monitors	Residential staff prompt and monitor daily
Coaching in crisis	Clinician (by phone)	Clinician or residential counselors on site
Structuring the environment	Informal, as needed	Formal point and level system based on DBT targets
Family therapy and skills training	Not included except by Miller et al. (2007)	Family therapy on site two times/month; family DBT skills training monthly
Consultation team	All clinicians on team	Agency DBT director, clinician, and all residence staff
Pharmacotherapy; case management	Outpatient, as needed	Provided on site

didactic instruction. A behavior management point and level system based on DBT targets is used to provide more trials for skills practice and generalization. All residential staff are trained in the DBT principles of validation. Their counseling focuses on conveying acceptance, while fostering the learning of new skills that reduce problem behaviors and enhance quality of life. The residence also offers family therapy and skills training with parents and children participating conjointly. The emphasis is on generalization of DBT skills to the home environment during treatment and postdischarge.

Despite these modifications, the program strives to provide DBT according to protocol. Core DBT skills were maintained in the protocol, but there were differences in the way these skills were developed and the staff's role in promoting the skills' generalization to daily activities. As with standard DBT, individual therapy in the residence focuses on the standard DBT targets and uses chain analyses and diary cards tailored to the needs of each youth. Also, the DBT skills training covers all the skills in the manual within a 6-month time period, consistent with Linehan's outpatient time frame.

PRELIMINARY OUTCOME DATA FOR THE GROVE STREET PROGRAM

Given that there is an absence of empirical research on the treatment of self-injury and related problems in group home settings, we thought it important to present some preliminary data regarding the Grove Street program. These data are from 5 years of program operation (2001–2006). During this period, the program has served 42 adolescents. Of these, 31 have been females and 11 have been males. The age range has been 13 to 19 years old, with a mean of 17.1 ($SD = 1.53$). The funding source for the program, the Massachusetts Department of Mental Health, refers all clients, and the program has no right of refusal. The majority of these adolescents came to this program from restrictive treatment settings (locked residential treatment programs or psychiatric hospitals). All clients referred to the program had received multiple diagnoses according to the *Diagnostic and Statistical Manual of Mental Disorders* (4th ed., text rev.; American Psychiatric Association, 2000), with the following distribution for the 42 clients: major depressive disorder, 42.5%; bipolar disorder, 33.3%; oppositional–defiant disorder, 33.3%; posttraumatic stress disorder, 30.9%; substance abuse, 26.1%; attention-deficit/hyperactivity disorder, 22.1%; anxiety disorder, 14.2%; and eating disorder, 9.5%. Grove Street does not provide its own diagnoses for clients. Length of stay for the clients ranged from 1 month to 26 months, with a mean of 10.75 months ($SD = 5.11$).

Because Grove Street is a single DBT adolescent residence with no sustained waiting list, there was no opportunity to assign participants randomly to different treatment conditions. We did devise an alternative strategy that permits some statistical comparisons. We noticed early in the process of operating the program that clients seemed to do better when they had participated in, and in most cases completed, two full courses of DBT. A course consisted of 6 months of treatment during which all the skills in the DBT manual were covered. Our interpretation was that the first round of DBT allowed the clients to learn the skills in a preliminary way, and the second round enabled them to consolidate this learning and to apply the skills in their day-to-day lives more consistently and effectively. The second round also offered more opportunity to generalize the use of the skills to the home environment postdischarge.

We therefore decided to compare two groups of clients comprising those who had participated in two rounds of DBT treatment (defined here as 7 months or more of residential care) versus those who had received one round or less (i.e., 6 months or less). The first group is referred to here as the *more treatment group*. Their lengths of stay in the program ranged from 7 to 20 months with an average of 12.3 months ($SD = 4.14$). The comparison group is referred to as the *less treatment group*. Their lengths of stay ranged from 2 to 6 months with a mean of 4.0 months ($SD = 3.16$).

The outcomes that we examined were the number of NSSI episodes, number of suicide attempts, number of psychiatric hospitalizations, and the total number of days that clients spent in the hospital. NSSI was clearly differentiated from high-lethality suicidal behavior in this program. Instances of NSSI included cutting, self-hitting, abrading, hitting, burning, scratching, self-piercing, and picking. A single incident of NSSI frequently involved inflicting more than one wound. Suicidal behavior included acts such as overdose, hanging, jumping from a height, or ingestion of a poison. Our hypothesis was that clients who completed more treatment would do better on all outcome variables.

The more treatment group consisted of 29 individuals, or 69% of the total served. This group included 20 female (69%) and 9 (31%) male participants; the racial composition was 25 Whites, 1 Latino, and 1 Black. For the less treatment group, there were 11 female (85%) and 2 (15%) male participants, and the races were 11 Whites, 1 Latino, and 1 Black. Therefore, the two groups were different as to sex, but quite similar as to race.

All outcome variables were assessed during three time periods: the 6-month period immediately preceding admission to the Grove Street program, the period corresponding to the first round of DBT treatment (up to 6 months of treatment), and the 6-month period following discharge from the program. A series of 2 (more treatment vs. less treatment groups) × 3 (time) repeated measures analyses of variance were conducted to determine whether there were significant differences between the treatment groups or whether there were significant differences in outcome measures across the three time periods. There were no significant group × time interactions for any of the analyses reported here.

A major goal of the Grove Street program is to eliminate clients' NSSI. There were no significant differences between the more treatment and less treatment groups in the number of self-injurious behaviors, $F(1, 40) = 1.22$, but there was a significant difference across the three time periods, $F(2, 80) = 12.70, p < .001$. Post hoc comparison of the time periods revealed a significant linear effect, $F(1, 40) = 17.09, p < .001$, indicating a significant decrease in the occurrence of self-injury behaviors for both treatment groups (see Figure 14.1). It is noteworthy that NSSI continued to decline for both groups during the 6-month period following discharge from the Grove Street program.

We recoded the self-injury variable to determine whether there were differences between the more treatment and less treatment groups in the number of clients who had any occurrence of NSSI during the 6-month period after discharge from Grove Street. There was a significant difference between the groups in the number of clients who self-injured during the follow-up period, $\chi^2(1) = 4.01, p < .05$. Only one client (3%) in the more treatment group self-injured after discharge from the program, but 23% of the clients in the less treatment group engaged in self-injurious behavior after discharge.

The occurrence of high-lethality suicidal behavior is another important clinical issue for these clients. For this outcome, there were no significant differences between the more treatment and less treatment groups in the number of suicide attempts, $F(1, 41) = 3.08$. Moreover, there were no significant

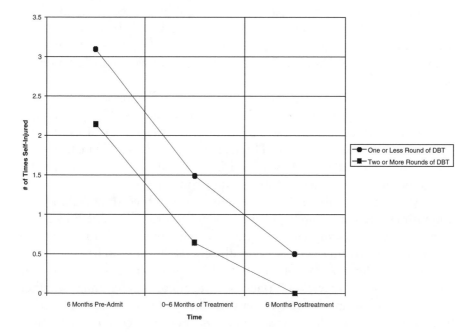

Figure 14.1. Comparison of clients who received one or two rounds of dialectical behavior therapy (DBT) for number of self-injury episodes.

differences in the number of suicide attempts across the three time periods, $F(2, 82) = 1.35$. Figure 14.2 presents the graphs for suicide attempts for the more treatment and less treatment groups. Inspection of the graph for the group that received less treatment shows a U-shaped curve. For this group, suicide attempts appear to decrease during treatment at Grove Street but then increase following discharge from the program.

We recoded the suicide-attempt variable to examine whether there were differences between the more treatment and less treatment groups in the number of clients who attempted suicide during the 6-month period after discharge from Grove Street. During the 6-month follow-up period, there were no differences between the treatment groups in the number of clients who attempted suicide, $\chi^2(1) = 2.12$. No clients in the more treatment group attempted suicide, and only one client from the less treatment group had done so. However, this adolescent attempted suicide nine times by overdose and was admitted to a long-term locked facility.

Overall, the findings indicate that suicidal behavior was unlikely to occur while these adolescents were in treatment at Grove Street. With the exception of the one client in the less treatment group, suicidal behavior did not occur during the 6-month follow-up period.

We also examined whether there were changes in the rates of psychiatric hospitalization because many of these adolescents had a history of hospitalization prior to referral to Grove Street. With regard to the number of

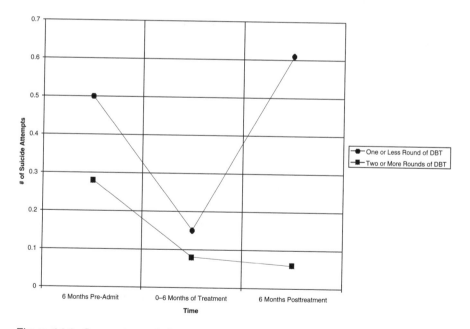

Figure 14.2. Comparison of clients who received one or two rounds of dialectical behavior therapy (DBT) for number of suicide attempts.

psychiatric hospitalizations, there was a significant difference between the more treatment and less treatment groups, $F(1, 40) = 10.85$, $p < .005$. As shown in Figure 14.3, the less treatment group had a significantly higher number of psychiatric hospitalizations across the three time periods, $F(2, 80) = 0.03$. This indicates that psychiatric hospitalization did not change during treatment at Grove Street or during the 6-month follow-up period.

We recoded the hospitalization variable to examine whether there were differences between the more treatment and less treatment groups in the number of clients who had been hospitalized during the 6-month period following discharge from the program. During the follow-up period, 14% of clients in the more treatment group were hospitalized at least once, and 39% of clients in the less treatment group were hospitalized at least once. However, this difference in the number of clients who were hospitalized during the follow-up period was not statistically significant, $\chi^2(1) = 3.24$.

We also examined the number of days that clients spent in a psychiatric hospital. There were no significant differences between the groups in the number of hospital days, $F(1, 40) = 0.66$, but there was a significant difference across the three time periods, $F(2, 80) = 3.96$, $p < .05$. Post hoc comparison of the three time periods revealed a significant quadratic effect, $F(1, 40) = 4.32$, $p < .05$. As shown in Figure 14.4, there is a U-shaped pattern, with a significant decrease in the number of days clients spend in a psychiatric hospital from the 6-month pretreatment period to the first round of

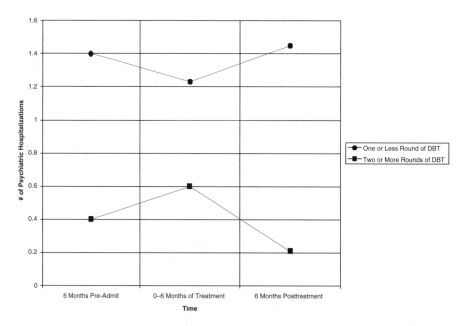

Figure 14.3. Comparison of clients who received one or two rounds of dialectical behavior therapy (DBT) for number of psychiatric hospitalizations.

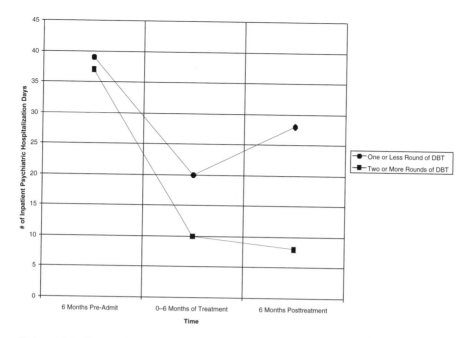

Figure 14.4. Comparison of clients who received one or two rounds of dialectical behavior therapy (DBT) for total number of inpatient psychiatric hospitalization days.

DBT treatment at Grove Street. However, the number of days in a psychiatric hospital increased following discharge from Grove Street. Inspection of Figure 14.4 reveals that the less treatment group had an increase in the number of hospital days following discharge, whereas the more treatment group remained the same. This finding suggests that clients in the less treatment group had a weakening of treatment effects after leaving the Grove Street program.

Overall, these findings indicate that the number of times that these adolescents were hospitalized did not change during the treatment and follow-up periods. However, the total number of days that these adolescents spent in an inpatient psychiatric facility decreased significantly while they were engaged in the first round of DBT treatment. In other words, the number of psychiatric hospitalizations remained the same, but the average duration of each hospitalization was shorter when clients were engaged in the first round of DBT treatment.

This decrease in the total number of days of inpatient psychiatric treatment was maintained during the 6-month follow-up period for the adolescents who received more DBT treatment. In contrast, the total number of days of inpatient psychiatric treatment increased somewhat for adolescents who received less treatment during the 6-month follow-up period. Even though the number of days of inpatient treatment for adolescents in the less treatment group increased during the 6-month follow-up period, these adolescents still spent fewer days in an inpatient psychiatric facility than they did during the 6-month period that preceded their referral to the Grove Street Program.

The findings suggest that DBT can be effectively adapted to a residential treatment program to reduce self-injury and other problem behaviors in adolescents. The adolescents who were treated showed a significant decrease in NSSI after they entered the Grove Street program. It is particularly noteworthy that self-injurious behaviors continued to decrease during the 6-month period following discharge from the program.

The absence of a control group requires that these findings be interpreted cautiously. Other factors besides the DBT treatment provided at Grove Street may account for these findings. It is important to recognize, however, that these adolescents were referred to this program because the severity of their disturbance was expected to worsen without intensive intervention. Hence, spontaneous remission or the passage of time probably cannot explain the improved outcomes for these clients.

Our hypothesis that clients who completed two rounds of DBT would have better outcomes than clients who completed one round or less (i.e., 6 months or less of treatment) was generally supported. For adolescents who received one round of DBT, the decrease in the number of self-injury incidents was comparable to the decrease exhibited by adolescents who received more treatment. However, during the follow-up period, there were significant differences in the number of clients who self-injured. During the 6-month period after discharge, only 3% of clients who received two rounds of DBT self-injured, whereas 23% of clients who received less treatment did so.

A similar pattern was found for rates of psychiatric hospitalization. The adolescents who received two rounds of DBT had a fewer number of hospitalizations than the adolescents who received less treatment. Moreover, 14% of adolescents who received two rounds of DBT were hospitalized at least once during the 6-month period following discharge from Grove Street, but 39% of the adolescents who received less treatment were hospitalized at least once following discharge from Grove Street. This difference was not, however, statistically significant.

Although the findings suggest that clients who received two rounds of DBT tended to have better outcomes than clients who received less treatment, it would be premature to conclude that longer or more intensive treatment produces more improvement because clients were not randomly assigned to receive one or two rounds of DBT. In some instances, clients who received treatment for 6 months or less were discharged to locked psychiatric facilities because they were unable to handle the demands of residential treatment. Adolescents who received less treatment had significantly higher rates of psychiatric hospitalization at all three time periods than adolescents who received two rounds of DBT, which suggests that adolescents who received less treatment exhibited more severe disturbance.

Even though we cannot conclude that longer treatment produces better outcomes for these adolescents, our findings provide some valuable clinical insights. For example, these findings suggest that clients who have more extensive histories of psychiatric hospitalization may need additional services to succeed in a residential treatment program such as Grove Street. Alternatively, these clients may need additional treatment components or interventions that expand the focus beyond NSSI (e.g., more intensive family therapy, substance abuse treatment, cognitive–behavioral therapy for major depression).

This study represents the first evaluation of DBT for self-injury in a residential treatment program for adolescents. As is often the case with this kind of initial evaluation, there are multiple limitations to the results presented here. The sample was small and from a single treatment setting in Massachusetts. Two groups were compared as to treatment effects, but there was no random assignment. The two groups were not comparable as to sex distribution. Moreover, there was some evidence that the less treatment group was more dysfunctional in the 6 months before admission, in that substantially more of the less treatment group came from inpatient or locked residential settings. In addition, the less treatment group had higher rates of hospitalization in the 6 months prior to admission than the more treatment group. Therefore, better outcomes for the more treatment group may have been due to preexisting differences in the level of disturbance and dysfunctional behavior in the two groups. It is possible that the less treatment group experienced poorer outcomes not because they received less treatment but because they were substantially more impaired.

Other influences that could have played a role in the positive outcomes for the more treatment group include historical and contextual influences that are unknown. Another concern is that treatment was evaluated only at 6 months postdischarge. Ideally, additional assessments would have been performed 1 and 2 years postdischarge.

On the positive side, the data and results reported here do represent a step forward. This study appears to be the first regarding the treatment of NSSI and related problems in a community residential setting. The findings are encouraging because residential DBT treatment appeared to work quite well for a large portion of clients in terms of reduced rates of self-injury, hospitalization, suicidal behavior, and successful return to family living. This contribution is important in that large numbers of self-injuring youth are treated in such settings, and empirical evaluation is warranted. Future studies in such residential settings should include larger, more diverse samples; include randomized assignment and control groups; and perform more sophisticated statistical analyses.

SELF-INJURY CONTAGION IN RESIDENTIAL PROGRAMS

A final topic for this chapter is the phenomenon of social contagion of self-injury. As just reviewed, one advantage of residential treatment settings is that intensive treatment can be provided over extended periods of time. However, congregate living can also lead to an exacerbation of problems. One such dilemma that has been frequently reported in the literature is the social contagion of self-injury. Ross and McKay (1979), Walsh and Rosen (1988), Favazza (1987), Taiminen, Kallio-Soukainen, Nokso-Koivisto, Kaljonen, and Helenius (1998), and Walsh (2006) have all written on the topic of self-injury contagion. Walsh and Rosen defined the phenomenon in two ways: (a) when acts of self-injury occur in two or more persons within the same group within a 24-hour period (Rosen & Walsh, 1989) and (b) when acts self-injury occur within a group in statistically significant clusters or bursts (Walsh & Rosen, 1985). These two definitions have different emphases and are not incompatible.

Contagion episodes have generally been reported in children, adolescents, or young adults living in institutional or treatment settings such as orphanages (Holden-Davis, 1914), inpatient units (Crabtree & Grossman, 1974; Offer & Barglow, 1960; Taiminen et al., 1998), prisons (Virkunnen, 1976), juvenile detention facilities (Ross & McKay, 1979), group homes (Walsh & Rosen, 1985), or special education schools (Rosen & Walsh, 1989). Unfortunately, self-injury contagion has yet to be studied in normative settings such as public schools, universities, and the community at large.

Although the phenomenon has been reported anecdotally for almost 100 years, Walsh and Rosen (1985) were the first to provide some empirical evidence of self-injury contagion. They studied a group of 25 adolescents in a community-based group home over a 1-year period. They found that self-injury occurred in statistically significant clusters or bursts, whereas other problems, such as aggression, substance abuse, suicidal talk, and psychiatric hospitalizations, did not.

Taiminen et al. (1998) replicated our findings in Finland. They studied a group of 51 adolescent psychiatric inpatients over a 1-year period. They also reported that self-injury occurred in statistically significant clusters. Of particular interest in their report was that two individuals self-injured for the first time while on the psychiatric unit. Taiminen et al. concluded that a majority of self-injury events in closed adolescent units may be triggered by contagion and that self-injury can spread to adolescents previously naive to self-injury. Thus, treatment programs can be hotbeds of contagion in which iatrogenic effects emerge. Clients who go to such settings to receive help may instead acquire new problematic behaviors such as self-injury. Such risks make the need to understand, manage, and prevent contagion all the more important.

Motivations Regarding Self-Injury and Contagion

One way to better understand contagion is to explore motivations for self-injury. This has been a fertile area for recent research. When individuals have been asked why they self-injure, they usually cite intrapersonal (i.e., internal psychological) reasons as being most important, with interpersonal functions of self-injury having a secondary role. For example, Osuch, Noll, and Putnam (1999) studied a sample of 75 adult inpatients who engaged in self-injurious behaviors. Their factor analysis of self-report data looked at motivations for self-injuring. Six factors emerged in the order of (a) affect modulation, (b) desolation (i.e., a desire to escape feelings of isolation or emptiness), (c) self-punishment and other motivations, (d) influencing others, (e) magical control of others, and (f) self-stimulation. Thus, the first three and the last concerned intrapersonal dimensions, whereas the fourth and fifth factors concerned more interpersonal motivations. For this sample, the interpersonal motivations were present but of secondary importance.

Nock and Prinstein (2004) also found intrapersonal motivations to be more powerful than interpersonal in predicting self-injury. They proposed and evaluated four primary functions of NSSI: (a) automatic negative reinforcement (e.g., removal of unpleasant affect), (b) automatic positive reinforcement (e.g., to feel something better, even if it is a different form of pain), (c) social negative reinforcement (e.g., to avoid punishment from others), and (d) social positive reinforcement (e.g., to gain attention from others or communicate unhappiness).

Nock and Prinstein (2004) ran analyses on 89 adolescents admitted to an inpatient psychiatric unit who had self-injured at least once. The authors performed a factor analysis on patient self-report data and found that "scores on the automatic-positive reinforcement subscale were significantly higher than both social reinforcement subscales" (p. 888). More than half of those who engaged in self-injurious behavior reported doing so "to stop bad feelings." Items on the automatic reinforcement subscales were endorsed by 24% to 53% of the participants, whereas items on the social reinforcement subscales were endorsed by only 6% to 24% of the participants. They concluded that the participants "reported engaging [in self-injury] in order to regulate emotions much more frequently than to influence the behavior of others" (p. 889).

Rodham, Hawton, and Evans (2004) reported similar results in their study of adolescents performing deliberate self-harm (with or without suicidal intent). Their sample included 220 15- and 16-year-old individuals who engaged in self-cutting from school settings in England. The most frequently selected reasons for cutting (which were chosen from a list of eight options) were intrapersonal in nature. These included such items as, "I wanted to get relief from a terrible state of mind" and "I wanted to punish myself." Interpersonal items such as, "I wanted to find out if someone really loved me," "I wanted to get some attention," and "I wanted to frighten someone" were cited much less frequently (Rodham et al., 2004, p. 82). The authors concluded that youth who self-cut were more likely to cite depression, escalating affective pressure, or a need to take one's mind off problems than interpersonal items such as reacting to arguments with others or seeking attention (Rodham et al., 2004).

Although such research suggests that interpersonal factors are of secondary importance for most self-injury, when contagion episodes occur, the interpersonal influences appear to become more salient. An important line of future research would be to identify what contributes to social factors becoming especially prominent during contagion episodes.

Walsh (2006) speculated that the following dimensions may influence social contagion of self-injury:

- desire for acknowledgment (e.g., "Pay attention to me"),
- desire to change the behavior of others (e.g., "If you don't do X, I'll cut myself"),
- desire to punish (e.g., "See what you've made me do?"),
- desire to produce withdrawal (e.g., "Perhaps now you'll leave me alone"),
- anticipation of aversive consequences (e.g., "If I assault someone, I'll go to jail; if I cut myself, the penalties are modest"),
- competition for caregiver resources (particularly in residential settings in which staff resources can be scarce),
- peer competition (e.g., peers compete to see who is the "best" at NSSI),
- direct modeling influences (i.e., behavior influenced by modeling alone without apparent contingencies), and
- disinhibition (e.g., those who are striving not to self-injure are disinhibited by witnessing self-injury in others).

Note that the first seven items in this list can be conceptualized as consistent with Nock and Prinstein's (2004) functional approach. These influences for self-injury contagion involve negative social reinforcement (e.g., producing the withdrawal of others or avoiding aversive consequences) or positive social reinforcement (e.g., receiving attention, coercing others). However, the role of modeling effects such as direct imitation or disinhibition may not fall within their framework.

Nonetheless, the important topic pertaining to self-injury contagion in residential settings is how to prevent it when possible and how to manage it when not. Walsh (2006) provided a school protocol that can serve as a prototype for responding to self-injury in group settings of diverse types. The basic principles for preventing self-injury contagion are as follows:

1. Encourage patients who self-injure to stop talking about the behavior with peers, explaining that such talk is triggering, conducive to contagion, and may thereby hurt their friends.

2. Instead, those who self-injure should talk with trusted adults such as counselors, therapists, or parents about their self-injury.
3. Consistent with this approach, when in a milieu, those who self-injure should be expected to cover up wounds, scars, and bandages because these visual cues can also be triggering.
4. Group treatment methodologies should concentrate on skills training and avoid or prohibit discussions of self-injury.
5. Individual therapy should be the modality in which self-injury is worked on in depth.

An Empirical Study of Self-Injury Contagion at Grove Street

In the Grove Street DBT program, we have striven to be consistent with the five principles just listed. Toward this end, the program has clear rules about client communication regarding self-injury. Within the program, it is a major rule violation for clients to discuss self-injury or exhibit their wounds or scars in the midst of peers. In addition, skills training groups have strict rules about not discussing details of self-injury or other self-harm behaviors. Instead, self-injury is discussed at length in individual DBT therapy with emphasis on data collection using diary cards and behavioral chain analyses. Problem-solving and skills practice in individual therapy prioritizes learning healthy emotion regulation and interpersonal effectiveness skills to replace self-injury. Data have already been presented indicating that the program appears to be successful in reducing rates of self-injury.

To measure whether NSSI contagion was occurring in the program, we conducted an empirical study replicating the design of Walsh and Rosen's (1985). For a 2.5-year period, we collected data on daily basis regarding the occurrence and nonoccurrence of self-injury. We then analyzed the distribution of NSSI occurrences to determine whether the behavior had occurred in statistically significant clusters or bursts. The result was that no significant clustering was found; rather, the distribution of acts of NSSI appeared to be entirely random. Given previous problems with self-injury contagion in group settings (Rosen & Walsh, 1989; Walsh & Rosen, 1985), we tentatively concluded that the strategies to prevent social contagion of NSSI identified earlier have been effective.

CONCLUSION

In this chapter, we reviewed the modest amount of empirical data related to self-injury in residential settings. The benefits and potential risks of treating self-injury in residential programs have been discussed. A brief summary of a rare empirical study of treatment outcomes regarding NSSI in a DBT group home setting has been presented.

Clearly, there is a pressing need for further research regarding the treatment of NSSI in residential settings. Future studies in such residential settings should include larger, more diverse samples; include randomized assignment and control groups; and perform more sophisticated statistical analyses. Also, in the study reported here, NSSI was measured using simple behavioral counts. In the future, it would be advisable to use validated instruments to measure NSSI such as the Suicide Attempt Self-Injury Interview (Linehan, Comtois, Brown, Heard, & Wagner, 2006) or the Self-Injurious Thought and Behaviors Interview (Nock, Holmberg, Photos, & Michel, 2007).

Residential programs may offer considerable benefits in treating NSSI in that such settings can be intensive, highly structured, positive learning environments for seriously disturbed individuals. However, these settings also can pose serious risks of social contagion of problematic behaviors such as NSSI. Empirical research is one's best ally in weighing the risks and benefits of residential treatment.

REFERENCES

American Psychiatric Association. (2000). *Diagnostic and statistical manual of mental disorders* (4th ed., text rev.). Washington, DC: Author.

Barley, W. D., Buie, S. E., Peterson, E. W., Hollingsworth, A. S., Griva, M., & Hickerson, S. C. (1993). Development of an inpatient cognitive–behavioral treatment program for borderline personality disorder. *Journal of Personality Disorders, 7,* 232–240.

Bohus, M., Haaf, B., Simms, T., Limberger, M., Schmahl, C., & Unckel, C. (2004). Effectiveness of inpatient dialectical behavior therapy for borderline personality disorder: A controlled trial. *Behaviour Research and Therapy, 42,* 487–499.

Bohus, M., Haaf, B., Stiglmayr, C., Pohl, U., Bohme, R., & Linehan, M. (2000). Evaluation of inpatient dialectical-behavior therapy for borderline personality disorder: A prospective study. *Behaviour Research and Therapy, 38,* 875–879.

Connor, D. F., Doerfler, L. A., Toscano, P. F., Volungis, A. M., & Steingard, R. J. (2004). Characteristics of children and adolescents admitted to a residential treatment center. *Journal of Child and Family Studies, 13,* 497–510.

Crabtree, L. H., & Grossman, W. K. (1974). Administrative clarity and redefinition for an open adolescent unit. *Psychiatry, 37,* 350–359.

Crowe, M., & Bunclark, J. (2000). Repeated self-injury and its management. *International Review of Psychiatry, 12,* 48–53.

D'Zurilla, T. J., & Goldfried, M. R. (1971). Problem solving and behavior modification. *Journal of Abnormal Psychology, 78,* 107–126.

D'Zurilla, T. J., & Nezu, A. M. (2001). Problem solving therapies. In K. Dobson (Ed.), *Handbook of cognitive–behavioral therapies* (2nd ed., pp. 211–245). New York: Guilford Press.

Favazza, A. R., (1987). *Bodies under siege: Self-mutilation and body modification in culture and psychiatry*. Baltimore: John Hopkins University Press.

Favazza, A., DeRosear, L., & Conterio, K. (1989). Self-mutilation and eating disorders. *Suicide and Life-Threatening Behavior, 19*, 352–361.

Hawton, K., Arensman, E., Townsend, E., Bremner, S., Feldman, E., Goldney, R., et al. (1998, August 15). Deliberate self-harm: Systematic review of efficacy of psychosocial and pharmacological treatments in preventing repetition. *BMJ, 317*, 441–447.

Holdin-Davis, D. (1914). An epidemic of hair-pulling in an orphanage. *British Journal of Dermatology, 26*, 207–210.

Katz, L. Y., Cox, B. J., Gunasekara, S., & Miller, A. L. (2004). Feasibility of dialectical behavior therapy for suicidal adolescent inpatients. *Journal of the American Academy of Child & Adolescent Psychiatry, 43*, 276–282.

Linehan, M. M. (1993a). *Cognitive–behavioral treatment of borderline personality disorder*. New York: Guilford Press.

Linehan, M. M. (1993b). *Skills training manual for treating borderline personality disorder*. New York: Guilford Press.

Linehan, M. M., Armstrong, H. E., Suarez, A., Allmon, D., & Heard, H. L. (1991). Cognitive–behavioral treatment of chronically parasuicidal borderline patients. *Archives of General Psychiatry, 48*, 1060–1064.

Linehan, M. M., Comtois, K. A., Brown, M. Z., Heard, H. L., & Wagner, A. (2006). Suicide Attempt Self-Injury Interview (SASII): Development, reliability, and validity of a scale to assess suicide attempts and intentional self-injury. *Psychological Assessment, 18*, 303–312.

Miller, A. L., Rathus, J. H., & Linehan, M. M. (2007). *Dialectical behavior therapy with suicidal adolescents*. New York: Guilford Press.

Muehlenkamp, J. J. (2006). Empirically supported treatments and general therapy guidelines for non-suicidal self-injury. *Journal of Mental Health Counseling, 28*, 166–185.

Nock, M. K., Holmberg, E. B., Photos, V. I., & Michel, B. D. (2007). Self-Injurious Thoughts and Behavior Interview: Development, reliability, and validity in an adolescent sample. *Psychological Assessment, 19*, 309–317.

Nock, M. K., & Prinstein, M. J. (2004). A functional approach to the assessment of self-mutilative behavior. *Journal of Consulting and Clinical Psychology, 72*, 885–890.

Offer, D. O., & Barglow, P. (1960). Adolescent and young adult self-mutilation incidents in a general psychiatric hospital. *Archives of General Psychiatry, 3*, 194–204.

Osuch, E. A., Noll, J. G., & Putnam, F. W. (1999). The motivations for self-injury in psychiatric inpatients. *Psychiatry, 62*, 334–345.

Pao, P. N. (1969). The syndrome of delicate self-cutting. *British Journal of Medical Psychology, 42*, 195–206.

Podvoll, E. M. (1969). Self-mutilation within a hospital setting: A study of identity and social compliance. *British Journal of Medical Psychology, 42*, 213–221.

Rodham, K., Hawton, K., & Evans, E. (2004). Reasons for deliberate self-harm: Comparison of self-poisoners and self-cutters in a community sample of adolescents. *Journal of the American Academy of Child & Adolescent Psychiatry, 43*, 80–87.

Rosen, P., & Walsh, B. (1989). Relationship patterns in episodes of self-mutilative contagion. *The American Journal of Psychiatry, 146*, 656–658.

Ross, R. R., & McKay, H. R. (1979). *Self-mutilation.* Lexington, MA: Lexington Books.

Taiminen, T. J., Kallio-Soukainen, K., Nokso-Koivisto, H., Kaljonen, A., & Helenius, H. (1998). Contagion of deliberate self-harm among adolescent inpatients. *Journal of the American Academy of Child & Adolescent Psychiatry, 37*, 211–217.

Virkkunen, M. (1976). Self-mutilation in antisocial personality disorder. *Acta Psychiatrica Scandanavica, 54*, 347–352.

Walsh, B. (2006). *Treating self-injury: A practical guide.* New York: Guilford Press.

Walsh, B., & Rosen, P. (1985). Self-mutilation and contagion: An empirical test. *The American Journal of Psychiatry, 142*, 119–120.

Walsh, B., & Rosen, P. (1988). *Self-mutilation: Theory, research and treatment.* New York: Guilford Press.

15
PSYCHOPHARMACOLOGIC TREATMENT OF NONSUICIDAL SELF-INJURY

CURT A. SANDMAN

Intentional acts of harm to self, evident in many species, have no known cause and no agreed-on treatment. Nonsuicidal self-injury (NSSI) is associated with numerous clinical manifestations, including genetic syndromes, psychological, personality and developmental disorders, and chronic pain. However, it is most prevalent among individuals with neurodevelopmental disorders (NDD), specifically autism, and among individuals with personality disorders, particularly borderline personality disorder (BPD). The most definitive pharmacological studies of the onset, expression, and topology of NSSI have been conducted with institutionalized individuals whose behavior can be directly observed and measured. However, it is not known whether the motivations and antecedents for NSSI exhibited by individuals who are institutionalized are shared by individuals within the community or with typically developing individuals.

It also is not known whether the motivations for NSSI are similar across the life span. Self-injuring behavior is exhibited both by infants who develop typically and by infants who develop atypically (Berkson, Tupa, & Sherman,

Preparation of this chapter was supported in part by award HD-48947 from the National Institute of Child Health and Human Development. The assistance of Shervin Bazmi is appreciated.

2001). Episodes of self-injury were not maintained by social consequences among a group of 2- to 4-year-old children observed over a 2-year interval with monthly functional analysis probes (Richman & Lindauer, 2005). These findings suggest that self-injurious behavior that develops early in life has an internal or biological drive, but it is not known whether this same motivation persists into later childhood and beyond. For instance, self-injurious behavior may emerge for the first time in early childhood, during adolescence, and even later in life (Lamprecht, Pakrasi, Gash, & Swann, 2005; Murphy, Hall, Oliver, & Kissi-Debra, 1999; Sansone, Gaither, & Songer, 2002). There is evidence that it decreases during middle adolescence among patients with NDD (Griffin et al., 1987), but at the same age, it becomes more prevalent among another group of patients (i.e., those with BPD; Sansone et al., 2002).

Guess and Carr (1991) described the evolution of behavioral disorders, including self-injury, in an elegant three-level model. The most primitive expression of self-injury (Level 1 of their model) presumes that NSSI and other maladaptive movements (e.g., stereotypy) are internally regulated or biologically motivated. Guess and Carr argued that over time the function of behaviors such as NSSI may change. Individuals may progress from lower (i.e., internally regulated behavior) to high (i.e., homeostatic and operant) levels because of either maturation or effective intervention. Individuals also may exhibit shorter term transitions between levels. Behavioral treatment was assumed to be most effective for NSSI maintained by operant factors (i.e., reinforcement such that behavior controlled others; Level 3 in their model), but individuals with internally regulated patterns were predicted to be resistant to behavioral treatment and better treated with pharmacological interventions.

In addition to the problems of not knowing the causes of NSSI present for treatment, individuals exhibiting NSSI engage in a panoply of methods of harm that include cutting, hitting, or biting themselves; ingesting foreign objects; hurling themselves to the ground and banging their head against solid objects, resulting in broken bones; disfigurement; blindness; and even loss of life (Claes & Vandereycken, 2007; Sandman, Spence, & Smith, 1999; Thompson, Hackenberg, Cerutti, Baker, & Axtell, 1994). This broad spectrum of self-harm phenotypes, the range of methods used to commit these acts, and the multiple motivations for exhibiting NSSI militate against attempts to develop a single treatment.

These are critical issues because the rational application of pharmacological agents to treat NSSI should be based on knowledge of the mechanisms motivating the behavior. Despite the lack of consensus and the absence of consistent findings, there are two general schools of thought about the underlying mechanisms. The most prevalent view is that there are environmental–social antecedents for NSSI. This view asserts that individuals intentionally injure themselves to receive attention or escape demands.

Behavioral and cognitive interventions are based on this belief, and there is clear evidence that behavioral strategies can be effective (Hanley, Iwata, & McCord, 2003; Iwata, Roscoe, Zarcone, & Richman, 2002). A second view is that NSSI is motivated by an underlying biological disturbance either in the pain and pleasure system (Bohus et al., 2000; Sandman & Touchette, 2002; Sandman, Touchette, Lenjavi, Marion, & Chicz-DeMet, 2003) or in the dissipation of anxiety or generation of arousal (Nixon, Cloutier, & Aggarwal, 2002). There are other plausible motivations, related to these general explanations, for individuals to self-injure, including attempts to mitigate chronic pain (Theodouloua, Harriss, Hawton, & Bass, 2005), self-punishment for guilt or shame (Klonsky, 2007), or that self-harm may be a component of a stereotypic ritual or a compulsive act (King et al., 1998).

All of these facts collide with the intense pressures on clinicians to reduce and eliminate expression of self-harm and conspire against the development of a rational pharmacological intervention. Acute treatment for self-harm in patients ages 7 to 24 in emergency rooms reflects a range of approaches from gastric lavage, intravenous fluids, a variety of antidotes and psychotropic medications, primarily anxiolytics, and antidepressants (Olfson, Gameroff, Marcus, Greenberg, & Shaffer, 2005). Outside the emergency room, a somewhat chaotic pharmacological approach to the longer term treatment of NSSI in those with and without NDD has emerged and is illustrated in Tables 15.1 and 15.2. These relatively recent studies are presented primarily to illustrate the general lack of focus, or agreement, in the application of pharmacological agents for treating NSSI. The actual clinical situation is much more confused than what is illustrated in the tables. We (Lott et al., 2004) documented the prevalence of polypharmacy in the treatment of maladaptive behaviors (including NSSI) in a community population. It is not unusual—in fact, it is very common—for individuals with high rates or severe manifestations of NSSI to receive several psychotropic medications. One patient referred to our clinic was administered 13 psychotropic medications in an attempt to control his behavior. To add a further complication to treating NSSI, individuals (especially those with NDD) exhibiting self-injuring behavior often respond in unpredictable ways to medications, and paradoxical reactions have been reported to several classes of neurotropic agents (Barron & Sandman, 1983). Not only does the clinical practice of treating NSSI, especially in the intellectually impaired population, often continue without consideration of the motivation for the behavior, it continues with little concern about the interaction among the various medications.

It is important to first acknowledge that several intervention studies conducted with NDD populations included direct observations of behavior and none relied on self-report. In contrast, few intervention studies in the non-NDD population included direct observations of patients, and most collected self-report ratings, observer ratings of core traits, or both. The opportunity to

TABLE 15.1

Examples of Pharmacological Treatment With Results for Patients With Borderline Personality Disorder (BPD)

Study	Patient/patient group	Medication	Results of treatment
Thurauf and Washeim (2000)	1 patient with BPD	Morphine	The application of morphine abolished the perception of pain during self-injury and intensified self-injurious activities.
Philipsen, Schmahl, and Lieb (2004)	9 female patients with BPD	Naloxone	After injection of either naloxone or placebo, dissociative symptoms significantly decreased. There were no significant differences between naloxone and placebo in the reduction of symptoms. Patients with the most prominent response to naloxone fulfilled the highest number of criteria for BPD.
Bohus et al. (1999)	13 female patients with BPD	Naltrexone	Highly significant reduction of the duration and intensity of dissociative phenomena and tonic immobility as well as a marked reduction in analgesia during treatment with naltrexone. Six of nine patients reported a decrease in the mean number of flashbacks per day.
Nickel et al. (2006)	52 patients with BPD	Aripiprazole	The aripiprazole group had a significantly greater rate of change than the placebo group on rating scales. Before therapy, 7 of 26 people in the aripiprazole group and 5 of 26 people in the placebo group self-injured. After therapy, 2 of 26 people in the aripiprazole group and 7 of 26 in the placebo group self-injured.

Study	Sample	Drug	Results
Philipsen, Richter, et al. (2004)	14 female patients with BPD	Clonidine	Aversive inner tension and urge to commit self-injurious behavior before administration of clonidine were strong. After administration of clonidine in both doses, aversive inner tension, dissociative symptoms, urge to commit self-injurious behavior, and suicidal ideations decreased. Blood pressure, aversive inner tension, and dissociative symptoms were correlated before and after clonidine administration.
Chengappa Ebeling, Kang, Levine, and Parepally (1999)	7 female patients with BPD hospitalized from severe self-mutilation	Clozapine	After clozapine treatment, there were statistically significant reductions in incidents of self-mutilation (restraint), seclusion, the use of as-needed antianxiety medications, and injuries to staff and peers. Four patients were subsequently discharged from hospital.
Cordás, Tavares, Calderoni, Stump, and Ribeiro (2006)	2 female patients with bulimia nervosa, self-mutilation	Oxcarbazepine	Case 1 showed a more impressive response to oxcarbazepine. Not only did self-mutilating behavior remit but reports of serenity and reflection seemed to go beyond the patient's usual self, suggesting action at personality level, that is, impulsive traits. Although clinically relevant, Case 2 reported a less dramatic change, restricted to self-mutilating behavior, after oxcarbazepine administration.

TABLE 15.2

Examples of Pharmacological Treatment With Results for Patients With Neurodevelopmental Disorders

Study	Patient/patient group	Medication	Results of treatment
Hammock, Levine, and Schroeder (2001)	2 adult men with profound mental retardation	Clozapine	Both adults showed a dose-related suppression of self-injurious behavior and aggression while on clozapine, with only mild side effects at a minimum effective dose of 200 mg/day.
Markowitz (1992)	21 severely to profoundly mentally retarded persons with aggression and self-injurious behavior	Fluoxetine	Marked improvement occurred in 13 patients, moderate in 4, mild in 2, and no improvement in 2 patients treated for a minimum of 3 months. Positive changes occurred in the areas of self-injury, agitation, emotional lability, and aggression.
Janowsky et al. (2005)	38 adults with MR	SSRIs and clomipramine	Significant decreases in the ratings of global maladaptive behavior and aggression, self-injurious behavior, destruction/disruption, and depression/dysphoria occurred in the patient group after the initiation of antidepressants.
Janowsky, Shetty, Barnhill, Elamir, and Davis (2003)	22 institutionalized adults with severe or profound MR	Topiramate	Significant decreases in global severity scores and in the cumulative aggression occurred in the patients after starting topiramate.
Sandman, Touchette, Lenjavi, Marion, and Chicz-DeMet (2003)	19 institutionalized individuals with severe or profound MR and self-injurious behavior	Naltrexone	A significant number of the patients displayed at least a 25% reduction in self-injurious behavior, at each dose of naltrexone. A significant number of patients displayed a 50% or greater reduction in self-injurious behavior for at least one dose of naltrexone. Three patients responded positively to all three doses, and three patients failed to respond to any dose.

Symons et al. (2001)	4 institutionalized adult men with severe and profound MR and daily self-injurious behavior	Naltrexone	Significant reductions (i.e., 33%) in self-injurious behavior rate for three of the four patients. For all patients, magnitude of the sequential dependency between staff behavior and self-injury was significantly greater during treatment with naltrexone than during treatment with a placebo.
Sandman, Hetrick, Taylor, Marion, and Chicz-DeMet (2000)	12 institutionalized individuals with MR and self-injurious behavior	Naltrexone	The degree of coupling between POMC fragments was related to response to naltrexone. Elevated beta-endorphin relative to ACTH predicted positive response to naltrexone.
Canitano (2006)	11 children with autistic disorder and severe self-injurious behavior	Risperidone	Nine children presented a mild improvement in self-injurious behavior, and two did not show any variation. A decrease in self-injurious behavior was mainly due to the reduction of frequency. Intensity did not change significantly, and global duration of self-injurious behavior was unchanged. Side effects were not severe.

Note. MR = mental retardation; SSRIs = selective serotonin reuptake inhibitors; POMC = proopiomelanocortin; ACTH = adrenocorticotropic hormone.

determine the rate and frequency of self-injury by direct observations has several methodological advantages over self-report and observer ratings; however, findings from the studies using direct observations (primarily in the NDD population) may not generalize to other groups. Furthermore, the development of the opiate hypothesis for NSSI in patient populations is much further advanced than for other systems. That is, there is a specific link proposed between the opiate system and self-injury (i.e., the perception of pain), whereas with many other interventions, the influences on NSSI are secondary and nonspecific (e.g., sedation).

THE PAIN AND PLEASURE SYSTEM

Pain

Although it is not a universal observation, most individuals who self-injure do not exhibit the usual signs of pain after their injurious behavior. Despite inflicting serious physical damage to their bodies, many of these individuals do not grimace, cry, or show other symptoms that they are experiencing pain. Bohus et al. (2000) demonstrated that patients with BPD who reported analgesia during episodes of self-injury had reduced sensitivity to pain in a laboratory challenge (involving cold pressor and laser-evoked pain). The pain threshold was higher (i.e., less perceived pain) when patients were calm versus when they were distressed. A recent study (Ludäscher et al., 2007) confirmed these findings in patients with BPD using electrical stimulation as a painful probe. One serious consequence of elevated pain thresholds among adolescent patients diagnosed with personality disorders and exhibiting self-injury is increased risk of subsequent suicide attempts (Nock, Joiner, Gordon, Lloyd-Richardson, & Prinstein, 2006).

The absence of response to self-inflicted injury may reflect insensitivity to pain and general sensory depression induced by either elevated endogenous opiates or supersensitive opiate receptors (Cataldo & Harris, 1982; Deutsch, 1986; Sandman, 1988; Sandman et al., 1983). This possibility is supported by classical findings that opiate receptor blockers (a) reverse congenital insensitivity to pain (Dehen, Willer, Boureau, & Cambier, 1977), (b) normalize hypothalamic–peptide dysfunction coexisting with elevated pain threshold (Dunger, Leonard, Wolff, & Preece, 1980), and (c) increase brain responses to sensory information (Arnsten et al., 1983). These observations are consistent with a venerable animal literature proving that opiate blockers lower pain threshold (e.g., see Sandman et al., 1979). In summary, these findings support an analgesia (or pain) hypothesis that implies that individuals who self-injure do not feel pain, perhaps because of chronically elevated endogenous opiates or opiate receptor down-regulation.

Addiction

It is possible also that the addictive properties of elevated endogenous opiates are responsible for maintaining NSSI. In a study of hospitalized adolescents diagnosed with BPD, Nixon et al. (2002) found that patients with repetitive self-injury were unwilling or unable to stop cutting themselves. The frequency and severity increased as tolerance developed. The patients reported a sense of relief on self-injuring that implied a "self-medication" role for their behavior. If it is presumed that NSSI results in pain and that the experience of pain results in the release of opiates, then it can be argued that individuals commit self-inflicted harm to receive the euphoric (i.e., pleasurable) effects of increased circulating opiates. From this perspective, self-injury is an addiction to the endogenous opiate system because the consequences supply a "fix." It has been known for more than 25 years that endogenous opiates have addictive properties as indicated by the development of tolerance (Madden, Akil, Patrick, & Barchas, 1977), physical dependence (Wei & Loh, 1976), and euphoric-like effects (Belluzzi & Stein, 1977) after repeated administration. The repetitive, often compulsive and ritualistic patterns of self-injury (e.g., injury to one area of head or body, stereotyped patterns of behavior, catastrophic responses if the environment is slightly changed) are similar to rituals and compulsive patterns often associated with addictive behaviors. The addiction hypothesis maintains that individuals inflicting NSSI may endure the pain to enjoy the pleasure it produces as well as to avoid a withdrawal effect. The addiction hypothesis predicts that NSSI may be reinforced both positively and negatively because it gains the individual access to the narcotic effect of endorphins while simultaneously allowing the individual to escape the unpleasant sensory consequences commonly associated with the absence of opiates following chronic and sustained access.

Stress

The endogenous opioid system is tightly coupled with the general stress response. Evidence from several laboratories indicates that functioning and processing of a stress-related molecule (i.e., proopiomelanocortin [POMC]) in the hypothalamic–pituitary–adrenal axis may be perturbed among subgroups of individuals exhibiting self-injury (Bouvard et al., 1995; Ernst et al., 1993; Gillberg, 1995; Leboyer et al., 1994, 1999; Sandman, Barron, Chicz-DeMet, & DeMet, 1990; Sandman, Barron, DeMet, Chicz-DeMet, & Rothenburg, 1990; Sandman et al., 1999; Sandman, Hetrick, Taylor, Marion, & Chicz-DeMet, 2000; Verhoeven et al., 1999). In humans, most POMC is produced in the pars distalis of the anterior pituitary but also by hypothalamic neurons and neurons in the amygdala and pituitary stalk. POMC is a well-characterized 31K dalton, bioinactive protein-like molecule that is posttranslationally converted by enzymes into biologically active fragments, including the endogenous opiate, beta-endorphin (BE), and adrenocorticotropic hormone (ACTH; Bertagna, 1994; Bicknell, Savva, & Lowry, 1996; Boutillier, Monnier, Koch, & Loeffler, 1994; Sandman et al., 1999; Seidah & Chretien, 1992; Seidah et al., 1991). Normally, BE is coreleased from the anterior pituitary with ACTH in response to a variety of stressors. However, elevated BE either at rest or after a behavioral episode, but not ACTH, is associated with self-harmful behavior (Sandman et al., 2003; Sandman & Hetrick, 1995; Sandman, Hetrick, Taylor, & Chicz-DeMet, 1997). This suggests that one consequence of NSSI is the disregulation of the arousal system.

An uncoupled arousal pattern is unusual because cleavage of POMC is tightly controlled, occurs in a specific order (Mains & Eipper, 1999), and usually results in highly coupled expression of ACTH and BE (Strand, 1999). Disruption of the coexpression of ACTH and BE can be attributed to lesions of the medial basal hypothalamus (Barna, Koenig, & Davis, 1992), stress-induced increases in circulating levels of corticotropic-releasing hormone (Hargreaves, Flores, Dionne, & Mueller, 1990; Sasaki et al. 1987), and mutations that alter the three-dimensional conformation of the POMC molecule (Rosenblatt & Dickerson, 1997). The most likely source of disregulation of POMC expression, however, is the pattern and order of proteolytic processing of POMC by the prohormone convertases PC1 and PC2. Both convertases are present in the fetus by midgestation, but the great differences in the distribution of PC1 and PC2 that are evident prenatally begin to disappear as organisms reach adulthood (Zheng, Streck, Scott, Seidah, & Pintar, 1994). Because all elements of this POMC–PC–peptide system unfold early in fetal life, uncoupling of POMC fragments or abnormal concentration of POMC products may be evidence of disturbances expressed during the prenatal period (Bicknell et al., 1996) or epigenetically expressed later in life.

The validity of the pain, addiction, and stress hypotheses is not known, but they have encouraged treatments, including opiate receptor blockers, designed to regulate the opiate system as a means to control self-injury.

OPIATE BLOCKERS

Naloxone and naltrexone hydrochloride (NTX) are pure opioid antagonists with primary affinity for mu-opioid receptors and few, if any, agonist effects. Both drugs reversibly block the effects of opioids by competitive binding at mu-, kappa-, and gamma-opioid receptors. These drugs block the subjective and addictive effects of intravenously administered opioids and are known to antagonize the effects of endogenously mediated opioid activity. The primary metabolite of NTX, 6-beta-naltrexol, has weaker opioid antagonist effects, but a longer half-life. On a weight basis, the antagonist activity of NTX is reportedly 2 to 9 times more than that of naloxone. In a dose-dependent fashion, single doses of NTX block the pharmacologic effects of intravenously administered heroin for periods as long as 24 hours at 50 mg and 72 hours at 150 mg.

Efficacy of Opiate Blockers in the Treatment of Nonsuicidal Self-Injury

Acute Treatment With Opioid-Blocking Agents

In a review of pre-1991 studies (Sandman, 1990/1991), 6 of 8 published studies reported that injectable naloxone significantly reduced self-injury. However, in these eight studies, the entire sample consisted of only 10 individuals, but 7 of these decreased their self-injury. In that same review, 12 published studies of orally administered NTX to autistic and NDD individuals were summarized. At that time, 45 individuals (at least 28 with NSSI) had been treated with NTX, and 38 individuals had positive responses of various degrees, including a reduction in self-injury, in 24 of the 28 patients. A separate review of 13 studies (including several in the Sandman review; Sandman, 1990/1991) concluded that about one third of the patients tested with NTX had a decrease in their self-injury (Verhoeven & Tuinier, 1996). Several studies in this later review included juvenile patients under age 8 (Campbell et al., 1993) and patients with primary behavioral problems related to aggression and agitation (Zingarelli et al., 1992).

Most recently, a thorough review of the recent scientific literature, which used rigorous criteria for inclusion, concluded that the effects of opiate blockers on self-injury could be evaluated in 86 patients (Symons, Thompson, & Rodriguez, 2004). Eighty percent of the patients were reported to have improved relative to baseline (i.e., self-injury was reduced) during NTX administration. Of the patients who improved, 47% exhibited a reduction in self-injury by 50% or more. Male patients were more likely than female patients to respond. No significant relations were found between treatment outcomes and autism status or methods of self-injury.

Two relatively large, placebo-controlled studies with direct observations of behavior included in this review contributed to these conclusions. Sandman et al. (1993) reported that 18 of 21 individuals exhibiting NSSI responded favorably to at least one dose (range: 0.5–2.0 mg/kg) of NTX (time-sampled video records provided direct observations of the participants). Acute treatment (1 week at each of three doses) with NTX reduced the frequency of self-injury without major side effects. Activity, stereotypy, involuntary movement, and neurological status were not influenced by NTX. There were two central findings. First, the highest dose (2 mg/kg) was the most effective, confirming earlier results in this population (Sandman, Barron, & Colman, 1990;

Sandman et al., 1983). Second, participants with the most frequent self-injurious behavior were the most positive responders to higher doses of NTX. A small minority of participants responded most favorably to lower doses. These results confirmed that at least 50% of the individuals decreased their self-injury after treatment with opiate blockers.

The second relatively large study (Thompson et al., 1994) reported that treatment with NTX reduced head hitting, head banging, and self-biting in eight individuals. Improvement was observed in 77% of the head-hitting and head-banging episodes and 100% of the self-biting forms. Episodes of high-frequency self-injurious behavior also were more sensitive to treatment with NTX. The 100-mg (high) dose was more effective than the 50-mg (low) dose in reducing self-harmful behavior. For several individuals, some forms of self-injury (e.g., head hitting, self-biting) decreased after NTX but other forms (e.g., throat poking) did not change. Four of the participants in this trial received concomitant treatment with clonidine (alpha-2-adrenergic agonist), but no effects on their behavior and no interactions with NTX were observed. These findings complement previous studies and caution that although NTX is effective in reducing self-injury, not all forms of self-inflicted harm may be controlled by blocking the opioid system.

In the single study that has evaluated the effects of NTX using time-series analysis, Symons et al. (2001) reported that three of the four patients evaluated had at least a 33% reduction in their self-injury (the fourth patient had a 17% reduction in self-injury). Second, and most interesting to note, they discovered that there was an increase in the sequential dependence between staff behavior and the manifestation of self-injurious behavior. One possible conclusion from these findings is that NTX exerts its effects on behavior, in part by the opioid-mediated reinforcing influences of social interactions.

Two reports of NTX treatment among patients with BPD yielded mixed results. In the first study of 13 patients, treatment with 25 to 100 mg of NTX resulted in a highly significant reduction over 7 days in the duration and the intensity of self-reported dissociative phenomena and tonic immobility, as well as a marked reduction in analgesia (Bohus et al., 1999). In the second study of nine patients, a single dose of 0.4 mg naloxone, administered intravenously, was compared with placebo in a double-blind crossover study (Philipsen, Schmahl, & Lieb, 2004). Self-reported scales for assessing dissociative symptoms and aversive inner tension were administered before and 15 minutes after naloxone or placebo. In addition, an observer-based scale was completed by a clinician. Significant improvement in both self-reported and observed dissociative symptoms were detected after treatment, but there was no difference between naloxone and placebo. Patients with the most improvement after treatment, however, fulfilled the largest number of *Diagnostic and Statistical Manual of Mental Disorders* (*DSM–IV*; 4th ed.; American Psychiatric Association, 1994) criteria for BPD.

Long-Term Treatment With Opioid-Blocking Agents

Most published studies of long-term treatment of NSSI with NTX have been either case studies or open-label designs, and they have generated mixed results. Two types of studies comprise the long-term evaluations of NTX: either prolonged treatment with NTX or extended observations following brief periods of treatment. With these procedures, six of eight patients examined in several studies exhibited long-term benefits in varying degrees from treatment with NTX (Barrett, Feinstein, & Hole, 1989; Crews, Bonaventura, Rowe, & Bonsie, 1993; Symons et al., 2001). In the first report, a total of 24 days of NTX treatment resulted in elimination of self-injury that persisted for at least 22 months in a 12-year-old girl (Barrett et al., 1989). A similar finding was reported after 1 year of continuous treatment with NTX in a 28-year-old woman with severe self-injury. Not only did treatment eliminate self-injurious behavior, but the near-zero rate persisted through placebo and no-drug phases of the study (Crews et al., 1993). In their retrospective study of 56 patients, Casner, Weinheimer, and Gualtieri (1996) discovered that 57% of their patients treated with NTX between 3 and 878 months were considered to be positive responders, and 25% of these met objective criteria as responders.

We (Sandman, Hetrick, Taylor, Marion, Touchette, et al., 2000) examined the residual (12-month) effects following acute treatment with NTX and then assessed the effects of subsequent long-term treatment with NTX. Following acute treatment, participants were followed for a 12-month, drug-free period, and then they were enrolled in a multiple baseline design with a single most effective dose (determined in the acute phase) that was administered to each participant for two 3-month periods over an 18-month interval with placebo periods separating the treatment phases. We found that 7 of 15 patients exhibited persisting effects (as much as 75% decreases in self-injury) in the 12 months after acute treatment with NTX. Patients with greatest improvement after acute treatment had the worst response when readministered NTX.

The precise mechanisms for this complex pattern of response to NTX are unknown, but several factors should be considered. First, in the acute trial, NTX was administered intermittently (i.e., every other day). There is clear evidence that chronic or daily administration of NTX up-regulates opiate receptors but that intermittent administration generates a more complex binding pattern. Second, opiate receptors of individuals exhibiting self-injurious behavior may be congenitally up-regulated and therefore have diminished plasticity in response to challenge (Sandman & Hetrick, 1995). Third, the effects of opiate blockers are regulated by the level and chronicity of exposure to (endogenous) opiates. The exacerbation of self-injury after re-exposure to NTX among the patients who exhibited a persisting reduction following acute (intermittent) exposures may reflect the consequences of nearly complete opiate receptor blockade. If up-regulation of opiate receptors is not possible because they are congenitally fixed or because the endogenous opiate levels are high, then blocking the receptors with NTX will result in individuals increasing their self-injury to achieve the reinforcing effects.

Is There a Specific Endophenotype That Predicts Response to Opioid Blockers?

We have reported that patients with the highest change in plasma levels of BE immediately after a self-injuring act had the most positive response to high doses of NTX (Sandman et al., 1997). These results were consistent with several other reports. First, Ernst et al. (1993) reported that baseline levels of BE were positively related to changes in behavior (assessed with the Clinical Global Impressions rating scale) after treatment with NTX in five young autistic children. Second, Bouvard et al. (1995) found that C-terminal BE decreased after NTX in good responders only. Third, Scifo et al. (1996) found that increases in self-injury and response to NTX in some patients were related to high levels of endogenous opiates (i.e., good responses to NTX were observed in patients with high levels of BE). Fourth, Cazzullo et al. (1999) reported that patients responding with decreased BE levels after treatment with NTX had better and more pervasive behavioral improvement than patients who did not have physiological changes after NTX.

Subsequently, we (Sandman et al., 2003) reported that low doses of NTX were effective in reducing self-injury only in either those who did not exhibit a surge in BE after a behavioral episode or those who had elevated baseline levels of BE. These findings suggest that the high doses of NTX were most effective in patients who had elevated BE after a behavioral episode (state) and that low doses of NTX were most effective in patients with elevated baseline levels (trait).

We (Sandman, Hetrick, Taylor, Marion, & Chicz-DeMet, 2000) found similar effects in long-term studies of NTX. Patients with lower levels of BE after initial exposure to NTX had persisting improvement in their behavior. Chronic administration of NTX to this group was associated with increased rates of self-injury and elevated levels of BE. Patients with elevated basal BE levels did not have long-term improvement after acute treatment, but they did improve after chronic treatment with NTX.

If opiate blockers are presumed to be an effective treatment for NSSI, then it can be argued that opiate agonists would exacerbate the symptoms of self-injury. Although anecdotal reports of paradoxical responses to medications have been reported among individuals with self-injury, including response to sedatives and hypnotics (Barron & Sandman, 1983), only one small study has documented this with an opiate agonist. In that study, administration of morphine to a patient diagnosed with BPD abolished her perception of pain during self-injury but increased her self-injurious activities (Thurauf & Washiem, 2000).

AROUSAL–ANXIETY AND THE DOPAMINE
AND SEROTONIN SYSTEMS

In an elegant series of studies, Breese and collaborators (Breese et al., 2005; Breese & Traylor, 1972) discovered that intracisternal administration of 6-hydroxydopamine (6-OHDA) to neonatal (but not adult) rats resulted in lesions to norepinephrine (NE) and dopamine (DA) containing neurons. Subsequently, they found that rats depleted of DA as neonates developed self-injuring behavior (self-biting) when administered a DA agonist (i.e., the DA receptors were supersensitive). Moreover, they isolated the effects to the sub-population of DA_1 agonists but ultimately found that it was the coupling between the DA_1 and DA_2 receptor subtypes that induced self-injury in their model animals. When a link was reported (Lloyd et al., 1981) between brain DA reduction and a genetic disease (Lesch–Nyhan disease) associated with serious self-injury, primarily self-biting, the neonatal 6-OHDA model became a test system for various pharmacological treatments.

This model also may be useful for understanding the role of serotonin in self-injury because neonatal animals with 6-OHDA lesions exhibited an increased in sprouting of serotonergic neurons. Serotonin depletion promotes aggressive behavior in animals (Breese et al., 2005), blocking serotonin is implicated in self-injury in humans (Denys, van Megen, & Westenberg, 2003; Janowsky, Shetty, Barnhill, Elamir, & Davis, 2005) and several medications for self-injury described in the sections that follow have been engineered to target both the DA and the serotonin systems.

TYPICAL ANTIPSYCHOTIC MEDICATIONS

Most of the patients exhibiting NSSI have been tried on a number of medications to control their behavior. The most common intervention, historically, has been antipsychotic medication. These medications, also known as neuroleptic agents, are used to manage psychosis related to schizophrenia, delusional disorder, and brief psychotic disorder. They are major tranquillizers. The mechanism of action involves many brain receptors, but these medications typically are associated with the blockage of DA or the subgroup of D_2 receptors. Because there is a substantial risk with cumulative dosing of developing extrapyramidal symptoms (EPS), including tardive dyskinesia, these drugs have become much less prevalent for treating psychiatric disorders and NSSI. Typical antipsychotics have been classified according to potency and anticholinergic side effects (e.g., blood pressure, dizziness, constipation). Lower doses of high-potency drugs are required to treat the positive symptoms of psychosis.

ATYPICAL ANTIPSYCHOTIC MEDICATIONS

Typical antipsychotics (haloperidol, chlorpromazine, thioridazine, fluphenazine) have been replaced over the past decade with atypical antipsychotic medications (see Jensen, Buitelaar, Pandina, Binder, & Haas, 2007, for a review). Compared with the typical antipsychotics, these medications appear to be equally effective in reducing positive symptoms such as hallucinations and delusions but are better at treating symptoms such as withdrawal and lack of energy. Their mechanism of action is unknown and differs among the drugs within the class. In general, the atypical antipsychotics decrease DA blockade in specific brain regions and tend to enhance serotoninergic activity. However, it is not that simple. For instance, the oldest atypical antipsychotic, clozapine (Clozaril), has a high affinity for the D_4 receptor but interferes with binding of the D_1, D_2, D_3, and D_5 receptor. In contrast, it is believed that the efficacy of one of the newer atypical antipsychotic agents, aripiprazole (Abilify), is mediated by a partial agonist activity at D_2 and $5HT_{1A}$ (serotonin) receptors and antagonist activity at the $5\text{-}HT_{2A}$ serotonin receptor. These different medications with varied receptor profiles are grouped together because of their decreased tendency to cause EPS.

Risperidone

Statistically significant reductions of disruptive behavioral disorder (DBD), which includes conduct disorder, oppositional–defiant disorder, and DBD—not otherwise specified, have been reported consistently after treatment with the most widely prescribed atypical antipsychotic medication in pediatric populations, risperidone (Hellings et al., 2006; Pandina, Bossie, Youssef, Zhu, & Dunbar, 2007; Pandina et al., 2007). None of these studies, however, or those included in excellent reviews (Jensen et al., 2007; Pandina, Aman, & Findling, 2006), incorporated direct measures or specific assessments of self-injury. Only a small handful of studies have examined the effects of atypical antipsychotic medication specifically on self-injury.

A double-blind study of 20 individuals treated with two doses of risperidone over a 22-week period (Zarcone et al., 2001) found that half of the participants had at least a 50% decrease in aberrant behaviors as assessed on a rating scale. Five individuals were directly observed for 30 minutes several times a week during acute dosing and then at less regular times over a longer time period. A composite behavioral variable was measured that included self-injury, but the independent effects of treatment on self-injury was not possible to determine. Nevertheless, aberrant behavior decreased significantly in two participants, two showed no change, and one increased aberrant behavior during and after treatment with risperidone. In an open-label trial, a group of 11 children diagnosed with autistic disorder were treated for 6 months with risperidone (Canitano, 2006). All participants were selected because they exhibited self-injurious behavior, including head hitting and hand biting. Of the 11 children, 9 reduced their self-injury (scores on the Yale–Paris Self-Injurious Behavior Scale) and 2 did not show improvement. Despite the improvement in nine children, the author concluded that "There was a decrease in the frequency of [self-injurious behavior] in this study, however intensity and duration were barely modified and none of the children showed complete remission" (p. 430).

Clozapine

Significant reductions in the frequency of NSSI, incidents of seclusion, the use of antianxiety medications, and injuries to staff and peers were reported following clozapine treatment in seven hospitalized patients with BPD (Chengappa, Ebeling, Kang, Levine, & Parepally, 1999). All patients previously had received trials of many psychotropic agents, often in combination, without benefit. A single-blind study (Hammock, Levine, & Schroeder, 2001) of two patients who failed to respond to risperidone in the Zarcone et al. (2001) study exhibited marked reductions in self-injury and aggression following treatment with clozapine at a dose of 200 mg/day. In this study, behavior was observed directly by staff for 24 hours a day, 7 days a week. Among the atypical antipsychotic agents, clozapine carries the highest risk profile, which limits its usage. A small but significant number of patients who are administered clozapine develop agranulocytosis, a condition in which white blood cells drop and patients become susceptible to infection. Frequent blood tests are required to monitor risks.

Aripiprazole

Nickel et al. (2006) split 52 patients (43 women and 9 men) diagnosed with BPD into two groups and randomly assigned them to treatment with aripiprazole (Abilify, 15 mg/day) or placebo for 8 weeks. Improvement in symptoms after active treatment was confirmed on measures of depression, anxiety, and anger. Baseline measures of self-injury were observed in five patients in the placebo group and in seven patients in the aripiprazole group. After treatment, two patients in the active treatment group and seven in the placebo group exhibited self-injury. These findings are among the strongest support for the efficacy of an atypical antipsychotic in the treatment of NSSI, and the authors concluded that "aripiprazole appears to be a safe and effective agent for improving not only the symptoms of borderline personality disorder but also the associated health-related quality of life and interpersonal problems" (p. 836).

If drugs that block DA transmission are effective treatments for NSSI, then DA agonists may precipitate or exacerbate it. It is well documented in animal models that psychostimulants can precipitate self-injury (Breese et al., 2005; Halladay et al., 2003; Kasim & Jinnah, 2002; Kita et al., 2000); however, this has not been reported in humans. Karila et al. (2007) reported that cocaine abuse (which prevents the reuptake of DA) in a 44-year-old woman was associated with repeated NSSI of her forearms. There was no evidence of childhood trauma or personality, including BPD, in her history. Thus, the authors argued, this was an example of DA-mediated self-injury and inferentially supported the use of DA antagonists in the treatment of NSSI.

SELECTIVE SEROTONIN REUPTAKE INHIBITORS—ANTIDEPRESSANTS

The main indication for selective serotonin reuptake inhibitors (SSRIs) is clinical depression, but they often also are prescribed for anxiety disorders including obsessive–compulsive disorder (OCD) and eating disorders. SSRIs have largely replaced other antidepressants (tricyclics) because of lower toxicity and fewer and milder, especially cardiovascular, side effects. SSRIs inhibit the reuptake of serotonin (5-HT) into the presynaptic cell, which results in an increase of serotonin in the synaptic cleft and activation of the postsynaptic receptors.

Serotonergic involvement in aggression and self-injury is supported by animal studies in which serotonin depletion promotes aggressive behavior, and drugs acting as agonists may be effective treatments (King, 2000). Moreover, drugs that increase brain levels of serotonin are effective in reducing OCD, consistent with the compulsivity hypothesis of self-injury (King, 1993). Despite the development of newer SSRIs, fluoxetine (Prozac) remains the most widely prescribed. Fluoxetine has been shown to be tolerated among children and may be effective in treating some symptoms of autism. DeLong, Ritch, and Burch (2002) conducted a comprehensive study of the efficacy of fluoxetine in autistic children and reported benefits among responders to be "improved emotional stability; increased happiness; more social interaction; improved tolerance of varieties of food; improved social response (getting a haircut, going to a restaurant, relating to grandparents), attention, and awareness or understanding" (p. 653). Even though the children remain autistic and cannot participate in mainstream education, parents in the responder group have elected to continue their children on the medication for more than 6 years. DeLong et al. (2002) described another subgroup as moderate responders and a smaller subgroup as poor responders who may actually have an unfavorable response including hyperactivity or agitation.

An early study (Markowitz, 1992) of 21 persons with severe to profound mental disabilities who engaged in aggression and self-injurious behavior reported that treatment with daily does of 20 to 40 mg of fluoxetine had beneficial effects and few side effects. Marked improvement was reported for 13 patients, moderate improvement for 4 patients, mild improvement for 2 patients, and no improvement in 2 patients over a 3-month period. The positive responses included decreased self-injury, agitation, emotional lability, and aggression. Subsequently, Bodfish and Madison (1993) reported decreases in self-injury and aggression in 7 of 10 adults with mental disabilities following fluoxetine administration.

Janowsky et al. (2005) reported the results of treatment response to a variety of serotonergic antidepressants (see Table 15.2) in 38 adults with intellectual disabilities who were institutionalized. Treatment effectiveness was determined by a retrospective review of records "in which global and specific maladaptive behaviours were rated on a 1- to 7-point scale, and by psychologists' ratings of target behaviours." Treatment with SSRIs was related to a decrease in "behavioural ratings, in global ratings of maladaptive behaviour and in aggressive, self-injurious, and destructive/disruptive behaviours and in depression/dysphoria" (p. 37). A significant percentage of the sample had at least a 25% reduction in global ratings of their maladaptive behavior.

There is evidence from double-blind, placebo-controlled trials that fluoxetine is an effective treatment for pathological skin picking (Hendrickx, Van Moffaert, Piers, & von Frenckell, 1991; Simeon et al., 1997). However, two case reports indicated that skin picking may actually be exacerbated by fluvoxamine and paroxetine (Denys et al., 2003). The reason for the increased behavior is unknown, but it could be a dermatological side effect, a displacement behavior or a serotonin-induced impulse. Moreover, there is evidence that some SSRIs (e.g., paroxetine) may be effective in reducing self-injury and aggression initially, but that after a month or so of treatment, behavior will reemerge and even rise above baseline levels (Davanzo, Belin, Widawski, & King, 1998). The development of tolerance to clomipramine also has been reported among persons with Lesch–Nyhan syndrome (Nyhan, Johnson, Kaufman, & Jones, 1980).

OTHER PSYCHOACTIVE AGENTS

Philipsen, Richter, et al. (2004) reasoned that self-injurious behavior may be the result of acute states of inner tension. They administered clonidine, a centrally acting alpha-2 agonist to reduce catecholamine production resulting in lowered heart rate and blood pressure in 14 women meeting DSM–IV criteria for BPD. They found that 75 and 150 mg of clonidine reduced dissociative symptoms, urges to commit self-injury, and suicidal ideation for up to 60 minutes after receiving medication. The emotional ratings were correlated with the reduction in blood pressure. Recent animal studies (Blake et al., 2007) indicated that a medication that rapidly lowered blood pressure, nifedipine (Procardia), was effective in the treatment of self-injury induced by four unrelated models, and the improvement was not a side effect of sedation.

Anticonvulsants have mood-stabilizing properties and often are effective in the treatment of bipolar disorder, especially in younger, adolescent patients. Topiramate is related to fructose and quickly absorbed after oral administration. Topiramate enhances gamma-aminobutyric acid–activated chloride channels and inhibits excitatory neurotransmission because of its actions on kainate and alpha-amino-3-hydroxy-5-methyl-4-isoxazole propionic acid receptors (accounting for its antiseizure effects). Its mood-stabilizing properties are achieved at lower doses than its anticonvulsant properties. The efficacy of topiramate (Topamax) was evaluated in a retrospective chart review of 22 institutionalized patients with disruptive, including self-injurious, behaviors (Janowsky, Kraus, Barnhill, Elamir, & Davis, 2003). Significant decreases in maladaptive behavior were observed that persisted for at least 6 months in these NDD patients, who were ages 25 to 70 years. In an open-label, 8-week trial, topiramate was associated with decreased self-injury in three patients with Prader–Willi syndrome (Shapira, Lessig, Murphy, Driscoll, & Goodman, 2002). Oxcarbazepine (Trileptal) is another anticonvulsant with mood-stabilizing properties that has been administered to individuals exhibiting NSSI. It is a derivative of carbamazepine (Tegretol) with fewer side effects but essentially the same mechanism of action—sodium channel inhibition that reduces brain cell excitability. Cordás, Tavares, Calderoni, Stump, and Ribeiro (2006) reported that NSSI was controlled with oxcarbazepine in two women diagnosed with bulimia nervosa.

CONCLUSION

The simplest conclusion is that there is no agreed-on pharmacological treatment for NSSI. A recent, comprehensive review of the BPD treatment literature concluded, "We have far to go before a clearly effective pharmacological treatment of [NSSI] is available" (Nose, Cipriani, Biancosino, Grassi, & Barbui, 2006, p. 352). In a thorough review of the pharmacological studies with BPD patients, Binks et al. (2006) concluded, "There were as many definitions of improvement as there were studies." They also opined that "if offered medication, people with BPD should know that this is not based on good evidence from trials" (p. 19). A rational pharmacological approach to treatment requires that one understands the biochemistry of self-injury (Klonsky, 2007). Some arguments suggest that this may not be possible and that "intervention efforts should be tailored to reducing individual issues that contribute to NSSI and building alternative skills for positive coping, communication, stress management, and strong social support" (Lloyd-Richardson, Perrine, Dierker, & Kelley, 2007, p. 37).

An even gloomier picture may exist. Most of the studies reviewed indicated that some improvement, often modest, in self-injury was achieved with the various medications. However, it is unknown how many negative trials exist that have not been reported. So, against the background of minimal efficacy is the unknown number of never-reported negative effects.

A more sober conclusion is that the evidence indicates there are examples of successful attempts to develop a rational psychopharmacology of self-injury. The proposals that pain and pleasure are confused in individuals with self-injury, and that this balance may be moderated by opiate blockers, have produced positive results among patients with NDD and, to a modest degree, among patients with BPD. The suggestion that DA–serotonin imbalance may result in anxiety or psychological tension and that this can be restored with atypical antipsychotic or antidepressant medications has produced positive results among both patients with and those without NDD.

In fact, it could be considered remarkable that any positive effects are seen in the patients tested in the pharmacological studies reviewed here. For the most part, the patients selected for these protocols have been treatment failures: They often are considered treatment resistant in that they continue to self-abuse or have disturbing urges to self-injure despite all forms of psychological, behavioral, and pharmacological treatments. Most of the patients in these studies are on the extreme end of the spectrum in terms of clinical severity.

One issue that was not considered here is the complex topic of drug interactions. Many of the patients in these trials also were on maintenance medications. In prospective studies of difficult patients who are a danger to themselves, it is often the protocol to add a medication without disturbing the maintenance regimen (even though it is frequently ineffective). The interaction among medications is far from an exact science, and the effects of adding or combining medications can result in iatrogenic NSSI. Thus, the fact that many of the patients in the studies presented here may have been on medications that interacted with the medications of interest complicates the ability to interpret the results. For instance, opiate blockers can enhance SSRI-induced analgesia (Singh, Patil, Jain, Singh, & Kulkarni, 2003), so this combination may increase NSSI if the motivation is to generate opiate-mediated euphoria, even though in isolation each medication may reduce self-injury.

Finally, it is important to reemphasize that a major obstacle to the development of rational and coherent treatment plans is the difficulty in understanding the motivations of self-injury. Not only may the motivations to commit acts of self-harm vary within a diagnostic group, it is not established that the motivations for NSSI are similar or different between diagnostic groups. Studies of mechanisms of complex behavioral disorders are challenging, perhaps impossible, in patient groups, and although animal models are useful, they cannot duplicate the intricacies of the human condition. One approach is to develop distinctive behavioral phenotypes that are associated with unique biological patterns. We (Kroeker, Touchette, Engleman, & Sandman, 2004; Marion, Touchette, & Sandman, 2003) have described self-perpetuating patterns of contagious self-injury, sequentially dependent patterns of self-injury in a subgroup of NDD patients that were not related to environmental or social contingencies. Subsequently, elevated levels of POMC fragments were reported in individuals with sequentially (Sandman, Touchette, Marion, & Chicz-DeMet, in press) and temporally (Kemp et al., 2008) dependent patterns (unrelated to frequency of occurrence) of self-injury, but not in other patients who self-injured. Developing treatments based on behavioral phenotypes, especially if there is an association between behavior and a biological marker, is one strategy for developing a rational pharmacology of NSSI.

Research Recommendations

Application of a rational psychopharmacological strategy cannot develop in the absence of understanding the motivation for NSSI. It is probable that individuals exhibit self-injury for several reasons. Research that identifies specific phenotypes, or endophenotypes, may provide one avenue for explaining individual differences in the motivation for these maladaptive behaviors. In this chapter, I presented several examples of biological and behavioral phenotypes that predicted response to treatment, but these studies are difficult to implement and therefore infrequent. Nevertheless, they are critically important if the causes (and cures) of self-injury are to be established.

Another obvious area of research is the assessment of new psychotropic medications for treating NSSI. There is a never-ending stream of new medications available for behavioral applications. Although rational psychopharmacology is the goal, pragmatic pharmacological treatment is the practice. This is a necessary approach and one that could lead to understanding the motivation for self-injury. For instance, if a miracle drug is discovered for eliminating self-injury, and its mechanism of action is known, an important step will be taken toward understanding the motivation for this behavior.

Perhaps the least known factor relating to the pharmacological treatment of self-injury (and almost every other behavioral or psychiatric condition) is the influence of drug interactions. It is unlikely that complex human (maladaptive) behavior will be controlled or determined by one ligand or one receptor. Medications interact, but little is known about whether the interactions produce positive or negative influences—it is likely both are produced depending on the medications and the target symptoms. This area of research is virtually unstudied and may be the most important area in which an advance can be made. A rational approach to the study of drug interactions (i.e., systematically controlling which drugs, and at what dosages, are administered) requires a controlled environment and a degree of risk. These important studies will have to balance the possible risk of exacerbating self-injury with the low probability of an eventual benefit.

Clinical Recommendations

The most cavalier clinical recommendation is to pay attention to the research literature. The most useful advice from the literature is to understand that one pharmacological treatment does not fit all patients. The choice of treatment should include careful observations of the target patient to detect the possible motivation for self-injury. In the clinical situation, functional analyses of behavior are often cited but rarely performed. However, even less rigorous observations than functional analyses can be illuminating with respect to motives, and therefore in the choice of treatment for self-injury in individual cases.

Combining pharmacological with behavioral interventions should be considered in many cases. There are at least two reasons for this. First, there may be more than one cause of the behavior, so more than one treatment should be entertained. This strategy almost necessitates that these difficult patients be seen by a team of experts. Second, this strategy might work because medications may reduce ancillary behaviors such as agitation or anxiety and make the individuals more receptive to behavioral and cognitive therapies.

REFERENCES

American Psychiatric Association. (1994). *Diagnostic and statistical manual of mental disorders* (4th ed.). Washington, DC: Author.

Arnsten, A. F., Segal, D. S., Neville, H. J., Hillyard, S. A., Janowsky, D. S., Judd, L. L., & Bloom, F. E. (1983, August 25). Naloxone augments electrophysiological signs of selective attention in man. *Nature, 304,* 725–727.

Barna, I., Koenig, J. I., & Davis, T. P. (1992). Effects of mediobasal hypothalamic lesion on immunoreactive ACTH/beta-endorphin levels in cerebrospinal fluid, in discrete brain regions, in plasma and in pituitary of the rat. *Brain Research, 593,* 69–76.

Barrett, R. P., Feinstein, C., & Hole, W. T. (1989). Effects of naloxone and naltrexone on self-injury: A double-blind, placebo-controlled analysis. *American Journal on Mental Retardation, 93,* 644–651.

Barron, J. L., & Sandman, C. A. (1983). Relationship of sedative–hypnotic response to self-injurious behavior and stereotypy in mentally retarded clients. *American Journal on Mental Retardation, 88,* 177–186.

Belluzzi, J. D., & Stein, L. (1977, April 7). Enkephalin may mediate euphoria and drive-reduction reward. *Nature, 266,* 556–558.

Berkson, G., Tupa, G., & Sherman, L. (2001). Early development of stereotyped and self-injurious behaviors: I. Incidence. *American Journal on Mental Retardation, 106,* 539–547.

Bertagna, X. (1994). Proopiomelanocortin-derived peptides. *Endocrinology and Metabolism Clinics of North America, 23,* 467–485.

Bicknell, A. B., Savva, D., & Lowry, P. J. (1996). Pro-opiomelanocortin and adrenal function. *Endocrine Research, 22,* 385–393.

Binks, C. A., Fenton, M., McCarthy, L., Lee, T., Adams, C. E., & Duggan, C. (2006). Pharmacological interventions for people with borderline personality disorder. *Cochrane Database of Systematic Reviews, 1,* CD005653. doi: 10.1002/14651858. CD005653

Blake, B. L., Muehlmann, A. M., Egami, K., Breese, G. R., Devine, D. P., & Jinnah, H. A. (2007). Nifedipine suppresses self-injurious behaviors in animals. *Developmental Neuroscience, 29,* 241–250.

Bodfish, J. W., & Madison, J. T. (1993). Diagnosis and fluoxetine treatment of compulsive behavior disorder of adults with mental retardation. *American Journal on Mental Retardation, 98,* 360–367.

Bohus, M. J., Landwehrmeyer, G. B., Stiglmayr, C. E., Limberger, M. F., Bohme, R., & Schmahl, C. G. (1999). Naltrexone in the treatment of dissociative symptoms in patients with borderline personality disorder: An open-label trial. *Journal of Clinical Psychiatry, 60,* 598–603.

Bohus, M. J., Limberger, M., Ebner, U., Glocker, F. X., Schwarz, B., Wernz, W., & Lieb, K. (2000). Pain perception during self-reported distress and calmness in patients with borderline personality disorder and self-mutilating behavior. *Psychiatry Research, 95,* 251–260.

Boutillier, A. L., Monnier, D., Koch, B., & Loeffler, J. P. (1994). Pituitary adenyl cyclase-activating peptide: A hypophysiotropic factor that stimulates proopiomelanocortin gene transcription, and proopiomelanocortin-derived peptide secretion in corticotropic cells. *Neuroendocrinology, 60,* 493–502.

Bouvard, M. P., Leboyer, M., Launay, J. M., Recasens, C., Plumet, M. H., Waller-Perotte, et al. (1995). Low-dose naltrexone effects on plasma chemistries and clinical symptoms in autism: A double-blind, placebo-controlled study. *Psychiatry Research, 58,* 191–201.

Breese, G. R., Knapp, D. J., Criswell, H. E., Moy, S. S., Papadeas, S. T., & Blake, B. L. (2005). The neonate-6-hydroxydopamine-lesioned rat: A model for clinical neuroscience and neurobiological principles. *Brain Research Reviews, 48,* 57–73.

Breese, G. R., & Traylor, T. D. (1972). Developmental characteristics of brain catecholamines and tyrosine hydroxylase in the rat: Effects of 6-hydroxydopamine. *British Journal of Pharmacology, 44,* 210–222.

Campbell, M., Anderson, L. T., Small, A. M., Adams, P., Gonzalez, N. M., & Ernst, M. (1993). Naltrexone in autistic children: Behavioral symptoms and attentional learning. *Journal of the American Academy of Child & Adolescent Psychiatry, 32,* 1283–1291.

Canitano, R. (2006). Self injurious behavior in autism: Clinical aspects and treatment with risperidone. *Journal of Neural Transmission, 113,* 425–431.

Casner, J. A., Weinheimer, B., & Gualtieri, C. T. (1996). Naltrexone and self-injurious behavior: A retrospective population study. *Journal of Clinical Psychopharmacology, 16,* 389–394.

Cataldo, M., & Harris, J. (1982). The biological basis for self-injury in the mentally retarded. *Analysis and Intervention in Developmental Disabilities, 2,* 21–39.

Cazzullo, A. G., Musetti, M. C., Musetti, L., Bajo, S., Sacerdote, P., & Panerai, A. (1999). Beta-endorphin levels in peripheral blood mononuclear cells and long-term naltrexone treatment in autistic children. *European Neuropsychopharmacology, 9,* 361–363.

Chengappa, K. N., Ebeling, T., Kang, J. S., Levine, J., & Parepally, H. (1999). Clozapine reduces severe self-mutilation and aggression in psychotic patients with borderline personality disorder. *Journal of Clinical Psychiatry, 60,* 477–484.

Claes, L., & Vandereycken, W. (2007). Self-injurious behavior: Differential diagnosis and functional differentiation. *Comprehensive Psychiatry, 48,* 137–144.

Cordás, T. A., Tavares, H., Calderoni, D. M., Stump, G. V., & Ribeiro, R. B. (2006). Oxcarbazepine for self-mutilating bulimic patients. *International Journal of Neuropsychopharmacology, 9,* 769—771.

Crews, W. D., Jr., Bonaventura, S., Rowe, F. B., & Bonsie, D. (1993). Cessation of long-term naltrexone therapy and self-injury: A case study. *Research in Developmental Disabilities, 14,* 331–340.

Davanzo, P. A., Belin, T. R., Widawski, M. H., & King, B. H. (1998). Paroxetine treatment of aggression and self-injury in persons with mental retardation. *American Journal of Mental Retardation, 102,* 427–437.

Dehen, H., Willer, J. C., Boureau, F., & Cambier, J. (1977, August 6). Congenital insensitivity to pain, and endogenous morphine-like substances. *The Lancet, 2,* 293–294.

DeLong, G. R., Ritch, C. R., & Burch, S. (2002). Fluoxetine response in children with autistic spectrum disorders: Correlation with familial major affective disorder and intellectual achievement. *Developmental Medicine & Child Neurology, 44,* 652–659.

Denys, D., van Megen, H. J., & Westenberg, H. G. (2003). Emerging skin-picking behaviour after serotonin reuptake inhibitor-treatment in patients with obsessive–compulsive disorder: Possible mechanisms and implications for clinical care. *Journal of Psychopharmacology, 17,* 127–129.

Deutsch, S. I. (1986). Rationale for the administration of opiate antagonists in treating infantile autism. *American Journal on Mental Retardation, 90,* 631–635.

Dunger, D. B., Leonard, J. V., Wolff, O. H., & Preece, M. A. (1980, June 14). Effect of naloxone in a previously undescribed hypothalamic syndrome. A disorder of the endogenous opioid peptide system? *The Lancet, 1,* 1277–1281.

Ernst, M., Devi, L., Silva, R. R., Gonzalez, M. N., Small, A. M., Malone, R. P., & Campbell, M. (1993). Plasma beta-endorphin levels, naltrexone, and haloperidol in autistic children. *Psychopharmacology Bulletin*, *29*, 221–227.

Gillberg, C. (1995). Endogenous opioids and opiate antagonists in autism: Brief review of empirical findings and implications for clinicians. *Developmental Medicine & Child Neurology*, *37*, 88–92.

Griffin, J., Ricketts, R., Williams, D., Locke, B., Altmeyer, B., & Stark, M. (1987). A community survey of self-injurious behavior among developmentally disabled children and adolescents. *Hospital and Community Psychiatry*, *38*, 959–963.

Guess, D., & Carr, E. (1991). Emergence and maintenance of stereotopy and self-injury. *American Journal on Mental Retardation*, *96*, 299–319.

Halladay, A. K., Kusnecov, A., Hichna, L., Kita, T., Hara, C., & Wagner, C. C. (2003). Relationship between methamphetamine-induced dopamine release, hyperthermia, self-injurious behavior and long-term dopamine depletion in BALB/c and C57BL/6 mice. *Pharmacology and Toxicology*, *93*, 33–41.

Hammock, R., Levine, W. R., & Schroeder, S. R. (2001). Brief report: Effects of clozapine on self-injurious behavior of two risperidone nonresponders with mental retardation. *Journal of Autism and Developmental Disorders*, *31*, 109–113.

Hanley, G. P., Iwata, B. A., & McCord, B. E. (2003). Functional analysis of problem behavior: A review. *Journal of Applied Behavior Analysis*, *36*, 147–185.

Hargreaves, K. M., Flores, C. M., Dionne, F. A., & Mueller, G. P. (1990). The role of the pituitary beta-endorphin in mediating corticotropin-releasing factor-induced antinociception. *American Journal of Physiology*, *258*, 235–242.

Hellings, J. A., Zarcone, J. R., Reese, R. M., Valdovinos, M. G., Marquis, J. G., Fleming, K. K., & Schroeder, S. R. (2006). A crossover study of risperidone in children, adolescents and adults with mental retardation. *Journal of Autism and Developmental Disorders*, *36*, 401–411.

Hendrickx, B., Van Moffaert, M., Piers, R., & von Frenckell, R. (1991). The treatment of psychocutaneous disorders: A new approach. *Current Therapeutic Research, Clinical and Experimental*, *49*, 111–119.

Iwata, B. A., Roscoe, E. M., Zarcone, J. R., & Richman, D. M. (2002). Environmental determinants of self-injurious behavior. In S. R. Schroeder, M. L. Oster-Granite, & T. Thompson (Eds.), *Self-injurious behavior: Gene–brain–behavior relationships* (pp. 93–103). Washington, DC: American Psychological Association.

Janowsky, D. S., Kraus, J. E., Barnhill, J., Elamir, B., & Davis, J. M. (2003). Effects of topiramate on aggressive, self-injurious, and disruptive/destructive behaviors in the intellectually disabled: An open-label retrospective study. *Journal of Clinical Psychopharmacology*, *23*, 500–504.

Janowsky, D. S., Shetty, M., Barnhill, J., Elamir, B., & Davis, J. M. (2005). Serotonergic antidepressant effects on aggressive, self-injurious and destructive/disruptive behaviours in intellectually disabled adults: A retrospective, open-label, naturalistic trial. *International Journal of Neuropsychopharmacology*, *8*, 37–48.

Jensen, P. S., Buitelaar, J., Pandina, G. J., Binder, C., & Haas, M. (2007). Management of psychiatric disorders in children and adolescents with atypical antipsychotics. *European Child and Adolescent Psychiatry, 16*, 104–120.

Karila, L., Ferreri, M., Coscas, S., Cottencin, O., Benyamina, A., & Reynaud, M. (2007). Self-multilation induced by cocaine abuse: The pleasure of bleeding. *La Presse Medicale, 36*, 235–237.

Kasim, S., & Jinnah, H. A. (2002). Thresholds for self-injurious behavior in a genetic mouse model of Lesch–Nyhan disease. *Pharmacology Biochemistry and Behavior, 73*, 583–592.

Kemp, A. S., Fillmore, P. T., Lenjavi, M., Lyon, M., Chicz-DeMet, A., Touchette, P. E., & Sandman, C. A. (2008). Temporal patterns of self-injurious behavior correlate with stress hormone levels in the developmentally disabled. *Psychiatry Research, 157*, 181–189.

King, B. H. (1993). Self-injury by people with mental retardation: A compulsive behavior hypothesis. *American Journal on Mental Retardation, 98*, 93–112.

King, B. H. (2000). Pharmacological treatment of mood disturbances, aggression, and self-injury in persons with pervasive developmental disorders. *Journal of Autism and Developmental Disorders, 30*, 439–445.

King, B. H., Cromwell, H. C., Ly, H. T., Behrstock, S. P., Schmanke, T., & Maidment, N. T. (1998). Dopaminergic and glutamatergic interactions in the expression of self-injurious behavior. *Developmental Neuroscience, 20*, 180–187.

Kita, T., Matsunari, Y., Saraya, T., Shimada, K., O'Hara, K., Kubo, K., et al. (2000). Methamphetamine-induced striatal dopamine release, behavior changes and neurotoxicity in BALB/c mice. *International Journal of Developmental Neuroscience, 18*, 521–530.

Klonsky, E. D. (2007). The functions of deliberate self-injury: A review of the evidence. *Clinical Psychology Review, 27*, 226–239.

Kroeker, R., Touchette, P. E., Engleman, L., & Sandman, C. A. (2004). Quantifying temporal distributions of self-injurious behavior: Defining bouts vs. discrete events. *American Journal on Mental Retardation, 109*, 1–8.

Lamprecht, H. C., Pakrasi, S., Gash, A., & Swann, A. G. (2005). Deliberate self-harm in older people revisited. *International Journal of Geriatric Psychiatry, 20*, 1090–1096.

Leboyer, M., Bouvard, M. P., Recasens, C., Philippe, A., Guilloud-Bataille, M., Bondoux, D., et al. (1994). Difference between plasma N- and C-terminally directed beta-endorphin immunoreactivity in infantile autism. *The American Journal of Psychiatry, 151*, 1797–1801.

Leboyer, M., Philippe, A., Bouvard, M., Guilloud-Bataille, M., Bondoux, D., Tabuteau, F., et al. (1999). Whole blood serotonin and plasma beta-endorphin in autistic probands and their first degree relatives. *Society of Biological Psychiatry, 45*, 158–163.

Lloyd, K. G., Hornykiewicz, O., Davidson, L., Shannak, K., Farley, I., Goldstein, M., et al. (1981). Biochemical evidence of dysfunction of brain neurotransmitters in the Lesch–Nyhan syndrome. *The New England Journal of Medicine, 305*, 1106–1111.

Lloyd-Richardson, E. E., Perrine, N., Dierker, L., & Kelley, M. L. (2007). Characteristics and functions of non-suicidal self-injury in a community sample of adolescents. *Psychological Medicine, 37*, 1183–1192.

Lott, I. T., McGregor, M., Engelman, L., Touchette, P., Tournay, A., Sandman, C., et al. (2004). Longitudinal prescribing patterns for psychoactive medications in community-based individuals with developmental disabilities: Utilization of pharmacy records. *Journal of Intellectual Disability Research, 48*, 563–571.

Ludäscher, P., Bohus, M., Lieb, K., Philipsen, A., Jochims, A., & Schmahl, C. (2007). Elevated pain thresholds correlate with dissociation and aversive arousal in patients with borderline personality disorder. *Psychiatry Research, 149*, 291–296.

Madden, J., IV, Akil, H., Patrick, R. L., & Barchas, J. D. (1977, January 27). Stress-induced parallel changes in central opioid levels and pain responsiveness in the rat. *Nature, 265*, 358–360.

Mains, R. E., & Eipper, B. A. (1999). Peptides. In G. J. Siegal, B. W. Agranoff, R. W. Albers, S. K. Fisher, & M. D. Uhler (Eds.), *Basic neurochemistry: Molecular, cellular and medical aspects* (6th ed., pp. 363–382). Philadelphia: Lippincott Williams & Wilkins.

Marion, S., Touchette, P., & Sandman, C. A. (2003). Lag sequential analysis reveals a unique structure for self-injurious behavior. *American Journal on Mental Retardation, 108*, 301–313.

Markowitz, P. I. (1992). Effect of fluoxetine on self-injurious behavior in the developmentally disabled: A preliminary study. *Journal of Clinical Psychopharmacology, 12*, 27–31.

Murphy, G., Hall, S., Oliver, C., & Kissi-Debra, R. (1999). Identification of early self-injurious behaviour in young children with intellectual disability. *Journal of Intellectual Disability Research, 43*, 149–163.

Nickel, M. K., Muehlbacher, M., Nickel, C., Kettler, C., Gil, F. P., Bachler, E., et al. (2006). Aripiprazole in the treatment of patients with borderline personality disorder: A double-blind, placebo-controlled study. *The American Journal of Psychiatry, 163*, 833–838.

Nixon, M. K., Cloutier, P. F., & Aggarwal, S. (2002). Affect regulation and addictive aspects of repetitive self-injury in hospitalized adolescents. *Journal of the American Academy of Child & Adolescent Psychiatry, 41*, 1333–1341.

Nock, M. K., Joiner, T. E., Jr., Gordon, K. H., Lloyd-Richardson, E., & Prinstein, M. J. (2006). Non-suicidal self-injury among adolescents: Diagnostic correlates and relation to suicide attempts. *Psychiatry Research, 144*, 65–72.

Nose, M., Cipriani, A., Biancosino, B., Grassi, L., & Barbui, C. (2006). Efficacy of pharmacotherapy against core traits of borderline personality disorder: Meta-analysis of randomized controlled trials. *International Clinical Psychopharmacology, 21*, 345–353.

Nyhan, W. L., Johnson, H. G., Kaufman, I. A., & Jones, K. L. (1980). Serotonergic approaches to the modification of behavior in the Lesch–Nyhan Syndrome. *Applied Research in Mental Retardation, 1*, 25–40.

Olfson, M., Gameroff, M. J., Marcus, S. C., Greenberg, T., & Shaffer, D. (2005). Emergency treatment of young people following deliberate self-harm. *Archives of General Psychiatry, 62,* 1122–1128.

Pandina, G. J., Aman, M. G., & Findling, R. L. (2006). Risperidone in the management of disruptive behavior disorders. *Journal of Child and Adolescent Psychopharmacology, 16,* 379–392.

Pandina, G. J., Bilder, R., Harvey, P. D., Keefe, R. S., Aman, M. G., & Gharabawi, G. (2007). Risperidone and cognitive function in children with disruptive behavior disorders. *Biological Psychiatry, 62,* 226–234.

Pandina, G. J., Bossie, C. A., Youssef, E., Zhu, Y., & Dunbar, F. (2007). Risperidone improves behavioral symptoms in children with autism in a randomized, double-blind, placebo-controlled trial. *Journal of Autism and Developmental Disorders, 37,* 367–373.

Philipsen, A., Richter, H., Schmahl, C., Peters, J., Rusch, N., Bohus, M., & Lieb, K. (2004). Clonidine in acute aversive inner tension and self-injurious behavior in female patients with borderline personality disorder. *Journal of Clinical Psychiatry, 65,* 1414–1419.

Philipsen, A., Schmahl, C., & Lieb, K. (2004). Naloxone in the treatment of acute dissociative states in female patients with borderline personality disorder. *Pharmacopsychiatry, 37,* 196–199.

Richman, D. M., & Lindauer, S. E. (2005). Longitudinal assessment of stereotypoic, proto-injurious, and self-injurious behavior exhibited by young children with developmental delays. *American Journal on Mental Retardation, 110,* 439–450.

Rosenblatt, M. I., & Dickerson, I. M. (1997). Endoproteolysis at tetrabasic amino acid sites in procalcitonin gene-related peptide by pituitary cell lines. *Peptides, 18,* 567–576.

Sandman, C. A. (1988). Beta-endorphin disregulation in autistic and self-injurious behavior: A neurodevelopmental hypothesis. *Synapse, 2,* 193–199.

Sandman, C. A. (1990/1991). The opiate hypothesis in autism and self-injury. *Journal of Child and Adolescent Psychopharmacology, 1,* 235–246.

Sandman, C. A., Barron, J. L., Chicz-DeMet, A., & DeMet, E. (1990). Plasma B-endorphin levels in patients with self-injurious behavior and stereotypy. *American Journal of Mental Retardation, 95,* 3–10.

Sandman, C. A., Barron, J. L., & Colman, H. (1990). An orally administered opiate blocker, naltrexone attenuates self-injurious behavior. *American Journal of Mental Retardation, 95,* 93–102.

Sandman, C. A., Barron, J. L., DeMet, E., Chicz-DeMet, A., & Rothenburg, S. (1990). Opioid peptides and development: Clinical implications. *Annals of the New York Academy of Sciences, 579,* 91–108.

Sandman, C. A., Datta, P., Barron, J. L., Hoehler, F., Williams, C., & Swanson, J. (1983). Naloxone attenuates self-abusive behavior in developmentally disabled clients. *Applied Research in Mental Retardation, 4,* 5–11.

Sandman, C. A., & Hetrick, W. P. (1995). Opiate mechanisms in self-injury. *Mental Retardation and Developmental Disabilities Research Reviews, 1*, 1–7.

Sandman, C. A., Hetrick, W. P., Taylor, D. V., Barron, J. L., Touchette, P., Lott, I., et al. (1993). Naltrexone reduces self-injury and improves learning. *Experimental and Clinical Psychopharmacology, 1*, 224–258.

Sandman, C. A., Hetrick, W. P., Taylor, D. V., & Chicz-DeMet, A. (1997). Dissociation of POMC peptides after self-injury predicts responses to centrally acting opiate blockers. *American Journal on Mental Retardation, 102*, 182–199.

Sandman, C. A., Hetrick, W., Taylor, D., Marion, S., & Chicz-DeMet, A. (2000). Uncoupling of proopiomelanocortin (POMC) fragments is related to self-injury. *Peptides, 21*, 785–791.

Sandman, C. A., Hetrick, W. P., Taylor, D. V., Marion, S., Touchette, P., Barron, J. L., et al. (2000). Long-term effects of naltrexone on self-injurious behavior. *American Journal of Mental Retardation, 105*, 103–117.

Sandman, C. A., McGivern, R. F., Berka, C., Walker, J. M., Coy, D. H., & Kastin, A. J. (1979). Neonatal administration of beta-endorphin produces "chronic" insensitivity to thermal stimuli. *Life Sciences, 25*, 1755–1760.

Sandman, C. A., Spence, M. A., & Smith, M. (1999). Proopiomelanocortin (POMC) disregulation and response to opiate blockers. *Mental Retardation and Developmental Disabilities Research Reviews, 5*, 314–321.

Sandman, C. A., & Touchette, P. E. (2002). Opioids and the maintenance of self-injurious behavior. In S. R. Schroeder, M. L. Oster-Granite, & T. Thompson (Ed.), *Self-injurious behavior: Gene–brain–behavior relationships* (pp. 191–204). Washington, DC: American Psychological Association.

Sandman, C. A., Touchette, P. E., Lenjavi, M., Marion, S., & Chicz-DeMet, A. (2003). B-endorphin and ACTH are dissociated after self-injury in adults with developmental disabilities. *American Journal on Mental Retardation, 108*, 414–424.

Sandman, C. A., Touchette, P. E., Marion, S. D., & Chicz-DeMet, A. (in press). The role proopiomelanocortin (POMC) in sequentially dependent self-injurious behavior. *Developmental Psychobiology*.

Sansone, R. A., Gaither, G. A., & Songer, D. A. (2002). Self-harm behaviors across the life cycle: A pilot study of inpatients with borderline personality disorder. *Comprehensive Psychiatry, 43*, 215–218.

Sasaki, A., Sato, S., Murakami, O., Go, M., Inoue, M., Shimizu, Y., et al. (1987). Immunoreactive corticotropin-releasing hormone in human plasma during pregnancy, labor, and delivery. *The Journal of Clinical Endocrinology & Metabolism, 64*, 224–229.

Scifo, R., Cioni, M., Nicolosi, A., Batticane, N., Tirolo, C., Testa, N., et al. (1996). Opioid–immune interactions in autism: Behavioral and immunological assessment during a double-blind treatment with naltrexone. *Annali dell'Istituto Superiore di Sanità, 32*, 351–359.

Seidah, N. G., & Chretien, M. (1992). Proprotein and prohormone convertases of the subtilisin family. *Trends in Endocrinology and Metabolism, 3*, 133–140.

Seidah, N. G., Marcinkiewicz, M., Benjannet, S., Gaspar, L., Beaubien, G., Mattei, M. G., et al. (1991). Cloning and primary sequence of a mouse candidate pro-hormone convertase PC1 homologous to PC2, Furin, and KEX 2: Distinct chromosomal localization and messenger RNA distribution in brain and pituitary compared to PC2. *Molecular Endocrinology, 5,* 111–122.

Shapira, N. A., Lessig, M. C., Murphy, T. K., Driscoll, D. J., & Goodman, W. K. (2002). Topiramate attenuates self-injurious behaviour in Prader–Willi syndrome. *International Journal of Neuropsychopharmacology, 5,* 141–145.

Simeon, D., Stein, D. J., Gross, S., Islam, N., Schmeidler, J., & Hollander, E. (1997). A double-blind trial of fluoxetine in pathologic skin picking. *Journal of Clinical Psychiatry, 58,* 341–347.

Singh, V. P., Patil, C. S., Jain, N. K., Singh, A., & Kulkarni, S. K. (2003). Paradoxical effects of opioid antagonist naloxone on SSRI-induced analgesia and tolerance in mice. *Pharmacology, 69,* 115–122.

Strand, F. L. (1999). *Neuropeptides: Regulators of physiological processes.* Cambridge, MA: MIT Press.

Symons, F. J., Tapp, J., Wulfsberg, A., Sutton, K. A., Heeth, W. L., & Bodfish, J. W. (2001). Sequential analysis of the effects of naltrexone on the environmental mediation of self-injurious behavior. *Experimental and Clinical Psychopharmacology, 9,* 269–276.

Symons, F. J., Thompson, A., & Rodriguez, M. C. (2004). Self-injurious behavior and the efficacy of naltrexone treatment: A quantitative synthesis. *Mental Retardation and Developmental Disabilities Research Reviews, 10,* 193–200.

Theodoulou, M., Harriss, L., Hawton, K., & Bass, C. (2005). Pain and deliberate self-harm: An important association. *Journal of Psychosomatic Research, 58,* 317–320.

Thompson, T., Hackenberg, T., Cerutti, D., Baker, D., & Axtell, S. (1994). Opioid antagonist effects on self-injury in adults with mental retardation: Response form and location as determinants of mediation effects. *American Journal on Mental Retardation, 99,* 85–102.

Thurauf, N. J., & Washeim, H. A. (2000). The effects of exogenous analgesia in a patient with borderline personality disorder (BPD) and severe self-injurious behaviour. *European Journal of Pain, 4,* 107–109.

Verhoeven, W. M., & Tuinier, S. (1996). The effect of buspirone on challenging behaviour in mentally retarded patients: An open prospective multiple-case study. *Journal of Intellectual Disability Research, 40,* 502–508.

Verhoeven, W. M., Tuinier, S., van den Berg, Y. W., Coppus, A. M., Fekkes, D., Pepplinkhuizen, L., & Thijssen, J. H. (1999). Stress and self-injurious behavior: Hormonal and serotonergic parameters in mentally retarded subjects. *Pharmacopsychiatry, 32,* 13–20.

Wei, E., & Loh, H. (1976, September 24). Physical dependence of opiate-like peptides. *Science, 193,* 1262–1263.

Zarcone, J. R., Hellings, J. A., Crandall, K., Reese, R. M., Marquis, J., Fleming, K., et al. (2001). Effects of risperidone on aberrant behavior of persons with developmental disabilities: I. A double-blind crossover study using multiple measures. *American Journal on Mental Retardation, 106,* 525–538.

Zheng, M., Streck, R. D., Scott, R. E., Seidah, N. G., & Pintar, J. E. (1994). The development expression in rat proteases furin, PC1, PC2, and carboxypeptidase E: Implications for early maturation of proteolytic processing capacity. *The Journal of Neuroscience, 14,* 4656–4673.

Zingarelli, G., Ellman, G., Hom, A., Wymore, M., Heidorn, S., & Chicz-DeMet, A. (1992). Clinical effects of naltrexone on autistic behavior. *American Journal on Mental Retardation, 97,* 57–63.

AFTERWORD

MATTHEW K. NOCK

Nonsuicidal self-injury (NSSI) is a behavior problem that has appeared in the historical record for thousands of years. Unfortunately, it has escaped serious scientific attention until only recently. Fortunately, however, the scientific and clinical attention devoted to NSSI in recent years has generated significant advances in the understanding of NSSI and in the ability to assess and treat this problem effectively.

This book was written with the purpose of summarizing what is known about NSSI. The contributors laid out definitions and a classification system for self-injurious behaviors, documented the prevalence of NSSI, reviewed current theories on why people engage in NSSI, outlined empirical evidence supporting each theory, and described the most promising assessment and treatment approaches currently available. This book is more comprehensive and scientifically based than any other volume available on this topic, and I believe it will serve as a useful point of departure for scientific work on NSSI for years to come.

I will not reiterate here the main findings reported by the contributors, because they do a much better job of describing this work than I could possibly do. However, I do want to make several concluding remarks on what has been learned, and what is yet to be learned, about NSSI.

Although NSSI is a complex phenomenon, research has provided a good initial understanding of why it occurs and what factors influence its development and maintenance. As outlined and described in detail throughout the pages of this book, people engage in NSSI for different reasons (such as to regulate thoughts and feelings and to influence the behavior of other people). In addition, NSSI is clearly a multidetermined behavior that is influenced by a wide range of developmental, psychological, social, and biological factors—all of which come together to produce NSSI in ways that are not yet fully understood. The chapters of this book were organized around reviewing and synthesizing work on each class of factors; however, the reader will have noticed that no effort was made to integrate all of these factors into one overarching theoretical model. It is simply too early to do so, and there is not yet enough knowledge about each area to put together such a model with any serious degree of certainty. It is hopeful that over the next several years, research will continue to advance in each of these areas and will do so in ways that begin to draw connections across these different domains. Examples from other areas of research include work on gene-by-environment interactions and the uses of biological and behavioral tests to predict responses to different types of behavioral and pharmacological treatment approaches. The causes of NSSI undoubtedly span various domains, and so it is important that the scientists and clinicians studying this problem do so as well.

Mental health professionals still have a lot to learn about NSSI. Although this book is filled with new and exciting advances in the understanding and treatment of NSSI, it is clear that there is a long way to go before full comprehension and effective management of this problem is achieved. A few humbling facts serve as reminders of the early stage of understanding currently facing them.

1. Most scientific and clinical work continues to rely on self-reports to detect and assess NSSI.
2. To date, no psychological or pharmacological treatments have convincingly demonstrated an ability to reduce the likelihood of NSSI, and no treatments for NSSI appear on existing lists of evidence-based treatments.
3. Few prevention programs have been evaluated, and none have demonstrated an ability to effectively reduce the rates of NSSI.

In closing, I think that the best way to characterize the current level of progress is to say that mental health professionals have reached a point of basic understanding about the nature and functions of NSSI and about some of the reasons it occurs and the factors that influence it; they now have reliable and valid methods for assessing NSSI and some good ideas about how to treat it. Indeed, the purpose of this book was to consolidate and disseminate this fundamental information about NSSI. It is my and the contributors' hope that this book will provide a platform from which to launch the next generation of scientific and clinical work that will bring a better understanding of the origins, assessment, and treatment of NSSI.

INDEX

Dialectics, 231
Diana, Princess, 33, 140
Differential reinforcement (DR), 165
Discriminant stimuli, 227, 237
Dishion, T. J., 90–91
Disinhibition theory, 150–151
Disruptive behavioral disorder (DBD),
    306
Dissociation, 126
Dissociative identity disorder, 99
Distress, NSSI as signal of, 71
Distress tolerance training, 231, 259
Dopamine (DA), 305, 308, 311
Dopaminergic system, 104–105
DR (differential reinforcement), 165
DSHI (Deliberate Self-Harm Inventory),
    193
Duke University, 232
Durand, V. M., 166
Durham Veterans Administration
    Medical Center, 232
Durkheim, Émile, 143
DVD players, 141
Dynorphin, 101

Eating disorders, 99, 100
Ebeling, T., 295
Elamir, B., 296
Eliade, Mircea, 22
Emergent norm theory, 149–150
Emotional reactivity, 225
Emotional regulation training, 231, 259
Emotional sensitivity, 225
Emotions, negative, 224–226
Endogenous opioid system (EOS), 127
England. See United Kingdom
Environmental factors, 185
EOS (endogenous opioid system), 127
Epilepsy, 22
Episodic NSSI, 15
EPS (extrapyramidal symptoms), 305
Ernst, M., 304
Escape extinction, 166–167
Establishing operations, 226
Ethnicity, and prevalence of NSSI,
    54–55
Euphemisms, benign, 215

Europe, 55–56
Evans, E., 285
Exposure, behavioral, 241
Extinction, in dialectical behavior
    therapy, 237–238
Extinction bursts, 237–238
Extrapyramidal symptoms (EPS), 305

FA. See Functional analysis
Factiva, 145
FAI. See Functional Assessment
    Interview
Family therapy, 263–264
FASM. See Functional Assessment of
    Self-Mutilation
FAST (Firestone Assessment of Self-
    Destructive Thoughts), 193
Favazza, A. R., 15, 29, 32–33, 272
FBA. See Functional behavior
    assessment
FCT (functional communication
    training), 166
Feminism, 26
FFM. See Four-function model
Film, self-injury references in, 139–140,
    145, 147, 148
Finland, 55, 284
Firestone Assessment of Self-Destructive
    Thoughts (FAST), 193
Fluoxetine, 296, 308
Fluphenazine, 306
Food deprivation, 226
Foot binding, 26
Four-function model (FFM), 66–68
    physiological and behavioral studies
        supporting, 69–70
    self-report studies supporting, 68–69
France, 55
Freedman, J. L., 150
Function (term), 67, 68
Functional analysis (FA), 68, 160–164,
    168, 170
Functional analytic psychotherapy, 223
Functional Assessment Interview (FAI),
    159–160
Functional Assessment of Self-Mutilation
    (FASM), 191, 195, 202

Norepinephrine–sympathetic–adrenal–
medullary (NE-SAM) system,
126–127
Norway, 55
NSSI. *See* Nonsuicidal self-injury
NSSI thoughts (term), 13
NTVS. *See* National Television Violence
Study
NTX. *See* Naltrexone hydrochloride
Nurturance, prompting of, 228

Obsessive–compulsive disorder (OCD),
252, 308
6-OHDA (6-hydroxydopamine), 305
Ohman, A., 226
Older adults, prevalence of NSSI in,
49, 50
Old Testament, 24
Olino, T. M., 88
Omnibus measures, 187–191
Operant conditioning, 227
Opiate blockers, 300–304
acute treatment with, 300–302
endophenotype and response to, 304
long-term treatment with, 303–304
Opioids, 100–103
Organizational model of NSSI, 120–123
Osuch, E. A., 88, 285
Otto, Rudolph, 31
Outpatient therapy, individual,
259–260
"Overdetermined" behavior, NSSI as,
80
Oxcarbazepine, 295, 310

Pain, chronic, 30
Pain perception, 101–102, 227–228,
298. *See also* Analgesia
Parasuicide, 13, 14, 55, 273
Parent reports, 253
Parepally, H., 295
Parkinson's disease, 22
Paroxetine, 103, 104, 309
Pattison, Mansell, 28
Peer-group support, 214–215
Peer influence, 72, 88–91
Penile mutilation, 23, 26

Philipsen, A., 294, 295, 309
Phillips, D., 143
Phobias, 252
Physiological studies, 69
Picture Exchange Communication
System, 166
Pidjandjana, 26
Plains Indians, 24
Platt, S., 55
Podvoll, E., 30
POMC. *See* Proopiomelanocortin
Popular culture, 33–34
Positive reinforcement, 67
Posttraumatic stress disorder (PTSD),
68, 69, 99
Prader–Willi syndrome, 104, 310
Prevalence of NSSI, 14–15, 37–57, 252
in children and adolescents, 40–46
determination of, 37–39
and ethnicity, 54–55
future research, directions for, 56–57
gender differences in, 49, 51–54
international differences in, 55–56
in older adults, 49, 50
in young adults, 46–49
Primates, NSSI in nonhuman, 100–102,
104
Prinstein, M. J., 87, 171, 285, 286
Problem-solving skills, 85–86, 212–213,
262
Problem-solving therapy (PST),
272–273
Proopiomelanocortin (POMC), 105,
299–300
Prose Edda, 31
PST. *See* Problem-solving therapy
Psychiatric hospitalization, 282
Psychoanalytic antisuicide model,
65–66
Psychological model of development
and maintenance of NSSI,
74–75
Psychopharmacologic treatment of
NSSI, 291–313
anticonvulsants, 310
antipsychotic medications, 305–308
clinical recommendations, 313

ABOUT THE EDITOR

Matthew K. Nock, PhD, is the John L. Loeb Associate Professor of the Social Sciences and director of the Laboratory for Clinical and Developmental Research in the Department of Psychology at Harvard University in Cambridge, Massachusetts. Dr. Nock received his doctorate in psychology from Yale University and completed his clinical internship at the New York University Child Study Center—Bellevue Hospital Center. His research focuses primarily on the etiology, assessment, and treatment of nonsuicidal self-injury, suicidal behaviors, and aggressive behaviors. Dr. Nock has authored more than 75 scientific articles on these topics, and his research is funded by the National Institute of Mental Health, the American Foundation for Suicide Prevention, and the Talley and Clark Funds at Harvard University. In addition to his research and clinical work, Dr. Nock teaches courses at Harvard on self-destructive behaviors, statistics, research methodology, developmental psychopathology, and cultural diversity.